FROM ALEPH TO ZE'EV

Praise for *From Aleph To Ze'ev*

WRITTEN WITH HUMOR AND VERVE, these short excursions into Jewish culture, history, rituals and beliefs will both intrigue and amuse you. They may not answer every question on Jewish background that has crossed your mind, but the brief essays are sure to enlighten you on topics you didn't know you were interested in: In what language did Abraham speak to Sarah? How did the 10th Century's "garlic" cities of the Rhineland contribute to Jewish history? Which commandments did the Arkansas House of Representatives intend to use when they approved posting the Ten Commandments in public buildings?

You don't have to be Jewish to enjoy the broad array of cultural and historical topics the author explores. From Aleph to Ze'ev would make an excellent choice for book clubs and discussion groups.

Marion Lewenstein, Professor of Communication, Emerita; Stanford University

❖

THIS COLLECTION IS RICH WITH inquiry. Both serious and playful, it is driven by a curiosity which points the author in every direction of matters Jewish. Ze'ev Orzech is a lover of ideas, who like our sages of old probes questions with openness and precision. In addition, he is an *ohev Yisrael*, a lover of the Jewish People. To encounter through his eyes such diverse details of Jewish life—be they historical, linguistic, ritual, or theological—is a journey full of surprise and appreciation. Regardless of your knowledge of Judaism, you will find yourself enlightened by its offerings. As both a student and a teacher of Jewish tradition, I am grateful for its presence in my library.

Rabbi Benjamin Barnett, Rabbi, Beit Am Jewish Community in Corvallis, OR.

❖

I HAVE READ – RATHER STUDIED – this extraordinary book by Professor Ze'ev Orzech, and heartily recommend it to Jew and non-Jew, students and enthusiasts of Jewish culture in its many facets. Like a diamond that glitters as the sun or light brushes against its edges, this book casts a vivid beam that will enlighten and educate the reader. It takes us across the centuries and across the globe from the dawn of an ancient people's history to the ongoing saga of Israel reborn after the Holocaust. Nothing Jewish is foreign to the mind of this original thinker. This is a wondrous book. Read it, enjoy it... its pages will educate, inform and uplift both mind and spirit.

Rabbi Israel Stein. Rabbi Emeritus of Congregation Rodeph Sholom of Bridgeport, CT. Professor of Homiletics and Practical Rabbinics at The Jewish Theological Seminary.

(Collaborated on books by Rabbi Joseph Telushkin; Bible Commentaries *by renowned scholars such as Everett Fox, Jacob Milgrom, Robert Alter; and* The Torah, *published by The Central Conference of American Rabbis).*

⁂

TO DIP INTO ZE'EV ORZECH'S *From Aleph to Ze'ev* is a sheer delight. These 110 short essays are simultaneously learned and witty, accessible and challenging. The book covers a vast array of subjects reflecting the complexity and beauty of Judaism's millennial-old traditions and history. Orzech's talent lies in shedding light on the more obscure and curious aspects of Jewish ritual and in offering appreciative and nuanced interpretations of historical events and persons. While the book is encyclopedic, the essays—infused as they are with the author's personality and passion—are anything but dry encyclopedia entries. To all those who might complain that history is "boring" or "irrelevant" in the modern world, *From Aleph to Ze'ev* is the perfect answer. This book is everything you wish you had learned in Hebrew School—and more.

Jonathan Katz, Chair of History Department, Oregon State University. Author of Dreams, Sufism and Sainthood: The Visionary Career of Muhammad al-Zawawi *and* Murder in Marrakesh: Emile Mauchamp and the French Colonial Adventure.

⁂

WHETHER HE'S EXPLORING BIBLICAL HISTORY, Jewish customs, or European streets haunted by memories, Ze'ev Orzech mines his subjects with great care and intelligence, and comes back bearing riches. Full of verve, wit and appealing directness, these excursions into all facets of the Jewish experience both delight and edify.

Marjorie Sandor, winner of the 2004 National Jewish Book Award in Fiction

❖

I HAVE READ *From Aleph to Ze'ev*, always with interest and often with delight. Ze'ev Orzech becomes in these pages a tour guide through the whole sweep of Jewish life from the formal and historical to the light-hearted and arcane. Orzech takes us from the battlements of the Masada to the origins of Hebrew curse words, from heinous acts of persecution to the ins and outs of Jewish cooking. And to use a cooking analogy, each subject is presented in a bite-sized chunk, just enough to whet the appetite and make the reader ready for more. Orzech's writing style is a joy: lively, informative, well-researched without ever becoming pedantic.

As a Christian minister with Jewish family roots, my interest in this book has been both personal and professional. I would recommend this book for any church's library, where it can be a significant resource for Church school teachers and Confirmation classes, as well as a satisfying read for congregation members who want to explore some of the Jewish roots of Christianity or better understand our Jewish neighbors.

The Rev. Elizabeth Oettinger, Senior Minister, First Congregational United Church of Christ of Corvallis

❖

From Aleph to Ze'ev IS A POCKET-BOOK of *Everyman's Jewish Learning*; a wonderful collection of excellent essays written in an easily – even painlessly – digestible style. It would make a superb Bar Mitzvah gift. But then again, it would be a superb gift to anyone and everyone, regardless of age.

Rabbi Simchah Roth, Rabbi Emiritus, Torat Hayim Masorti Congregation, Herzliya, Israel

From Aleph to Ze'ev

Excursions into Jewish Culture, History, Rituals, and Beliefs

by

Ze'ev Orzech

From Aleph to Ze'ev
by Ze'ev Orzech

ISBN 0615464572

Printed in USA
 Published by Beit Am Publications *
P.O. Box 1143, Corvallis, Oregon 97339-1143
בי״ת עם www.beitam.org/publications

Book and cover design by Ellen Perlis
Illustrations by Diane Wenzel

*To my beloved wife, Mimi,
our children and grandchildren.*

Table of Contents

Rules by Which We Live

The Way We Do Things: Customs and Rituals

How Others See Us

Upon Re-reading the Bible

Time, Calendars and Holidays

Superstitions and Other Odd Notions

Preface

FROM ALEPH TO ZE'EV IS a compilation of short articles I wrote for *Kol Ha'am*, the monthly newsletter of Beit Am, the Jewish Community in Corvallis, Oregon. When I agreed to become the newsletter editor, more than sixteen years ago, I resolved to make *Kol Ha'am* more than the usual listing of community announcements, Hebrew School news and Shabbat candle-lighting times. I wanted to add a regular, educational component to it, one that would be of interest to our members and would keep me engaged in what is essentially a routine task. (I had retired not long before from thirty-two years of teaching Economics at Oregon State University and was looking for something that would keep me intellectually challenged.)

There is no overriding theme for this book. I wrote about whatever interested me at the time, sometimes in response to specific questions. The articles were geared to a readership with varying degrees of Jewish knowledge including those with no Jewish background whatsoever.

Finding answers to the questions that inevitably arose in writing each column was not always easy in a place like Corvallis. The Oregon State University library has a fair collection of Judaica, and over the years, I have tried to fill the most obvious lacunae in my own library. The *Encyclopedia Judaica* has been an invaluable resource. Everything changed with the arrival of the internet which offers an ever-increasing number of online Jewish resources.

Given the space limit of the monthly columns, I decided from the beginning not to overload them or burden my readers with footnotes and keep references to a minimum. This book does not purport to be a textbook that completely covers the various subjects it presents. On the contrary, the constraints forced me to be selective and look for the most important and interesting points about each topic.

Because the original articles were written over a period of years, they covered, at times, points that were repeated in different contexts. In the book, I brought together articles into chapters that are loosely connected thematically and eliminated most of the duplications. In several places, I combined articles that had originally appeared in two or three consecutive issues of *Kol Ha'am*. Mostly, I withstood the temptation to elaborate and add to the original material.

From Aleph to Ze'ev does not have to be read from A to Z, that is, sequentially. Each of the chapters stands alone and can be savored like pieces of candy — two or three a day. It is my hope that there are many candy lovers all over the world who will enjoy the treat.

Researching and writing these articles has kept me engaged and learning over many years. Perhaps I have managed to educate a few of my readers as well. Editing the newsletter and creating this collection has been a labor of love. All proceeds from the book will go directly to Beit Am. This is my gift to the Jewish community.

Ze'ev B. Orzech
Corvallis, Oregon

Technical Note

TO DESIGNATE TIME, I USE the scholarly, religion-neutral terms B.C.E. (Before the Common Era) and C.E. (Common Era) instead of B.C. and A.D. For a discussion of this convention, see Chapter 89, "The Times We Live In: A.D. or C.E.?"

Hebrew words appearing in these articles are pronounced according to the *Sephardi* or Modern Israeli usage. In general, the spelling, capitalization and italicization of these terms and of proper names follow the rules of the *Encyclopedia Judaica*.

Transliterating Hebrew words into the alphabet of another language presents certain problems. With few exceptions, I use the conventions suggested by the Academy of the Hebrew Language in Jerusalem: An apostrophe indicates the presence of either of the two silent letters, *aleph* and *ayin*, as in *ha'aretz* and *tish'ah*. (Technically, the *aleph* is a glottal stop; the *ayin* is not but is pronounced that way by Ashkenazic Jews.)

Instead of the Germanic "ch," I use a dotted h (*ḥ*) for the letter *ḥet*, and "kh" for the letter *khaf*. This usage has become common in recent transliterations of Hebrew texts. I chose not to follow the Academy's rules where the transliteration would look strange to American readers or where a Hebrew term has entered the English language. Thus, the letter *tsadeh* is rendered by "tz" (as in kibbutz) rather than by a dotted z.

Acknowledgements

IT IS A PLEASURE TO thank the many good friends and members of my family who were so generous in providing substantial help and advice in making this collection of articles into a book.

Even before this book was a gleam in anyone's eye, my dear friend, Alex Fischler, reviewed many of the articles with a pencil in his hand before they were published in *Kol Ha'am*. His feel for language and his willingness to ask "what did you mean by this?" led me to make changes that added to the clarity of the newsletters and this book.

Several people read the manuscript in its entirety. Long-time friends Ken Krane and Judy Wilcox spent many hours highlighting inconsistencies in style and spelling, as well as duplications in material that was written over a period of sixteen years. I am deeply in their debt. I have greatly benefitted from Rabbi Israel Stein's knowledge of Jewish sources and his sage advice. It was his enthusiasm that finally convinced me to publish this book.

I owe a special debt to Rabbi Simchah Roth of Herzliya, Israel, with whom I've had the privilege of studying Mishnah online for the last 15 years (via his *Bet Midrash Virtuali*). My work is informed by the ideas and knowledge I gained from him. His inspiration is particularly apparent in the several columns in which I mention his name. In addition, it was his emendations which removed what I hope are the last misstatements in the book. It goes without saying that all remaining errors and deficiencies are mine alone.

All of my family have been involved in this literary enterprise. They have given freely of their wisdom and expertise. My wonderful wife Mimi read each article before it saw the light of day in the newsletter and was always able to come up with the right phrase when words escaped me. My daughter Sarah, patient editor and critic par excellence, was always ready to discuss a book-related idea or problem and applied her uncommon common sense to editing the manuscript in its final stages. My son Dan, given his métier as a writer, offered critical guidance early in this project and used his skills to tighten the writing and, thereby, improve the final product. My son Joe, my computer guru, devoted long hours to solving the technical problems I encountered while preparing the manuscript for publication. Thank you doesn't begin to express my appreciation to them; it is not an exaggeration to say this book would not exist without their participation, support and encouragement.

Proverbs 27:10 states that "a close neighbor is better than a distant brother." This does not hold in my case. My brother David's careful proofreading caught at least one not-so-funny blooper that would have seriously compromised the credibility of much that I had written: he pointed out that Tel Aviv really lies north of Jaffa and not south of it where I had placed it. I, of course, having lived there, knew this little fact, but somehow....

Finally, thank you to my *mekhuteneste*, Therese Polan. (It is too bad that English lacks a word for this most important family member—the "other" mother-in-law.) Therese made this the first project in her proposed post-retirement career as a proof editor. She was unfailingly complimentary in her comments to me and gentle in her corrections. This book is much the better for her labors.

I am grateful to the many members of our wonderful Beit Am community who never in all these years commented on a boring article, but often were quick to mention something they especially liked in what I had written. I particularly want to thank five members for donating their professional services to this project: Ellen Perlis, who with tender loving care performed magic and transformed my Microsoft Word manuscript into a book; Diane Wenzel, whose illustrations enhance the looks of the book and beautifully complement the text; Ken Bronstein and Dan Vega, who modified the Beit Am website to support the new publication; and Nadine Davison, who managed the legal aspects of this donation to our community.

History

King Hezekiah's Tunnel

ABOUT 2,700 YEARS AGO, THERE occurred one of those moments in Jewish history when the continued existence of the Jewish people hung in the balance. Only an impressive feat of construction engineering prevented what could easily have spelled the complete extinction of the Jewish people and of Judaism. That moment occurred in the year 701 B.C.E., when the Kingdom of Judah, under King Hezekiah, faced the mighty army of Assyria, the superpower of those days.

First, a bit of history: Hezekiah ruled over a tiny part of what once was the great Jewish state put together by King David's army and his son Solomon's talent for diplomacy. Together, they established a kingdom that extended from the Red Sea to the shores of the Euphrates River. But that was 300 years before and now only a small part of that extensive empire remained.

To build and maintain his vast domain, including the magnificent Temple in Jerusalem, and to finance his sumptuous life style, King Solomon required large revenue and resources. He acquired these by levying crushing taxes on his people and imposing a system of forced labor. The discontent, which had already begun during his lifetime, finally erupted upon his death into a full-blown tax revolt. Unfortunately, his son, Rehoboam, who succeeded him at age 41 (928 B.C.E.) refused to ease the burden. As a result, the United Kingdom which had stood for barely 100 years split into the southern Kingdom of Judah (encompassing the tribal areas of Judah and Benjamin) and the northern Kingdom of Israel (encompassing the areas of the other ten tribes).

The breakup and the subsequent civil war between the two kingdoms weakened both, and as a result many of the nations that David had conquered broke away and regained independence. Ultimately, the Kingdom of Israel fell to the Assyrians in the year 722 B.C.E. The population through deportation into exile, intermarriage and assimilation gradually disappeared from the stage of history. This gave rise to the myth of the "Ten Lost Tribes." The Kingdom of Judah became a vassal of Assyria, paying tribute to that powerful empire.

This brings us to the end of the eighth century. Hezekiah, who had ascended the throne of Judah at age 25 (in 716 B.C.E.), was an exemplary king. He brought about a religious reawakening and strengthened the country by rebuilding and extending its defenses. However, he made a serious political blunder and joined in an anti-Assyrian alliance with Babylon and Egypt.

He faced his moment of truth when Sennacherib, the new ruler of Assyria, set out to conquer Egypt. On his sweep down the coast he had defeated Babylon, and laid waste to all the fortified Judean towns. In 701 B.C.E. he turned toward Jerusalem.

The City of David (Jerusalem) was well situated defensively. On three sides, it was protected by deep valleys and on the fourth by one of the city walls. The weak point was the city's main water source, the Spring of Gihon, which was located *outside* the city walls. The city was thus in danger of being cut off from its vital source of water during a prolonged siege.

Hezekiah, in an ingenious move, sealed off the spring, disguised its location and dug a tunnel which channeled the water from the Gihon Spring to the Siloam Pool within the city walls.

The remarkable story of the tunnel did not come to light until 1880 when a stone tablet with an inscription in biblical Hebrew, on which Hezekiah commemorates the event, was accidentally discovered on one of the tunnel walls. The tablet was removed by the Turkish authorities, who ruled Palestine at that time, and is now preserved at the Museum of the Ancient Orient in Istanbul. Here is what it says:

> The boring through is completed. And this is the story of the boring: while yet they plied the pick, each toward his fellow, and while yet there were three cubits [4½ feet, ed.] to be bored through, there was heard the voice of one calling to the other, that there was a hole in the rock on the right hand and on the left hand. And on the day of the boring through the workers in the tunnel struck each to meet his fellow, pick against pick. Then the water flowed from the spring to the pool twelve hundred cubits, and the height of the rock above the heads of the workers was one hundred cubits.

Hezekiah's tunnel represents an engineering feat of the first order. The tunnel, which runs 1,800 feet through solid rock over a circuitous route and drops 66 feet, was started at both ends simultaneously. The diggers worked toward one another until they met, almost exactly in the middle!

Hezekiah's stratagem worked: After a prolonged siege Sennacherib withdrew his forces and returned to Nineveh. Whether the plague among his troops—as described in the Bible—was the result of the lack of water or the "miraculous salvation" promised by the prophet Isaiah, a contemporary of Hezekiah, remains a moot point. What is beyond dispute, though, is the likelihood that, had Sennacherib crushed Jerusalem then, the Jews of Judah, the "last remnant," would have been scattered to the winds. Because the final writing and editing of the Bible was not yet completed at that time, the Jewish exiles would have lacked the spiritual foundation upon which to base their hope for a return to Zion. Had Judah fallen then, we might now be telling fanciful tales of the "Twelve Lost Tribes."

2 Masada

KING HEROD'S FRIENDS MUST HAVE snickered behind his back when he announced that he would build himself a magnificent palace somewhere in the Judean Wilderness. But Herod had the last laugh. "Herod the Great" who ruled Judea from 37 to 4 B.C.E. was one of the great builders of antiquity. He greatly enlarged and beautified the Temple in Jerusalem and fortified the city with a new citadel. He built fortifications in strategic places all over the country and hollowed out a whole mountain for his own burial place, Herodion. He built a beautiful city, Caesarea, which recent underwater archaeology has shown to have had the biggest deep-sea harbor in the eastern Mediterranean. The characteristic "framed" ashlars of this period (some weighing as much as 60 tons) that can still be seen in the lower courses of the Temple Mount's Western Wall are known as "Herodian stones."

The most spectacular of Herod's projects was the magnificent palace complex he built on a towering plateau overlooking the Dead Sea, at the edge of the Judean desert. Herod was not a man loved by his people. He came from a family that had converted to Judaism and was, therefore, not a direct descendent of King David. He ruled only by grace of the Roman suzerain. Fearing for his safety—probably with some reason—he fortified the plateau with a thick outer wall and 38 towers. The place became known as Masada, the Fortress.

The palace walls, decorated with colorful frescoes, the storerooms, the Roman baths and a swimming pool, all of which have been excavated and partially reconstructed, testify to the life of luxury led by the royal household on top of Masada. Huge cisterns hewn into the rock held the water that was collected during the rainy seasons. These same cisterns also provided water to the *mikva'ot* (Jewish ritual baths) that served those living on Masada.

The sides of Masada fall off precipitously, descending on the east side more than 1,300 feet down to the Dead Sea. Because all the approaches were narrow and difficult, the fortress was practically impregnable, making it an ideal refuge for a nervous king. For the same reason, after Herod's death it would become the last stronghold of the Jews in their war against Rome. Two thousand years later, the story of Masada and those Jews would become a national symbol of Israel's determination to survive.

Thanks to a clever ruse, the Roman garrison stationed atop Masada during the Jews' "Great Revolt" was defeated by a group of Jewish Zealots. As city after city in Israel was taken by the Romans, Masada became the refuge for many who were in danger of being captured. In 70 C.E., after a prolonged siege and several major battles against the famous Tenth Legion—the best troops of the Roman Empire led by Titus—Jerusalem finally fell and the Temple was destroyed. For three long years afterwards, Masada alone held out against the Roman onslaught.

We have a detailed record of this war from the writings of the first century Roman-Jewish historian Josephus Flavius who recounted the last days of Masada in his book, *The Jewish War*.

For three years after the fall of Jerusalem, the Tenth Legion, along with other Roman forces and tens of thousands of Jewish prisoners of war, laid siege to Masada. During these years, a massive earthen ramp was constructed by Jewish slave labor along which the Roman siege tower, with its iron battering ram, inched toward the wall of the fortress. This ramp still exists today and provides the relatively easy access to the top that most tourists take.

When it became clear that the wall would soon be breached, the commander of Masada, Eleazar Ben-Ya'ir, assembled the 960 men, women and children and gave a deeply stirring farewell speech. The group pledged "never to be servants to the Romans, nor to any other than God Himself" and decided to kill themselves rather than be captured. Each man would kill his wife and children and ten men were chosen by lot to kill the men. The ten then cast lots to see who among them would kill the others, set the fortress afire and finally kill himself. When the Romans finally took Masada, they found storerooms full of food and water and close to a thousand corpses. Thus, the last defenders of Jewish freedom died. Only two women and five children who had hid in a cave survived. It is from them that Josephus claims to have the details of the last days.

There are several puzzling aspects to this account. In all the modern excavations, only 25 skeletons have been discovered. On the other hand, Josephus' description of the physical layout on top of Masada is amazingly accurate. Moreover, a number of small pottery shards each inscribed with a name (one of which was Ben-Ya'ir) have been excavated. Could these have been the lots the men cast? Yet, how could the two hidden women possibly have known about the suicide lottery? (They could, of course, have heard the discussions of the plan and then decided to hide, with or without the knowledge of their husbands.)

Most important though is the question whether a group of highly religious Zealots would commit suicide (and murder children!) not for the sake of *Kiddush HaShem* (the Sanctification of the Holy Name) but for the secular sentiment that "It is nobler to die free than to live as a slave!"

Masada and the heroic death of its defenders have become powerful symbols. Elite units of the Israeli Defense Forces take their oath of allegiance on the spot that represents the last national freedom for almost 2,000 years. Clearly, the young recruits take on a heavy commitment when they swear that, "Masada shall not fall again!"

3 After the Destruction: Rabbinic Judaism

THE YEAR WAS 130 C.E. and it was not the best of times. Sixty years had passed since Jerusalem had been laid waste and the Holy Temple destroyed by the mighty Roman army. Jerusalem had been the capital and therefore the political center of the Kingdom of Judah. But it had been much more than that. The Temple in its midst had been the spiritual center of the nation. It contained the Ark of the Covenant and was regarded as the site of the Divine Presence. The people's religion had been centered on it and it was the only place where sacrificial offerings could be brought.

The trauma of that terrible loss was intense. Only a few old men and women remembered, but the whole nation was still in shock. When Judea fell to the Romans, it was the end of the country in a political sense. But it was not the many who perished during the war, not the large numbers sold into slavery, nor the physical destruction in the country and the ruin of the country's economy, it was rather the loss of the spiritual institutions that brought Judaism close to being wiped off the face of the earth. With the destruction of the Temple (the Destruction), religious practices such as the daily sacrifices, the three annual pilgrimages, the system of taxation and all observances which had been focused on the Temple, disappeared or became meaningless. The High Priesthood, which had managed the Temple's affairs, lost all power, and the Sanhedrin, the assembly of 71 ordained rabbis, which had served as both legislature and Supreme Court, ceased to function. The Destruction marked the loss of Jewish nationhood and, some maintain, the beginning of *galut* (the exile).

With the passage of time, though, several developments took place that helped reduce, if not heal, the loss of religious identity. Jews still lived in their native land and tried their best to rebuild their ruined lives. Attempts were made to unify the various factions in the country, gather support from Jewish communities abroad and, as we shall see, regain political independence and freedom. Villages were rebuilt, agriculture revived at an impressive rate and the population increased considerably in the three generations following the Destruction.

The most important development, though, the one to which we owe the survival of the Jewish people, was the development of rabbinic Judaism. It changed the nature of Judaism in fundamental ways and created the religion we practice today. Before the Destruction, communal power was concentrated in the hands of the *kohanim*, the priestly families who comprised the social elite. Many of them identified with the views of the Sadducees, the political party that represented the wealthier elements of Judean society. After the fall of Jerusalem, the power shifted to the popular, grass-roots party, the Pharisees. As a result, the leadership of the Jewish people shifted from the priests to the Sages or, to use the title by which they were addressed, the Rabbis.

Rabbi Yohanan Ben-Zakkai, a Pharisee, was the leading sage at the end of the Second Temple period. We know that he fervently preached peace and was opposed to the uprising against Rome. Possibly because of his pro-peace stance he was able to secure from the Roman authorities the safety of Yavneh, a small town south of Jaffa, known for its academy and its sages. Yavneh replaced Jerusalem, which was out-of-bounds to Jews, and became the new location of the reconstituted Sanhedrin, the chief legislative body dealing with religious and political matters.

Under the leadership of Ben-Zakkai and of those who followed him, the rabbis of the Sanhedrin wrought fundamental changes in both Jewish ritual and the body of Jewish law, changes that define our daily lives to this day. In ritual, they substituted prayer for the sacrifices that were offered in the Temple. Of course, the rabbis realized that prayer often is the spontaneous outpouring of emotion from the human heart. This kind of prayer (*tefillah*) was not circumscribed or limited in any way. However, they did add prayers that were patterned after the various Temple offerings (*avodah*). These were stylized, with prescribed contents and order. They were often designated for special times of the day or days of the year. Moreover, introducing a radical change, the rabbis decreed that prayers could now be offered anywhere, not only in Jerusalem. The synagogue (*bet knesset* or gathering place) thus became the substitute for the Temple that had held the people together in the past.

AT THE SAME TIME THESE changes in ritual were taking place, a much more fundamental change, the development of the Oral Law, was under way in the *yeshivot* (academies) that were established both within *Eretz Israel* (the Land of Israel) and outside of it (mainly in Babylon). It was this expansion of law, from the "Written Torah" to the "Oral Torah," which enabled Judaism, and therefore the Jewish people, to adapt to the drastic changes and survive after the Destruction.

Interpretation of the Written Torah dates back to long before the fall of Jerusalem in 70 C.E. Orthodox doctrine maintains that the Oral Torah was also given by God to Moses on Mount Sinai together with the Written Torah. Interpretations, though, could not be written down and had to remain oral. Therefore, no coherent body of Jewish law other than the Written Torah was transmitted to the lawgivers of the Sanhedrin.

The great contribution of the rabbis was that they created a method of interpreting the Torah and provided an extensive body of their own interpretations (which, at the time, were still memorized and orally transmitted). Above all, they insisted that these interpretations, the Oral Torah, be accepted as of equal sanctity and validity as the Written Torah.

By the second century C.E., Jewish law and tradition were no longer based on a literal reading of the Torah, but on the combined oral and written traditions. "As Jews, we do not live by Torah Law," my teacher, Rabbi Simchah Roth, puts it, "we live by Torah Law as interpreted by our Sages." To quote him at some length (with his permission):

> The Written Torah is the ideological basis of Judaism and the Oral Torah is an organic continuation of the Written Torah. The immutable Written Torah is not the rule by which Israel lives: the Torah, as understood and interpreted by the oral tradition is Israel's rule of law. In this way, the Written Torah is constantly being re-understood by the rabbis, its licensed practitioners. The Oral Torah (rabbinic law) is, in essence, developmental-dynamic and not static; it is a living continuation of the Written Torah. The Oral Torah is the means whereby the Written Torah is made constantly relevant.

THERE ARE SEVERAL GOOD REASONS why the Torah by itself is an insufficient guide to Jewish life. One: it is silent on many important subjects. For example, nowhere in the Torah is a marriage ceremony recorded. Only in the Oral Law do we find details on how to perform a Jewish wedding. Two: even where certain laws are mentioned in the Torah, they would be incomprehensible without an oral tradition. Example: In the first paragraph of the *Shema*, the Torah instructs us concerning the *tefillin* (phylacteries): "And you shall bind them for a sign upon your hand, and they shall be for frontlets between your eyes" (Deuteronomy 6:48). The Hebrew word for "frontlets" is *totafot*. Interestingly, although the word occurs three times in the Bible, it is always in connection with the *tefillin*. The derivation of the word is unknown and its meaning obscure. Thus, from the text, we cannot know what the word could possibly mean, or what "between your eyes" refers to. Only through the Oral Law, that is, rabbinic interpretation, do we learn the proper use of the two small black boxes during weekday morning prayer.

Finally, even where the Torah is very specific, it may be necessary to re-interpret certain categorical laws (or render them ineffective) to limit the damaging results if these laws were applied literally. It is impossible to know whether the Bible's cryptic demand of "an eye for an eye" was ever taken literally, yet it took the Oral Law to "explain" the verse in terms of money payments in compensation for damages. The same holds true for many other safeguards which the Torah does not include in its jurisprudence. According to biblical law, a husband can divorce his wife at will and send her from his home. It was the rabbis who at first required a pre-nuptial agreement, the *ketubbah*, to assure the woman some financial security in case of a divorce, and later added the requirement that the wife must consent to the divorce. The same holds true for laws concerning the rebellious son, the wife accused of infidelity and many others. In all these cases, the rabbis, although unable to annul an objectionable biblical law, were able to mitigate its harmful effects by heaping on it restriction upon restriction.

THE ORAL LAW COULD NOT remain oral forever. The amount of material grew beyond what even scholars with exceptionally good memories could recall. Toward the end of the second century C.E., Rabbi Yehudah ha-Nasi, the President of the Sanhedrin, produced a revolution by arranging the *halakhot*, the vast legal material, into six "orders" according to subject matter. This voluminous collection (which could now be passed on in written form) was edited, codified and published about the year 200 C.E. It became the Mishnah, the main subject of study for the academies. Eventually, in the year 500 C.E., the extensive rabbinic deliberations and elaborations on the Mishnah were edited and published as the Gemara. Together, the Mishnah and the Gemara, make up the Talmud.

Rabbinic Judaism formed the Judaism we practice today. By the end of the third century C.E., the rabbis had essentially completed the canonization of the Bible. After lengthy discussions, they had decided which books to include and which books not to include in our Sacred Writings. By creating the massive, multi-volume Talmud they opened the way for future re-interpretations. Rabbinic Judaism thereby provided a way of "updating" the Torah. The Oral Law has not only kept Judaism alive after the Destruction, but has provided it with the mechanism to keep it ever fresh and able to renew itself.

The Bar Kokhba Revolt

AFTER THE DESTRUCTION OF THE Temple and the loss of an independent Jewish State in the year 70 C.E., rabbinic Judaism developed a system of laws (known as *halakhah*) that kept the Jewish people functioning. Less tangible but just as powerful a factor was the pervasive hope, or rather the firm conviction, that Jerusalem would be rebuilt and the Temple restored within their own lifetimes. This hope was only partly based on wishful thinking or on the belief in the imminent coming of the Messianic Age. To a large extent, it was based on a series of assurances, or what the Jews believed to be assurances, that were given to them over the years by the Roman authorities, promising to rebuild the Temple and grant them some measure of political independence.

Toward the end of the reign of the Roman Emperor Trajan, in the years 115–117 C.E., violent clashes between Diaspora Jews and the pagan Greek minorities broke out in several cities and developed into armed rebellions against the authorities in at least three provinces of the Empire. Trajan ordered Lusius Quietus, a distinguished general, to restore order. Quietus crushed the rebellions with savage cruelty and as a reward was appointed Governor of Judea. When Hadrian succeeded Trajan as emperor in 117 C.E., he removed Quietus from his post in Judea. The Jews saw this as a hopeful sign, because Quietus had ruled Judea with an iron fist and was much hated. Their hope seemed justified when Hadrian announced that he was going to rebuild Jerusalem and the Temple.

But joy quickly turned into disappointment and despair. Hadrian rebuilt Jerusalem as a pagan city and rebuilt the Temple as a shrine to the Roman god Jupiter. He changed the name of the city to Aelia Capitolina and renamed the country Palestina after the Philistines who had migrated there from Greece. Hadrian wanted to wipe out all memory of Judea, the name by which the country had been known for over a thousand years. Blow followed blow! Hadrian outlawed circumcision (on threat of death), the keeping of the Sabbath and holidays, study and public reading of the Torah, and the ordination of new rabbis.

He sought to eradicate Judaism and saw these measures as bringing Hellenism and, therefore, civilization to a backward part of his empire. The Jews saw it as the death of everything they valued.

Judea had never resigned itself to Roman rule, but for 60 years the Jews of *Eretz Israel* had been patient, trusting the Roman promises. They had even refrained from joining the uprisings of their brethren in the Diaspora. Now, Rome had become the enemy (the Talmud uses the term "The Evil Empire"). The mood of the people was despondent and disappointment had changed to profound resentment. They longed for a *melekh mashi'ah* (anointed king, Messiah) to lead them, throw off the yoke of the heathen, and restore Judea to its former glory. And so, in the year 132 C.E., the country exploded in revolt.

The uprising against Rome was led by a charismatic leader, Shim'on Bar Kokhba. It was not the work of a small group of revolutionaries, but involved large parts of the population. Shim'on Bar Kokhba, a national hero and a descendent of the House of David, rallied the forces of resistance and led the fight. He decimated the occupying Roman legions, conquered Jerusalem and proclaimed an independent Jewish state. Coins were struck which celebrated the "First Year of the Deliverance of Israel."

The large number of troops that Rome threw into the war put a heavy strain on the resources of the Empire. The second-to-third-century Roman historian, Cassius Dio, relates that the insurrection, which was well organized, spread until the whole of Judea was in revolt in a fierce and protracted war.

Who was this man under whose command Jewish fighters held out against the might of Rome for three and a half years? From letters discovered in the Judean Desert in 1952–1961, we learn that Bar Kokhba signed himself "Bar Koseva." The Talmud refers to the coins that were struck to celebrate Bar Kokhba's liberation of Jerusalem as "Koseva coins." Rabbi Akiva, the leading sage of the period and one of the spiritual leaders of the uprising, proclaimed Bar Koseva to be the Messiah and, in a neat pun, re-named him Bar Kokhba (belonging to a star). It is an allusion to the verse (Numbers 24:17): "There shall step forth a star (*kokhav*) out of Jacob" — a direct reference to the Messiah. Indeed, Rabbi Akiva firmly believed that Bar Kokhba was the savior, finally come to redeem his people as prophesied in Scripture, and he referred to him as *ha- melekh ha-mashi'ah* (the anointed king or Messiah). Rabbi Akiva was, of course, not alone; most of the Sages, and certainly many of the people, shared his belief.

It is important to remember that during the Roman period the Jewish idea of a Messiah was still that of an "anointed king." He was a human warrior, the descendant of King David, who would be raised up by God to break the yoke of the heathen and to reign over a restored Kingdom of Israel to which all the Jews of the Exile would return.

The euphoria did not last long. Rome brought in additional legions, some from as far away as Britain, and re-conquered the land town-by-town and district-by-district. "In the fourth year after liberation" as the Talmud puts it, the revolt was finally crushed. Bar Kokhba died in the fall of Beitar, a fortified town in the Judean Hills, where the Jews had made their last stand. The defeat was absolute. Talmudic sources speak of half a million massacred, and with so many sold into slavery, that the price of a Jewish slave fell to the cost of "a day's ration for a horse." The land was devastated with hundreds of towns and villages destroyed. Cassius Dio claims that the Roman legion destroyed 985 Jewish villages! Severe religious persecutions followed the war, so much so that *Eretz Israel* lost most of its Jewish population. Rabbi Akiva and many of his fellow rabbis were martyred by the Romans. The quality of Jewish life was now worse than it had been before the revolt. The fall of Beitar is still mourned to this day on *Tish'ah be'Av* (the ninth day of the month of Av) together with the destruction of the First and Second Temples (in 586 B.C.E. and 70 C.E.).

Not everybody had seen Bar Kokhba as the Messiah, nor had all the Sages been in favor of the uprising. Those rabbis of the Sanhedrin, who were not, referred to him in another pun on his real name, as *Bar Kozivah* (the deceitful one) and pronounced him a false Messiah. Still, he remains one of the great heroic figures in Jewish history. The Bar Kokhba Revolt was, without doubt, the greatest war of liberation Jews fought in ancient times. The defeat ended Jewish independence until the State of Israel was founded eighteen centuries later.

5 Josephus and his *Testimonium Flavianum*

My HIGH SCHOOL IN TEL-AVIV did not have forensics as an after-school activity. However, in our history classes we had something that served almost the same function. We staged mock trials of historic figures and sometimes even of ideas. Three students served as judges, we had teams of prosecutors and defenders and the rest of the class constituted the jury which, at the end of the trial, had to bring in the verdict of history. Both prosecutors and defenders could call witnesses who would present evidence to bolster their case. The exercise came as the concluding step of a unit of study, after much reading and preparation, and provided an exciting way to summarize what we had learned.

One of the figures we tried was Yoseph Ben-Matityahu ha-Kohen, better known by his later, Roman name, Josephus Flavius. Yoseph was born in Jerusalem in 38 C.E., son of an aristocratic priestly family. He was well versed in Jewish literature and was at home in the Roman culture as well. After many years of seething discontent, the war against Rome broke out in 66 C.E. The Sanhedrin (supreme political and judicial body) in Jerusalem commissioned him as commander of the Judean forces in the Galilee, despite his youth and opposition of the local officers. But the country was not prepared for war. As one after another of the Jewish strongholds crumbled, further resistance against the mighty Roman army seemed futile. Yoseph persuaded the few surviving defenders of Jotapata, the last stronghold in the Galilee, to commit suicide rather than surrender to the enemy. Then, by deceitfully manipulating the order in which his comrades slew one another, he saved himself and defected to the enemy!

Had this been the end of the story, the verdict of our high-school class would have been swift and unequivocal: Yoseph Ben-Matityahu was a traitor, pure and simple. Why waste time on him?

But this is not the picture by which history remembers him. When he was taken to Rome, he was quickly accepted in the highest social circles and enjoyed the patronage of the Emperor Vespasian whose family name he adopted. The Emperor granted him Roman citizenship, provided him with a lifelong state pension and commissioned him to write a detailed account of the Roman war against the Jews.

Josephus was a highly talented and well-educated person. He knew Jerusalem, Judea, the internal politics of his day and the developments leading up to the war from first-hand experience. During the siege of Jerusalem, he was outside the walls with Titus, commander of the Roman troops. Moreover, it seems clear from his writings that he had access to the Roman military archives, as well. In his classic *The Jewish War*, he was thus able to give a detailed account of the years leading up to the revolt, and practically a day-by-day description of the fateful battles which culminated in the fall of Jerusalem in 70 C.E.

The Jewish War comprises seven books, the last of which covers the Jewish revolt and the fall of Masada in 74 C.E. So accurate and complete were Josephus' descriptions of Herod's palace and the other installations of the fortress, that archeologist Yig'al Yadin used them as blueprints for his excavations on top of Masada in the 1960s. It is therein that the great contribution to history of Josephus Flavius lies.

Recent scholarship, however, has thrown doubt on the accuracy of many of Josephus' accounts. There is no question that *The Jewish War*, written under imperial patronage, was slanted to bolster the image of the Emperor and to support the foreign policy of the empire. Although his writings may have bought Josephus a place at court, he was despised and hated by his fellow Jews, both in Rome and in *Eretz Israel*.

Still, to be fair, we must consider several points in his favor. True, he did urge the defenders of Jerusalem during the Roman siege to lay down their arms and surrender the city. It is, however, entirely possible that he was sincere and acted out of concern for Jerusalem, as he claims he did, and not primarily to seek favor with the aggressors. And who knows? Had Jerusalem surrendered, Titus might actually have spared the city and not destroyed the Holy Temple!

Also, not all of his books were written to pander to the Emperor's ego. In *Contra Apionem*, Josephus writes a detailed response to the accusations of Apion, the fanatical, first century, anti-Jewish propagandist. (In his vitriolic book, *Against the Jews*, Apion was the first to level the nefarious Blood Libel myth against our people. See Chapter 63.) In his other important work, *Jewish Antiquities*, Josephus tries, to explain Judaism to the Greek and Roman world.

GIVEN THE CHARACTER OF JOSEPHUS' work and the period it covers, it is not surprising that Christian scholars would comb it eagerly for proof of the historicity of Jesus. Christian sources, the New Testament and the writings of the Church Fathers all bear a later date, and in any case, do not provide independent evidence of the existence of Jesus. Indeed, two references to Jesus do appear in *Jewish Antiquities*, Josephus' history from Adam to his own times. The first, known as the *Testimonium Flavianum* is by far the most hotly-debated passage in all the five works by Josephus and refers to *Antiquities* 18.3.3 §63–64:

> Now there was about this time Jesus, a wise man, *if it be lawful to call him a man*, for he was *a doer of wonderful works*, a teacher of *such men as receive the truth with pleasure*. He drew over to him both many of the Jews, and many of the Gentiles. *He was the Christ*, and when Pilate, at the suggestion of the principal men among us, had condemned him to the cross, those that loved him at the first did not forsake him; *for he appeared to them alive again the third day; as the divine prophets had foretold these and ten thousand other wonderful things concerning him*. And the tribe of Christians so named from him are not extinct at this day.

Most scholars doubt the authenticity of the passage and maintain that it was an early Christian insertion into the text. They point to the italicized passages and maintain that Josephus, who formerly was part of the religious Jewish establishment, in fact a Pharisee, could not have written them. They, therefore, reject the whole passage. Others are willing to concede the point and accept the passage without the italicized words as authentic. Many, however, reject this argument, as well as the many others advanced against the *Testimonium*, and accept it as authentic.

The second, much shorter passage refers to James, "the brother of Jesus the so-called Christ," and is equally suspect. There is a vast literature dating back as far as the sixteenth century dealing with these controversial passages.

Finally, whether we accept the *Testimonium* as authentic or not, it is clear that, although he undoubtedly distorts the truth in his accounts of the war, Josephus the historian provides us with much insight into an important period in Jewish history. Moreover, his descriptions, corroborated by the archeological findings at the sites, are our only source for the heroic events at the two Jewish fortresses—Gamla in the Galilee and Masada in the Judean desert. Thus, Yoseph Ben-Matityahu ha-Kohen, defector to the enemy and betrayer of his people, left us the legacy of two of our most cherished symbols of Israel's past glory. I value the contributions he made to our understanding of his age.

6 Dura-Europos Revealed

FEW PEOPLE HAVE HEARD OF Dura-Europos. Yet the discovery of this once-bustling town in Syria was one of the most significant archaeological finds of the twentieth century. Although historians had long been aware of its existence from documents and literary references, the exact location of this Roman stronghold on the right bank of the Euphrates River had remained concealed for almost 2,000 years until it was accidentally unearthed in 1932. The site has been called the "Pompeii of the East" for the richness of its finds and the perfect state of their preservation.

Among the most exciting discoveries at Dura, and without question the most significant for Jewish history—second only to the discovery of the Dead Sea Scrolls—was the discovery of the Dura-Europos synagogue. From the moment of its discovery, adjectives such as "amazing" and "magnificent" have been used to describe it. So sensational was the discovery of this ancient synagogue, that the American archaeologist, Clark Hopkins, who directed the dig, was moved to write, "It was like a page from the Arabian Nights. Aladdin's lamp had been rubbed and suddenly from the dry, brown bare desert had appeared paintings, not just one nor a panel nor a wall, but a whole building of scene after scene, all drawn from the Old Testament in a way never dreamed of before."

From the synagogue and the rest of the excavations, we can piece together an accurate picture of Jewish life in the Eastern Mediterranean Diaspora during the third century C.E. At that time, Dura was a fortified Roman town and regional capital with a highly diverse population. Besides the descendents of the original Greek colonists, who had founded the city 500 years earlier, there were many groups of Semitic peoples indigenous to Mesopotamia. There was also a large Roman population, administrators, legionnaires and civilians, who had been settled there since Rome had conquered the area in 165 C.E. Dura was a complex multicultural city that was religiously tolerant and in which, from all evidence, the inhabitants got along with one another.

The Jews were not newcomers to that mixture: coins found in the excavations indicate that the Jewish population dates back to, at least, the victory of the Maccabean Revolt in 164 B.C.E. They may have come to Dura as traders, for the city served as a "refueling station" on what later became known as the Silk Road (the trade road connecting Southern Europe, the Middle East and Asia). They may have come as mercenaries, for Jews were often employed in that capacity during the Hellenistic period, or they may have been brought into the area as slaves. In any case, by the time of the Roman occupation, the Jewish community was well established. It was in communication with other Mesopotamian Jewish communities and spiritually nourished by the Sages that passed through, from time to time, on their way from Babylon (the great center of Jewish learning) to *Eretz Israel*.

The synagogue that served this community was originally a private residence which had been enlarged and converted to communal use. There was no women's balcony and the experts are agreed that men and women worshipped together. It served as a center for communal activities, as the building contained spaces for offices, classrooms, a kitchen and a dining hall. A feature found at Dura — also found in most contemporary synagogues — was the prominent display of the names of large donors and synagogue officials. Many decorated ceiling tiles were inscribed with these names, the inscriptions being in Aramaic, Greek and Persian. The main assembly room of the Dura synagogue held about 120 worshippers. Interestingly, the niche that held the *aron kodesh* (Holy Ark) was in the western wall, which, of course, makes sense for that is the direction pointing to Jerusalem.

The unique feature, though, which sets the Dura Synagogue apart from any other, was the stunning frescoes that covered all the walls. Displayed in vivid colors were scenes from throughout the *Tanakh* (Hebrew Bible): the exodus from Egypt, the history of the Ark, famous battles in which the Israelites overcame their enemies. Many of the picture panels are thematically linked and tell a story similar to a modern cartoon strip. For instance, there are illustrations of the life of Moses from his infancy, being pulled from the Nile by Pharaoh's daughter, to all the dramatic events in his later life. Similarly, we find the stories of Abraham and the binding of Isaac, the prophet Samuel anointing King David, and many others.

Unfortunately, only twelve years after the completion of the artwork, the synagogue had to be abandoned. To prepare for an imminent attack by the neighboring Sasanian Persians, the Romans fortified the existing city walls by completely filling all the houses built adjacent to them (among them the synagogue) with sand. To no avail! Dura fell in 256 C.E., the inhabitants were carried off into slavery and the abandoned city sank beneath the desert sands. This entombment preserved the paintings in their pristine state.

When Dura was accidentally discovered 1,700 years later and subsequently dug out by Yale archeologists, the Syrian authorities refused to grant an export license for the synagogue. The gorgeous Dura-Europos paintings were transferred to Damascus, where they hold the pride of place in the country's national museum. Yale had to settle for copies.

Benjamin of Tudela

IN THE UPSCALE NEIGHBORHOOD OF Rehavia in Jerusalem where we lived for
a year during a sabbatical leave from Oregon State University, there is
a street named *Binyamin mi-Tudela*. Who was this Benjamin of Tudela to
have streets in several cities in Israel named for him? Was he a famous
rabbi? One of the founders of modern Israel? He was neither. Benjamin
lived in the small town of Tudela in southern Spain, in the second half
of the twelfth century, and his fame rests exclusively on the account
he has left us of his wide-ranging travels. His book, *Sefer ha-Massa'ot*
(*The Book of Travels*), gives us a vivid description of the places he visited
during an extensive journey that covered many countries in southern
Europe, North Africa, the Middle East and Asia.

Except for his name, Binyamin Ben-Yona, and the fact that he started
out from Tudela we know practically nothing about him. There is even
disagreement about the exact dates of his travels. From context, most
scholars set his departure at about 1165 C.E. and agree that he returned
to Spain in 1172 or 1173.

In contrast to other famous medieval travelers, such as Marco Polo,
whom he preceded by more than 100 years, Benjamin rarely uses the
first person singular in his accounts. He describes the places he visits,
mentions important trade routes and gives the distances between stops
on his itinerary. He describes the more than 300 cities and towns he
passed through, reports on the major occupations of the people and
comments on the forms of government he encountered.

Benjamin never fails to document the condition of the Jewish
populations of the towns on his route. He meticulously records not only
the size of the communities but also the names of their leaders and the
Torah sages among them. For example, in his description of the town of
Lunel, in southern France, he speaks of one of the community leaders, a
"Rabbi Asher, the recluse, who dwells apart from the world; he pores over
his books day and night, fasts periodically and abstains from all meat.
He is a great scholar of the Talmud." The town obviously deserved the

international reputation that it had as a seat of learning, for Benjamin continues: "The students that come from distant lands to learn the Law are taught, boarded, lodged and clothed by the congregation, so long as they attend the house of study. The community has wise, understanding and saintly men of great benevolence, who lend a helping hand to all their brethren both far and near. The congregation consists of about 300 Jewish families—may the Lord preserve them."

Benjamin's *Book of Travels* does not read like an adventure tale. Unlike many pilgrims' tales of the period, he does not report having been captured by pirates and held for ransom; neither does he mention having been entertained by royalty. He did not see any fanciful creatures and did not meet up with unicorns. To the contrary, his descriptions are highly reliable, a fact that is greatly appreciated by the many historians, ethnographers and geographers who have pored over his accounts. (In several places, though, he does report, as hearsay, tales about the Ten Lost Hebrew Tribes.)

We do not know what prompted Rabbi Benjamin (as he is often called—though there is no evidence that he was ever ordained) to set out on his grand tour. Undoubtedly, one of his goals was to make a pilgrimage to the Holy Land. Yet his itinerary was considerably longer than necessary had this been his only purpose. Perhaps he wanted to see how his Jewish brethren were faring throughout the Diaspora. Moreover, there is the question of how he financed his long voyage. Jews often engaged in international trade in the Middle Ages because many had family members in different countries with whom they had commercial ties and shared a common language. It seems reasonable, therefore, to assume that Benjamin carried some high-priced, low-weight merchandise with him for trading purposes—possibly diamonds.

BENJAMIN'S ITINERARY LED HIM THROUGH both Christian kingdoms and Muslim caliphates. His descriptions reveal how the attitudes toward his Jewish brethren differed in these two realms.

The twelfth century was a pivotal period in the history of Christendom. By the time Benjamin set out on his long journey, the driving Islamic expansion into Europe had long been stopped and Christianity was now the dominant religion in most European countries. Christian beliefs (and prejudices) and venomous anti-Jewish sentiments were firmly rooted in the minds of the people. These turned into frequent acts of oppression and persecution at this time. The century opened with the First Crusade, called by Pope Urban II to free the Holy City of Jerusalem from Muslim rule, a crusade which rapidly assumed the "mission" of massacring Jewish communities along its route. It is interesting that Benjamin, although he traveled along the Rhine River in Germany, did not visit either Mainz or Speyer—both cities in which the crusading hordes had wiped out long-existing Jewish communities about seventy years before he set out on his voyage.

The century also saw a series of ritual murder accusations leveled against the Jews. The first case of blood libel in the Middle Ages occurred in Norwich, England in 1144. Not long afterwards, in 1171, the Jewish community of Blois, France was accused of ritual murder and 33 men, women and children were burned at the stake.

The twelfth century was but the opening chapter of the history of Jewish suffering and bloodshed. The expulsion of Jews from England in 1290, from France in 1306, and the well-known expulsions from Spain and Portugal in 1492–97 are examples of the exclusion of Jews from Western European countries. These expulsions were usually preceded by staged, public religious disputations in which Jews were bound to lose. Forced conversions, confiscation of properties, book burnings and *autos-da-fé* (burning of non-believers at the stake as acts of faith) were common outrages of the later Middle Ages.

Compared with the above, the attitude toward the Jewish populations in Muslim countries was benign. Although there were exceptions, there was little persecution because both Jews and Christians were accorded the status of *dhimmi*, (protected religious minorities). As "People of the Book," who accepted the Bible as sacred, they were not subject to forced conversion to Islam. *Dhimmi*, however, did not have the same legal and social rights as their Muslim neighbors: they had to pay a special tax, had to submit to certain degrading restrictions and, most importantly, could not testify against Muslims in a court of law. Still, they enjoyed freedom of religion (though forced conversions did occur at times in several of the Muslim countries), freedom of occupation and internal communal authority. In fact, Jews refer to the period of Moorish rule in Iberia as the Golden Age of Spanish Jewry. It was a period in which Jewish communities prospered and Jewish scholarship, both in science (most notably, medicine) and in the arts (philosophy, poetry, etc.) flourished.

From what Benjamin writes, and from what he fails to mention, we can learn much about the differences in attitude toward Jews. In his account of Constantinople, one of the largest and wealthiest cities in Christendom at the time, he describes the ghetto: "In the Jewish quarter are about 2,000 families. No Jews live in the city, for they have been placed behind an inlet of the sea. An arm of the Sea of Marmora shuts them in on the one side, and they are unable to go out except by way of the sea, when they want to do business with the inhabitants." On the other hand, in his description of the city of Damascus, which he credits with a Jewish population of 3,000 families, no ghetto is mentioned. Similarly, about the 40,000 Jewish families in Baghdad he writes: "...they dwell in security, prosperity and honor under the great Caliph, and amongst them are great sages, the heads of Academies engaged in the study of the Law. In this city there are ten Academies." Again, no mention of a ghetto. There were, of course, Jewish quarters in some Muslim cities for Jews found it convenient to live close to one another for religious and social reasons. This was by choice, however, and not forced upon them.

A curious mistake occurs in the number of Jews supposedly living in Jerusalem at the time. Translations based on transcriptions of the original manuscript mention 200 families. This number is patently wrong, for Jerusalem was out of bounds for Jews during the 100-year period that the Crusaders ruled the city. In his book, *The Itinerary of Benjamin of Tudela**, Nathan Adler explains the error by pointing out the great similarity between the Hebrew letter ר (*resh*) whose numeric value is 200, and the letter ד (*dalet*) whose value is 4. In a hand-written, yellowed parchment that is hundreds of years old, it is easy to mistake these letters for each other.

Finally, it is noteworthy that among all the occupations in which Jews engaged, money lending does not appear. Benjamin mentions the dyers in Brindisi, the silk-weavers in Thebes, the tanners in Constantinople, the glass-workers in Aleppo and Tyre and many others in other crafts. Indeed, in *both* Christian and Muslim countries Jews engaged mainly in commerce and industry. It was only toward the end of the Middle Ages, when they were excluded from the craft guilds and when commerce was taken over by the newly developed corporations in the Christian countries, that Jews were forced into what was practically the only occupation left open to them— lending money at interest.

The Book of Travels by Binyamin Ben-Yona, the world traveler from Tudela, was written in Hebrew, translated into Latin and from there

---

**The Itinerary of Benjamin of Tudela*, edited by Marcus Nathan Adler, M.A., (London, 1907). This is a critical text, translation plus commentaries that are very helpful in understanding the medieval text. The book can be accessed as an e-book at no cost through the "Project Gutenberg" which makes available on-line books in the public domain.

into most European languages. It is still a primary source book for all medieval historians.

8 The Garlic Cities of the Rhineland

THE FIRST TIME THAT I became aware of stalks of garlic as Jewish symbols was during a trip to Germany, on a visit to the Jewish Museum in the town of Worms. Worms (pronounced Vorms) is a town of 73,000 situated on the west bank of the Rhine River in Southern Germany. Today, there are no Jews in Worms. Of the 1,016 who lived there in 1933, all but a few perished in the Holocaust. Only the artifacts and documents in the museum bear witness to the long and important history of Jews in Worms. The town is the site of the oldest Jewish cemetery in Europe, dating back to the tenth century.

During that time and the succeeding centuries, the scholars of Worms were connected in a unique alliance with two other important Jewish communities along the Rhine: Mainz (35 miles to the north) and Speyer (pronounced Shpire, 28 miles to the south). The three communities were known as the Garlic Cities, a name made up of the initial letters of the Hebrew names of the cities. This acronym (*shin* for **Sh**pire, *vav* for **V**orms and *mem* for **M**ainz) spells *shum*, the Hebrew word for garlic. The *Shum* alliance encompassed mutual defense agreements for the inevitable times of trouble and arrangements for periodic rabbinical conventions.

By the middle of the eleventh century C.E., the flourishing Jewish community of Worms was already so well known as a seat of learning that it attracted Rashi (acronym of the name R. Solomon Ben-Isaac) who came from France to study in its *yeshivah*. Rashi was the foremost exegete and commentator on the Bible and Talmud, and his presence lent luster to Worms while he resided there.

It is hard to exaggerate the importance of the work Rashi left behind. He wrote extensive commentaries on every book of the Bible and on most of the tractates of the Babylonian Talmud. His explanations are couched in simple, lucid language and he was the first to use the rules of Hebrew grammar to increase his understanding of the texts. His commentary on the *Ḥumash* (Five Books of Moses) is the first known Hebrew work to have been printed. The work was published in 1475 by a Christian print shop (Jews were prohibited from joining the craft guilds). By that time his fame had spread to non-Jewish scholars. Today, no serious student would "learn" either Torah or Talmud without Rashi.

When Rashi returned to Troyes, his birthplace in France, the center of Jewish learning moved with him. However, after his death, leadership of the Jewish communities slowly returned to the Rhineland.

The *Shum* conventions were often called upon to draft communal regulations, which were binding not only on the three communities of Speyer, Worms and Mainz but, because of the reputation of the shum rabbis, had wide-ranging influence and were binding on all of Ashkenazic Jewry. These changes in the law were called *Takkanot Shum* and amounted to amendments to Torah law. Clearly, no rabbi or group of rabbis could ever directly overturn a prohibition of the Torah, i.e., permit something that the Torah expressly forbids. However, *takkanot* could prohibit something that the Torah permits when, in the rabbis' estimation, circumstances demanded it.

Many of these *takkanot* are associated with the name of R. Gershom Ben-Yehudah of Mainz, also known as *Me'or ha-Golah* (Light of the Exile, c. 960–1028), one of the first great German talmudic scholars and *halakhic* authorities. Most famous of his *takkanot* is the two-part ḥerem (ban) against bigamy and divorcing a wife without her consent. Well known, too, is the ḥerem forbidding the unauthorized reading of private letters. One *takkanah*, which reveals much about the times, is the prohibition against reminding Jews who had been converted by force, but later repented and returned to the fold, of their transgressions.

The histories of the Garlic Cities, though not parallel in every detail, resemble a roller-coaster. Periods of relative tranquility and prosperity in which the kings protected the Jewish communities, and, in some cases, even afforded them a large degree of self-government in exchange for heavy payments to the royal treasuries were inevitably followed by periods of almost complete annihilation of these communities. Dates commemorating the First Crusade (1096), the anti-Jewish violence at the time of the Black Death (1349) and many others in between and after, were observed as days of mourning in the *Shum* cities. And always, after each calamity, the cities revived. Ultimately, though, it was the Nazis who succeeded in wiping out 1,500 years of vibrant Jewish life in the Rhineland.

Haym Salomon: Forgotten Revolutionary War Hero

ALONG THE RIVERWALK IN CHICAGO, there stands an interesting monument commemorating the Revolutionary War. The statue, erected in 1941, shows General George Washington flanked by two civilian gentlemen. One is Robert Morris, the Superintendent of Finance of the newly formed Department of Finance, which Congress created to straighten out the desperate American wartime finances. The other is Haym Salomon, a Jewish patriot and hero who played a vital part in the success of the Revolutionary War. Salomon's contribution consisted of providing the critical resources necessary for the colonies to continue waging the war against England, thereby assuring the ultimate victory of the American Revolution.

After retreating during the Battle of Germantown, Washington's army encamped for the winter in Valley Forge. The winter of 1777–1778 was extremely cold, and the troops suffered greatly from cold and hunger. In a letter to Governor George Clinton, written from his headquarters in Valley Forge and dated February 16, 1778, General Washington refers to the "dreadful situation of the army for want of provisions," and speaks of famine among his soldiers whom he describes as "naked and starving." Congress had problems supplying the American army. The desperate conditions even led to several (fortunately short-lived) mutinies among the soldiers.

The cause of this pitiful state was the fact that Congress had no practical means for financing the revolution other than printing vast amounts of paper money. This, of course, caused the value of the currency—the Continental—to fall precipitously. Therefore, to maintain the army, Congress issued short-term bonds (i.e., IOU's) and the twelve colonies represented in the Congress promised to share in repaying these bills. This is where Haym Salomon enters the picture.

Haym Salomon was born in Leszno, Poland, in 1740 to a *Sephardi* family. He was an ardent fighter for freedom and at age 32 was forced to flee for his life due to the active role he played in the fight for Polish independence from Russia. He emigrated to New York where he set up in business provisioning the British army with food and drink. Salomon joined the Sons of Liberty, a group of revolutionary patriots, and through his business connections with the British and wealthy loyalists in New York, was able to pass much valuable information to the Revolutionary government. When the war started in 1776, the British arrested him and imprisoned him as a spy. He was released after a short time because the authorities needed him as a translator (he spoke several European languages). He continued to supply information to the colonists and repeatedly helped prisoners escape British captivity. In 1778, he was arrested yet again, tried as a spy and condemned to death. With some outside help, he managed to escape and settled in Philadelphia.

In Philadelphia, Salomon engaged in a very profitable financial brokerage and commission business and soon amassed a great fortune. He was appointed financial agent in America for the French Government, which was assisting the revolutionaries with large amounts of money. In 1781, he became an assistant to Robert Morris, superintendent of the Office of Finance for the Continental Congress. As mentioned, Congress had no power to tax the Colonists in order to raise money for Washington's troops and it looked as if defeat was imminent. Salomon used his own money and monies he raised from Jewish communities both in the colonies and in France to provide food and material aid for the troops. He repeatedly made interest-free loans to government officials such as James Madison, Thomas Jefferson and others and advanced huge sums of money to the government to carry on the war.

It is not clear exactly how much money Salomon advanced to the government. The amounts mentioned in the literature range from $200,000 to over $600,000 with $300,000 the most often quoted sum. This is an enormous amount, equaling over $7.5 million in today's purchasing power. What is quite clear, however, is the fact that after the war, Congress defaulted on its war bonds and Salomon was never repaid. When he died (at the age of 45), the man who is said to have changed the course of American history died penniless and left his family destitute.

Two hundred years later, on March 25, 1975, in connection with the Bicentennial Celebration, the United States Government was finally moved to honor Haym Salomon by putting his picture on a ten-cent stamp. The reverse side of the stamp, the gummed side, was imprinted with the following tribute taken from the Congressional Record of that date: "Haym Salomon, businessman and broker, was responsible for raising most of the money needed to finance the American Revolution and later save the nation from collapse." This, clearly, is a very effective way of internalizing American history.

Salomon was devoutly religious and fought actively for political rights for the Jews. According to a plaque on the cemetery wall of the *Sephardi* congregation *Mikveh Israel*, in Philadelphia, he is buried there in an unmarked grave. He was a major contributor to the congregation's first synagogue built in 1782.

10 The Golden Land and the Humor it Inspired

MOST JEWS LIVING IN THE United States today trace their ancestry to Poland, Russia or some other European land. That was not always the case. For almost 200 years, the majority of Jews in the United States were of Spanish ancestry. A group of 23 *Sephardi* Jews (*Sepharad* is Hebrew for Spain) who arrived by boat in New Amsterdam more than 300 years ago, were the first Jews in North America. They fled from Brazil where they had been living securely under Dutch rule until 1654 when Portugal conquered that country and the Inquisition spread into the New World. These were the Jewish Founding Fathers. Because of the great contributions to Jewish culture made in Spain during the Golden Age, which ended with the Expulsion in 1492, American *Sephardi* Jews have always regarded themselves as the "The Grandees"—the American Jewish elite.

After having been confronted with religious restrictions in the American colonies, the emancipation of the Jews came as part of the independence and liberation gained through the American Revolution. The *Sephardi* communities prospered and established the first synagogues in many of the eastern, southern and, to a lesser extent, western cities.

The second wave to come to our shores were German Jews, the original *Ashkenazim* (*Ashkenaz* is Hebrew for Germany). In the 1830s through 1850s, many Western European countries were convulsed by social unrest and liberal revolutions. The backlash that followed these uprisings led many Jews to leave their homelands. Like many non-Jews, they came to the United States in search of a more liberal society and greater economic opportunities. Many of these immigrants joined the westward movement and followed the expanding American frontier. There were Jewish farmers (some in areas in which they were the only Jews for miles around), communities of Jewish chicken farms and, of course, Jewish peddlers. These peddlers were the real pioneers. They often traded their wares, carrying their whole inventory on their backs or on pushcarts, in thinly populated areas or in Indian territories as far as the West Coast or New Mexico. From these modest beginnings sprang such retail empires as Gimbels and Bloomingdale's in New York City, Neimann-Marcus in Dallas, and I. Magnin in San Francisco.

By 1860, there were an estimated 150,000 German Jews in this country. Most of them were already well established (though by no means wealthy) by the time the Civil War broke out. They certainly left their mark on this country. If nothing else, they gave us the ubiquitous Levi jeans and other ready-to-wear, off-the-rack clothing that fit. And, of course, they gave us Reform Judaism.

Starting in the 1880s, driven by poverty and anti-Jewish violence in Eastern Europe, and lured by the promises of *Die Goldene Medineh* (the Golden Land), two million Jews entered the United States between the Civil War and World War I. The stories here are endless: tales of the Yiddish theater, the vibrant life of the Lower East Side, tailors and sweatshops. What a rich legacy this group of impoverished Jews left us!

Once they were accepted to American universities, that for a long time had strict quotas on Jewish enrollment, their contributions to science and medicine were out-of-proportion to their numbers. Many, coming from working-class backgrounds and driven by their yearning for a better life for themselves and their children, left their mark on the social movements in the United States. They greatly influenced the American labor movement and brought us the eight-hour workday. They contributed much to American culture, established the American movie industry and gave us much good music. On the lighter side, their influence can be felt in the dozens of Yiddish words and idioms that have entered the English language and in many of the deli foods we love to eat. The list is endless.

ONE WAY TO TRACE THE history of Jews in America is through their humor. I restrict myself to the latest wave of immigrants, the Yiddish-speaking Jews of Eastern Europe. As one would expect, their humor tended to mirror both the early hardships and the later successes that they experienced. Early on came the jokes about *die greener*, the new immigrants from the *shtetl* (small town or village in Eastern Europe) and the problems they encountered in their new lives. For instance, the crowded condition in which families lived on the Lower East Side, and the inevitable border who shared their quarters, gave rise to a whole genre of jokes, some of them quite risqué. Leo Rosten, in his incomparable *The Joys of Yiddish*, tells the following: At his wife's graveside, Mr. Berman wept copiously. Mr. Berman's border, a Mr. Kipnis, wept even more—and, indeed, carried on so hysterically that Mr. Berman said, "Kipnis, don't take it so hard! I'll get married again."

With the imposition of immigration quotas in 1921 and then again in 1924, the number of new immigrants slowed to a trickle. Those who had been in the *Goldene Medineh* for a while, were starting to "make it" in the new country and slowly moved out of the Lower East Side into the middle class. In trying to behave in keeping with their new status, they became the butt of a new, indulgent kind of joke. Leo Rosten tells the story of the new immigrant who'd been making weekly deposits into his savings account, signing his deposit slips with XX. Over the years, his deposits had been growing and one day he comes into the bank and signs his check with an XXX. "Why the change?" asks the bank teller. "Well," he shamefacedly admits, "now that we can afford it, my wife wants me to take a middle name."

Jokes about such *alrightniks*, Jews who had become prosperous and were trying to fit into American society, now took on a new dimension. They poked fun at individuals changing the family name, having "nose jobs" and, ultimately, trying to "pass"—be accepted as Gentiles. Usually though, the punch line was that such attempts were doomed to failure; persons trying to pass would slip up somehow in the end. An example tells about Yankel who had not only converted to Catholicism but had entered the priesthood. The bishop, commenting on the first mass the new priest offered, said: "That was very well done, Father Jacob. But next time, don't start your sermon with 'Fellow *Goyim*....'"

Jewish jokes were often quite sarcastic and self-disparaging. There's the one about a black woman who won the lottery and goes into a fancy dress shop to buy herself a mink coat. She looks at herself in the mirror for a long time then asks the saleslady: "Do you think it makes me look too Jewish?" Now there's a racist joke, no doubt; but is it anti-black or anti-Jewish—or both?

In attempting to assimilate, at least partially, many Jews also shed the orthodoxy that characterized *shtetl* society. Their jokes tended to make fun of organized religion—usually alleging hypocrisy among Orthodox rabbis and ignorance among Reform rabbis. One of the classic jokes showing the contempt for the latter is about the Reform Temple which during the High Holy Days, Rosh Ha-Shanah and Yom Kippur, displayed a sign saying, "Closed for the Holidays."

The humor of the period, as Jewish humor in general, was not of the belly-laughter, side-splitting sort. It was often bitter-sweet, introspective and self disparaging. It, undoubtedly, provided a partial antidote to the stresses and hardships this group of immigrants to the *Goldene Medineh* had to endure.

11 Zionism Without Zion

IN ISRAEL THESE DAYS, WHEN the conversation turns to the question of giving up land, it does not take long before tempers heat up, voices rise and words like "betrayal" and "sin" are thrown about. Giving up even a small part of *Eretz Israel* is certainly an explosive issue; abandoning it completely is without question an unthinkable idea. Yet, the history of Zionism records a number of occasions when well-meaning people sought solutions to the "Jewish problem" away from Zion. The Uganda proposal at the beginning of the twentieth century was undoubtedly the most notable of these proposals.

When Dr. Theodor Herzl was sent by his Viennese newspaper to Paris in 1895 to cover the trial of Captain Alfred Dreyfus, who was falsely accused of high treason, he was struck by the venomous anti-Semitism of the French. He concluded that Europe was becoming a dangerous place for Jews. In his book, *The Jewish State*, published a year later, he proposes that the solution to the problem was the establishment of an autonomous Jewish state in *Eretz Israel*. This could be achieved only through political activity and to that aim he convened the First Zionist

Congress in 1897 in Basel, where the World Zionist Organization was founded. Jewish yearning for a homeland had now become a political movement — Zionism.

As elected president, Herzl worked tirelessly for the next six years pursuing diplomatic channels to achieve his goal. He made repeated offers to Sultan Abdul Hamid II of Turkey to sell Palestine, which was under his rule, to the Jews; he met with Kaiser Wilhelm II of Germany to enlist his support; and he discussed his plans with the British government, which was essentially in sympathy with them. All to no avail. Great Britain, which could not give him Palestine because it was not theirs to give, offered him several other areas for possible settlement. Herzl rejected these unequivocally. Zionism without Zion was unthinkable.

Yet Herzl changed his mind when, at Easter time 1903, news of the pogrom in Kishinev, the capital of Bessarabia, became known. Under the active leadership of high-placed government officials, and with the incitement of local newspapers, a terrible slaughter took place—over 50 Jews killed and many more injured, thousands of houses and businesses looted and 2,000 families left homeless. It was then that Joseph Chamberlain, British Colonial Secretary, offered Uganda, an East-African colony, for a possible settlement area. Herzl brought the offer to the Sixth Zionist Congress when it met in Basel in August of that year.

The Uganda Plan burst upon the delegates like a bombshell. Although Herzl presented it as a temporary measure (an "overnight shelter") until *Eretz Israel* became available for settlement, the opposition considered this an abhorrent suggestion. Surprisingly, it was the Russian delegates, including those from Kishinev, who felt most strongly that no alternative to the ancient and historic homeland was acceptable. At the end of the day, the Congress could agree only that a delegation of three be sent to investigate Uganda for possible settlement (292 for, 177 against, 132 abstentions).

We know now that the Uganda Plan came to naught. At the time, though, it came close to tearing the new Zionist Organization apart. Although Herzl closed the session with an emotional declaration of the Psalmist's words, "If I forget thee, O Jerusalem, may my right hand wither!" the East-European delegates left feeling betrayed. Emotions ran so high that at a Hanukkah party three months later a young Russian Jew tried to assassinate Max Nordau, Herzl's close friend and second-in-command. Nordau, who did not believe in the Uganda Plan and supported Herzl only out of a sense of loyalty, narrowly escaped the two bullets fired at him.

The bitter rift was partially healed during the Seventh Zionist Congress (London, 1905), when the Uganda Plan was finally laid to rest. Still, Israel Zangwill, the noted British author, and 40 other delegates walked out in protest and founded the Jewish Territorial Society. Its aim was to establish an autonomous Jewish entity somewhere other than in *Eretz Israel*. During the twenty years of its existence, the society explored possibilities for settlement in Surinam, Iraq, Canada, Australia, Mexico and several other countries.

As in the case of Uganda, all of these territorialist suggestions were rejected. In the final analysis, Zionism without Zion, that is, without the Land of Israel, was never an acceptable solution.

THE UGANDA PLAN WAS NOT the first attempt to save Russian Jews from the devastating forces which beset their society. Twenty years before, in the early 1880s, another movement had evolved in response to those same forces: officially sanctioned anti-Semitism and the resulting periodic pogroms, which ravaged the *shtetlakh* (small Jewish towns) of southern Russia. The movement, which called itself *Am Olam* (the Eternal People), was founded by a group of young idealists who believed that it was not enough to escape the continual Cossack massacres and general wretchedness of Jewish life in Russia. To revitalize and normalize Jewish society required a return to the soil, to physical labor and to those occupations from which Jews had been shut out since the Middle Ages.

Am Olam were young men and women who believed in the ideals of Utopian Socialism, that is, absence of private property, no hired labor, and a communal sharing of all they produced. Moreover, they believed that the United States was the place in which to convert their vision into reality. They were dreaming of a Jewish region in this "Land of the Free."

So, in 1881, several hundred of them set out from Odessa and other Russian cities to establish communal agricultural settlements in America. On the whole, they were not very successful. Of the four settlements they founded, "New Odessa," in southern Oregon (between Medford and Ashland), flourished the longest. It functioned for over five years, got along well with its neighbors (who were fascinated by these Russian Jewish farmers) but, finally, started breaking up because of ideological squabbles in 1886. *The Jews of Oregon* by S. Lowenstein devotes a chapter to "New Odessa," and refers to valuable archival materials.

Although *Am Olam* was an attempt at organized, *mass* emigration from Russia for the purpose of establishing Jewish agricultural settlements in the New World, there were, of course, many individual Russian immigrants to the Americas. Some of these who had come earlier and many who followed had tried their hand at agriculture. Baron Maurice de Hirsch, the fabulously wealthy German Jewish banker and philanthropist, had much to do with this.

De Hirsch had offered the czarist government 50 million francs to improve the miserable economic conditions of Russian Jews. When his offer was rejected, de Hirsch founded the Jewish Colonization Association (ICA, 1891) whose aim it was to help Russian Jews emigrate and become farmers in the Americas. Many of the families helped by his fund settled in various places in the United States. His focus, though, was Argentina. He proposed to transfer three million Jews to that country and set up a "sort of Jewish State." Although his grandiose scheme did not even come close to reaching its objective, by the time of his death in 1896, the ICA had established five large colonies in Argentina in which almost 7,000 Jews lived as farmers.

Theodor Herzl, founder and president of the World Zionist Organization, had met Baron de Hirsch and had tried to interest him in the Zionist idea. De Hirsch thought the idea of Jewish settlements in *Eretz Israel* (Palestine) insane.

It is surely one of the supreme ironies of history that for a fraction of what the ICA spent to settle Jews worldwide, it could have acquired the whole of Palestine from the sultan of Turkey. Herzl and the Zionist organization were unable to raise the five million pound sterling the Sultan demanded for the area at the time.

In 1881, the year that *Am Olam* was founded, another movement was born in Russia—Ḥibbat Zion, (Love of Zion). It differed from *Am Olam* in one important respect: its dreams, and the efforts to realize them, were directed toward *Eretz Israel*. Only there could a meaningful independent existence, a national renaissance of the Jewish People, be achieved.

It was *Ḥibbat Zion* that generated the first wave of mass immigration to *Eretz Israel*. Its members, facing great physical hardships, founded the first agricultural settlements: Rishon le-Zion, Petaḥ Tikvah, Gederah, Reḥovot, Rosh Pinnah, and many others—places that have long since become prosperous towns. They were the men and women who insisted that Hebrew become the language of the land and, by not accepting any *ersatz* Zions, laid the foundation for the rebirth of Israel.

THERE WAS ONE OTHER IMPORTANT attempt to create a geographic Jewish entity. This one, however, was imposed from the outside and it too was doomed to failure.

The Soviet Union had been granting national autonomy to minority groups who constituted the majority of the population in a given area. Although Russian Jews were not concentrated in any one part of the country, the Soviet government was eager to have them settle in and near Manchuria in order to develop it as a line of defense in the East. To that purpose, it recognized the Jewish population as a National Minority in 1928 and established a national district (*okrug*) for them in Birobidjan. In 1934, the status of the area was raised to that of a region (*oblast*) with the following declaration: "Soviet Jewish statehood is being developed and consolidated in forms corresponding to the national and traditional conditions of the Jewish people." To that end, Yiddish was declared one of the official languages, used by several schools and even by the Kaganovich State Theater.

Even at its height the project had attracted only about 30,000 Jews. Today, only a few thousand are left. It is clear that most Russian Jews never viewed Birobidjan, an underdeveloped area in eastern Siberia, as their national homeland. The scheme left a bitter legacy from which Russian Jews suffer even today: The word "Jewish" appears where personal identification cards ask for "Nationality." This has facilitated discrimination against Jews starting with Stalin's purges in the '50s until this very day.

12 A Windmill Stands in Jerusalem

IN A SMALL, WELL-KEPT PARK in modern Jerusalem, there stands a windmill. The windmill looks across the valley to Mt. Zion and the Old City of Jerusalem, to which it indirectly owes its existence. The arms of the windmill have stood still for over a century and a half, and today the beautiful three-story high structure serves mainly as a photo spot for tourists and for Israeli couples who like to have their wedding pictures shot at this romantic view-point. The windmill also serves as a museum which recalls the life of the man who transplanted it from England to the Middle East — Sir Moses Montefiore.

Moses Montefiore was born in 1784, the oldest son of a wealthy *Sephardi* merchant family in London. During his long life — he died at age 101 — he became a close friend and counselor to Queen Victoria and was highly respected all over Europe and beyond. He was a well-known philanthropist who greatly influenced the development of the modern city of Jerusalem.

Montefiore retired at age 40 after having amassed great wealth as one of only a handful of Jews on the London stock exchange. From then on, he devoted his life to humanitarian endeavors and charitable enterprises, helping both Jews and non-Jews in distress. With a member of the Rothschild family he provided a huge loan to the British Government that enabled it to implement the Slave Emancipation Act of 1833.

In 1840, he successfully negotiated for the release of innocent Jews accused in the infamous Blood Libel suit in Damascus. A Capuchin monk had disappeared without a trace and Jews were accused of having used his blood in the making of *matzah* (unleavened bread) for Passover. In recognition of his success in this scandal, which had outraged all of Europe, Queen Victoria allowed Sir Moses, the first Jew ever to be knighted, to add the word *Yerushalayim* (Jerusalem) in Hebrew to his family crest. He expended similar efforts on behalf of the Jews of Morocco, Persia and of czarist Russia.

His main love, however, was reserved for the Holy Land, which he visited a total of seven times and which bears his stamp to this day. On his first visit to Jerusalem in 1827, he was appalled at the squalor and filth in which most of the inhabitants lived. The Talmud states that ten measures of beauty descended on the world: nine were bestowed on Jerusalem and one upon the rest of the world. That may have been the case during the time of Herod's Temple, but nineteenth-century travel accounts all agree on the filth and the lack of sanitation that characterized the city of Jerusalem. The Turkish bureaucrats who ruled the city were interested only in filling their own coffers with bribes.

Montefiore resolved to improve the situation by inducing Jews to leave their hovels and move outside the city walls. He built various industrial enterprises (a printing press, a textile mill, a sewing school, etc.) to provide employment to the overcrowded and impoverished population. None of these succeeded. On his fifth visit, in 1855, he imported a windmill from England to provide cheap flour for the residents of Jerusalem and employment outside the city. Below it, he built *Mishkenot Sha'ananim* (Restful Residences)—two long buildings with small apartments for the workers and their families. Despite the fact that the buildings were surrounded by a wall, and that he paid a bonus to those who moved into them, he still did not succeed in luring the residents of the city out of their squalid environment into the fresh air. Afraid of Arab marauders and wild animals, they scurried back every night to the protection of the city walls. At least two of the workers were murdered during this period.

The windmill, too, was a failure. Mill owners in town, afraid of the competition from the modern contraption, hired a woman known to have the Evil Eye to cast a spell on the windmill—and, sure enough, after a few years it ceased to operate. It is also true that the mechanism was not suited for the tough Middle Eastern wheat and soon broke down for lack of maintenance and spare parts.

Mishkenot Sha'ananim did not expand until ten years later in 1865 when a cholera epidemic broke out in town. When 15 percent of the inhabitants of the Jewish Quarter died, but nobody living in *Mishkenot*

Sha'ananim even fell ill, people started to concede the value of fresh air and clean water. They moved into the residences and more housing units were added. This became the first Jewish settlement outside the walled Old City of Jerusalem.

Today, *Mishkenot Sha'ananim* is the pride of modern Jerusalem. It houses the beautiful apartments to which the City of Jerusalem invites special guests—artists, composers, authors, etc. from all over the world—to spend a sabbatical year at the City's expense and pursue their creative interests.

Next to it is another quarter which carries Sir Moses' name: *Yemin Moshe*. Established in 1891, on land which he had acquired, it provided housing for poor Turkish immigrants for many years. After the Six-Day War, it turned into an artists' colony and subsequently into a beautifully landscaped, high-priced neighborhood for Israeli yuppies.

The windmill, one of the many enterprises Montefiore established to help develop *Eretz Israel*, is a fitting memorial to this man of great vision.

Finland: Where Jews Fought on the Side of the Nazis

ON OUR TRIP TO THE Scandinavian capitals, my wife and I spent some time in Helsinki, the capital of Finland. While there, we visited the Great Synagogue and had a chance to talk at length with the Cantor, Mr. André Zweig, who showed us around the complex of which the synagogue is part. In recounting the history of Finnish Jews, he told us a most bizarre story: during the Second World War, Finnish Jews fought on the side of the Nazis against the allies. Before taking a look at this strange episode, a bit of background is in order.

Jewish history in Finland does not go back very far. Until 1809, Finland was part of Sweden. For centuries, Sweden had kept Jews from living within its borders in order, as one historian puts it, "to protect its pure Lutheran faith." Only toward the end of the eighteenth century were Jews allowed to settle there, and then only in the three major cities. Special laws restricted their freedom of movement and their entrance into most occupations. Moreover, they could not hold government positions and did not have the right to vote. In 1809, when Finland became part of Russia, the anti-Jewish laws were kept in force.

THE FIRST JEWISH SETTLERS IN Finland were *Cantonists*—Russian soldiers who had been stationed there, had completed their army stint, and remembered enough of their Jewishness to return to it after 25 years of forced service in the Russian army. *Cantonists* were the victims of one of the most cruel attempts by the Russian czars to force the Jewish population, specifically Jewish children, to convert to Christianity. To fill the government's draft quota for Jews, children as young as eight or nine-years old were snatched from their families, placed in *Cantonist* units (army live-in schools) until the age of eighteen, after which they were inducted into the czar's army for 25-year terms of service. The express objective of the government was to turn these boys away from their Jewish roots and force them into baptism. Several eyewitness accounts describe the misery of these youngsters. Kidnapped from loving Jewish families, half of them died on the forced marches to the

Cantonments. Most of those who survived succumbed to the unrelenting pressure of privation and torture and "consented" to be baptized. It has been estimated that, between 1827 and 1854, approximately 70,000 Jewish men were conscripted. Of these, 50,000 were minors sent first to the *Cantonments.*

A few of the *Cantonists* returned to Judaism at the end of their army service. Those who had served in Finland and opted to be discharged there, constituted the first Jewish community in that country. They still needed special residence permits that had to be renewed every three months. For a living they were restricted to deal only in used clothing. It was not until the Communist Revolution overthrew the Russian government in 1917, and Finland became independent for the first time in its history, that the 1,200 Finnish Jews received full civil rights. By 1940, the Jewish community had grown to about 2,000 persons who were fully integrated into the economic, political and cultural life of their country.

IN 1939, WHEN THE SOVIET Union attacked Finland, Jews, of course, fought to repulse the invaders of their homeland. Again, in 1941, when Germany and Russia went to war with each other, Finland entered the war against Russia on the side of Germany. This was a purely pragmatic step based on an empty Nazi promise that the Finns could annex southern Karelia, a territory the Soviets had previously taken from them. And so it came about that Finnish Jews fought on the side of the Nazis who had sworn to make Europe *Judenrein* (cleansed of Jews).

Later, the Germans put pressure on Finland to surrender its Jews, and, in fact, readied ships in Helsinki harbor to transport them to Germany. Finland refused to yield—and no Finnish Jews died in the Holocaust. (Eight Jewish immigrants to Finland who had fled Russia at the beginning of the war could not be saved in this fashion. A kibbutz in Israel, Yad Hashemonah, keeps their memory alive.)

Today, about 1,350 Jews live in Finland. About 850 are members of the synagogue in Helsinki, the rest are affiliated with the *shul* in Turku. But Turku's community is dying a slow death as a result of a 99 percent intermarriage rate. In contrast, from what we were able to observe, the Helsinki congregation seemed to be quite vital. The community center, which we visited, houses the synagogue (the congregation is Orthodox), a smaller chapel for a daily *minyan,* a sixteen-bed hospital and a *mikveh* (ritual bath). A 90-student school offers a general curriculum as well as instruction in Hebrew, Judaism and Jewish history. The building also contains two kosher kitchens that serve 200 meals a day, a 5,000-volume library and a large social hall for special events.

World War II days are forgotten by all but a few of the Finnish Jews. Those who remember maintain, "We did not fight *with* the Nazis, we fought *against* the Russians."

14 A Synagogue They Call "The Ruin"

UNTIL 1948, THREE IMPOSING DOMED buildings graced the Old City of Jerusalem—each representing one of the three major religions that call the city "holy." Each of these buildings symbolized all the things that make Jerusalem, the Holy City, meaningful to the faithful of that particular religion.

For Christianity, it was the Church of the Holy Sepulcher which, according to Christian tradition, stands on Golgotha, the place of the crucifixion of Jesus and contains the tomb in which he was buried and from which he rose.

In Islam, the Temple Mount with its magnificent Dome of the Rock, is the third holiest place on earth, after Mecca and Medina. Below the golden dome lies the Rock of Foundation from which, according to Muslim tradition, the Prophet Muhammad was lifted to heaven by the Archangel Gabriel.

Situated in the heart of the Jewish quarter of the Old City, the third building, known as the Ḥurvah (ruin) provided the center of gravity for the religious life of the large number of Ashkenazi Jews of Jerusalem. It was to this synagogue that Sir Herbert Samuel, the first High Commissioner to Palestine under the British Mandate, came to pray on his first Sabbath in Jerusalem in 1920. The Ḥurvah, whose high arching dome was a landmark of Jewish Jerusalem that could be seen from afar, was destroyed in a senseless act of brutish vandalism by the Jordanian forces after the Jewish Quarter surrendered to them in the War of 1948.

Where did the Ḥurvah get its strange name? A letter by the Spanish scholar Naḥmanides dated 1267, which describes the plight of the tiny Jewish population of Jerusalem at the time, recounts that he converted an existing structure into a synagogue to serve that community. Two centuries later, the synagogue collapsed after a heavy rain in 1474 and was rebuilt 50 years later. At that time, it was the only synagogue in Jerusalem. This time, it served for only about 60 years until it was closed in 1586, on the order of the Turkish governor of Jerusalem. It seems that the bribes offered his Highness were not high enough for him to allow infidels to pray in the Holy City.

The *Ḥurvah's* modern—and fascinating—history starts in the year 1700. In that year, Rabbi Yehudah the Pious left Poland to settle in Jerusalem in order to hasten the coming of the Messiah. He must have been a charismatic person, for 1,300 of his disciples and their families followed him to the Holy Land. Their dream was to build a large synagogue for their community and devote themselves to prayer and study. To that end, they collected pledges of support from the various European communities they passed on their route.

Unfortunately, things did not go well: Rabbi Yehudah died three days after arriving in Jerusalem (some say he was bitten by a snake while immersing himself in a *mikveh*) and, consequently, much of the promised money never materialized. In desperation, his followers borrowed money from Arab moneylenders to bribe the authorities to grant them a building permit and to buy construction materials. Being *Ashkenazi* Jews, they spoke no Turkish, Arabic or Ladino (the language of the local *Sephardi* Jews), and were greatly taken advantage of by everyone they dealt with. Their debts kept rising, year after year, until the moneylenders' patience ran out. On November 8, 1720—a Shabbat—the Arabs broke into the synagogue, burned the Torah scrolls and tore down the building. After that, all *Ashkenazi* Jews were banned from Jerusalem and moved to Safed.

The *Ḥurvah* remained a ruin until the 1830s by which time much had changed: *Ashkenazim* had drifted back into Jerusalem, a new law had wiped out the old debts and the *Qadi* (Muslim religious leader) of Jerusalem, under pressure from several European governments, ruled that the area in question belonged to the *Ashkenazi* community. By 1837, they were allowed to build a small synagogue which quickly proved inadequate in size. It took years of petitions and pressure, and repeated payments of large bribes, for the Ottoman authorities to give

permission to enlarge the building. Donations were collected from all over the world, with more than half of the total amount needed contributed by Yeḥezkiel Re'uven, a *Sephardi* Jew from Baghdad.

The resulting structure was an imposing building. Designed

in the Byzantine style, built of the finest materials and beautifully decorated, it was large enough to accommodate 300 male worshippers in the large hall and 150 women on the various balconies that ran along the inside of the great dome.

When the Jordanians destroyed the building after it was surrendered to them in 1948, they also brought down the four arches which had supported the dome of the synagogue. Only one of the arches has been rebuilt. For many years, it stood alone as a graceful, sweeping reminder of the glory that once was known as "The Ruin."

In the year 2000, the Israeli government approved the rebuilding of the synagogue in its original style, and paid part of the cost of reconstruction. The rest of the funds were donated by a Ukrainian Jewish businessman and philanthropist, Vadim Rabinovitch. Early

in 2010, the full restoration of the Ḥurvah was completed.

In some people's opinion, it was the wrong thing to do. They felt that the ruined Ḥurvah standing in stark contrast to the rest of the beautifully rebuilt Jewish Quarter, would have provided a most dramatic memorial to the indecencies sustained in the War of Independence. Yet Naomi Ragen, the Israeli author and Journalist, attending services there on *Yom HaZikaron* 5770 (Memorial Day 2010), writes movingly: "It reminded me of Ezekiel's vision of dry bones rising from the dead full of life once more."

NILI: A Jewish Spy Ring

NOT MANY PEOPLE OUTSIDE ISRAEL have heard of an organization called NILI or are aware of the important role it played in the establishment of the State of Israel. NILI was a Jewish espionage ring which operated during the First World War in *Eretz Israel* (then called Palestine). Its goal was to help the British war effort by providing intelligence about Turkish fortifications and troop movements in the area. The hope was that Britain and its allies (France, the United States, Russia and others) would win the war against the Central Powers (Germany, Austro-Hungary and the Ottoman Empire), and that England would wrest Palestine from Turkish rule.

Palestine had been part of the Ottoman Empire since 1517 when the Ottoman Turks conquered the area and extended their rule over the Middle East. Palestine, which at that time was a backward, impoverished province of Syria with fewer than 1,500 Jewish households, prospered under the Ottoman rulers. The Sultan welcomed large numbers of Jewish refugees expelled from various Catholic countries of Europe and Jewish communities were founded throughout the Empire. They were assured religious freedom and, with some restrictions, granted equal civil rights. The communities felt secure and flourished.

This was true also of the Jewish communities in *Eretz Israel*. At that time, the city of Tzefat (Safed) became an important center of Jewish learning, particularly for the Kabbalists, students of Jewish mysticism. Jerusalem was greatly rebuilt and beautified by the early sultans.

Unfortunately, these favorable conditions did not last long. Already by the end of the sixteenth century, Palestine was suffering from political and economic decay and the Jews were singled out for special harassment. The Turkish governor of the region and the rulers of the various towns were corrupt and enriched themselves at the expense of the country. They extorted large sums of money from the Jewish inhabitants, many of whom were then forced to depend on handouts collected from Jewish communities abroad. The Sultan and his central government were too weak to stop the corruption.

The impoverishment of Palestine and its Jewish population continued over the course of the next three centuries. It was actually part of the decline of the Ottoman Empire as a whole. Turkey had failed to keep up with the industrial progress in Europe and its rate of economic development had slowed greatly. The empire had lost many of the states it had conquered and was beset by civil strife within its shrinking borders. The corruption of its administration was a byword in diplomatic circles and from about the middle of the nineteenth century, Turkey was known as "the sick man of Europe."

By 1914, the condition of the Jews in Palestine was grave indeed. As non-Muslims, they had been subject to discriminatory taxes and legal restrictions even before World War I. They had been victims of scattered anti-Jewish violence, repeated burnings of synagogues, and, of course, the infamous Blood Libel suit of Damascus in 1840. When Turkey entered the war in October 1914 on the side of Germany, the Jews' problems were greatly exacerbated. The survival of the *Yishuv*, the Jewish community in *Eretz Israel*, was now in doubt. It was cut off from the major sources of new immigrants and, except for monies collected in the United States, from the sources of financial aid. Access to European markets for the products of the recently established agricultural settlements became impossible during war time.

About half of the 85,000 Jews in Palestine were Russian citizens and the Ottoman government treated them as enemy aliens. The laws protecting them as foreign nationals were revoked. They were forced to become Turkish citizens or leave the country. Most chose to become naturalized, but about 10,000 were expelled amidst much cruelty. In November 1914, the government compelled the Jews to surrender all the arms in their possession on threat of very severe punishment. Since these arms served as the means of self-protection from Arab attacks, the *Yishuv* at first refused to give up the weapons but eventually was forced to comply.

By 1917, people had become very anxious. The United States had entered the war and thus the last source of financial aid was cut off. The publication of all Hebrew-language newspapers was suspended and explicit anti-Jewish and anti-Zionist sentiments were expressed by government officials. In March of that year, the government expelled all but a small fraction of the 11,000 Jewish inhabitants of the city of Jaffa and its recently-founded suburb, Tel Aviv. The realization started to grow in the *Yishuv* that the situation closely resembled the one that had led to the Turkish slaughter of a million and a half of its Armenian Christian citizens. (Information about the massacre had become public the previous year.)

THESE, THEN, WERE THE PRECARIOUS conditions—both political and economic—which the *Yishuv* faced with the outbreak of World War I in 1914. This situation was the reason why a small group of young Jewish men and women were willing to risk their lives to help the British armed forces defeat the Turkish rulers of Palestine. The organizer of the secret intelligence organization was Aaron Aaronsohn, a renowned agronomist who was joined by his sister Sarah, who had recently left an unhappy marriage to a Turkish businessman and returned to *Eretz Israel*. Both Aaron and Sarah had personally witnessed the atrocities against the Armenians in Turkey. They feared an Islamic holy war against non-Muslims and were convinced that the best chance for a Jewish homeland in *Eretz Israel* lay with the British rather than the Turks. They were joined by their younger brother, Alexander, by Avshalom Feinberg, an assistant in Aaron's agricultural experiment station and by several friends of the family. The Aaronsohns were residents of Zikhron Ya'akov, which, at the time, was a small village situated on the western slope of the Carmel mountain range. Slowly, the size of the group grew, always through personal recruitment of family members and close personal friends. NILI, the name they chose for the group, is an acronym of the biblical phrase: *netzah yisrael lo yeshakker* (the Strength of Israel will not deceive) taken from 1 Samuel 15:29.

Although the British forces were massed in Egypt, they seemed unwilling to push their attack through the Sinai desert into Palestine. From July 1915 on, members of NILI made repeated attempts to contact the British High Command and volunteer their assistance. All their overtures were rebuffed and their offer rejected. Finally, in the summer of 1916, Aaronsohn was able to reach London and persuade the military that the offer of his group was sincere. He transferred to British headquarters in Cairo where he contributed much valuable information about water resources in the Sinai desert that he had gathered during his many professional explorations in the area.

In January 1917, Feinberg and another NILI member, Josef Lishansky, disguised as Arabs, tried to make their way to Egypt to renew contact with Aaronsohn. They were attacked by Bedouins in the Sinai desert. Feinberg was killed and Lishansky, though badly wounded, succeeded in reaching the British lines. Fifty years later, Feinberg's remains were definitively identified and repatriated to *Eretz Israel*.

From Cairo, Aaronsohn was able to set up a regular channel of communication with NILI members by means of a British ship that dropped anchor off the coast, opposite Zikhron Ya'akov. Starting in February 1917, at prearranged meetings, NILI members relayed information on troop strength and movement that the network had gathered. The ship fulfilled an additional, very important function: it enabled Aaronsohn to transfer sums of money that he had collected from various charitable organizations (mainly in the United States) to support the beleaguered *Yishuv*. With the expulsion from Tel Aviv, families had lost their livelihood and had become homeless. Although many found shelter in the villages and towns inland, their situation was desperate. Four months after the forced evacuation, in early August 1917, Lishansky reports in a letter to Aaronsohn: "Children by the dozen are dying of starvation...."

The sea connection was maintained until September 1917, when the Turks intercepted a carrier pigeon carrying a coded message sent by Sarah Aaronsohn. This spelled the end of NILI. Shortly thereafter, Na'aman Belkind, a cousin of Feinberg, was caught on his way to Egypt. He broke under torture. On October 1, Turkish soldiers surrounded Zikhron Ya'akov and arrested numerous people including Sarah. After four days of cruel torture, Sarah, fearing that she might reveal information about additional members of NILI, committed suicide. She managed, on the way to the bathroom, to lay hands on a revolver hidden in a secret cabinet and shot herself through the mouth. She died three days later. Josef Lishansky managed to escape, but was later captured by the Turks. He and his cousin Belkind were both hanged in Damascus on December 16 of that year.

It is one of the ironies of history that the tragic end of NILI and the death of so many of its members came only days before the victory for which they fought. The British forces led by General Allenby, finally pushed across the Sinai and captured Beersheba on October 31, 1917. They took Tel Aviv and Jaffa on November 16, and on the 10th of December, 1918, the first day of Hanukkah, accepted the surrender of the Turkish forces in Jerusalem.

Does this mean that the NILI members died in vain? Not when one considers their achievements and the veneration in which they are held today in the State of Israel.

Throughout its existence, the attitude of the *Yishuv* was hostile toward the group. The commanding officer of the Turkish forces in Palestine was known for his cruelty; the leaders of the *Yishuv* believed that NILI was endangering the Jewish population by their illegal activities and refused to lend support to the group. In fact, when the Turkish army threatened to burn Zikhron Ya'akov to the ground unless the village surrendered Lishansky, many of the farmers were willing to hand him over. They were spared this shameful act because by this time he was not there any longer.

NILI was a small organization. It has been estimated that even at its height, the group never numbered more than a couple of dozen active members and no more than 150 supporters. (Of course, there may have been a much larger number of sympathizers among the general population, but this is hard to assess.)

Today, NILI and its members are revered as one of the heroic pre-State groups that helped bring about the independent State of Israel. This small number of men and women helped overthrow Turkish rule in Palestine and, according to a British estimate after the war, saved the lives of 30,000 British soldiers. In addition, NILI smuggled into the country and distributed the financial aid that enabled the *Yishuv* to survive when it was completely cut off from all other Jewish communities.

Sarah Aaronsohn has been called "Israel's favorite pre-State martyr-heroine" and there is hardly a town in Israel in which a street is not named for her. The Aaronsohn house is maintained as a museum of the NILI group, and is the major attraction of the town of Zikhron Ya'akov. The secret wall cabinet in which Sarah had hidden the gun with which she committed suicide to save her comrades is still being shown by tour guides.

Aaron Aaronsohn, the founder of this Jewish spy organization and the only one of its leaders to see its goal achieved, died in an aircraft accident over the English Channel six months later.

16 The Little Blue Boxes

NOT SO MANY YEARS AGO, there was hardly a Jewish home outside of *Eretz Israel* that did not boast a "Little Blue Box." The blue *pushke*, as it was affectionately called in Yiddish, was the tangible symbol of the connection of Diaspora Jewish families to *Eretz Israel*. It was the major means by which the Jewish National Fund collected the monies required to purchase and develop land in what was then called Palestine.

The fund to buy land in Turkish-ruled Palestine was created by the Zionist Federation at the Fifth Zionist Congress in Basel, in 1901. The Jewish National Fund—Keren Kayemet LeYisrael (JNF–KKL)—was established to purchase land for the Jewish People in *Eretz Israel*. The Hebrew name of the organization is most apt. It is taken from a passage in the Talmud which promises a reward for certain good deeds "in this life, while the principal remains intact (*hakeren kayemet*) for the Life to Come."

The JNF is a unique institution. The land it bought became "public land" in the truest sense of the word. It is not government land. It is land purchased with the nickels and dimes and, more often than not, the pennies of hundreds of thousands of Jewish families who, even when impoverished themselves, put their contributions on a regular basis into the little tin collection boxes. It is land that belongs to the Jewish People as a whole. JNF land is not resold to private owners, but leased for long periods of time, usually 49 years.

In the period between the two World Wars, about one million Blue Boxes had pride of place in Jewish homes throughout the world. The little *pushkes* did their job well. From the first small parcel of 800 acres, which it acquired in the spring of 1903, the JNF grew to become the largest non-government owner of land before the establishment of Israel. In 1948, the Fund owned 13 percent of all Jewish land in *Eretz Israel*, about half of which had been paid for with monies collected in the Blue Boxes. It should be noted that up to the War of Independence, when the six neighboring countries attacked the newly-founded state, every single square-foot of land was bought—usually at exorbitant prices—from the original owners. These owners were often absentee landlords, rich Arabs who lived in Beirut, Cairo, Paris or London. They were not greatly concerned about the fate of the *fellahin* (small farmers) who worked the land on a share-cropping basis.

Much of the land was barren and uninhabited at the time it was bought. It became fertile agricultural land through the efforts of the JNF. From its very birth, the organization focused on developing agriculture and greening the land. Whenever a new plot was acquired trees were planted on it. This reforestation effort—over 230 million trees—changed the ecology of the land. It pushed back the ever-encroaching desert and reversed the ecological damage that 400 years of Turkish rule and neglect had wrought. Israel is the only country in the world that entered the twenty-first century with more trees than it had 100 years earlier!

In 1926, the Jewish National Fund formed a partnership with Hadassah, the Women's Zionist Organization of America. Both organizations shared the Zionist dream of redeeming *Eretz Israel* for the Jewish People. Both also shared an interest in research and education to improve life for the people. Over the years, Hadassah has been the Fund's largest single contributing organization.

With the creation of the State of Israel, the focus of JNF activities has shifted from acquisition of land to solving ecological and environmental problems. Reforestation is still a high priority, especially in view of the fact that recent wars and deliberately set fires by Arab arsonists have taken a devastating toll on forested areas. The emphasis, however, is on reclamation projects that have created hundreds of parks, recreation areas and trails, for relaxation and nature study. An important feature of these areas is the fact that they are easily accessible to the large number of disabled—many of them victims of the wars Israel had to fight for its existence.

An overriding concern in recent years has been the critical water shortage Israel faces. JNF, besides constructing 180 reservoirs to conserve this precious resource, uses cutting-edge science to develop new recycling and desalinization methods to better utilize the water available. This is in line with its next great mission, developing the parched southern portion of Israel, the Negev.

Theodor Herzl, the father of modern Zionism, in laying out his vision of a homeland for the Jewish People, declared: "If you will it, it is no dream." The creation of the Jewish National Fund—and the Blue Boxes which became such an important part of it—helped to make his dream a reality.

A Tale of Two Cities

IS THERE A CONNECTION BETWEEN the name of a European synagogue and the name of the city of Tel Aviv? There is, indeed—a very direct connection. The synagogue to which I am referring is the *Altneuschul* (Old-New *shul*), which stands in what used to be the Jewish quarter in the city of Prague. It is the oldest still functioning synagogue in Europe. Records show that it was built in 1270, though recent scholarship suggests that the south annex had existed as a single-naved synagogue as early as 1230.

The origin of the curious name of the *Altneuschul* is not quite clear. A pamphlet put out by the State Jewish Museum in Prague traces the name to the seventeenth century when another synagogue was built in the Jewish ghetto, known as the New Synagogue. Folk etymology, however, hears in the name the Hebrew expression, *al-tnai*, (on condition), and explains that stones from the ruins of the Holy Temple in Jerusalem, which was destroyed in the year 70 C.E., were lent for the construction of the *Altneuschul*, on condition that they be returned upon the coming of the Messiah and the rebuilding of the Temple.

For centuries the *Altneuschul* has captured the interest of artists, scholars and travelers. Many paintings and old prints exist which depict the interior and furnishings of the synagogue. Much history and many legends are connected with the place. Sentimental tourists believed they saw the blood of victims of the pogrom of 1389—when a large number of the Jews of Prague were murdered in the *shul* on the last day of Passover—splattered on the walls.

The most famous story concerns Rabbi Judah Loew, also known by the acronym *MaHaRal*, who, in 1594, at the age of 80, became Chief Rabbi of Prague. Rabbi Loew is said to have fashioned an artificial being in human form out of clay, the famous *golem*, who saved the Jews of Prague repeatedly from impending disaster. It was only when the *golem* got out of control and started killing indiscriminately that Rabbi Loew had to destroy it. It is almost certain that Frankenstein's monster, who hails from the same region, is based on the *golem* legend.

WE NOW SHIFT TO *FIN-DE-SIÈCLE* Vienna. Theodor Herzl, who was destined to become the father of modern political Zionism, had established a reputation as a fine journalist by the time he was 30 years old, in 1890. He had grown up in an assimilated Jewish home in Vienna and was not much interested in "the Jewish Question." All this changed abruptly in 1891 when his newspaper, the *Neue Freie Presse*, sent him to Paris to cover the Dreyfus Affair. Alfred Dreyfus, a captain in the French army, was falsely accused of selling military secrets to the Germans. Dreyfus was Jewish and provided a convenient target for the French General Staff looking for a scapegoat. The trial provoked an unbelievable wave of anti-Semitism in France, with mobs in the streets of Paris howling "Death to the Jews!"

Herzl dates his own raised consciousness of the "plight of a people without a homeland" to this period. He devoted the rest of his life to trying to make his dream of a Jewish State a reality. He called for and, against vast opposition, managed to organize and convene the first Zionist Congress. It met in Basel, Switzerland on August 29, 1897 and was, in Abba Eban's words, "the first official and world-wide gathering of Jews since their dispersion." It is worth noting, that it was on this occasion that the 197 delegates and hundreds of observers first saw the white flag with the two horizontal blue stripes and the *Magen David* in its center—the flag that was later adopted as the official flag of the State of Israel.

Besides his enormously important book *Der Judenstaat* (*The Jewish State*), which outlined his reasoning and plan of political action, Herzl wrote a utopian novel—a detailed description of his vision of the Jewish State. Two travelers who visit Palestine are dismayed by the primitive conditions, the decay and the backwardness of that part of the Ottoman Empire to which Palestine then belonged. They return 20 years later to find a modern state with advanced technology, glittering cities, thriving ports, etc. A new social and economic order has been established with equal rights for women, full employment, cooperative ventures, free education, Jews and Arabs living together in friendship—true social-science fiction! The title of the book was to be *The New Zion*. But on August 30th, 1899, Herzl thought of a better title. We find the following entry in his diaries for that date: "Today, on the rattling omnibus, the title of my Zion novel came to me: *Altneuland*—a throwback to the *Altneuschul* in Prague. It will become a famous word."

And indeed it did. We now have a straight connection from the Old-New Synagogue in Prague to the Old-New Land of Herzl. But where is the last link that brings us to Tel Aviv? In his translation of Herzl's utopian novel into Hebrew, the writer Nahum Sokolow, a pioneer in modern Hebrew journalism, named the novel *Tel Aviv*. This is a reference to the name of a settlement of Jewish exiles in Babylon, mentioned in the Bible (Ezek. 3:15). The name combines two Hebrew words: *tel* (an archaeological mound), in this case standing for the "Old," and *aviv* (spring) standing for the "New." Put together, the words constitute a clever translation of Herzl's book title, *Altneuland*. In 1909, a modern city was founded on the sand dunes north of Jaffa on the Mediterranean seashore. Its founders were inspired by Herzl's diary entry of ten years before, and quickly agreed to give the new city—the first all-Jewish city in over 1,800 years—the fitting name of Tel Aviv.

18 Aliyah Bet: "Illegal" Immigration

ON THE COASTAL HIGHWAY, JUST south of Haifa, stands a small museum which documents one of the most heroic chapters in the struggle for Jewish independence and the difficult path to Statehood—the *Aliyah Bet* Museum. This museum tells the story of the "illegal" immigration which spirited over 100,000 Jewish survivors of the death camps out of Europe and ultimately into *Eretz Israel*. As we shall see, the impact of the events preserved by the pictures, documents and personal accounts in the collection was far out of proportion to the short time span, 1945–1948, in which they took place.

In May 1945, the war in Europe ended. Germany had lost the war, but the *real* losers were the Jews of Europe. As shown by the figures that slowly emerged after the war, six million of them had been murdered in what came to be known as the *Shoah* (Holocaust). Whole communities, once flourishing centers of Jewish life and learning, were wiped out with nothing Jewish left in them but their cemeteries, and sometimes, not even those.

After the war, those who had survived the starvation, the gassing and the inhumane surgical operations came out of the concentration camps. They, and the few who had survived in hiding with Gentile neighbors, had passed for Christians (often after having been baptized) and those who had fought the Nazis as partisans or in the underground resistance, ended up in camps again. They had become Displaced Persons, people torn from their roots, with no place to go.

Unlike the non-Jewish DPs who could not wait to return to their native lands from where they had been brutally transported by the Germans, the Jewish survivors no longer had any homes. Those who returned to their former homes often found a new expression of the old anti-Semitism: their homes, businesses and other possessions had been appropriated by people who had no intention of returning them to their rightful owners. They terrorized the Jewish survivors and, evidence shows, in many cases murdered them.

Broken in body and in spirit, locked out from many countries and unable or unwilling to rebuild their lives in their former home towns and villages, many of the Jewish survivors longed to go to the one place where they could live as Jews among Jews, to the one place that was eager to accept them — *Eretz Israel*. But the British Government made it impossible for the vast majority of the Jewish refugees to enter the land — at least openly and legally.

For 400 years, Palestine had belonged to Turkey until it was conquered by Great Britain at the end of World War I. In April of 1920, the League of Nations awarded the Mandate for Palestine to England, making it her responsibility to foster Zionist aspirations and help reconstitute a Jewish National Home in Palestine. The mandatory power was expected to establish Jewish self-government institutions, to facilitate immigration to *Eretz Israel* and encourage settlement of Jews on the land.

At first, mandatory administrations were indeed pro-Zionist and tended to carry out the provisions of the mandate. Hebrew, together with English and Arabic, was recognized as one of the official languages, immigration was free and open and Jews could acquire land wherever Arab or previous Turkish owners were willing to sell it.

Unfortunately, this attitude changed in less than a decade. Whenever Arab extremists decided to go on rampages of killing and destruction, Britain, which at first had armed the *Yishuv* to help quell these "disturbances," gradually succumbed to the entrenched anti-Semitism of the British Foreign Office. Its policies now aimed at appeasing the Arabs by restricting Jewish self-government, immigration and land purchases.

This gradual change in attitude culminated in the infamous White Paper put out by the British Government on May 17, 1939, a few months before the outbreak of World War II in Europe. The new policy restricted sale of land to Jews in large parts of *Eretz Israel*, and limited immigration to a mere 75,000 over the next five years, to continue thereafter only with the consent of the Arabs!

The White Paper of 1939 came as a severe blow to the *Yishuv*. Although the full, horrible truth about the death camps did not become known until after the end of the war, enough was known about the fate of German Jews for the *Yishuv* to be outraged. It was clear that the provisions of the White Paper had to be fought — even at a time when the democracies were girding up to fight Nazism. Ben-Gurion, then Head of the Jewish Agency, put it succinctly: "We shall fight the war as if there were no White Paper, and we shall fight the White Paper as if there were no war."

The publication of the White Paper meant, in essence, that the British mandate on Palestine was dead. The mandate had imposed on Britain the obligation to foster Zionist aspirations in Palestine. Yet, by severely restricting Jewish immigration, Britain dashed the hopes of thousands of European Jewish refugees of finding a haven in *Eretz Israel*. More generally, it dealt a severe blow to the hope of attaining political independence in the foreseeable future. The same year, *haMossad le'Aliyah*, the Organization for Immigration, was set up in reaction to the White Paper.

HaMossad le'Aliyah was a remarkable development with far-reaching effects. Besides the strikes and protest meetings that were held throughout the country, the leaders of the *Yishuv*, the Jewish community in *Eretz Israel*, decided actively to oppose the mandatory powers. With the creation of the *Mossad*, "political Zionism was transformed" in Ben-Gurion's words, "into militant Zionism." Its chief purpose was to force open the gates of Palestine that the British White Paper had slammed shut.

The *Mossad* was unique in one respect: it brought together all the different factions of the *Yishuv*. Ideologically-opposed groups, such as the mainstream *Histadrut* (General Federation of Jewish Labor) and the right-wing Revisionist movement, cooperated with each other. Their respective fighting units, the *Haganah* and their former rivals, the "terrorist" groups, *Irgun* and *Lehi*, — all outlawed and driven underground by Britain — joined forces to bring in the *ma'apilim* (illegal immigrants).

When the war broke out in Europe in September 1939, the focus of the *Yishuv* shifted to supporting the war effort. Despite British unwillingness to recruit Palestinian Jews into its fighting forces, tens of thousands of them volunteered and many others carried out secret missions, gathering intelligence and organizing guerilla groups behind enemy lines. Finally, in 1944, after years of bitter negotiations, Britain agreed to establish the Jewish Brigade. This gave the thousands who had volunteered the chance to fight the Nazis under their own Jewish flag. Moreover, it provided them with the experience and the skills which were to prepare them when, with the establishment of the State, *Tzahal* (the Israel Defense Forces) was formed.

The efforts to save Jewish refugees continued even during the war though on a much reduced scale. The *Mossad* smuggled 10,000 *ma'apilim*, mainly from Islamic countries, on overland routes into Palestine. By ship, it helped over a thousand Greek Jews flee to safety and brought more than 4,000 Jews out of Bulgaria and Rumania. Several of the overcrowded ships were lost at sea. Refugees who reached *Eretz Israel*, and were not detected by the British, were quickly dispersed among the *kibbutzim* and took on new identities. Those who were caught were deported to Mauritius, a British colony in the Indian Ocean.

Unbelievable as it may sound, Britain that had denied all entreaties to help bring refugees to the land with the refrain "there's a war on and we can't spare any ships" suddenly found enough ships to exile the unfortunate *ma'apilim*.

With the end of the war, in May 1945, most of the Jewish survivors were interned in "Displaced Persons" camps. In a letter dated August 31 of that year, President Truman wrote to General Eisenhower: "We have a particular responsibility toward these victims of persecution and tyranny who are in our zone." On September 18, Eisenhower responded: "Dear Mr. President, With respect to the Jews I found that most want to go to Palestine." When Britain rejected repeated pleas to accept 100,000 refugees (instead of the monthly quota of 1,500), the clandestine operations resumed in earnest.

The three-year period, from the end of the war to the establishment of the State of Israel in May 1948, was one of stark heroism. The *Haganah* collected groups of refugees and led them clandestinely under the most difficult conditions, often across several national borders, to port cities around the Mediterranean or the Black Sea. From there, ships refitted to accommodate four to five times the number of passengers for which they were originally designed and often barely seaworthy, set sail for Palestine.

And then Britain extended its prevailing pro-Arab and anti-Jewish policies in Palestine to extremes. The newly-elected, post-war British Labour Government, on whom the *Yishuv* had hung so much hope, declared war on the survivors of the Holocaust whose only desire was to reach *Eretz Israel* and there build a new life for themselves. Royal Navy ships and airplanes went into action to detect and hunt the refugee ships. Even the Foreign Office got into the act by successfully pressuring the governments of France, Italy, Greece and others to harass the *Haganah* ships by withholding exit permits, insisting on repeated and unnecessary safety inspections, and forbidding them to refuel or restock supplies.

British Marines often boarded the ships on the high seas, in violation of international law, and forced them to return to their ports of departure. If detected, the passengers whose ships reached the shores of Palestine, were forced off their ships, interned and deported to detention camps in Cyprus. Except for the few who were admitted on the paltry monthly quota, they languished there, once again behind barbed wire, until the State of Israel was founded.

From the end of World War II in May 1945 to the end of 1947, 64 ships carrying in excess of 70,000 *ma'apilim* attempted to run the British blockade. This amounts to one ship every ten days—a heroic effort indeed. Of these ships, only six managed to evade the British forces. All the rest, aside from those lost at sea, were returned and their passengers interned in British concentration camps on Cyprus.

Each of these ships had its own dramatic story to tell. The well-known story of the SS Exodus stands out because of the direct effect it had on the creation of the State of Israel. On July 18, 1947, this refugee ship packed with 4,554 persons was towed into Haifa Harbor. It had been captured and boarded on the high seas after a fierce battle in which three Jews were killed and many wounded.

Four days earlier, a United Nations Special Commission on Palestine had arrived in Jerusalem to study the Palestine problem and propose a solution. Fortuitously, two members of the commission were present in Haifa Harbor and witnessed the despondent refugees being dragged to the deportation ships. The images they saw that day, plus the news that the refugees ended up being returned to a camp in Germany (a fact which provoked outraged protests from around the world), influenced in large measure the Commission's report. Their solution proposed the end of the British Mandate and the partition of Palestine into a Jewish and an Arab state.

In her autobiography, *My Life*, Golda Meier writes: "The State of Israel might not have come into being for many years if that British war-within-a-war had not been waged so ferociously and with such insane persistence." In the end, the all-out commitment of the *Yishuv* to promote *Aliyah Bet*, which brought 115,000 "illegals" to *Eretz Israel*, hastened the founding of the independent State of Israel.

19 *Krav Maga: A Personal Memoir*

IT'S STRANGE HOW THESE THINGS happen. I hadn't thought of *krav maga* for about 60 years when, in the short span of a few weeks, I ran across the words on three separate occasions. *Krav maga* (pronounced *krahv maGA*) is Hebrew for contact combat, and refers to the official self-defense system of the Israeli Defense Forces. One day, a good friend of mine, a member of *Beit Am*, told me she had joined a *krav maga* training facility right here in Corvallis. "It is not the usual martial arts studio which also offers *krav maga* classes," she explained, "it is rather a facility devoted exclusively to this Israeli import."

Next, I saw the name and its derivation discussed in an article by Philologos, the linguist who writes a weekly column on Hebrew and Yiddish in the Jewish newspaper *The Forward*. "What a coincidence?" I thought, harkening back nostalgically to my late-teen years in *Eretz Israel* (then Palestine). Finally, when *HealthNOW* carried a full-page article entitled "*Krav Maga*... it's about life!," I started to suspect that my "sightings" were more than a coincidence, that *krav maga* was a new phenomenon on the American scene.

What is *krav maga* and what explains the interest in it in the United States? *Krav maga* is not one of the traditional martial arts, it is rather a hand-to-hand combat system designed to teach Israeli military conscripts, with a minimal amount of training, how to protect themselves effectively against attacks. It is dead-serious: it is meant as a defense against sudden chokeholds and grabs as well as against attacks with weapons such as guns, knives and sticks. It is not a sport with rituals of bowing to one's opponent and to the referee, but rather a method akin to street-fighting that aims at disarming the assailant in any way possible.

WHAT DOES ALL THIS HAVE to do with my distant past? When I was growing up in *Eretz Israel* during the war (that's the Second World War!), it became clear that England could not hold on to Palestine for very much longer and that after the war, she would have to give up the mandatory power granted her by the League of Nations. It was also clear that, at that time, two events would take place: the *Yishuv* would establish an independent Jewish state, Israel, and the surrounding Arab countries would attack the new state. To prepare for these developments, the training of the *Haganah* was stepped up. (The *Haganah* was the clandestine military organization of the *Yishuv* established as early as 1920 to protect the Jewish population throughout *Eretz Israel*.)

During the war, another paramilitary organization, the *Gadna* (acronym of *Gedudei No'ar*, Youth Corps), was established for training thirteen to eighteen-year olds in defense and national service. Although it always remained a voluntary organization, the *Gadna* worked in collaboration with schools and the various youth groups. I was a high school student at the time, and joined the *Gadna*—as did most of my friends—almost as a matter of course. That was where I first encountered *krav maga* training. Because the possession of weapons by Jews was illegal in British-ruled Palestine, our training in Tel Aviv, where I lived, consisted mainly of *kapap* (acronym for **krav panim-el-panim**, hand-to-hand combat) as *krav maga* was then called. It was only during the summer vacations, when the group as a whole went to one of the *kibbutzim*, that we could train with guns. But even that was highly dangerous, for British patrols often combed the areas looking for weapons. We worked half-days in the fields, which paid for our keep, and trained for the remainder of the day.

I am sure that nobody had any illusion about the training we received with shepherd-staffs. We knew they would not be of much avail against the weapons our enemies were sure to use. On the other hand, some of the credit for winning the War of Independence must go to the *krav maga* training and some of the noncombat goals it promoted. The official Web site of the *Krav Maga* Association of America lists them as follows: to develop self-confidence, increase physical fitness and foster "technical, tactical, physical and mental growth and improvements."

In the United States, this method of countering aggression is now being taught to large numbers of law enforcement and security officers, military personnel, correction-facilities officers, and, increasingly, to private citizens of both sexes and of all ages.

20. "The Wall"

"A CITY SET APART, WITH a wall at its heart." Thus the song, *Jerusalem of Gold*, by Naomi Shemer, describes Jerusalem and the Western Wall. However, *ha-Kotel*, to use its Hebrew name, stands not only at the heart of Jerusalem, but has a place in the heart of every Jew who feels connected to the Holy City, or, for that matter, to Judaism. For the *kotel* represents the glory that once was and the tragedy of 2,000 years of exile. For many, it represents a promise as well: whether of a unified Jerusalem now or of a hope for the Messiah at "the end of days."

The story of the *kotel* is fascinating. When the Roman legions, under Titus, finally captured Jerusalem in the year 70 C.E., they laid waste to the city and destroyed the Temple. The Second Temple had been greatly enlarged by King Herod and was of legendary beauty. What the legions could not destroy were the four massive retaining walls Herod had built to enclose the Temple Mount—an enormous area measuring more than 35 acres—which held the Temple and several spacious plazas, any one of which could accommodate the tens of thousands of pilgrims who flocked there during the festivals.

Rome not only destroyed the city, it built a Roman city, Aelia Capitolina, on its ruins and the Emperor Hadrian forbade Jews from living in it or visiting the Temple ruins. Jews could gaze at the Temple Mount and mourn their loss only from the Mount of Olives to the east, and across the Kidron Valley. Later on, it became the custom to pray at the *Shushan* Gate in the eastern wall of the Temple Mount and at the Ḥuldah gate in the southern wall because these were accessible without entering the city proper.

When Rome became Christianized in the fourth century, the Byzantine Empire continued to enforce Hadrian's edict: No Jews in Jerusalem! Jews prayed only at the eastern and southern retaining walls of the Temple Mount.

The situation changed with the Arab conquest of Jerusalem in year 628 C.E. Under Muslim rule, Jews were again allowed to live in the city, and the ravages on the Temple Mount (mostly caused by the Byzantines) were repaired. At the end of the seventh century, the Arabs, following their custom of building mosques on conquered holy sites, built two magnificent structures, that still grace the Temple Mount: the *Al Aqsa* Mosque and the Dome of the Rock. The latter, by the way, is not a mosque at all; it is a memorial to Omar, the second Caliph, who had led the Arab conquest of the Middle East.

And the Jews? Some Jews had begun to return to Jerusalem and many more were making pilgrimages to the city. Still, the place for prayer remained at the southern and eastern walls. Although they could now approach the western wall, which was located inside the city, tradition and the fact that the area around the wall had been used for centuries for a garbage dump kept them at the old prayer places. Accounts by travelers and several inscriptions found on the walls attest to these facts.

The situation changed slowly while Jerusalem was ruled, successively, by the Crusaders, the Ayyub Muslims, the Tatars and the Mameluke Sultans of Egypt, that is, from 1099 to 1516. During this period, the focus of the small Jewish population started to shift toward the western wall, which was closer to where most of them lived. We find this described in an increasing number of travelogues. However, it was only under Ottoman (Turkish) rule that the *kotel* became officially recognized as a place of Jewish worship.

The first Ottoman ruler, Suleiman the Magnificent, had part of the wall dug out from under the garbage that covered it and raised its height significantly by adding several courses of stones. It now became the *kotel*, the Western Wall, which found its way into Jewish folklore, song and art. For almost 450 years, until the Jordanian Arab Legion conquered the Jewish Quarter of the Old City in 1948, Jews gathered in the narrow alley in front of the *kotel* to pray and mourn the loss of what once was the core of their spiritual life.

Praying at the *kotel* was not without its dangers: Worshippers were regularly harassed, even pelted with stones from above, by the inhabitants of the Arab slum quarter which abutted the Western Wall. Moreover, the Turkish authorities forbade the erection of any permanent structure in the space in front of the *kotel*. No *aron kodesh* (Holy Ark that holds the Torah scrolls), no *mehitzah* (physical barrier to separate the genders), not even benches could be left overnight.

However, all these difficulties pale in comparison with the trauma of the period of Jordanian occupation. In flagrant disregard of an explicit clause in the Armistice Agreement, which guaranteed Jews access to their holy places, Jordan sealed off the Jewish Quarter—and the holy places it contained—to Jewish visitors. For 20 long years, Jews could not approach and pray at their beloved and revered *kotel*. It was not until June 7, 1967 when the Israel Defense Forces recaptured the Old City that the *kotel* took its traditional place—more magnificent than ever—in the heart of Jewish Jerusalem.

IT IS DIFFICULT TO EXAGGERATE the emotional impact of the three words "*har habayit beyadainu*" (the Temple Mount is in our hands) with which Brigade Commander Colonel Motta Gur announced the capture of the Old City of Jerusalem.

When Egypt had crossed into the Sinai in June 1967, Israel secretly appealed to Jordan not to join the war. But King Hussein miscalculated the odds and started the second front by shelling Jerusalem on June 5. Within two days of the beginning of hostilities, after fierce fighting north and south of Jerusalem, Israeli forces breached the walls of the Old City and captured the Temple Mount and the Western Wall on the morning of June 7.

Many of the soldiers were too young to have ever visited the *kotel* before 1948 when the Jewish Quarter fell into Jordanian hands. A whole generation had grown up that had been denied access to the Jewish holy places. And so, the soldiers gazed at the *kotel* with awe—many with tears in their eyes—and possibly with some disappointment: the legendary Wall was somewhat less imposing than they had imagined it.

Although the total length of the western retaining wall of the Temple Mount is 1,580 feet, only 66 feet were visible at that time. In front of the Wall was a narrow stone-paved alley, which bordered on an Arab slum quarter, the *Maghreb*. The *kotel* itself was 50 feet high, but clearly not all of it dated to the time of the Second Temple. Only the five lower courses of ashlars (huge stones) bore the characteristic sign of Herodian masonry work—the finely worked "frame" around the edges of each stone. These stones reached to a height of 16 feet. This is all that was left visible of King Herod's magnificent 100 foot high wall. On top of the original stones were four more courses of large stones, dating to the Muslim period of reconstruction in the seventh century and, finally, sixteen courses of much smaller stones added during the Ottoman rule.

ALL THIS CHANGED DRAMATICALLY WITH the victory of the Six Day War, when Israel retook the site. To accommodate the thousands of worshippers and visitors, the government cleaned up the area, removed the broken-down hovels of the *Maghreb* quarter (most of which were empty by this time) and created a magnificent plaza which now fronts on 200 feet of the *kotel* and extends clear to the Jewish quarter. Moreover, in cleaning up, two more courses of Herodian origin were excavated which lowered the level of the plaza—and raised the height of the Wall—by about seven feet. The area along the *kotel* is divided by a *meḥitzah* (a latticed fence), the southern third being reserved for women.

Since then, the wall that was once called "the Wailing Wall" has taken on an important additional function. Besides its traditional function as a place for both communal and individual prayer, it has become the symbol of a reunited Jerusalem and one of the focal points of national consciousness.

Primarily, however, people come to the *kotel* to pray, as they have for several hundred years. A talmudic *Midrash* holds that the *Shekhinah* (the Presence of God) has never left the Western Wall. Although the legend was originally told about the actual wall of the Temple, it has slowly been transferred in folk tradition to the Western Wall—the *kotel*. This explains in part why people feel a direct connection to Heaven in the presence of the ancient stones. Many insert personal notes with supplications or thanks into the cracks between the stones in complete faith that these will be answered more quickly there than anywhere else in the world. (As the old joke has it: "A phone call from Jerusalem to the Heavenly Throne is just a local call.") An Internet address is now available to which one can send messages that, for a small fee, so the advertising company promises, will be printed out and inserted into the Wall.

However, to insert anything between the ashlars of the *kotel* is not as easy as it sounds. Many of these stones weigh ten to fifteen tons, several as much as 40, and one giant block which forms the north corner of the wall is estimated to weigh close to 100 tons! The stones are so closely fitted to one another without the use of any binding material that it is hard to insert a knife edge between them except in the places that have weathered over time.

Lesley Hazleton points out in her book *Jerusalem Jerusalem* that of the many nations which have ruled Jerusalem since it fell to the Romans in the year 70 C.E., not one mourns the destruction of the City except for the Jews. But, clearly, it is not the loss of the ancient city's water system, nor that of King Solomon's stables that we mourn. It is the destruction of the Holy Temple in which the spiritual force of Judaism was centered—the force which, for many, informs the massive stones of the *kotel* today.

21 "Jerusalem of Gold"

BEFORE I LEFT ISRAEL (THEN Palestine) in 1947 to study in the United States, I visited Jerusalem to say "goodbye." I wandered through the city and among other places, stopped for a few minutes at the *kotel*, the Western Wall. In those days, the *kotel* was a dismal place: it was fronted by a short, narrow alley, barely ten feet wide, into which only a relatively small number of worshippers could fit. This holiest of all Jewish places was bordered by the *Maghreb* Quarter, one of the worst slum areas in the Muslim part of the Old City.

Even though the British mandate was still in force, the site was controlled by the *Waqf*, the Muslim religious authority, which put severe restrictions on the Jewish worshippers. It did not allow any ritual structures such as a Holy Ark to be erected in front of the Wall and did not even allow the sounding of the *shofar* at the Wall during the High Holy Days.

For nineteen years, from the War of Independence in May 1948, when the Jewish Quarter of the Old City fell into Jordanian hands, to the Six-Day War in June 1967, when Israel recaptured the Old City, Jews were prevented from approaching the Wall, much less organizing prayer services near it. The Jordanians did not honor the "freedom of access to the holy places," which had been guaranteed in the cease-fire agreement.

It was during these nineteen years, when the Jewish Quarter of Jerusalem languished under Jordanian occupation, that the song *"Yerushalayim shel Zahav"* ("Jerusalem of Gold") was composed. The song captures the anguish caused by the wanton destruction of Jewish holy places and the inaccessibility of the *kotel*, the Western Wall. Next to *"Hava Nagilah"* it is probably the best known and most beloved of all Israeli songs.

"Yerushalayim shel Zahav" has an interesting history. It was commissioned from the well-known Israeli composer, Naomi Shemer, for a very special occasion. The year was 1967, and the annual Israel Song Festival was to take place in Jerusalem on Independence Day that

year. In the six years since its inauguration, the festival had become an important occasion for artists to show off their talents and compete for prize-money, fame, and a chance to advance to the much larger Eurovision song competition. Mayor Teddy Kollek decided that only songs about Jerusalem would be performed in the non-competitive part of the festival that evening.

Naomi Shemer was a good choice: she had written a good number of songs, many of which had become popular hits. Although she was reluctant at first to take on the commission, she went ahead and composed the first three verses of the song. They perfectly expressed the special connection between the Jewish people and Jerusalem. The translation below by Haya Galai appears on the official web site of the Israel Ministry of Foreign Affairs.

The song was an immediate hit at the Festival. Twenty-one days later the song was on everybody's lips: On June 7, 1967, during the Six-Day War, the Israel army recaptured Jerusalem and the soldiers sang it spontaneously upon reaching the Western Wall. When Naomi Shemer then added the fourth stanza to celebrate the reunification of Jerusalem, *"Yerushalayim shel Zahav"* practically became a second national anthem. In fact, Uri Avneri, member of the Knesset (Israel Parliament), introduced a bill to have the song replace *"Hatikvah"*, the national anthem of the State of Israel. Naomi Shemer was flattered, but not in favor of the idea.

THE TERM "JERUSALEM OF GOLD" has ancient roots. The Talmud mentions it several times, referring to a golden diadem in the shape of a city wall surmounted by turrets. In *Nedarim* (50a), we are told a beautiful tale about the great scholar, Rabbi Akiva (c. 50-135 C.E.) who promised to buy his wife a Jerusalem of Gold if he ever had enough money. Akiva, who had started as an illiterate, poor shepherd working for a rich man, had fallen in love with his employer's daughter. When she married him against her father's wishes, the father withdrew all support and the couple lived in abject poverty. His wife sold her own hair to enable Akiva to pursue his studies at the Academy. When Akiva became well known and well off, he remembered his promise and bought his wife the expensive, beautiful head ornament.

There is an interesting sequel to the story. The wife of Rabban Gamaliel HaNasi, president of the *Sanhedrin* at that time, was jealous of Rabbi Akiva's wife and complained to her husband. He reacted by saying: "Had you done for me what she did for him, I too would have bought you a Jerusalem of Gold!"

JERUSALEM OF GOLD
by Naomi Shemer

The mountain air is clear as water
The scent of pines around
Is carried on the breeze of twilight,
And tinkling bells resound

The trees and stones there softly slumber,
A dream enfolds them all.
So solitary lies the city,
And at its heart—a wall.

Refrain:

Oh, Jerusalem of gold, and of light and of bronze,
I am the lute for all your songs.

The wells ran dry of all their water,
Forlorn the market square,
The Temple Mount dark and deserted,
In the Old City there.

And in the caverns in the mountain,
The winds howl to and fro,
And no-one takes the Dead Sea highway,
That leads through Jericho.   *(Refrain)*

But as I sing to you, my city,
And you with crowns adorn,
I am the least of all your children,
Of all the poets born.

Your name will scorch my lips for ever,
Like a seraph's kiss, I'm told,
If I forget thee, golden city,
Jerusalem of gold.   *(Refrain)*

The wells are filled again with water,
The square with joyous crowd,
On the Temple Mount within the City,
The shofar rings out loud.

Within the caverns in the mountains
A thousand suns will glow,
We'll take the Dead Sea road together,
That runs through Jericho.   *(Refrain)*

22 Oasis of Peace

OVER THE PAST FEW DECADES, much effort has been expended to bring about peace in *Eretz Israel*, the Holy Land. Most of the recent, and not-so-recent, schemes to settle the Jewish-Arab conflict involved drawing lines on a map. It was hoped that partition of the land into separate political entities would solve what appeared to be an intractable problem.

There is, however, a different approach, which was proposed in the past and which has its proponents today. Instead of dividing the land between Jews and Arabs, find a way for them to live together in harmony. Already in the 1930s, Judah Magnes, the highly respected first President of the Hebrew University in Jerusalem, headed a movement that proposed the creation of a bi-national state in which the two peoples could live together peacefully. He believed that people with different languages, different religions, and different cultures could learn to coexist in a democratic state as is the case today in Switzerland or Belgium.

In Israel, even in cities such as Haifa or Jaffa where both Jews and Arabs live, the groups live side by side and are not integrated in the American sense. Towns and villages are populated by distinct ethnic groups: a Jewish *moshav* here, an Arab town there or a Druze village in the Upper Galilee. In this mosaic, there is one village that is unique: *Neve Shalom* or, by its Arabic name, *Wahat al-Salam*. Both names mean Oasis of Peace. *Neve Shalom* is a cooperative village in the central part of Israel in which Arabs and Jews live together and, beyond that, dedicate their lives to the quest for peace in a personal way.

Neve Shalom was founded in 1972 by Fra Bruno Hussar, a Catholic monk (1911–1996). Bruno Hussar was born a Jew in Egypt, converted to Catholicism, and was admitted to the Dominican Order in 1950. He came to Israel in 1953 and established a center for biblical research and the study of the theological and historical aspects of Jewish-Christian relations. Then, in 1967 after the Six Day War, in his own words: "It was impossible to imagine a communal life shared by Jews and Christians in Israel without taking into account those other sons of Abraham, the Arabs, both Muslim and Christian, who live in the country. So the idea of *Neve Shalom* began to take shape."

Neve Shalom is located about halfway between Tel Aviv and Jerusalem on a pleasant hilltop overlooking the Valley of Ayalon where Joshua once bid the moon to stand still. The land, about 100 acres, is leased from the nearby Trappist monastery at Latrun (known for the wines it makes) for the symbolic rent of five cents a year for a 100-year period.

As of now (2010), 60 families have settled in Neve Shalom—half Palestinian Arab couples (Israeli citizens) and half Jewish couples. According to their mission statement, about 300 couples are on the waiting list hoping to make the community their home. Whereas the original settlement had a slight "hippie" character, the majority of the members of *Neve Shalom* today are professionals. Most commute to jobs in Jerusalem or fill the administrative and educational positions in the village.

Education is an important aspect of the task the village members have set for themselves. The nursery, the kindergarten and the primary school are all completely bilingual. The school instills in each child not only a knowledge of his/her own culture, but promotes a knowledge of, and respect for the other cultures represented in the student body. The school enrolled 220 students in 2010, of whom only 36 belong to member-families, the rest come from 19 separate communities, both Arab and Jewish, in the area.

The success of the system is attested to by the fact that the Israel Education Ministry, in 1997, designated the school an experimental school, which recognizes it as a possible model for new educational trends. The school's achievements in bilingual and bicultural education have led to other bilingual programs to be set up in Israel. Also, it has drawn to it educators from abroad (*e.g.*, Macedonian, Albanian and Greek) who come for in-service training in the teaching of tolerance and mutual acceptance and appreciation. The village itself has been officially recognized by the Ministry of the Interior in 1989.

Equally important to its vision of "establishing a more humane, just and equal society" is the School for Peace (SFP), which *Neve Shalom/Wahat al-Salam* conducts. The SFP is a major educational outreach institution dealing with the Israeli/Palestinian conflict. Since its establishment in 1979 it has reached over 25,000 Arabs and Jews through joint activities and encounters which it organizes throughout Israel and increasingly in the Palestinian territories.

The main and largest project of the SFP has been its youth encounter program, which brings together sixteen and seventeen-year old Jews and Arabs for four-day residential encounter workshops. There are also academic courses conducted in conjunction with the social psychology departments of all the major universities in Israel. SFP programs reach many population groups besides high school and university students. In recent years, workshops in mediation and conflict resolution have attracted international interest and participants.

Does all of this activity amount to anything? It is easy, of course, to be cynical about *Neve Shalom/Wahat al-Salam* and its programs. One could argue that they are as effective as standing at the brink of hell and throwing down ice cubes. And yet, in a landscape in which the Palestinian National Charter states that "Claims of historical or religious ties of Jews with Palestine are incompatible with the facts of history" or, on the other side, where religious Jewish groups view giving up even one square-foot of land as a sin, the Oasis of Peace provides a glimmer of hope. The 2,000 Jews and Arabs that the School for Peace reaches each year may not end up loving one another, but they might constitute the core of the critical mass necessary to bring a stable peace to the region.

Language:
The Holy—
and Not So Holy
—Tongue

What Language did Abraham Speak?

SOMETHING THAT HAS PUZZLED ME for a while is the question: "In what language did Abraham speak to his wife Sarah and to the rest of his household?" In the Torah, of course, all his conversations are reported in Hebrew. But where did he learn Hebrew? He was born in the city of Ur of the Chaldeans (in modern-day Iraq), which he left with his father, Terah, and wife, Sarai (Sarah's original name), to settle in Haran (now Syria) before he migrated into Canaan. Did they speak Hebrew in Ur? In Haran? Did he learn it in Hebrew School?

Our Sages must have been puzzled by the same question for there is an old Midrash (homiletic interpretation of Scripture) which provides an answer. It recounts that when Abraham was born, all the dignitaries at the court of King Nimrod wanted to destroy him and he was hidden in a cave for thirteen years. When he came out of the cave he spoke Hebrew.

Well and good! But now let us go a bit further back and ask: In what language did God speak to Adam and Eve, and in what language did they speak to one another? Here, according to Jewish tradition, the answer is clear. In *Genesis Rabbah* we find the following unequivocal statement: "The world was created in the holy tongue" (18:4); they all spoke Hebrew to one another. (This, by the way, means that the snake—in one of the only two instances in the Bible where animals speak—must have spoken Hebrew too!)

The belief that Hebrew was the *Ursprache* (original language) from which all other languages developed was generally held by Jews and non-Jews alike during the Middle Ages. William Chomsky, in his book, *Hebrew: The Eternal Language*, tells of several experiments conducted to lay to rest any doubts in this matter. Among others he cites are those by the German Emperor Frederick II (thirteenth century) and by King James IV of Scotland (fifteenth century). The latter had two newborn babies isolated with a mute woman on the island of Inchkeith. When they emerged several years later, the children spoke perfect Hebrew. Proof that Hebrew was "the natural tongue of humankind"—the

Mother of all Languages! (The origin of all other languages is, of course, explained by the Bible's interesting tale of the Tower of Babel.)

The trouble with this assertion is that several other peoples have similar beliefs that validate their own ethnocentric convictions. Thus, the Chinese, the Greeks, the Turks and others each believe that their own language deserves that honor, and conducted experiments similar to the one described above to prove their point.

The question of a single, prehistoric language from which all other languages sprang is a controversy of long standing among linguists. Fortunately, we are concerned with far simpler questions: What language did Abraham speak, and where did he learn it?

Archaeology and comparative linguistics provide what I consider a surprising answer: After Abraham heeded the Lord's call to "Go forth from [his] native land and from [his] father's house" and migrated to Canaan, the "Promised Land," he found that the language spoken there was Hebrew.

Hebrew belongs to the Middle-Semitic or Canaanite branch of the language tree. During the Middle Bronze Age (the period of the Patriarchs with which we are dealing), Hebrew, or languages very similar to it were spoken by the Emorites, Ammomites, Moabites, Midianites and others, all of whom inhabited Canaan. The Bible confirms this when it refers to Hebrew as the "Language of Canaan." Along with other migrating (or invading) groups, Abraham's household adopted the language as well as some of the cultures of the older and more settled civilizations they encountered.

Did Abraham and his household have a difficult time learning Hebrew? Most probably not, for linguistic analysis shows that the Canaanite Hebrew of that period (1800–1600 B.C.E.) was closely related to Ugaritic, the mother-tongue they brought with them from Haran. So, in his later years Abraham spoke Hebrew and, like countless immigrants after him, it was in the land that was to become *Eretz Israel* that he learned the language!

Pitfalls of Translating the Bible

TRANSLATING A PIECE OF WRITING from one language into another is always a tricky business. Usually, when a translation is true to the original, it does not read well in the new language, and if it reads well, it often is not a faithful translation. When it comes to translating the Bible, these difficulties are multiplied: besides the usual linguistic problems, doctrinal considerations often enter the picture. Here are some examples of English translations from the Hebrew Bible to illustrate the point.

We start with the image of the "Horned Moses" (see Chapter 97). When Moses comes down from the mountain with the tablets of the Law, the Bible tells us that "his face beamed." Now the Hebrew word *keren* stands both for a beam of light and for the horn of an animal. The Christian translator chose to use the second meaning and so we find Moses depicted in numerous paintings and statues with a pair of horns sprouting from his forehead. The horns may have been an innocent mistake or, alternatively, meant as a symbol of power and leadership, yet in the Middle Ages they served to equate Moses—and Jews in general—with Satan.

Of greater consequence is a mistranslation that has become one of the fundamental tenets of faith in Christianity. In Isaiah (7:14), the prophet, speaking to King Ahaz, says: "Look, the *almah* (young woman) is with child and about to give birth to a son. Let her name him Immanuel." Christians have translated the word *almah* as virgin and base the belief in the "Virgin birth" on this translation. It is clear that early Christianity, in order to establish Jesus as the Messiah, son of the House of David, had to link him to the prophesies of what to them was the Old Testament. Because the origins of legendary heroes, gods, etc. were ascribed in many cultures to virgin births, Isaiah's prophecy of the pregnant young woman was made to serve that purpose.

Another example in which the Jewish Bible (and Jewish translations of it into English) differs from Christian Bibles is the sixth commandment. The Hebrew clearly says: "Thou shalt not murder," yet many translations render it as "Thou shalt not kill." The word "kill", of course, exists in Hebrew but it does not appear in the Ten Commandments. The Bible *does* allow killing in certain instances, such as in self-defense, in a just war and as punishment for certain transgressions.

If we continue comparing the Hebrew Bible with some of the translations, we discover a peculiar phenomenon. The translators often add details that do not exist in the original. For instance, everybody knows about the apple with which Eve tempted Adam. Yet the Hebrew original speaks only of "a fruit" and does not specify which. Over the centuries there have been various speculations as to the nature of this fruit. Most Jewish commentators believe that the "fruit of a goodly tree" of which the Bible speaks was a date. In Austrian German the tomato is called a *Paradiesapfel* (apple of paradise) and is believed to have been that fateful piece of dessert.

Again, in the story of Jonah, the Bible speaks of a "big fish" swallowing Jonah—not of a whale. Now, granted that it is hard to imagine any animal big enough to provide temporary digs for a grown man. Still, why specify at all?

In Chapter 37 of Genesis, we read about Jacob giving his favorite son, Joseph, a "striped shirt (or tunic)." When the Hebrew was translated it must have become colorized at the same time, for the striped tunic became a "coat of many colors." The addition of this colorful detail is not unique to Christian versions. In Jewish Bibles it goes back to the *Septuagint*, the oldest Greek translation of the Bible (third century B.C.E.) which, by the way, was made by Jews for Jews. It is almost as if the scholars involved in translation all remembered the admonition of their Writing 101 instructors, "Don't be vague! Be specific!"

The King James (or Authorized Version, 1611) which has so enriched the English language, has also introduced some idioms into the language that are based on mistranslations. The well-known "voice [that] calls in the wilderness" owes its existence to a misplaced colon! The Hebrew original (Isaiah 40:3) reads: "A voice calls: 'In the wilderness clear a road for the Lord...'" On the other hand, when King Solomon, the purported author of the Song of Songs, says in his description of spring-time that "the voice of the turtle is heard in our land" (Song of Solomon 2:12) it is not a mistake at all. In Old English "turtle" stood for the modern turtle dove, which is the correct translation of the Hebrew word *tor*.

There is a peculiar geographic error in the translations of the story of the Exodus. The route the Israelites took to the Promised Land did not come close to the Red Sea—nor does the Hebrew Bible claim it did. It speaks of the *Yam Soof*, where *soof* is the plant from which papyrus used to be made. The correct translation, therefore, is the "Sea of Reeds" or the "Reed Sea," and refers to the Nile delta region in which this plant grows in abundance.

There are many more examples of errors of this kind besides the ones I have mentioned. It is true, of course, that not everyone may be able to read the Bible in the original. Still, serious students must be aware of the possible problems inherent in reading a translated version. It is ludicrous to say—as someone once said to me when I suggested clarifying a point by checking it in the Hebrew Bible: "If English was good enough for Jesus, it's good enough for me."

Eliezer Ben-Yehudah: Father of Modern Hebrew

UNTIL LESS THAN 100 YEARS ago, Hebrew was a dead language. For nearly 2,000 years no children had played hide-and-go-seek in it, no one had used it to shop for groceries or to exchange recipes, and it was not the language in which the idlers in the coffeehouses discussed the latest government scandals.

All this changed at the end of the nineteenth century. Because of the vision and missionary zeal of one man who devoted all of his adult life to it, Hebrew became a language in which modern ideas and terms of modern science and industry could be easily expressed. That man was Eliezer Ben-Yehudah, who was born Eliezer Perelman in Luzhky, Lithuania, in 1858. Eliezer started out with a conventional Jewish education, but quit the *yeshivah* for a more secular, French-style lycée high school, eventually going to Paris to study medicine at the Sorbonne. It was there, in the ferment of Paris in the 1870s, that he was exposed to the European national freedom movements and inspired to formulate his own dream of Jewish national independence and a national language.

Ben-Yehudah laid out his ideas in a letter to the editor of *Ha-Shahar*, the monthly journal dedicated to the diffusion of Jewish Enlightenment and the Hebrew Language (Vienna, 1868–1884): "Let us increase the number of Jews in our desolate land; let the remnants of our people return to the land of their fathers; let us revive the nation and its tongue will be revived, too!" And speaking of Hebrew, he says: "...we cannot revive it with translations; we must make it the tongue of our children on the soil on which it once bloomed and bore ripe fruit."

This became his strategy. When he contracted tuberculosis and had to quit his studies, he decided to immigrate to *Eretz Israel*, the Land of Israel, which was then a minor province in the Turkish Empire. Before he left, he married the woman to whom he had been engaged since his student years and, on his honeymoon sailing down the Danube River, started teaching her Hebrew. He extracted a promise from her that they would speak only Hebrew at home and would bring up their children completely and exclusively in the Hebrew language.

Today, it is hard to imagine how heroic—or possibly foolhardy—that commitment must have been at the time. Hebrew was not nearly rich enough or flexible enough for everyday speech. And yet, Ben-Yehudah kept all neighbors and friends who wanted to speak Yiddish, Russian or French in his house, out of earshot of his young children. "Ours is the first Hebrew-speaking household in 2,000 years," he liked to say.

While trying to eke out a living as a teacher, writer and newspaper publisher, Ben-Yehudah labored mightily at increasing the number of words available in modern Hebrew, and at what was to become his major effort for the next 40 years—*The Complete Dictionary of Ancient and Modern Hebrew*. By the time he died, in 1922, five volumes had been published. The remaining twelve volumes, completed by his wife and son Ehud, were published in 1957.

In his autobiography, Ben-Yehudah recalls that the first word he invented was the word for dictionary: He had been jotting down the list of words he planned to work on in a notebook which he always carried. He referred to this notebook as his *sefer millim* (book of words, a direct translation of the German *Wörterbuch*). It was a happy choice when he coined the much more elegant, single word *millon* (from the same Hebrew root)—a word still in general use today.

Ben-Yehudah faced strong opposition in his fight to bring Hebrew back to life. Baron Edmund de Rothschild, the great benefactor who provided financial assistance to many of the new settlements and ventures in *Eretz Israel*, did not share Ben-Yehudah's Zionist vision. French Jewish circles, which supported the *Alliance Israélite* schools, demanded that the language of instruction be French. Other national groups who supported schools in the country insisted that it be German or English. At the end of the nineteenth century, few saw Hebrew as the primary language of the Jewish population of *Eretz Israel*, or believed it could ever achieve that status.

The main opposition, though, came from the *Ashkenazi* religious establishment. Orthodox Jews were outraged by Ben-Yehudah's efforts to change what they consider the Holy Tongue. They viewed the articles on theater, music and women's fashions, which were regular features in his newspaper, as sacrilegious. They argued for Yiddish as the *lingua franca* of the new state. The rabbis proclaimed a *ḥerem* (ban) against him and his newspaper, and denounced him to the Turkish government, accusing him of sedition. The Turkish authorities threw Ben-Yehudah into jail and closed down his paper for a prolonged period. He, on his part, attacked the *halukah*, the system of distribution of alms collected abroad which provided the main economic support of the Orthodox community. He considered it a parasitical way of life which ran counter to his notion of a national rebirth in *Eretz Israel*.

After a lifetime of effort, Ben-Yehudah could see his dream become a reality: The playgrounds and hallways of schools in *Eretz Israel*, which had taught Hebrew only as a foreign language, now resounded with it. In 1913, the Technion in Haifa adopted it as the language of instruction, despite the protests of its German financial backers who argued that only in German could science and technical subjects be adequately taught. And finally, in 1920, two years before Ben-Yehudah's death, the British mandate government adopted it as one of the official languages of Palestine (together with English and Arabic).

WHERE DID BEN-YEHUDAH FIND THE thousands upon thousands of new words necessary to make Hebrew a modern language? Some were direct translations from one of the European languages he knew. The word for vacuum cleaner, *sho'ev avak*, comes from the German *Staubsauger* (dust sucker), while the word for dentist, *ropheh shinayim* is a translation of *Zahnarzt* or tooth doctor.

In his quest for words, he read thousands of books in Hebrew, Arabic and other Semitic languages. Many of the words he discovered in ancient texts and writings had lain lost in the dustbins of history for centuries. Some of these words could be used "as is" in a modern context and to others Ben-Yehudah gave a slightly altered form, always consonant with Hebrew grammar and usage. The modern Hebrew word for electricity (*hashmal*), for example, actually occurs in the Bible, except that there it refers to a "shining substance," possibly amber. The ancient Greeks, who knew that rubbing amber creates static electricity, rendered the word in the first translation of the Bible into Greek (the *Septuagint*) as *elektron*. So, a word from the book of Ezekiel sparked a nineteenth-century scientific term.

In many other cases, Ben-Yehudah was able to use ancient Hebrew roots to create modern words. The word for newspaper, *itton*, is derived from the biblical word *eit* (time which echoes the German word *Zeitung*). Again, the root r-k-v, on which the biblical *rokheiv* (horseback rider) and *merkavah* (chariot) are based, yielded *rakevet* for railroad train and, later, *rekhev* in its modern use for vehicle.

When his wife, Hemda, who wrote a regular women's column in the newspaper he published, needed a Hebrew term for fashion, Ben-

Yehudah again turned to the Bible and converted the word *ophen* (manner, mode, way) into the modern term *ophnah* by the addition of a single letter. How many Israeli women who are *ophnah*-conscious are aware of their debt to Ben-Yehudah? A similar word, with a slightly different spelling, *ophan* (wheel), forms, with the addition of the dual ending -*ayim*, the word *ophanayim* (bicycle) and *ophno'a* (motorcycle). He coined the word for soldier, *hayal*, and even its feminine form, *hayelet*, from the biblical word *hayil* (strength).

Ben-Yehudah was greatly helped in disseminating his new words by the Hebrew weekly (later to become a daily) newspaper he founded in 1884, *Ha-Tzevi* (The Deer). He used the new terms in the articles he wrote and discussed them in a special column on language. Every issue of *Ha-Tzevi* provoked lively debates in the country. The new pioneers, who had been coming out of Russia after the pogroms in the 1880s to settle in *Eretz Israel*, were happy to see their newly adopted language, Hebrew, become richer and more flexible.

Some people grumbled: "Who does he think he is? Who gives him the authority to introduce new words into our language?" But Ben-Yehudah argued that only usage can validate a language, and that ultimately it was the Hebrew-speaking public that accepted or rejected each new word. And, indeed, not every word he proposed made it into his dictionary. For example, for "tomato" he proposed the Arabic word *bandurah*, which was in general use at the time. But in the settlements people had adopted the term *agvaniyah*—a felicitous choice, indeed. *Agvaniya* is derived from the biblical root *agav*, which stands for sensual love (see Ezekiel 33:31–32). The word evokes the idea of an aphrodisiac, which is mirrored in the European names for tomato: *pomme d'amour* and *Paradiesapfel*, or love apple.

Still, criticism led Ben-Yehudah to create the *Va'ad ha-Lashon*, the Hebrew Word Council, to which he invited influential persons from throughout the country. The *Va'ad* was to discuss and pass on each of the new words he coined. (It was this body that decided in 1909 to make the *Sephardi* pronunciation the standard for modern Hebrew.) With the establishment of the State of Israel, the *Va'ad* became the official Academy of the Hebrew Language, the national institution that is still the arbiter on all matters pertaining to the Hebrew language.

Even today, not all the words the Academy proposes are accepted in daily speech. Although it strives mightily to keep up with the vocabulary for new technology, it is sometimes too late. The Academy's suggestion for a word for computer chip was ignored by the general population, which had already begun using the word *jook* (rhymes with book), the Russian word used in popular Hebrew for cockroach. The "at" symbol, @, in e-mail addresses goes by the very graphic name of *strudel*.

We may be amused, or bemused, by the directions in which the Hebrew language is now developing, but without Eliezer Ben-Yehudah's stubborn dedication and unceasing labors to revive it, chances are that there would not be any need for new Hebrew words. It would still be a language used only for study and prayer. And without a common language, Israel today would likely be made up of disparate national Jewish communities, each speaking its own language, rather than a linguistically united Israeli nation.

Of Airplanes and Acronyms

LANGUAGES CHANGE OVER TIME. CONTEMPORARY English is very different from the English that Chaucer spoke and wrote in the second half of the fourteenth century. In fact, linguists view Chaucerian English as a different language from the one we speak today. Besides changes in spelling and pronunciation, our language has undergone changes in grammar and structure and, above all, has grown by the addition of many new words. This is true for all the 6,000 languages spoken in the world today—except for the many that are in danger of disappearing. In most cases, the process of change and growth is quite slow and not perceptible to the speakers of the language. Thus, we have little trouble understanding something written by our grandparents or even by people several generations before them.

Hebrew is one of the few languages that do not follow the rule. The change, especially in the number of words Hebrew contains, has been phenomenal and swift. For 2,000 years the vocabulary was essentially fixed because the language was not used for oral communication and there was little need to invent words to describe new concepts or phenomena that might have been observed. The language was used mainly for prayer and study, and the vocabulary handed down was sufficient to discuss new ideas or insights.

All this changed with the beginning of modern Zionism and the settlement of Jews in *Eretz Israel* at the end of the nineteenth century. A new country (in this case, our age-old homeland) required a new language (in this case, the age-old language of our forebears—Hebrew). Many people besides the lexicographer Eliezer Ben-Yehudah, the "Father of Modern Hebrew," came together to revitalize and modernize the Hebrew language.

The growth of a language takes many forms. Foreign words may be incorporated into the language unchanged. For example, Hebrew uses "telefon" and "microscope" to express modern concepts. The process may not always make sense, especially when a perfectly good word exists in Hebrew. For example, in driving through the north of Israel one often sees signs advertizing "*tzimerim lehaskir.*" Now the word *lehaskir* is perfectly good Hebrew meaning for rent, but *tzimerim* is the German word *zimmer* (room) plus the Hebrew suffix -*im*, to make the word a masculine-plural noun. Curiously, many Israeli youngsters, who speak neither German nor Yiddish, are unaware of the comical side of this combination. To whom are these signs directed? To German tourists? Then they should be printed in German. To Israeli travelers? For them the Hebrew word *ḥeder* (room) would do nicely.

Words may also be translated from a foreign language such as the Hebrew term for Israel's national sport, *kaduregel* (soccer). The word is a contraction of two words: *kadur* (ball) and *regel* (foot)—a direct translation of the British football. A language may use existing words or roots and give them a new twist to make them fit a new environment. For example, the words *aviron* (airplane) and *me'avrer* (ventilator) both derive from the Hebrew word *avir* (air), which, in turn, was introduced into post-biblical Hebrew from the Greek. There are yet other ways in which new words get added to a language. Hebrew uses all of them.

There is, however, one method, which, though not unique to Hebrew, is very characteristic of it: the creation of words through the use of acronyms, that is, words that are formed from the initial letters of the words in a phrase. The use of acronyms in Hebrew goes back a long way. It has been estimated that over 10,000 abbreviations occur in the rabbinic literature (Talmud and subsequent medieval writings) many of which became acronyms and are pronounced as words. For instance, the name for the Hebrew Bible, *Tanakh*, is an acronym that is composed of the first letters of the three components of the Bible—*Torah*, *Nevi'im* and *Ketuvim* (the *Pentateuch*, *Prophets* and *Writings*). The Talmud is also popularly referred to by the acronym *Shas*—made up of the first letters of the words *shisha sedarim*, (the Six Orders) into which R. Judah Ha-Nassi divided the Mishnah.

Early on, acronyms were used as names. Many of the medieval Sages are known and referred to by acronyms rather than by their full names. Thus Rabbi Shelomo Ben-Isaac (1040–1105), the leading commentator on the Bible, is best known as *Rashi*, and Rabbi Moshe Ben-Maimon (Spain, 1135–1204), the most illustrious figure in Judaism in the post-talmudic era, is known as *Rambam*. In more modern times we have Rabbi Israel Ben-Eliezer (c. 1700–1760), the founder of Hasidism in Eastern Europe, who is known as the **Ba'al Shem Tov** (the Miracle Worker) or by its acronym *Besht*. To be called by one's acronym was to be well-known and highly respected. Hundreds of such acronyms remain current.

Besides names, numbers (especially the calendar-years) are also traditionally expressed as acronyms. Each letter in the Hebrew alphabet has a numerical value, therefore, the years in a date can be represented by a series of letters. These lend themselves quite naturally to the formation of acronyms and are pronounced as words. For example, the year 2004 is 5764 in the Jewish calendar, and can be represented by the letters *heh* (5,000), *tav* (400), *shin* (300), *samekh* (60), *dalet* (4). Put together, the letters form the word *tashsad*, which is, the common way of referring to that year. The letter *heh* (5), which stands for the number of millennia, is most often implied and not pronounced. Two familiar examples are the holidays which are named for the dates on which they fall: *Lag ba-Omer* and *Tu bi-Shevat*. The *Lag* in *Lag ba-Omer* is composed of *lamed* (30) and *gimel* (3) and stands for the thirty-third day in the *Omer* period, and the letters in *Tu*, add up to 15—*tet* (9) and *vav* (6)—which is the date of the festival in the month of *Shevat*. These are familiar, traditional uses.

Modern Hebrew, in turn, has added (and keeps adding daily) a bewildering number of new words, many of which are acronyms. Whenever I return to Israel for a visit, I am struck by the number of times I have to ask, "What does this word mean, and where did it come from?" The Israel Defense Force (IDF) provides a good example, for its vocabulary is peppered with acronyms.

The IDF itself is best known and usually referred to by the acronym of its name: *Tzahal—Tzeva Haganah leYisrael*. Within *Tzahal*, almost every unit and rank is known by an acronym. Thus we have, to take just two examples, *Magav*—formed from *Mishmar ha-Gevul* (the border guard) and *Tzadal—Tzeva Derom Levanon* (the South Lebanese Army). A frighteningly descriptive term for weapons of mass destruction is the word *abakh* from *atomi*, *biologi* and *khimi*.

To keep up with the acronyms in use by the armed forces is daunting enough; add to it the soldiers' slang and even knowledgeable Israelis are in trouble. Who could guess that the term *hamshush* stands for a long weekend pass? The word is made up from the initials of *hamishi* (Thursday), *shishi* (Friday) and *shabbat* (Saturday).

Why is Hebrew so much more likely than English to turn a series of letters into an acronymic word? After all, English is also full of abbreviations; the internet has lists of thousands of them. Every field of activity creates its own jargon, using numerous abbreviations, yet, more often than not we tend to pronounce these as individual letters, not acronyms. SOP (standard operating procedure) remains "ess-oh-pee" and not "sop," POW (prisoner of war) is pronounced "pee-oh-doubleyou" and not "pow," and SUV (sport utility vehicle), is always "ess-you-vee" rather than "suv," or some word based on it.

The reason for this phenomenon is the fact that it is much easier to form acronyms in Hebrew than in English. The Hebrew alphabet contains only consonants. Vowels are indicated by dots and dashes above and below the letters and are not part of the alphabet. Therefore, any group of consonants can be turned into a word by (arbitrarily) assigning vowels to the letters. An example that is in common use is the word *eshel* that stands for per diem expense. *Eshel* is made up of the three consonants *aleph*, *shin* and *lamed*, the initial letters of *okhel* (food), *shenah* (sleep) and *linah* (accommodations). Or take my favorite construction: *sakum* (flat-ware), which stands for *sakeen* (knife), *kaf* (spoon) and *mazleg* (fork). Both words are short, functional and easy to remember; both have long since become part of the vocabulary of the Hebrew language.

In English, it is difficult to form an acronym if there are no vowels among the initial letters of a phrase. Of course there are phrases where the vowels fall into place just right, and in those cases acronyms are sometimes formed. We have, for instance, the old army expression from WWII, SNAFU (situation normal, all fouled up); from the field of computers which is full of acronyms, WORM (write once, read many [times]); and SCUBA (self-contained underwater breathing apparatus). All these, and many others, are pronounced as words. Yet, in proportion to the size of the two languages, Hebrew rather than English seems to be the more fertile soil for the proliferation of acronyms.

Curses and Invectives

HOW WOULD YOU TRANSLATE "C@#?&X!" into Hebrew? Answer: with great difficulty. Hebrew—and especially biblical Hebrew—is a powerful language. However, it is clearly deficient in the expletives and invectives that seem to go with modern life in Israel, or for that matter, in most countries in the world. That is not to say that the Bible does not contain curses. But can you just imagine even the most irate motorist in Tel Aviv, being side-swiped by someone and seeing a dent in his new car, shouting: "You'll betroth a wife, but another will bed her; you'll build a house, but never dwell there; you'll plant a vineyard, but not use its fruit!" (Deuteronomy 28:30)?

In biblical society, words were believed to have great power. Both curses and blessings were taken to be basic prayers, which invoked the power of God, and people were careful not to utter them lightly. (This is the sense of the Third Commandment—not to take the name of the Lord in vain.) So strong was the belief in the efficacy of curses that the Masoretes, who put together the final version of the Hebrew Bible in the tenth century, actually changed the original text in several places to avoid references to humans cursing God. For example, when Job was afflicted with severe inflammations from head to toe, his wife showed him a way out of his misery: "*Barekh Elohim vamut*" ("Bless God and die"). This, of course, makes no sense at all. Fortunately, most Bible translations choose to disregard the correction and render the passage in its original meaning, "Curse God and die!" (Job 2:9)

Let me point out that the Masoretes were concerned not only with blasphemy, but also with public sensitivity. For instance, the curse from Deuteronomy to which I referred above (…will bed her) uses the Hebrew root *shagal*, which best translates as to screw—a crude sexual term. Yet, when we *layn* (chant) the passage aloud on Shabbat morning, we substitute the verb *shakhav*—to lie with or to bed, a much tamer euphemism for the same activity. The Hebrew language uses the Aramaic expression *sagi nahor* for such substitutions of less hurtful or offensive language. Literally they mean full of light yet in practice they refer to a blind person.

But back to our motorist. The confrontation may start mildly enough with *hamor!* (you ass!) and escalate quickly to *ben zonah!* (son-of-a-whore). And here something interesting happens: since traditional Hebrew does not lend itself easily to obscene language, loan-words from other languages are brought in — especially Arabic and Russian terms. It seems that both these languages have a rich vocabulary dealing with the various body parts and their ingenious use in sexual activity. Details must be left to the reader's imagination.

Many Israelis use these foreign language expressions so freely that they're often surprised when told that they are not Hebrew. The story is told of two customs officials who watched a group of Russian immigrants exit a plane at Ben-Gurion airport when one of the group tripped and let out a resounding curse in his own language. "Amazing," said one official to the other, "they've only just arrived and already speak perfect Hebrew!"

Many of these expletives by now also exist in Hebrew. The root *ziyen* (to screw) appears in all the f-word variations we know in English. Moreover, army slang seems to expand this lexicon at a dizzying pace. Many of the swearwords in ubiquitous use cannot be found in any dictionary — even a dictionary of slang terms.

Interestingly, if someone tells you, *lekh la'azazel!* (Go to hell!), you may be offended — but not because it is bad language. Words such as hell, damn, devil and the like that are regarded as profanity in English, do not carry that connotation in Hebrew. This is, undoubtedly, because the concept of hell (and being damned to it) did not exist in biblical times. The Bible speaks of *She'ol* as a place where souls dwell after death, but not as a place of punishment, of fire and brimstone. Satan is not the Prince of Darkness reigning over hell but the accuser or prosecutor before the heavenly throne. Therefore, euphemisms such as heck, darn and dickens don't exist either. (*Azazel*, you may remember, was the place where, on Yom Kippur, the High Priest laid the sins of the people on the scapegoat which was then cast out in the desert.)

What is offensive in one culture may not be so in another. In all cultures, though, Mark Twain's dictum may be true, "In certain trying circumstances, urgent circumstances, desperate circumstances, profanity furnishes a relief denied often to prayer."

THERE IS ONE TERM IN Hebrew which, though not exactly a curse, is just as pejorative to those in the know. Some time ago, I started noticing that more and more people (locally and nationally) close their messages with *b'shalom*. Because the prefix *b* means in, I assumed they meant to say, in peace. I had not seen this usage before and could not explain why it left me feeling so uneasy. Then, Rabbi Simchah Roth, in response to an e-mail message that ended with *"b'shalom,"* posted the following:

> In Jewish tradition we speak of someone arriving *"**be**-shalom"* only to their grave. The traditional blessing of sending someone on his way is *"**le**-shalom."*

> In modern Israel it would be considered quite insulting to take your leave of someone (knowledgeable) by saying *"lekh be-shalom"* (go in peace), which is almost the equivalent of "drop dead." Under such circumstances the correct benediction is *"lekh le-shalom."*

> The source for my statements is: Talmud Bavli, *Berakhot* 64a. There, Rabbi Avin ha-Levi says, "When you take leave of a friend do not say *"lekh beshalom"* but say *"lekh leshalom."* This is what Jethro said to Moses (Exodus 4) and Moses went on to success; David took his leave of Absalom by saying *"lekh beshalom"* (2 Samuel 15:9), and Absalom went and got himself hanged! Rabbi Avin ha-Levi further says: when you take leave of the deceased (at the graveside) do not say *"lekh leshalom"* but rather *"lekh beshalom"* (based on Genesis 15:15).

> Sorry to be so pedantic, but to the knowledgeable Hebrew speaker it's uncomfortable when someone wishes you *"be-shalom."*

Only after reading R. Roth's explanation, did it occur to me that, yes, of course, I knew this from the Friday night liturgy. In the opening hymn, *Shalom aleikhem*, where we bid the angels to come in peace, we sing: *"bo'akhem le-shalom"* and not *"bo'akhem be-shalom"*!

28 A Modest Proposal

THERE IS AN ACADEMIC DEBATE raging in modern Israel that I personally find very interesting—a debate that, some claim, may ultimately affect the Jewish people as a whole. The debate concerns a proposal which would change the vowels in the Hebrew language and thereby, of course, change the language itself. Lest you think, "who cares?" let me point out that though the proposal has yet to be officially considered, newspapers in Israel are already devoting significant space to it. What may be more telling is that the Jewish media in the United States are starting to pick up on the issue. Philologos, who writes a weekly column on linguistics for the Jewish newspaper *The Forward*, devoted a column to it entitled "Questioning the Marks." The English-language magazine, The *Jerusalem Report*, which is published in Israel but aimed at an American audience, also covered the question in its July 26, 2004 issue in a lengthy article with the catchy title, "Ee, Oo, Ah, Eh and Oh No!"

The controversy revolves around the proposal by an Israeli linguist to simplify the Hebrew language by eliminating more than half the vowel signs from it. Traditionally, vowels are not part of the alphabet, but are represented by diacritical marks, that is, by dots and dashes placed under, next to or above the consonants they vocalize. Dr. Mordecai Mishor, an employee of the Hebrew Language Academy and a long-time member of its Grammar Committee, argues that many of the vowel marks of classical Hebrew are now redundant. For instance, the five basic vowels ("ah", "eh", "ee", "oh", "oo") appear in a short form and a long form. Originally, each of these forms probably represented a distinct sound. Some of these distinctions are still maintained in the Diaspora. For example the short *segol* (three dots in a triangle under the letter) is pronounced "eh" as in let, whereas its long equivalent, *tseyrey* (two horizontal dots under the letter), is pronounced as in late.

In modern Hebrew speech, however, especially as spoken in Israel, these distinctions have all but disappeared. The word *sefer* (book), for instance, which has two "eh" sounds in it—the first long, the second short—should be pronounced *seyfer*. Yet everybody says *"sefer."* We know that many of our Israeli friends have trouble hearing the difference between met and mate, doll and dole, live and leave, and so on. They have trouble hearing the differences in sound because the distinctions don't exist in their own language. Why, then, asks Mishor, retain symbols for vowels that are no longer part of the spoken language?

Mishor goes further. He suggests we eliminate the half-vowels which combine the *sheva* symbol (:) with either of the short vowels "ah", "eh" or "oh". (Examples of these abound: the word *Adonai* starts with such a vowel.) Although there are good grammatical reasons for the presence of these vowels, and although they undoubtedly once represented unique sounds, the distinctions have long since been lost. Finally, Mishor proposes to do away with the *dagesh*, the dot that may be placed inside most of the letters of the alphabet, depending on various grammatical factors. Historically, the *dagesh* changed the pronunciation of these letters. However, in modern, Israeli speech, the presence of the little dot changes the sound in only three cases: from *vet* (v) to *bet* (b), from *khaf* (kh) to *kaf* (k) and from *pheh* (f) to *peh* (p). These uses Mishor proposes to retain.

How can such revolutionary changes in the language be justified? In modern Hebrew the vowel signs are rarely used. Most written material such as newspapers, literature, even science textbooks use consonants only. (The exceptions are printed Bibles, prayer books, children's books and books of poetry—where the vowels affect the meter of the line.) Because of this, most Israelis are notoriously bad spellers when they must use the vowel signs. Dropping the diacritical marks that have outlived their usefulness would certainly remove a great source of confusion and make it easier to learn the language.

The purists, who see value in maintaining intact what some regard as the "Holy Tongue," are clearly opposed to the changes. The simplified spelling would make it increasingly difficult for Israelis—and for those communities abroad that accept the changes—to read traditional texts, especially the Bible. These will seem as strange and incomprehensible to them as Chaucer does to the average English-reader. The opponents therefore argue that "this horrible proposal" will further alienate the non-religious from their Jewish heritage. They see it as an attack on the Orthodox Jewish community and an attempt to isolate that community from mainstream Judaism. A dire consequence, indeed, of such a modest proposal in Hebrew spelling!

Immigrant Hebrew Words in English

THE MOVIE "MY BIG FAT Greek Wedding" features a running gag that consists of a person who is very proud of his Greek heritage and maintains that he can trace every word in the English language back to a Greek root. I make no such claims with respect to Hebrew, though it is true of course that a large number of words have entered our language from Hebrew. As one would expect, most of these loan-words come from the Hebrew Scriptures.

A Hebrew speaker would recognize many of these "English" words immediately because both their sounds and their meanings have remained exactly as they are in Hebrew. For instance, the word *halleluyah* (Praise the Lord) sounds the same in both languages. The same is true for *seraphim*, the six-winged angels that graced the cover of the Ark of the Covenant in the Temple in Jerusalem. Hebrew words such as *behemoth* and *shibboleth*, though possibly not on everyone's lips, can be found in any English dictionary. *Behemoth* is the mighty animal described in Job 40:15–24, a word we use for anything of monstrous size or power, and *shibboleth* was the test-word the poor Ephraimite soldiers could not pronounce because they lisped and, as a consequence, were identified as the enemy and slain by the Gileadites (Judges 12:6). We use *shibboleth* to indicate language, or even beliefs, specific to a particular group.

In other cases, the meaning in English is close but not quite identical to the original Hebrew. Thus, sabbatical of course refers to the Hebrew Sabbath and comes from the root *shavat* (to rest). I'm not sure, though, how my Dean would have reacted had I asked him, after six years of teaching, for a year's sabbatical leave in order to rest!

Sometimes, however, the Hebrew word that has crept into English has taken on a meaning quite different from that of the original. A good example is the word Hosanna. The Hebrew phrase *hoshi'a na!* is unequivocally a cry for help: "Save us!" In the Christian liturgy, though, the English phrase "Hosanna in the highest!" has become an exclamation of acclamation or adoration.

A common change in the pronunciation of Hebrew words is the result of a quirk of transliteration. The Greek alphabet has no letter for the "v" sound and uses a "ß" (b) instead of it. Therefore, when the Hebrew Bible was first translated into Greek (the *Septuagint*—middle of third century B.C.E.), the Hebrew letter *vet* was rendered as a "b." Latin followed suit and ultimately this spelling became the norm in English translations of the Hebrew Bible. It is because of this that Hebrew names such as *Avraham*, *Devorah*, *Ya'akov*, and *Avigayil* among hundreds of others, became Abraham, Deborah, Jacob and Abigail. This shift from "v" to "b", of course, holds true not only for personal names. For instance: the word for father in Hebrew is *av*, its plural is *avot*. Change the "v" to a "b" and we get abbot—the superior of a monastery addressed, as it were, in the plural! Another example is the Hebrew word *yovel*, which refers to the fiftieth year in which, according to biblical law, all land reverts to its previous owners, all debts are cancelled, all Jewish indentured servants are set free, etc. Changing the "v" to a "b" gives us Jubilee, the golden version of which we jubilantly celebrate after a half century of wedded bliss.

The name Beelzebub (a devil ranking right next to Satan), also, comes straight from the Hebrew. Here, both "b"s have undergone the "v"-to-"b" shift. *Ba'al* was the name of a Philistine god and is often translated as Lord and *zevuv* is the Hebrew word for that pesky insect, the fly. Change the "v"s into "b"s and we get *Ba'al zebub* or Beelzebub, a.k.a. "Lord of the Flies."

Most interesting is the derivation of the word abacus, which comes from the Hebrew word *avak* (dust or fine dirt). What is the connection between a calculating device that uses movable beads and the Hebrew word for dust? Philologos, the linguist who writes about words for the weekly *Forward*, traces the connection in his column of September 23, 2005. He cites the discussion in the Talmud concerning writing on the Sabbath where the term *avak* appears: Writing with ink, copper sulfate and other means which leave a permanent impression is forbidden, whereas writing with fruit juice, in ordinary dirt (*avak derakhim*) or in scribes' dust (*avak sofrim*) is permitted. *Avak sofrim* was a layer of fine dirt or sand spread on a tablet or in a box that scribes used to make temporary notes or to perform calculations. When the operation was finished, the sand was smoothed out and could be used again as in the modern children's toy, the Etch-a-Sketch. In the course of time, the Hebrew *avak* became the Greek *abax* (a slab), which we inherited as abacus.

It is always tempting to see connections in words that are homophones (or almost sound alike) and have related meanings in the two languages. But these words may be false cognates, the connections illusory. Thus, although the Hebrew word for the number seven is *sheva* (surely a sound-alike), the two words are not related. Again, we cannot trace the word ravenous to the Hebrew *ra'ev*. Despite the fact that both words refer to that empty feeling in the pit of one's stomach (or in one's soul), the former comes from the French verb *raviner* that crept into English in its current meaning from Latin, as early as the mid-sixteenth century. On the other hand, there is no proof that the American slang word, copacetic (excellent, going just fine) does not come from the overused Hebrew expression *hakol be-seder* (everything's in order, all right), as some claim. The venerable *Oxford English Dictionary*, though, lists the word and adds: "Origin unknown" and who can argue with that?

30 The Sabbath Planet

A QUESTION THAT HAS INTRIGUED me for some time is the connection between the English name of the seventh day of the week, Saturday, and the Hebrew name for the planet Saturn, which is *shabtai*. Saturday comes from the Latin name *dies saturni*, or Saturn's day, and *shabtai* derives from the Hebrew word *shabbat*, or Sabbath. In one case, the seventh day of the week is named for the planet Saturn, and in the other the planet is named for the seventh day. That there is indeed a connection seems beyond doubt.

The question is of the chicken or the egg variety — which came first? Did the ancient Romans call the seventh day "Saturn's Day" because they knew that the Hebrew word for the planet referred to the Sabbath, or did the Jews call the planet *shabtai* after the Roman name for that day?

I posed the question to Philologos, author of a column on Hebrew and Yiddish in the weekly Jewish newspaper, *The Forward*. On January 5, 2007, he answered my question in a column entitled, "The Sabbath Planet."

Philologos starts by trying to ascertain when the word *shabtai* entered the Hebrew language, and when Saturday entered Latin and from there into other European languages. The earliest Hebrew text in which he finds the names of the planets mentioned is *Genesis Rabbah* (commentaries that explain and enlarge on the first book of the Torah, Genesis). *Genesis Rabbah* dates to the second half of the fourth century C.E. but includes material dating back at least to the third century. (It is, of course, entirely possible that the names of the planets, and among them *shabtai*, go back much farther.)

Philologos then turns to the Latin names of the days of the week. He points out that even before the emperor Constantine adopted Christianity as the official religion of his empire in the early fourth century, Rome had a fixed eight-day week. In that week, the last day was known as the market day and the other seven days were named after the sun, the moon and the five planets known in antiquity. The seventh day of the week was named after Saturn and became our Saturday.

How far back do these names go? Philologos cites two early Roman authors who mention the name Saturday. Interestingly, both show a remarkable knowledge of Jewish customs and laws. The first, the Latin poet Tibullus (54–19 B.C.E.) refers to *dies Saturni sacra* (the holy day of Saturn). Since the Romans did not regard their own Saturday as holy, could he have referred to the Jewish Shabbat? The second reference comes from Tacitus, a Roman historian of the late first century C.E. Tacitus tells us that Jews rest every seventh day and let the earth lie fallow every seventh year in honor of Saturn, the seventh and highest of the heavenly bodies. He does not say that the Jews worship Saturn but does state that they consider it to be the planet with the most powerful influence on human life.

Since both Tibellus and Tacitus antedate *Genesis Rabbah* by several hundred years, Philologos concludes that Saturday is an older term than *shabtai*. It is therefore likely that, "even before the rise of Christianity, the Romans, aware that the Jews rested every seven days and wondering why they did, attributed this to the role played in their religion by Saturn and referred to the Jewish Sabbath as 'Saturn's day'." Philologos thus hypothesizes that the Romans named the seventh day of their own week on the basis of their understanding of the Jewish religion. He continues: "In the course of time the term *dies Saturni* would have influenced Jews, too, to associate their Sabbath with Saturn and to call the latter *shabtai*."

Whether Philologos is correct in his analysis or not, what is interesting in this scenario is the assumption that both Romans and Jews had a detailed knowledge of each other's culture. And indeed they did! Even before the Great War of the Jews against the Romans (which ended with the destruction of the Temple in the year 70 C.E.), large numbers of Jews had settled within the Greco-Roman world. And, as was the case throughout Jewish history, there was considerable interaction between the minority culture of the Jews and the majority cultures surrounding them. In the case of Hellenism and Judaism, the mutual influence of the two cultures upon each other was extensive. A good example to demonstrate this point is the very volume of Midrashim to which we referred above, *Genesis Rabbah*. Though written in a combination of Hebrew and Aramaic, it contains a large number of Greek words and expressions. It is certain that the Jews knew about Saturn Day and more than likely that many Romans knew about our Shabbat.

31 Which Way is Up in the Bible?

THE OTHER DAY, I JOKINGLY referred to the River Nile as "running uphill." Although it is clearly wrong, we often think of the direction North as being up and of South as being down. I started wondering: Has the Nile always run uphill? Has North always been "up"? If, instead of "a pillar of cloud by day and a pillar of fire by night," Moses had had a map to guide him during the 40-year trek through the desert, what would its orientation have been? What are the references to compass-directions in the Bible?

The Bible mentions all four major compass-points. As one would expect, East and West are defined in terms of the apparent course of the sun: East is *Mizrah*, from the root *zarah*, referring to the sunrise, and West is *Ma'arav*, related to *erev* (evening), and refers to the direction in which the sun sets at the end of the day. Many cultures have this same association. The two words, Orient and Occident, both derived from Latin for the rising and setting of the sun, are current in many languages.

The biblical word for North, *Tzafon*, derives from the root *tzafan* meaning to hide. North, then, was the hidden or dark region for our ancestors. It was from the North that the country was repeatedly invaded, at least twice defeated and its population carried off into exile. The prophet Jeremiah had it right when he warned in terse biblical language (1:14): "From the North shall come the evil," or, in the more dramatic translation of the Jewish Publication Society Bible: "From the North shall disaster break loose (upon all the inhabitants of the land!)." On the opposite side of North we have South, the word for which is *Darom*. It is of unknown origin and has no meaning other than South.

These four biblical words are still used in modern Hebrew for the major compass points. However, in addition to them, the ancient Israelites often used terms more closely related to their country's geography and history. Let us take them one at a time.

For West, rather than *Ma'arav*, we often find the word *Yama* (toward the sea). This directional adjective points to the Mediterranean Sea that defines the western border of the Land of Israel.

To indicate the East, rather than *Mizrah*, the Bible uses the interesting word *Kedem* (before), which suggests two, almost opposite, meanings. In the sense of "coming before" (both in time and place) it evokes the tribal past, the direction from which the Israelites entered and conquered the land of Canaan. However, in the sense of "in front of" or "forwards", it expresses the future and, possibly, the national aspirations, as exemplified, for example, by the direction of expansion of King David's empire.

The words for North and South indicate directions in surprising ways. In Arabic the word, *shamaal*, stands for both North and left (as in left-hand side). *Shamaal* is clearly a cognate of the Hebrew word *semol* (left). Thus, the terms north-side and left-hand side are closely related. We turn 180 degrees and what do we find? The Bible frequently uses the word *Teyman* for South. *Teyman*, however, not only refers to the country of Yemen—which does lie south of *Eretz Israel*—but also contains the Hebrew word *yamin* (right, as in right-hand side). The words for south-side and right-hand side are synonyms in biblical Hebrew.

South is indicated most often by reference to the Negev, the dry or desert-land which comprises the southern part of *Eretz Israel*. It is interesting, however, to note that both the directions North and South in Hebrew also echo the connotations we find in many cultures of the terms right-hand side and left-hand side. Right suggests favored, auspicious and (in Arabic) even lucky, as in the name Binyamin (Benjamin—son-of-the-right, or favored son) whereas left implies inept, inauspicious and even sinister (as in the quote from Jeremiah above).

Clearly, the biblical terms for the compass directions are consistent with one another: by facing in the direction that the Israelites called forward, that is, East, they had North on their left side and South on their right side.

DID THIS VIEW OF THE world carry over to the orientation of maps they may have constructed? On a visit to Jordan, I had the opportunity to see close-up the oldest surviving map of the Land of Israel—the famous Madaba map (see next page). This is a mosaic map of the whole Middle East that covers the floor of a 6th century church in Madaba, Jordan. The map shows the "Holy Lands" from Egypt to Lebanon, including the Sinai, Israel and Jordan. It was discovered accidentally in 1894 during the construction of a Greek-Orthodox church for the resident Christian-Arab population.

Unfortunately, large parts of the mosaic have been lost over the centuries. Yet, it still depicts more than 150 individual cities of interest to Christian pilgrims. The city of Jerusalem is shown in especially great detail. One can identify four of the city gates, the Church of the Holy Sepulcher, the Tower of David and other important religious sites. The map clearly

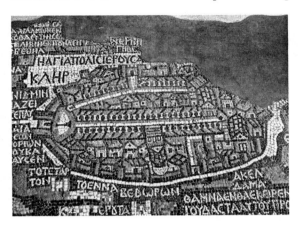

shows the *Cardo Maximus*, the column-lined main street that bisected the city in a straight north-south oriented line. It is noteworthy that on the map it runs from left to right. The Cardo was a characteristic feature of Roman city design and Jerusalem was a Roman city in the 6th century. Basing themselves on this 1,500-year old map, archeologists deduced the existence of the *Cardo Maximus* below the current street level of the city. And, indeed, in 1975, it was unearthed below a section of the Jewish quarter of the Old City of Jerusalem. Since then, several other landmarks depicted on the map have been excavated within the Old City walls.

We have focused on only the small detail of the Madaba map showing Jerusalem and, specifically, the *Cardo Maximus*, running from left to right along its north-south axis. From these, and from the location of all the other places shown on the Madaba map, we see that it is oriented with East on top. As our discussion would suggest, this is consistent with the biblical terminology and shows that north-flowing rivers, such as the Nile, did not run uphill in ancient times.

EXTENSION: According to the *Shulḥan Arukh* (Code of Jewish Law) Jews in the Diaspora have to face East, that is, in the direction of Jerusalem, during prayer. Rabbi Israel Stein reminded me, however, that in case a person is lost (in a deep forest, perhaps?) and cannot tell where East lies, our Sages held that any direction will do, so long as "the heart is directed toward Jerusalem."

Yiddish, the *Mame-loshn*

YIDDISH IS, WITHOUT DOUBT, ON the endangered-species list of languages. Over the course of history, many languages have disappeared, some leaving us only a written (or engraved) record and many not even that. What may be unique about Yiddish is the speed at which this endangered stage has been reached. Until the Second World War, Yiddish was a rich, vibrant language on which, to borrow a metaphor, the sun never set. Now, there is practically no new literature produced in it, and the average age of its speakers is advanced enough to secure senior-discount prices at the local deli.

Yiddish is one of maybe a dozen Jewish languages that were spoken by large numbers of Jews at various times and in different places. Besides Hebrew and Aramaic, the two Semitic languages spoken in the Land of Israel, we find languages such as Judeo-Greek, Judeo-Persian, Judeo-Italian, etc. In each case, the Jewish inhabitants adapted the vernacular of the country in which they lived for their own use by introducing words from Hebrew and other languages, which served their particular needs. The common feature of all these languages was the fact that they were all written in the Hebrew alphabet, from right to left.

For example, Judeo-Arabic was widely used by Jews in all Muslim countries after the spread of Islam in the seventh century. The great Jewish scholars, poets, philosophers and scientists of Moorish Spain, such as Sa'adia Ga'on, Ibn Gabirol and Maimonides, all wrote their major works in Arabic, using the Hebrew *aleph-bet*.

With the expulsion from Spain in 1492, the *Sephardi* (Spanish in Hebrew) Jews settled in various North African countries and around the Mediterranean. Over time, they added words in (among others) Turkish, Greek, Italian and Arabic to the Castilian language which they had brought with them. In this way evolved the Judeo-Spanish language called Ladino, which is still widely spoken today in *Sephardi* communities around the world.

Yiddish evolved in a similar fashion. About a thousand years ago, Jews from northern France settled in the area that was later to become Germany. Over the course of generations, they adopted the German language, but retained some elements of Old French. As always, they reached into their own background for words and idioms from the language of prayer and religion. This mixture was the earliest form of Yiddish. They were wary of the Latin alphabet as too monkish, and used Hebrew letters to write this Judeo-German language. Rashi, the venerated eleventh century scholar from Troyes, France, refers to it as *leshon Ashkenaz* (the German tongue).

Ironically, present-day scholars in some German universities are studying Yiddish for early forms of their own language, for Yiddish has retained much of its original Middle-High-German character. (It has been estimated that the language consists of 70% German words, 20% Hebrew and 10% Slavic—Russian, Polish, Ukrainian, Slovenian, etc.—loan-words.) The increased isolation of Jews into ghettos made it difficult for their language to keep pace with the changes in the German language proper.

The great flowering of Yiddish came with its expansion into the Slavic countries of Eastern Europe in the fifteenth and sixteenth centuries. By the eighteenth century, Poland was the spiritual center of the Jewish communities of Europe and definitely the center of Jewish learning. Yiddish became the *lingua franca* of European Jewry.

In Eastern Europe, Yiddish was the *mame-loshen*, (mother tongue). Much good literature was written in it, a broad spectrum of journals and newspapers was published in it and it became the linguistic vehicle for such mass movements as ḥasidism and, later, the Jewish labor movement and Zionism. Even the *Haskalah* movement (Jewish Enlightenment), which inveighed against Yiddish as a "backward ghetto tongue," had to use it, for it, and only it, was the language of the masses.

YIDDISH IS A VERY EXPRESSIVE language and is able to reflect, as no other can, both the joys and the unspeakable horrors of Jewish life in the East-European *shtetl*. Here is how Leo Rosten describes it in *The Joys of Yiddish*: "Yiddish is a language of exceptional charm... It is bright, audacious, mischievous... Steeped in sentiment, it is sluiced with sarcasm... It is a tongue that never takes its tongue out of its cheek."

Although Yiddish was spoken by millions, it was not universally held in such high esteem. German Jews despised it as a low-class vulgarization of the language of Goethe. The English author Israel Zangwill wrote in 1906: "I have never been able to understand how it is that a language spoken by perhaps more than half of the Jewish race should be regarded with such horror, as though it were a crime." When I grew up in pre-Israel Palestine, members of patriotic youth movements (including me) used to shout down speakers who came to town to deliver lectures in Yiddish. Yiddish was the language of the ghetto, of an ignoble past. We believed that it had to be forgotten and replaced by Hebrew to enable a new, free Jewish society to develop.

WHAT IS THE SITUATION TODAY? It has been estimated that 11 million Jews spoke Yiddish at the outbreak of World War II. Most of these perished in the Holocaust. In the United States today, despite the fact that many Yiddish words have entered mainstream American speech (_hutzpah_, _shlep_, _nosh_, _maven_, etc.), the heyday of the _mame-loshn_ has passed. Yiddish is spoken as a first language mainly by the ultra-Orthodox who cling to it because it is informed by the values of the past.

This is the case even in Israel, where the _haredim_ (ultra-orthodox) use Yiddish for secular matters and reserve Hebrew for prayer and study. With the recent influx of Russian immigrants, somewhat more Yiddish is heard on the street, and now there are even two Yiddish dailies published. However, once these immigrants are absorbed and at ease in Hebrew, the supply of new Yiddish speakers will, for all practical purposes, be nil. What is missing are the rich literary contributions of Yiddish writers of the past such as Sholom Aleichem, Sholom Asch, Isaac Bashevis Singer and many others.

THERE ARE SOME HOPEFUL SIGNS, however. Besides the recent revival of Yiddish music—mainly in the form of klezmer music—we find that Yiddish is being taught in some American universities, that many cities have regular Yiddish programs on radio, and that plays in Yiddish are revived every once in a while. In New York there are several _kindershuls_, connected with the Workers' Circle, in which the languages of instruction are both English and Yiddish. There are several Yiddish interest groups on the internet to which participants from all over the world contribute.

In 1980, a National Yiddish Book Center was established whose aim is to rescue Yiddish books and collect them before they are thrown away or destroyed as if the were of no more interest to anybody. The Center is housed at Hampshire College in Amherst, Massachusetts. With the help of a staff of 35, Aaron Lansky, who has dedicated his life to this rescue mission, has collected a 1.5 million books so far. The Center distributes books to libraries and schools all over the world to supplement existing collections, and to restore collections that were destroyed in the *Sho'ah* (Holocaust). Lansky hopes it will become a place to study the Yiddish language and the culture it represents, rather than a museum of a dead way of life.

Do all these developments point to the reversal of a trend? Possibly. Still, it is almost certain that never again will it be possible to step up to a Jew chosen at random, and ask: *Mistome ir red mame-loshn?* (Do you speak Yiddish by any chance?) and receive *avade, farshteyt zikh* (of course) for an answer.

Rules by Which We Live

Fit to Eat: Reason(s) for the Jewish Dietary Laws

ALTHOUGH MANY CULTURES HAVE PROSCRIPTIONS relating to food, the laws of *kashrut* (dietary laws) hold a very special place in Judaism. They are central to the Jewish religion, and like the religion itself, pervade all aspects of daily life. The laws of *kashrut*, which relate almost exclusively to animal foods, deal with the choice of foods, the proper way of killing the animal, the proper preparation of the food and the mixture of foods allowed for consumption.

The Torah presents these laws as *ḥukkim* (divine statutes) and does not provide an explanation for them. Still, many quite diverse explanations have been advanced to justify the dietary laws in rational ways. These explanations are not necessarily at odds with a perception of the divine nature of the laws, for something may be divinely inspired and still make sense in medical, ethical or cultural terms.

The most famous of those who believed in the health benefits of a kosher diet was Maimonides, the great twelfth century Egyptian sage who was also a physician. In his *Guide of the Perplexed*, he writes: "All the foods which the Torah has forbidden us to eat have some bad and damaging effects on the body...." He explains the various prohibitions against eating the fat of the intestines, the consumption of blood or the mixing of meat and dairy dishes in terms of human hygiene and medicine.

In the thirteenth century, Naḥmanides, a renowned Spanish scholar, also uses a medical explanation: "...fish without fins and scales [which are forbidden] usually live in the lower muddy strata.... They breed in musty swamps and eating them can be injurious to health."

A somewhat different but related argument was advanced by two Lubavitch Ḥasidim who visited our home some years ago. They relied on an argument found in the Talmud, namely that the dietary laws have an ethical intent and are meant to "refine a person." Food affects not only the body but also the soul, and "the consumption of impure animals dulls the finer appetites." The two young men argued in favor of a kosher home in terms of the personality traits the kosher foods would engender: "a person becomes what he eats." By refraining from consuming birds of prey and carnivorous animals, all of which are *treyf* (not kosher), and limiting oneself to herbivorous animals and certain fowl, a non-violent, just and peace-loving character will be developed. They assured us that, "children reared in a kosher home do not succumb to drug abuse or end up in jail."

Such arguments as "it's good for you" have been rejected by many: "God forbid that I should believe that the reason for forbidden foods is medicinal! For were it so, the Book of God's Law would be in the same class as any of the minor brief medical books" (quoted in Klein, *A Guide to Jewish Religious Practice*).

There may be disputes concerning the reasons for the existence of the laws of *kashrut*, but there is none regarding the effects these laws had on Jewish history. They operated as a powerful agent to assure the continued existence of the Jewish people. To paraphrase a well-known aphorism about the Sabbath: "More than the Jewish people kept the laws of *kashrut*, the laws of *kashrut* kept the Jewish people."

There are scholars who argue that the best explanation for the promulgation of the dietary laws in the Torah, and their subsequent amplification and extension in the Talmud, was the desire to "build a fence" around the Jewish people which would set them apart and, thus, keep them from being assimilated into the surrounding cultures.

The Rabbis of the talmudic period were concerned that the pressures of alien religions would dilute the ethnic purity and weaken the bond between "the unique God and His unique people." They were quite direct about this: "We should not eat their bread because we may be led thereby to drink their wine. We should not drink their wine because we may be led thereby to intermarry with them, and this will lead us to worship their gods." The Rabbis, therefore, forbade the eating of bread baked by Gentiles or even to buy wine, milk or cheese from them.

The dietary laws, thus, unquestionably had the effect of severely limiting the social and cultural contacts between Jews and non-Jews. Since a companion (in Latin) is literally one with whom one shares bread, it is clear that the laws of *kashrut* were designed to keep Jews from undesirable company.

The Torah puts it more positively by suggesting a connection between *kashrut* and holiness. In connection with the dietary laws, it says, "I am the Lord your God; sanctify yourself and be holy; for I am holy..." (Leviticus 11:44).

The Hebrew root of the word *kadosh* (holy) has the secondary meaning of "set apart." The divine promise is that being holy—in this case, by elevating the physical activities of eating and drinking to a discipline in holiness—assures the continued identity and, therefore, existence of the Jewish people. "You shall be holy unto me; for I the Lord am holy, and have set you apart from the people, that you should be mine" (Leviticus 20:26).

34 Fuzzy Sets and *Kashrut*

IN THE PREVIOUS CHAPTER, WE looked at traditional reasons for *kashrut*, the Jewish dietary laws. These were divided into arbitrary arguments, in the sense that no explanation could be known or was necessary, and pragmatic arguments that adduce beneficial effects for keeping kosher. In this column we look at a contemporary, anthropological approach to the subject.

We start with a series of Torah commandments that are known as *sha'atnez* or the mixed species laws (Leviticus 19:19, Deuteronomy 22:9–11). According to *halakhah* it is forbidden to plant together two kinds of seed (for food) which differ in name, appearance or taste. It is forbidden to graft one kind of tree onto the stock of another kind. The Torah forbids the crossbreeding of animals, or even the use of different animals yoked together for plowing or pulling. We are forbidden to spin, weave or wear any cloth that contains both wool and linen. These basic laws of the Torah are greatly expanded in tractate *Kilayim* of the Mishnah.

What reason is given for these prohibitions against the intermingling of different kinds of seeds, trees, animals and fibers? The laws are classified as *hukim*, divine decrees, which do not require an explanation.

In her book *Purity and Danger* (1966), Prof. Mary Douglas, anthropologist at Northwestern University, offers a general theory. Prof. Douglas argues that the biblical notion of holiness implies the ideas of wholeness and completeness. Since God created all growing things and animals "each according to its own kind," the world was so ordered as to represent "unity, integrity, perfection of the individual and of the kind." Holiness exists when the individual units conform to their general categories. Impurity is introduced when the taxonomy of creation is upset by blurring the boundaries between categories.

Prof. Douglas shows that the biblical legislators extended the idea of holiness to wholeness of appearance. A *kohen* (priest) had to be whole. One who was physically impaired was not allowed to approach the altar to bring sacrifices. Related to this is the requirement that animals also had to be without blemish to be fit to be sacrificed to the God of Israel.

Prof. Douglas applies this tendency of the ancient Israelites to see the world in stark categories—sacred and profane, pure and impure, ordered and chaotic—to an explanation of the laws of *kashrut*. This she does in the chapter entitled "The Abominations of Leviticus." As we saw in the previous chapter on *kashrut*, the dietary laws are directly tied to the idea of holiness of the people Israel. To fit her theory, the laws must therefore correspond to the scheme of unity and wholeness she sets up.

To be classified as clean, she argues, each animal we consume must accord as much as possible with the ideal of its class. Cloven-hoofed, cud-chewing ungulates define the category for domestic mammals. Wild animals are allowed as long as they correspond to the ideal. Animals which possess only one of these two traits blur the boundary of the set and are, therefore, not kosher. Thus, the rabbit chews its cud but does not have cloven hooves, and the pig has cloven hooves but does not chew its cud. Both are *treif*—not fit for human consumption.

Any class of creatures that is not equipped for the right kind of locomotion in its element is contrary to holiness. Fish have scales and propel themselves by means of fins. These two traits are the criteria for being kosher—and not whether the fish are predatory.

Land animals hop, jump or walk. Insects, though, despite their six-leggedness, fly and are therefore unclean. There is, however, a certain kind of locust that jumps and is therefore kosher. This insect used to be an important source of protein in the diet of Yemeni Jews.

Prof. Douglas does not deal with birds because the Bible does not define the group but simply enumerates a list of unclean birds. She concludes that, "In general, the underlying principle of cleanness in animals is that they shall conform fully to their class. Those species are unclean which are imperfect members of their class, or whose class itself confounds the general scheme of the world."

Robert Alter, of the University of California at Berkeley, in dealing with this subject, adds that, "Amphibians and reptiles are the prime model of unclean creatures in this gastronomic language of the holy because they belong to more than one element and because they exhibit an improper means of locomotion for their element, neither swimming nor walking but 'slithering and swarming'."

He extends this "principle of preserving sharp distinctions" to explain many other biblical laws such as the strong sentiment against transvestism, incest, homosexuality and bestiality. He writes: "These acts flagrantly involve human bodies and feelings in a confusion of identities and distortion of the dividing lines between natural kinds—male and female, human and animal" ("A New Theory of *Kashrut*," *Commentary*, August 1979). There is little doubt that biblical society would have been horrified had they known of such modern practices as genetic engineering and sex-change operations.

Alter adds a dynamic attribute to the clean categories—vitalism. He says: "God is a living God and His commandments, as the Bible tells us again and again, confer life on those who observe them." Therefore, anything that destroys life, such as a predatory animal, cannot possibly be Godlike or holy, that is, cannot possibly be kosher. He thus completes the *schema* that ties our dietary laws to the original act of creation.

Ketubbah: No Married Woman Should be Without One!

THERE ARE TWO PREREQUISITES FOR a Jewish wedding ceremony: The mutual consent of the two persons involved and a *ketubbah*. Consent is demonstrated by the bride accepting an object of value (usually a ring, these days) given to her by the bridegroom. This condition is interesting because it represents one of the few times a daughter may act contrary to her parents' express wishes. Marital happiness trumps the Fifth Commandment!

The other condition, the presence of a *ketubbah*, is interesting because it shows that as far back as the first century B.C.E., when it was first proposed, our Sages worried about safeguarding the rights of the woman in a marriage or, more precisely, upon the dissolution of the marriage. A *ketubbah* is a contract, a prenuptial agreement, which specifies the amount of money due to the wife upon the death of her husband or in case of a divorce. It is signed by two witnesses, read aloud during the wedding ceremony and handed by the bridegroom to the bride.

This legal protection was especially important because, according to biblical law, a widow was not a legal heir to her deceased husband's estate (Numbers 27:8–11). In post-talmudic times, this law has been changed by various amendments, and the wife now figures in the succession of inheritance. The *ketubbah* provides the wife an agreed upon sum of money that assures her an income after her husband's death.

The wife needed protection also in case of a divorce. According to *halakhah*, unchanged to this day, only a husband can initiate divorce procedures; a wife cannot divorce her husband. According to the Talmud, the *ketubbah* was to serve as a deterrent to arbitrary divorce. It was hoped that a husband would think twice before divorcing his wife for a capricious reason, knowing that he would have to assume a heavy financial obligation.

What financial details, then, does the *ketubbah* contain? First, it specifies a compulsory minimum to which the wife is entitled. The Talmud sets the sum at 200 *zuzim* for a virgin getting married and 100 *zuzim* in all other cases. This sum is referred to as the "main *ketubbah*" payment or simply as the *ketubbah*. In addition, and much more important, a voluntary increment (*tosefet*) is specified. This additional sum was usually the result of pre-betrothal negotiations between the groom (or his father) and the bride (or more probably her father).

However, regardless of the actual sums specified, Jewish courts tended (and still tend) to follow local custom in calculating the payments due the woman. In case they deemed the main sum and its increment insufficient (say, it was devalued over time by inflation), they would award the woman a sum sufficient to allow her to live in the style to which she was accustomed.

In addition to the above sums of money, the *ketubbah* records the amount of the *nadan* (dowry)—the financial assets the bride brought into the marriage. She was entitled to these, as well, upon the death of her husband or upon being cast out by him.

The Rabbis considered the protection provided by the *ketubbah* so important that they decreed that a couple could not live together for even one hour in case the *ketubbah* was lost or mislaid. Intercourse under such circumstances was likened to prostitution. A new deed had to be drawn up, duplicating the original in all respects, before normal relations could be resumed.

The Sages of the Talmud appended a caveat to the protection accorded to the divorced wife by her ketubbah. According to the Mishnah (*Ketubbot*, 7:6), she could lose the ketubbah payment due to her, as well as the dowry she had brought to the marriage, if she "transgressed the law of Moses and the practice of Jewish women." The second condition clearly translates into the requirement that she be a virtuous and chaste woman.

THE POSITION OF THE WIFE changed greatly in the tenth century when Rabbenu Gershom (Mainz, c. 960–1028 C.E.) passed a *herem* (ban) which became binding on all *Ashkenazi* Jews. It outlawed marrying multiple wives—a custom which had not been practiced by Jews other than in Muslim countries, anyway. More importantly, it decreed that a wife could not be divorced without her consent. So fundamental was this change that it was argued that there was no more need for "divorce insurance" to protect the wife. However, by that time the *ketubbah* had become so entrenched in Jewish law and tradition that it was retained anyway.

Little known is the fact that the wife could use the rights granted by her *ketubbah* as collateral for a loan. As with any other promissory note these rights could be sold with the payoff to the buyer contingent upon the premature death of the husband or upon divorce. Our medieval sages discuss, in surprisingly contemporary language, the factors that affect the value of the discounted *ketubbah*, such as life expectancy, health, marital happiness, etc. Thus, a woman married to an older man, or to one with a choleric temper, could expect to receive more money for her *ketubbah* than a wife happily-married to a younger husband.

A PUZZLING ASPECT (TO ME, at least) are the beautiful decorations with which *ketubbot* from past centuries are often adorned. Many are richly illuminated, the text carefully calligraphed and bordered by brightly colored illustrations. Because *ketubbot* were financial documents, it is unlikely that they were displayed in the home as is the custom so often these days with modern *ketubbot*. It must be the case, then, that these works of art, created for the exclusive, and possibly solitary enjoyment of the wife, were decorated to fulfill the *hiddur mitzvah* (the *mitzvah* of beautification of ritual objects), discussed in Chapter 44.

Divorce and the Agony of the *Agunah*

As WE NOTED IN THE previous chapter, according to biblical law, only a man can dissolve his marriage; a woman cannot. "A man takes a wife and possesses her. She fails to please him, because he finds something obnoxious about her, and he writes her a bill of divorcement, hands it to her, and sends her away from his house" (Deuteronomy 24:1). Except for minor limitations, a husband's authority to dissolve his marriage is absolute. This is, of course, very much in line with the legal codes of other cultures of that period, and fundamentally different from Western legal systems today in which a court grants the divorce.

Although in the Jewish tradition biblical laws cannot be repealed, they can be reinterpreted and hedged about so as to change their impact. This is what has happened over the centuries to the laws pertaining to divorce. By the time of the Talmud (second to fifth centuries), the simple *Bill of Divorcement* of which the Torah speaks had become a very complicated legal document—the *get*. Its wording, and the procedures connected with it, are highly exacting and time-consuming and, undoubtedly, were meant to minimize the occasions in which a husband divorced his wife on a whim or in the heat of the moment.

In certain cases a woman can initiate divorce proceedings. She can have a *bet din* (Rabbinical Court) compel her husband to give her a *get*. These include cases where the husband becomes physically repulsive to her because of some offensive medical condition or because of his occupation; where the husband does not carry out his marital obligations to provide her with food, shelter and conjugal relations; where the husband is habitually cruel to her and, finally, where his conduct is immoral.

Except in such cases, the position of the woman was one of impotence, for she could neither initiate a divorce nor withhold her consent to it. As we saw above, this situation changed radically with the *ḥerem* (ban) of Rabbenu Gershom, which mandated the consent of the wife to a divorce. The ban reduced the wife's vulnerability considerably and made her an active partner in the negotiations of any settlement. Rachel Biale in her comprehensive *Women and Jewish Law*, points out that this medieval innovation represents a total change in *halakhah*, for the Talmud states explicitly: "A woman may be divorced with her consent or without it" (*Yevamot*, 112b). With this change, a man can no longer send away his wife without her consent and, if he insists on the divorce, he may have to pay dearly for it.

The wife, though, cannot be completely unreasonable and withhold her consent under any conditions, for *batei din* (religious courts) have been known to threaten to set aside Rabbenu Gershom's ban. It is, after all, only a *takkanah* (amendment)—although it is binding on all *Ashkenazi* Jews.

ONE OF THE TRAGIC CONSEQUENCES of the fact that only a man can initiate a divorce—a consequence that has ruined (and still ruins) many Jewish women's lives—is the case of the *agunah* (the "fettered" or literally the anchored) wife. The *agunah* is a woman whose marriage has ended in every sense of the word, but who, because she cannot obtain a *get* from her husband, is not free to remarry. It is not hard to think of examples: Consider the plight of the tens of thousands of East-European wives whose husbands took off for America (*die goldene medineh*—the golden country) promising to send money to bring the family over. Some of these immigrants died on the trip, others took new wives. If, in the first case, two witnesses could not attest to the husband's death and, in the second case, the husband deserted his wife without benefit of a *get*, the wife was bound forever in a fictitious marriage.

The rabbis were sympathetic to the plight of these unfortunate women and looked for possible ways to annul their marriages. And yet, they were afraid to set up situations where a woman might be free to remarry and then find that her first husband was alive and that she had committed adultery. The problem is similar to that of a husband missing in action in a war. How long is long enough to give up all hope? In traditional Jewish law as it stands today there is no easy solution to the problem.

In Israel, it has been suggested that each (male) soldier hand his wife a conditional *get* when he starts his army service. Aside from certain *halakhic* problems connected with this plan, it was rejected by the army as injurious to the morale of its soldiers.

Especially disturbing is the case of a husband who, out of spite or in the hope of extorting large sums of money, refuses to give his wife a *get*. Since there is no legal way in Jewish law to compel him to do so, the unfortunate wife is truly "fettered." In Israel, the Rabbinate has persuaded the civil authorities to jail such a husband until he sees reason.

In the United States, the Conservative Movement has adopted a prenuptial agreement by which husband and wife agree that, if their marriage should end with a civil divorce, and one of the parties refuses to grant or accept a *get*, the marriage will retroactively become null and void. "*Get* laws" have been passed in New York and elsewhere that in effect insist that all impediments to remarriage be removed before a civil divorce is granted. Many Orthodox women's groups are agitating for changes in Jewish law that will finally free the *agunah*.

37 The *Mikveh*: A Pool of Clear Water

A HEBREW DICTIONARY GIVES THE first meaning of the word *mikveh* simply as "a pool or collection of water." In that sense we find it early in Genesis (1:10), where we read that God, on the third day of creation, "called the dry land Earth, and the gathering of waters (*mikveh*) He called Seas." The term, however, has entered our tradition as "a pool of clear water, immersion in which renders ritually clean a person who has become ritually unclean."

How does a person become ritually unclean? It is important to emphasize that a *mikveh* is a ritual bath; it is not meant to remove dirt or the perspiration of a day's hard labor. Rather, it belongs to the area of *tohorah* (purity) and *tum'ah* (impurity).

The Bible specifies that contact with the dead (or other defiling objects), an unclean flow from the body or childbirth renders a person unclean and therefore ineligible to enter the Sanctuary. With the destruction of the Temple, these laws of purity became inapplicable. In rabbinic Judaism, the emphasis shifted from the Sanctity of the Tabernacle to the idea of *tohorat hamishpaḥah* (family purity). The laws of purity, and with them the use of the *mikveh*, became a means of regulating sexual behavior.

For centuries, the main use of the *mikveh* was for a *niddah* (menstruating woman) who has to immerse herself in it before she can resume sexual intercourse. A bride, too, is obligated, to immerse herself before her wedding. This, according to Isaac Klein (*A Guide to Jewish Religious Practice*) prepares her "to enter marriage in a state of physical and mental purity."

In some observant groups (e.g., Ḥasidim) it is customary for men (and, to a lesser extent, women) to immerse themselves on the eve of Shabbat or the holidays, especially Yom Kippur, as an aid to spirituality. Recently, for the first time, a group of men from Beit Am used the Willamette River as a natural *mikveh* before the High Holy Days, to, as they put it, "recapture our heritage."

It is probable that in small Jewish communities like ours the primary knowledge of a *mikveh* stems from the immersion that seals the occasional conversion of a proselyte (female or male) to Judaism.

Ritual immersion was widely practiced by various groups (e.g., the Essenes) during Second Temple days, and a well-preserved *mikveh* can be seen on top of Masada, the mountain-top palace and fortress that King Herod I built in the Judean desert. A large literature traces Christian baptism and the Muslim laws of purity to the Jewish laws of immersion that obviously predate them.

To be kosher, a *mikveh* must meet rigid specifications. For instance, the minimum amount of water in it is specified (about 185 gallons)—enough water for a total immersion. Modern *mikva'ot* (pl.) are considerably larger, and can accommodate more than one person at a time.

Equally important is the source of the water. The minimum specified must be natural water, that is, rainwater, a spring, melted snow, etc. A river, lake or ocean can, of course, serve as a *mikveh*. Once the minimum quantity is met, additional water may be added from any source whatever.

Because of the central importance of the *mikveh* in Jewish life, the talmudic Sages devoted a whole tractate to discussions of its structure and operation, and to the laws governing family purity. The rabbis held that every Jewish community had to construct a *mikveh*—even before building a synagogue! In the ghettos and later in the East European *shtetls*, immersion after menstruation regulated family life for it enabled the couple to resume sexual intercourse after a hiatus of about two weeks. The *niddah* (menstruant) had to count seven clean days after menstruation before she could go to the *mikveh*. Only then could any physical contact between husband and wife take place. If her husband was away from home, the woman was not obligated to immerse herself. Yet, any delay designed "to torment her husband shall be severely punished."

There are stories of pious women living in isolated areas of Russia without a *mikveh* who underwent great hardship when the rivers froze over in the winter. If they were able to hack a hole in the ice, they performed the *mitzvah* of total immersion in the freezing water. The alternative spelled abstinence until the spring thaws.

Strictly traditional Orthodox women (or those trying to recapture their heritage) who still observe the laws of *tohorat hamishpaḥah* certainly have an easier time of it these days. Corvallis does not have a *mikveh*, but there is one in nearby Eugene. It is clean and well run. It has shower facilities for washing oneself before entering the pool. It is reasonably priced and, best of all, the water is heated!

38 Lighting the Sabbath Candles

THE FOURTH COMMANDMENT BIDS US to observe the Sabbath as a day of rest. Lighting the Sabbath candles is so much an integral part of our Sabbath observance that it may come as a surprise to learn that this *mitzvah* is not mentioned anywhere in the Bible. Yet in the *berakhah* (blessing) before lighting the candles we say: "Praised are You ... who has sanctified us with His commandments and commanded us to kindle the Sabbath light." Since it is not in the Torah, where does this commandment originate and what is the reason for it?

Kindling the Sabbath lights is one of the seven *mitzvot* that the Sages added on their own initiative. These are in addition to the traditional 613 commandments given in the Torah. Why did the Sages feel the need for the Sabbath lights? Was it in hopes of increasing the sanctity of the day?

The noted rabbinic authority, Maimonides (twelfth century, Egypt), writes in his *Hilkhot Shabbat* (Laws pertaining to the Sabbath, 5:1): "The lighting of the Shabbat lamp is not a voluntary act; it is, rather, a duty. For this is part of Shabbat joy (*oneg Shabbat*)." Clearly the Sages saw the light and the warmth contributed by a lamp as an integral and necessary part of the enjoyment of the Sabbath. Indeed, this preparation for the Sabbath was so important that Maimonides continues: "Both men and women must have a lamp burning in their home on Shabbat. Even if one does not have the wherewithal to eat one must beg from door to door to obtain oil to light the lamp."

In one of his lessons, Rabbi Simchah Roth comments extensively on this *mitzvah*:

> The Sages required a lamp to be burning in every Jewish home on the evening of Shabbat and this was considered so important to the enjoyment of Shabbat as a day of pleasantness that it was elevated to the degree of a rabbinical command (and there are only seven such commands in all). Shabbat would hardly be pleasant if one had to eat cold food without light or heat. Later on, the requirement of the Sages that a lamp be burning in the home was amplified to

having lamps burning in all places around the house where one might go during the hours of darkness on Shabbat. It is thus clear that the lighting of the Shabbat lamp was much more akin to our lighting of electric lights than to a religious ritual of lighting candles, as we now observe the custom. And, indeed, there are modern *poskim* (rabbinic decision makers) who hold that one can fulfill the *mitzvah* (including the *berakhah*) of Shabbat "candles" with the use of electric lights.

While I am quite aware that electric lights do not shed the same aura of religious feeling that candles do, I would certainly recommend reciting the *berakhah* over electric lights when candles are not available or not usable. (Such lights should be left burning and not turned off.) After all, surely the pious Jewish housewife of 250 years ago who lowered the chandelier over her dining room table before Shabbat in order to light the many candles it held, hauled it up again, and then recited the *berakhah*—surely she must have experienced the same or a similar religious aura as moderns do.

The Sages who did not want us to spend Friday evening in darkness and, therefore, required the lighting of a lamp, had to re-interpret Exodus 35:3, which expressly commands that, "You are not to let fire burn throughout all your settlements on the Sabbath day." They construed the verse as forbidding the "creation" of a fire, but not the enjoyment of the light and heat of an already existing fire. Most translations (though by no means all), therefore, have the verse saying: "You may not ignite any fire...." Kindling the Shabbat lamp (or candles, in our times) before the onset of Shabbat meets this condition and accomplishes the desired goal.

There are groups, however, who observe Shabbat as a day of rest but do not believe in the admissibility of Shabbat candles, even if lit before Shabbat starts. The Karaites, a Jewish sect that came into being at the beginning of the eighth century, deny the validity of the talmudic-rabbinical tradition. The Bible is the sole source of their creed and laws. They therefore reject the rabbinic interpretation of Exodus 35:3 and interpret the verse literally. Their Shabbat evenings are devoid of light and warmth. There are still several thousand Karaites settled in Russia, primarily in the area of the Black Sea. One cannot but wonder how much Shabbat enjoyment they experience in the depth of a Russian winter. (Karaite communities also still exist today in Israel, Turkey, and in the United States of America.)

Of Scribes and Scrolls and Authentic Texts

AFTER THE PUBLIC READING FROM the Torah is finished, say on a Shabbat morning, the *magbiha* is called to the *bimah*, the platform from which the Torah is read. The *magbiha* raises the Torah scroll up high, turns so that the written side of the scroll faces the congregation and unrolls it so that at least three columns of it are visible. The congregation, now standing, points to the holy scroll and sings: "*zot hatorah...*" ("This is the Torah which Moses set before the Israelites..."). This ritual is performed to confirm that the scroll from which the *ba'al koreh* (Torah reader) has just read was indeed a true copy of the Torah which Moses received on Mt. Sinai. For, according to Jewish tradition, God not only gave the Ten Commandments to Moses, but dictated the entire Torah to him on that mountain top.

Leaving aside the long-debated controversies about who really wrote the Bible and when it was edited in its final form and canonized, all we can be sure of is that the scroll presented to us represents the standard or authorized version of the Torah. This is the version known as the Masoretic text. How did this Masoretic version come about and how did it come down to us?

The text on the scroll we see before us cannot be printed. It is handwritten on parchment by a highly-skilled, devout person, the *sofer* (scribe), who painstakingly copies the *sefer torah* from a true, error-free model copy. The task is regarded as sacred and the *sofer* will have immersed himself in a *mikveh* before he started his work and will have worn a *tallit* and *tefillin* (prayer-shawl and phylacteries) while engaged in it. With this kind of devotion and the great care taken to reproduce the Holy Text without deviations, one might assume that the Torah scrolls we have today are identical to those of Second Temple days, or, at least, to those of the talmudic period (second–fifth centuries, C.E.). However, this is not the case.

FOR MANY CENTURIES, TORAH SCROLLS with significant variations among them existed and were in use. There was no standard version of the

Tanakh, the Jewish Bible. Generations of scribes, stretching back many centuries to Ezra the Scribe (sixth century B.C.E.), labored hard to standardize the transmitted text. The text that was ultimately accepted became known as the Masoretic text. It was produced by the Ben-Asher family in 930 C.E., and was selected by Maimonides from among several he examined as the authentic one.

Besides achieving uniformity, members of different scribal schools strove to make the text easier to read and therefore to understand. Originally, the scrolls were written without any spaces; the Masoretes divided the text into words, paragraphs, sections and books. They changed the previously cursive script to the square letters (the manuscript form) of the Hebrew alphabet. They prescribed the shape of the letters, whether they are decorated with a crown or not and the distance between letters and between words. They also fixed the number of lines in each column, the length of the lines and the size of the margins above, below and between the columns.

More important, the Masoretes standardized the spelling of the words. Moreover, by the eighth century, they had fixed the system of vowel signs which helped to pronounce the words. Here, again, diverse vowel systems were in use; the one in general use now is called the Tiberian System after the city of Tiberias where it was developed.

To facilitate the study of the Bible, the Masoretes divided the text into verses. Interestingly, the division into chapters was a Christian innovation by Stephen Langton, Archbishop of Canterbury (1150–1258). His divisions don't always make sense. In numerous instances new chapters start in the middle of a narrative, or fail to separate two clearly unrelated topics. Many Jewish publications of the Bible, though retaining the chapter numbering, now print the text with corrected chapter divisions. The Torah scrolls used in the synagogue for the public reading, of course, do not show either chapter and verse divisions nor, for that matter, any punctuation marks, vowels or musical notations for chanting the Torah (the *trope*).

BESIDES PUNCTUATION AND TROPE MARKS, a printed text of the Torah will also contain corrections of the errors in the hand-written Torah scroll. I realize that speaking of mistakes in the Torah sounds like heresy, yet the fact is that there are many scribal errors that crept into the text during repeated copying and became part of the final, codified Masoretic Text. We find spelling mistakes, grammatical errors, letters or words left out, and words or even strings of words repeated. In order to define the authentic text, the Masoretes had to correct these errors.

Yet, since Deuteronomy 13:1 explicitly enjoins us to "neither add to it nor take away from it," they could not correct them in the scroll. The Masoretes solved this problem by compiling numerous directives to the reader which are now printed as marginal notes (usually footnotes) in Hebrew Bibles. In essence they say that, "although the word in the scroll is 'he' you should read it 'she'."

An additional example of scribal emendations (*tikkun sofrim*) concerns several instances of indelicate words in the Holy Text. In cases where a term was felt to be offensive to public sensibilities, the Scribes, although admitting that the original text was the correct one, required the substitution of a less juicy term for public reading. Thus, in each of the several instances where the Bible uses the verb *shagol* (referring to sexual intercourse), the reader is instructed to substitute the less offensive *shakhov* (to lie with, to bed).

One might ask: "By what authority did the Masoretes edit the divinely revealed text? Should it not be read as given by God at Sinai?" To which our tradition answers: "Both the written version (*ketiv*) and the amended version (*keri*) are from Sinai!"

40 Divine Names in Print

ON A RECENT FLIGHT ON Alaska Airlines, I found, packed with my lunch, a card that quoted a verse from Psalms: "I will praise God's name in song and glorify him with thanksgiving (69:31)." For a while I idly wondered about the motivation of the airline company: Did they hope to make their food more palatable in that way? Was the card meant to serve as an antidote for the fear of flying? Then I started thinking about the word "God" in the message: would that present someone on the plane with a problem of how to dispose of the card? After all, in the Jewish tradition, a piece of paper containing the name of God may not be thrown away. Tattered Bibles, prayer books, etc., that is, sacred texts, are all carefully stored for a suitable occasion when they can be ritually buried in consecrated ground. What about secular texts that contain the word "God"?

Halakhah forbids the erasure of the name of God from a written document (*Shevu'ot* 35a). This leads directly to the prohibition of writing the name explicitly in any non-sacred document for such secular texts may be easily discarded and the name thereby erased. It would seem that the airline company was in serious trouble—at least according to *halakhah*. Fortunately, *halakhic* authorities hold that the prohibition of erasing divine names relates only to names in Hebrew!

Of course, some pious Jews guard against writing the names of the Deity even in English, and prefer such surrogate spellings as "G-d" and "L-rd." They choose to disregard the *halakhic* principle of *ko'ah de-hetera adif*, i.e., where there are two conflicting legal views, the view that is less stringent is preferred. Many (secular) books by Orthodox scholars do spell out the words "God" and "Lord" in full.

There are at least one hundred different names for God in Hebrew, ranging from the well-known biblical *Elohim* and *Adonai* to the many rabbinic appellations, such as *Ribono shel Olam* (Ruler of the Universe) and *HaKadosh barukh Hu* (The Holy One Blessed Be He), to the philosophic ones in the Kabbalah, such as *Ein Sof* (the Infinite One). Of all these names, only seven biblical names are specifically included in the prohibition of erasure, the rest may be used in secular writing and erased, even in Hebrew. The seven prohibited names are: *El, Elohim* (or its singular *Eloha*), *Ehyeh asher Ehyeh* (I Am that I Am), *Adonai, Shaddai, Tzeva'ot,* and, most important, the Tetragrammaton consisting of the four letters YHWH. Several important medieval scholars, among them Judah Halevi and Maimonides, insisted that YHWH is the only proper Name of God. The rest of the titles describe His attributes or actions, but only this Name "gives a clear and unequivocal indication of His essence" (*Guide of the Perplexed,* 1:61–64). In fact, *halakhah* holds that only this name is considered so holy that using it as a curse or swearword constitutes sacrilege.

There is little chance that anyone will commit this particular sacrilege, for the original pronunciation of the four letters YHWH has been irretrievably lost since the destruction of the Temple. Rabbi Simchah Roth expands on this:

> Whenever the term is used in the Bible or Prayer-Book we substitute for it the surrogate term "*Adonai*" (Lord). The Masoretes, who were responsible for transmitting the biblical text to us in its present format, added the vowel signs of the word *Adonai* to the letters of the Tetragrammaton in order to remind the reader to read the term *Adonai*. When non-Jews read the Hebrew text they misunderstood, and started construing this term as if it were a real word, thus creating the nonsensical proper noun "Jehovah." This word has no basis whatsoever in Jewish tradition.

Pious abbreviations are often employed in print. Thus, the Tetragrammaton is often replaced simply by a double *yod*. This term is also pronounced *Adonai,* though it is not one of the names of God. The abbreviation *yah* (the first two letters of YHWH) often occurs as a suffix, (as in *halleluyah*), or by itself in biblical poetry. Each letter in the Hebrew alphabet has a numerical equivalent, which for the combination *yah* amounts to 15 (*yod* = 10 and *heh* = 5). To avoid using the term for secular purposes, say to write a date, we replace it by a different combination of letters whose values also add up to 15: *tet* and *vav* (9 plus 6). This combination is pronounced "*tu*" and occurs, for instance, in the name of the holiday *Tu bi-Shevat.* The same stratagem is employed for the number 16 so as to avoid writing the combination *yu* in secular uses.

The pious circumlocutions that we find in everyday speech, such as: *Elokim* for *Elohim,* or the ubiquitous *Hashem* (the Name) for God, do not stem from the prohibition to erase. Rather, they are based on the Third Commandment, which forbids taking the name of the Lord in vain.

41 Cruelty to Animals

ON ITS WEB SITE, THE Royal Society for the Prevention of Cruelty to Animals proudly proclaims, "In 1822 Richard Martin MP sponsored the passage of the Animal Protection Act which outlawed cruelty to cattle, horses and sheep. *This was the world's first ever anti-cruelty law*" [my emphasis]. This statement could not be more false. True, Britain was the first "modern" state to pass such legislation. However, the first animal protection and anti-cruelty laws can be found in the Torah. These laws antedate the British laws by several millennia. They, and their later elaborations in the Talmud, make up the *halakhah* that deals with *tza'ar ba'alei ḥayim*, the prohibition on inflicting pain on animals.

Prohibition against inflicting physical suffering upon animals is only a small part of the large body of legislation dealing with this subject. As we shall see, *halakhah* is equally concerned with more subtle forms of suffering, such as mental anguish and even frustration, experienced by animals. As to physical suffering—it is forbidden, for example, to inflict a blemish on an animal (Talmud, *Hullin* 7b). This would rule out the branding of cattle as practiced on the open spaces of the West and, more importantly, castration. The *Encyclopedia Judaica* stresses the unique character of this legislation: "Judaism has always forbidden all forms of castration. Alone among the nations of antiquity, the Hebrews imposed a religious prohibition on the emasculation of men and even animals, a prohibition not found in the teachings of Buddha, Confucius, Christ, or Muhammad." The ban on castration covers all animals, domestic as well as wild.

Judaism not only forbids the infliction of pain on animals, but expects humans to behave with compassion and mercy and to relieve animals of suffering. Thus, when we see "the donkey [even] of him who hates [us] prostrate under its load," the Torah commands us to relieve it from its burden (Exodus 23:5). This principle is so important that we must perform the labor of unloading even on Shabbat. In fact, relieving an animal in distress is one of the few exceptions to the rule that forbids us to ask a Gentile to do that which we ourselves are forbidden to do on Shabbat. Therefore, arrangements have to be made (beforehand) to have one's cows milked on Shabbat. If this is impossible to arrange, we must milk the cows ourselves on the Sabbath—though the milk may not be used.

Far beyond what modern legislation dictates, the Torah is concerned with the "feelings" of animals. It prohibits us "to muzzle an ox as it threshes" (Deuteronomy 25:4). Compassion here goes beyond the alleviation of physical pain and deals with the frustration of an animal thus restrained. (This strikes me as a very humane principle, for such muzzling would be comparable to taking children into a candy store and then denying them a treat.) Again, to spare the feelings of the mother-bird, we are enjoined to shoo her away before we rob a nest of its fledglings or its eggs (Deuteronomy 22:6-7).

I sometimes wonder whether the prohibition, "do not boil a kid in its mother's milk," is not similarly motivated. Although the Bible gives no reason for this law, later commentators ascribe it to the need to differentiate Israel from the pagan nations surrounding her. This short sentence (Exodus 23:19) is, of course, the basis for the enormous superstructure of the Jewish dietary laws that forbid the mixing of dairy and meat foods. If the intent of the law was, indeed, to express compassion for the lamb, similar to the law which requires that "no animal from the herd or from the flock shall be slaughtered on the same day with its young" (Leviticus 22:28), then having meat cooked in the milk of a different animal might actually be kosher! But this is idle speculation.

When it comes to a well-deserved day of rest after six days of labor, the fourth of the Ten Commandments mentions humans and animals side by side. The Torah, however, does indicate that Shabbat was ordained chiefly to provide a day of respite for working animals. Exodus (23:12) is quite explicit: "on the seventh day you shall cease from labor so that your ox and your ass may rest."

In at least one way, *halakhah* favors animals over humans. When it comes to mealtime, the Rabbis of the Talmud, basing themselves on the verse "I will provide grass in the fields for your cattle, and you shall eat your fill" (Deuteronomy 11:15), taught that "it is forbidden for a man to eat before he has fed his animal because the animal is mentioned first" (*Berakhot* 40a).

The Torah measures a person's moral worth in terms of his attitude toward animals: "A righteous man cares for the needs of his animal…"

(Proverbs 12:10). Judaism regards the way a person treats animals as a good indicator of the way this individual treats human beings. A person who is cruel to a defenseless animal will most likely be cruel to defenseless people, and a person who cares for the lowest of creatures will certainly care for his fellow humans. In Genesis, Chapter 24, we are told that Abraham's trusted servant who was sent to Ḥaran to find a wife for his master's son, Isaac, chose Rebecca because, when he asked her for a sip of water, she proceeded to water all of his camels as well. (This, by the way, was no mean feat since the servant came with ten camels on his quest and the water to quench their thirst had to be drawn by the bucketful from a well!) The Bible presents this as a fitting character trait for someone destined to become one of Israel's matriarchs.

As is often the case, *halakhah* expands on Torah Law: it forbids a person to buy an animal unless he (or she) can properly provide for it. Judging from the frequent newspaper articles that describe the pitiful fate of neglected or abandoned pets and the overcrowded conditions in animal shelters, this twelfth-century Jewish law might not be out-of-place in contemporary society.

A recent news item reports that Holland is considering outlawing the practice of *sheḥitah* (the ritual slaughtering of animals according to Jewish law). I am no expert on ritual slaughter, but I do know that *sheḥitah* is based on the same laws that prohibit inflicting *tza'ar ba'alei ḥayim*. It has often been described as a humane and painless process. I am, of course, aware that there are dissenting views as well. Still, in view of the above discussion and given the timing of the legislation, I cannot escape the suspicion that the proposed law is (in part at least) politically motivated.

42 Not to Bring Shame on Others

I AM INDEBTED TO MY daughter Sarah who asked the questions prompting this column and to Rabbi Simchah Roth who covered some of the material in a different context in one of his Mishnah lessons.

To embarrass somebody in public is unacceptable behavior in most, if not all, cultures. There may be no entry in a code of law against such behavior, yet the code of good manners surely frowns on this kind of conduct. Judaism goes beyond this, however. Shaming a person in the presence of others is a grave ethical offence. The Sages of the Talmud regarded it as tantamount to murder. The Hebrew term for causing shame to somebody is *lehalbin panav*, to blanch his face. Shaming, then, like murder, causes a draining of blood (at least symbolically), and the punishment is severe: "loss of one's portion of the World to Come."

Certain rules of conduct to avoid shaming have been proposed. Thus, one of the Sages who saw a passerby hand a coin to a poor person on the street exclaimed: "It is better not to give charity than to shame someone." Not shaming a person in public is deemed more important than giving *tzedakah* (charity), which is one of the cornerstones of Jewish ethics. Based on this dictum, the Sages defined the optimal way of giving *tzedakah* as one where "the donor does not know the recipient and the recipient does not know the donor."

Communal practices reflect *halakhah* and indeed many of our customs are designed to avoid shaming individuals in the synagogue. The best example of not shaming people publicly is the repetition by the Cantor, or prayer leader, of the *Amidah*—the prayer said by each individual silently. The *Amidah* is the core of our liturgy and each individual is required to recite it at each of the three worship services. After all (or most) of the worshippers have concluded their own recitation, the Cantor repeats the *Amidah* aloud. This custom was introduced when prayer books were not generally available and when it could not be assumed that all were literate and able to fulfill their duty by themselves. The Cantor, therefore, repeats the *Amidah* aloud and everyone answers

"Amen" to the blessings, which is tantamount to saying, "I identify with what you have just said, it is as if I had said it myself." It would be unthinkably callous if, after everyone has had the opportunity to recite the Amidah, a general question were asked: "Is there anyone here who needs the Cantor to repeat the *Amidah* out loud?" No one would respond because of the shame involved! Hence, it was established that the *Amidah* must always be repeated. (This, by the way, does not hold for the evening service when the *Amidah* is not compulsory. Therefore, repeating it for the benefit of the unskillful at that time is regarded as *tirḥa de-tzibbura*, an imposition on the congregation's time).

One could ask whether today, when most people are literate, it is still necessary to repeat the *Amidah* aloud. It may not be necessary any longer, but some traditions are hard to change.

Reading the Torah in the synagogue provides us with several examples of procedures designed to avoid embarrassing the less knowledgeable. For instance, it is not customary to have the one honored with an *aliyah* (call to the Torah) read his or her own portion. This is so as not to shame those who cannot do so and require a reader to do it for them. The same reasoning holds for those honored with reading from the Prophets, the *haftarah*. In general, they do not read the concluding portion, the *maftir*, themselves, but leave it to one of the regular readers. Exceptions to this rule are *benei mitzvah*, who, of course, read their own portion to show what they have learned. Also, if a congregation has a regular reader who reads all of the week's portions, he or she does not have to forego the honor of an *aliyah*.

Finally, in the matter of correcting mistakes during the reading: *halakhah* requires that there should be no mistakes made in the public reading of the Torah. The reader who makes a mistake must repeat the word correctly before the reading may continue. Yet it would be too embarrassing to call the reader's attention to every mistake made. Therefore, the reading is stopped only for those mistakes that actually change the meaning of the passage.

The consideration given to people's feelings extends beyond their lifetime. Rabban Gamaliel of Yavne (latter half of the first century C.E.) was the president of the *Sanhedrin* and laid the foundation for the Mishnah (the legal part of the Talmud). He was also one of the wealthiest men of his time. Yet, to put an end to the ostentatious garb in which the rich were being buried, he expressly ordered that he be buried in a simple linen shirt with his face covered (*MK* 27b). The reason was to set an example that all could follow: the poor (whose faces in death were often gaunt from deprivation) would not be shamed at the poverty of their enshroudment. Jews follow the example set by Rabban Gamaliel to this day.

43 Jewish Bible vs. "Old Testament"

THERE ARE SIGNIFICANT DIFFERENCES BETWEEN the Jewish Bible and the Christian version of the Jewish Bible. Even the names by which these holy scriptures are called reveal these differences. Jews refer to their holy scriptures as the Hebrew Bible or the *Tanakh*, Christians refer to them as the "Old Testament". This last name is not interchangeable with the first two. The Jewish names, Hebrew Bible in English, and *Tanakh* in Hebrew, do not have theological implications; the term "Old Testament" does. This name is completely alien to the Jewish tradition. It is a thoroughly Christian name and makes an important Christian doctrinal point. Let us look at the names in turn.

It is a curious fact that what we know in English as the Hebrew Bible does not have a name, as such, in the language in which it was written. In Hebrew, we refer to it by the acronym of the names of the three parts, which make up our Holy Scriptures. Part one consists of the *Torah* (Teachings, or the Law), the second, *Nevi'im* (Prophets) and the third, Ketuvim (Writings). Their first letters, t-n-k, with the addition of two (arbitrary) vowels, form the word *Tanakh*, where the "k" at the end of the word changes to the throat-clearing "*kh*" sound. The name *Tanakh*, thus, is merely a mnemonic of the parts that constitute the Bible.

This differs radically from the name by which Christians refer to the same Bible. In "Old Testament", the term "old," as juxtaposed to "new" of the "New Testament," does more than differentiate the two works in terms of time. It refers to the belief that the "New Testament" has superseded the Hebrew Bible, which justifies calling the latter the "Old Testament". To supersede means to put aside, to make void or nullify. Supersessionism is the Christian belief that the Church has replaced Israel in God's plan for salvation. It is the belief that the coming of Jesus fulfilled the Hebrew Bible prophecy about the coming of the Messiah, and that the role of the Hebrew Scriptures is to validate the "New Testament". In essence, it means that the covenant between God and the people Israel is not valid any longer and has been replaced by a new covenant (covenant = testament) between God and those who accept Jesus. Jews are no longer God's Chosen People for Christian claims to that title supersede those of the "Old Testament".

To add weight to this claim, the Christian version of the "Old Testament" has rearranged the order of the books of the *Tanakh*. The *Tanakh* is made up of three parts, as we saw above. In the Jewish tradition, part one consists of the Five Books of Moses (*Ḥumash* in Hebrew, or *Pentateuch* in Greek). The second major part, Prophets, includes the Former Prophets (Joshua, Judges, Samuel and Kings) and the Latter Prophets (Isaiah, Jeremiah and Ezekiel, plus the twelve Minor Prophets. The designation minor does not refer to the importance of these prophets, but only to the lengths of their texts, which are far shorter than those of the major three.) The third part of the *Tanakh*, Writings, contains seven major books (Psalms, Proverbs, Job, Daniel, Ezra, Nehemiah and Chronicles) plus five books that are often referred to as The Scrolls (Song of Songs, Ruth, Lamentations, Ecclisiastes and Esther).

The Christian version reverses parts two and three so that the "Old Testament" ends with Prophets, which is directly followed by the "New Testament". This makes it appear as if the thrust and purpose of the "Old Testament" are the prophesies that Christians believe are fulfilled in the "New Testament".

There are several other changes in the sequence of the books in parts two and three. Both the Protestant and Roman Catholic versions of the "Old Testament" use the same inverted sequence of these parts. The Catholic version includes seven additional books (or parts of books), which did not become part of the Hebrew Bible (e.g., Books of the Maccabees). Martin Luther removed these from the Protestant version of the Bible and relegated them to the Apocrypha.

THE NEW SEQUENCE WAS QUICKLY adopted and canonized in the Christian Bible because of a major technological innovation that took place at about the first century C.E. — the appearance of the bound book, the Codex. Until then, books were written and stored on parchment scrolls. The books of the Bible, too, were stored on individual scrolls, even the five books of the Torah — as we learned from the Dead Sea Scrolls and other early manuscripts.

One advantage of a separate scroll for each book was ease of handling. The average length of a Torah scroll is about 30 feet. To combine all the books of the *Tanakh* on one scroll would have yielded an exceedingly long, heavy and unwieldy manuscript. Another advantage of separate scrolls was the flexibility this system provided. Neither the list of books included in the canon (the regulation edition), nor their order in it, had to be definitively established.

All this changed with the appearance of the bound Codex in which the individual columns of text in a scroll were cut apart and bound together as pages of a book. (It is interesting to note that the same Hebrew word, *amud*, stands for both column and page.) The codex was more efficient and cheaper to produce since text could now be stored on both sides of the page. The burgeoning faith of Christianity was quicker to adopt the Codex than its more conservative mother-religion. It has even been suggested that the handier form of the Christian Bible may explain, in part at least, the rapid spread of the new religion.

Judaism and Christianity are two distinct religions, two separate belief systems. To gloss over this fact by talking about Judeo-Christian this or Judeo-Christian that, or by claiming to be Jews who believe in Jesus, will not alter this fact. Judaism does not recognize Jesus as the Messiah, and Christianity does not recognize the special relationship between God and Israel which stands at the core of the Jewish religion. The very names by which the two religions refer to the Scriptures that give voice to their beliefs underscore their differences.

Hiddur Mitzvah: the Beautification of Ritual Objects

A GREAT PART OF JEWISH ART over the ages has been dedicated to the adornment of ritual objects. Of course, Jewish artists and artisans over the last 4,000 years have also created many beautiful objects for personal and secular use in the home. Still, a major part of their artistic genius and energy seems to have been devoted to the creation of objects that are used, whether in the synagogue or in the home, in connection with religious observances.

This is no accident: applying artistic skills to beautify *mitzvah*-related objects is itself a *mitzvah* and is known as *hiddur mitzvah*. Rashi traces the source of the talmudic injunction to embellish ritual objects to the biblical phrase, "This is my God, and I shall glorify Him" (Exodus 15:2). The Hebrew verb for glorify (*nun-vav-heh—naveh*) can equally well be translated as adorn or beautify. And so, a great part of Jewish art has always endeavored to glorify God by creating beautiful objects, such as a decorated curtain for the Holy Ark, a beautiful *seder* plate for the Passover meal or a colorfully decorated *sukkah* for the Sukkot festival.

The practice goes back to the early days of our history. Moses transmitted to Bezalel, the divinely inspired artist, God's personal instructions for building the desert Tabernacle, the Tent of Meeting and its furnishings. The blueprints called for precious metals and fine woods for construction, and for elegant textiles "of blue, purple and crimson" to adorn the walls. The descriptions of the various spaces and vessels make it clear that a high value was put on the esthetic enjoyment that was to accompany the service of God.

Ever since those early days, *hiddur mitzvah* has always been an important element of Jewish religious practices. For Friday night *kiddush*, a simple glass to hold the wine would have sufficed. Yet, we go out of our way to use a specially adorned cup for this *mitzvah*. At Beit Am, we make this our community present to

the new *Benai Mitzvah* in the hope that they will use and enjoy this *Kiddush* cup throughout their lives.

During services in the synagogue, we are surrounded with objects that exhibit the special charm that *hiddur mitzvah* implies. We wrap ourselves in a *tallit* that is decorated with an *atarah* (neckband). The *atarah* is decorative, often woven of silver thread, and may contain the special *berakhah* we pronounce when donning the *tallit*. We face the *aron kodesh* (Holy Ark), which is usually decorated with traditional symbols, the tablets of the Law, the lions of Judah, etc. The Torah scroll has its own beautiful accessories: the decorated mantel, the silver breastplate, the *rimonim* (finials) for the two *atzey ḥayim* (wooden rollers, literally, "trees of life") on which the scroll is wound, and the *yad* (pointer in the shape of a hand) with which the reader points to the text. Unlike many other manuscripts, including scrolls of the Book of Esther, *Haggadot* (for Passover), and *ketubbot* (marriage contracts) which are often illustrated, or illuminated, the Torah scroll itself is perfectly plain. The *hiddur* here comes from the meticulous calligraphy and the perfect materials (parchment, ink, etc.) used in its writing.

The Talmud discusses two examples of *hiddur mitzvah* that do not involve adornments. The first is the number of Hanukkah candles we light. The *mitzvah* requires only one candle a night for eight nights per family. That is the minimum, for families who cannot afford more. *Hiddur mitzvah* calls for one candle per night for each member of the household. A different extension of the *mitzvah*, one that is the general custom nowadays, calls for increasing the number of candles lit from one to eight over the eight days of Hanukkah. Those families who follow this custom, and light more than one *ḥanukkiyah* (Hanukkah lamp) each night, are among the *mehadrin dimehadrin*, maximum beautifiers! (Each night, of course, a *shamash* or service candle, must also be lit so that the Hanukkah lights will not be used for anything other than to publicize the miracle.)

In the second example, our Sages hold that Torah scholars have to give special attention to their appearance. For instance, they have to see to it that their clothing is neat, in good repair and order. This is their way of *hiddur mitzvah*, glorifying God. Similarly, regardless of how we dress during the week, we traditionally put on special clothes for the Sabbath and for holidays.

It is interesting that limits have been set on the amount of money one may spend on *hiddur mitzvah*. The Rabbis suggest that a person spend, at most, a third more than the ordinary cost of the object. Yet a quick look at one of the finely wrought spice-boxes used to help usher in the new week in the *Havdalah* service, or at a contemporary hand-woven, multi-colored *tallit*, suggests that considerably more than the limit was paid for them.

In the *Me'ah She'arim* quarter of Jerusalem, in the weeks before the Sukkot festival, it is not uncommon to see men pay more than a week's wages for one *etrog* (citron). No wonder, then, that each year, the local rabbis sternly remind their followers that the satisfaction of fulfilling this *mitzvah* may not come at the expense of the well-being of the family.

45 Legal Loopholes

WHILE WE WERE IN SEATTLE to celebrate *Pesah* with our son's family, I heard Rabbi Jill Borodin of Beth Sholom explain the concept of *eruv tavshilin* (mixing of cooked dishes) to her congregation. The need for the *eruv* arose from the fact that that year the first two days of Passover fell on Thursday and Friday that is, immediately preceding Shabbat. Now cooking is allowed on a holiday but only for the holiday itself. Because one is not allowed to cook on a holiday for any subsequent day, it would have resulted in a particularly joyless Shabbat of only cold meals. To remedy this, the Rabbis of old held that if the food preparation for the Shabbat was begun, even if only symbolically, on the day before the holiday and a declaration to that effect was made, cooking for the Shabbat meal was actually allowed during the Festival. So, Rabbi Borodin cooked one hard-boiled egg on Wednesday and set it aside with a piece of *matzah* symbolically as part of the Shabbat meal to be supplemented and expanded on Friday (the second day of Passover!) into a complete Shabbat menu.

In thinking about this symbolic act, my mind wavered between cynicism and admiration: cynicism about the ease with which the Sages were willing to bend the law to enable people to do what they wanted to do, and possibly might do anyway, and admiration for their ingenuity in finding ways to accommodate the law so as to prevent a real hardship for those trying to observe it. Was the *eruv* a loophole to get around the law or was it a way to make *halakhah* (traditional Jewish law) more attuned to the realities of living?

The laws of Passover provide us with another instance in which the letter of *halakhah* is strictly obeyed, yet made to correspond to reality via a legal fiction. The Torah prohibits the ownership of *hametz* (leaven) during *Pesah*. Therefore, Jewish housewives scrub and scour their homes, sometimes to exhaustion, to remove the last crumb of bread and other *hametz* before the Festival. But what about all the remaining packages of pasta, tins of crackers and cans of noodle soup? And what about the half-eaten cookie that went undetected in one of the kids' toy boxes? A custom has developed of "selling" all these forbidden foods to a non-Jew for a small, symbolic sum with the understanding that at the end of Passover the transaction will be reversed and possession revert to the original owner.

Here, again, the letter of the law is obeyed, for the "sale" constitutes a legal transfer of ownership even though the items don't necessarily leave the home. Yet is this what the Torah had in mind when it commanded us to rid our residences of leaven? Clearly not. Still, by interpreting "ownership" in the strictest sense, the Jewish housewife (and the rest of the family, of course) can go to sleep with a clear conscience knowing that they had done the best they could to clean the house of known ḥamets, and for the rest...well, for eight days it wasn't theirs to worry about.

Equally ingenious solutions make it possible to perform certain acts on Shabbat which a strict reading of the law would have forbidden. Consider, for instance, the question of "carrying." We read in Jeremiah (17:21): "This is what Adonai says: Be careful not to carry a load on the Sabbath day or bring it through the gates of Jerusalem. Do not bring a load out of your houses ...." The Sages interpreted this as a prohibition to carry objects on Shabbat from a private domain, say, one's residence, into an area that is defined as public domain. If the law were strictly observed, a person could not carry even a prayer-book or a *tallit*-bag walking from home to the synagogue, or, for that matter, pick up and carry a tired child. But since the verse speaks of bringing something "through the gates of Jerusalem," the Sages considered Jerusalem and, by extension, any walled city as one single domain within which, therefore, carrying was allowed. This way, certain hardships are alleviated while still preserving the sanctity and enjoyment of the Sabbath.

Here, again, we see that by slightly changing their interpretation, in this case by redefining "domain," the Sages made it possible to bring existing customs and traditions in line with *halakhah*. Interestingly, in modern times this process has been carried an amazing step further: many Jewish communities have established a "wall" (another example of an *eruv ḥatzerot*) by using the telephone or power lines which surround their communities to define the domain in which carrying is permitted. Where a gap exists in such a fence, communities have appealed to city authorities to be allowed to string wires between the tops of existing telephone poles to complete the symbolic wall.

The question arises: Is it really necessary to go through these "rabbinic acrobatics," as I've heard them called, to tweak *halakhah* so as to make it fit contemporary conditions? The answer to this question may define the essential differences between the various streams of modern Judaism.

46 Legislation to Heal the World

TORAH LAW, INCLUDES BOTH THE Written Law (the Torah) and the Oral Torah (the Talmud, which was codified toward the end of the 5th century C.E.) However, at times, it may be necessary to add new laws to Torah Law or to interpret existing laws so as to adapt them to contemporary problems. The most common way to modify the traditional legal structure is by means of takkanot.

The word *takkanah* (singular) has been variously translated as directive, regulation, or ordinance. The root letters of the word are *t-k-n*, which are also the root of the word *tikkun* as in *tikkun olam*. *Tikkun olam* is the Kabbalistic idea of repairing the world, that is, improving or healing it. Since *takkanot* are enacted "to correct an injustice or to improve the religious and ethical life of the community," they are, as it were, the legal means devised to bring about *tikkun olam*. *Takkanot* are enacted either to provide answers to problems which are not covered by the existing body of law, or to resolve difficulties of a social, economic or ethical nature which arise because of changed circumstances. They are exceptions to the law and supplement or amend it. In rare cases they even contradict it.

Takkanot have been enacted throughout Jewish history and have often changed our way of life drastically. For instance, Joshua ben Gamla, High Priest during the last days of the Second Temple, is credited with the *takkanah* which established universal public education in *Eretz Israel* by requiring communities to provide compulsory education for children from the age of six. A thousand years later, R. Gershom Ben-Judah (960–1040 C.E.), a French rabbi also known as "the Light of the Diaspora," passed a number of revolutionary ordinances. Among other social changes, he famously outlawed polygamy, a husband taking a second wife while still married to the first. In the same *takkanah* he decreed that a husband could not divorce his wife without her consent. This part of the *takkanah* had a much greater impact on Jewish society than the first, for in Europe monogamy was already generally accepted by that time. Still, it was a bold step, for both of these changes contravene Torah Law. The Bible does allow polygamy (remember, two of the three Patriarchs were polygamous) and it allows a husband to divorce his wife for any reason (didn't like her cooking!) or for no reason at all.

There is, however, a big difference between our first example, the *takkanah* governing education and the second, imposing monogamy. The first *takkanah* was enacted before the Talmud was codified (c. 500 C.E.) and is, therefore, as part of *halakhah*, binding on all Jews everywhere and for all times. On the other hand, the second is binding only on the community that accepts the authority of its author. Although Rabbenu Gershom was a highly respected *halakhic* scholar, his authority did not extend beyond the bounds of *Ashkenazi* Jewry. *Sephardi* and most Eastern Jewish communities sanctioned polygamy, in accord with the customs and laws of the Muslim countries in which they lived. (However, even there, a Jewish husband needed his wife's consent to bring a second wife into the family.) In the State of Israel, by the way, it is a criminal offense to be married to more than one wife at a time, though the law is not always enforced. Jewish immigrants from Yemen and Iran were often polygamous and, of course, the State has to honor the rights of its Muslim and Druze citizens.

OVER THE CENTURIES, THOUSANDS OF *takkanot* have been enacted in all areas of the law. How do the modern streams of Judaism deal with these extra-legal amendments to repair the world? Until about 200–250 years ago all *takkanot* came from rabbis or groups of rabbis that today would be labeled "Orthodox." Then, the 18th century saw the rise of European Emancipation, which granted civil rights to Jews in many countries. That, and the Jewish Enlightenment movement caused many Jews to forsake their faith "to keep up with modernity." Orthodox rabbis believed that passing laws which resolved the contradictions between Jewish tradition and the demands of modern life would in the end lead to assimilation and the demise of Judaism. Therefore, Orthodox Judaism, in effect, ceased to enact new *takkanot*. The movement insists on an ever-stricter interpretation of the existing laws. It has become more rigid and is more interested in counteracting modernity than in finding ways to live with it. In the 1980s, for instance, the Union of Orthodox Jewish organizations in America required all its member synagogues to erect *meḥitzot* (physical barriers between men and women during services).

Conservative Judaism also sees itself as a *halakhic* movement. In trying to find solutions to problems that confront the modern Jew it gives primary consideration to *halakhah* and to decisions handed down from tradition. Yet, it views *halakhah* as subject to change when specific problems can not be resolved on the basis of tradition. Responses to technological or social changes involved such radical *takkanot* as permitting congregants and rabbis to drive to the synagogue on Shabbat if the distance is too great to walk, counting women in the *minyan*, and, more recently, lifting all rabbinic prohibitions on homosexual conduct. Although, as we saw above, these changes are binding only on congregations that agree to abide by them, they have been generally accepted and have greatly changed the nature of worship and religious life for Conservative Jewry.

In contrast to the above movements, Reform and Reconstructionist Judaism view themselves as post-*halakhic* movements. They see Judaism as an evolving religious civilization which should not be defined or limited by conditions (or beliefs) which prevailed in the past. In the words of Mordecai Kaplan, the founder of Reconstructionism, the past should have "a vote, but not a veto." Since Reconstructionist and Reform Jews view *halakhah* as a rigid body of often-outdated laws, there is no need to pass *takkanot* to effect change. Rather, it is the importance of values such as democracy, equality and free choice by individuals to make ethical and ritual decisions that define their approach to Judaism.

WE SAW THAT THE VARIOUS streams in modern Judaism view *halakhah* and its applicability to our times very differently. However, all share one goal—though they may define it differently: to preserve the Jewish people by making Judaism more accessible and meaningful for all Jews. It may not be amiss to end with a talmudic story. The two famous academies, the House of Hillel and the House of Shammai, were at odds (as they were wont to be) about the interpretation of a certain biblical passage. They applied to Heaven to settle the argument. Then a Voice was heard from on high saying: "These as well as these are the words of the Living God."

The Way We Do Things:
Customs and Rituals

Yarmulka, Kippah: A Rose by any Other Name...

A NON-JEWISH VISITOR COMING TO a typical Synagogue service may be puzzled by the many different *kippot* (plural of *kippah*, head-covering) in the congregation. However, the different colors, styles and sizes do not signify anything. All *kippot* have but one function: to provide a head-covering, in this case during prayer. But why do Jews cover their heads in the first place?

Some evidence suggests that women may have covered their hair routinely as far back as biblical days, though there is no biblical law requiring them to do so. During talmudic times (second-fifth centuries C.E.), however, married women were expected to cover their hair as a sign of modesty and chastity. In the Mishnah this is referred to as a Jewish ordinance. If a Jewish woman wore her hair uncovered, it was assumed she was a virgin (*Ketubot* 2:10).

The Rabbis put such importance on the custom that they decreed that no blessing could be uttered in the presence of a woman whose hair was not covered. If a married woman went bareheaded outside of her home, her husband could divorce her forthwith without having to pay back her dowry!

According to Alfred Rubens' beautiful book, *Jewish Costume*, women started wearing wigs as beauty aids during talmudic times. Ultimately, these wigs took on the additional function of regularly worn head-coverings. Rabbi Leon of Modena (Venice, 1571–1648) writes about Jewish women of his day: "When they are married, upon their wedding day they cover their own hair, wearing either a *peruke*, ... or something else that may counterfeit hair according to the custom of the women of that place, but they are never to appear in their own hair more." This custom is still practiced today in very traditional circles, where girls have their hair cut on their wedding day and replace it with a *sheitel* (Yiddish: wig). Some of these *sheitels* are so elaborate and expensive that rabbis have inveighed against their use from the sixteenth century on—with mixed results.

The origin of head-covering for men is more controversial. Again, we find no biblical pronouncements requiring any kind of head-covering except for the priestly garb which included a head-cover.

During Mishnaic times (first and second centuries C.E.), men went bareheaded. The pictorial representations we have, for instance, the frescoes of the third century Dura Europos synagogue, show men at prayer without any head-covering. On the other hand, the Talmud mentions the *kova sheberosho* (head-covering) and the blessing to be said when putting it on. However this practice seems to have been a privilege reserved for scholars, scribes and rabbis. Bachelors using it were thought presumptuous (*Kiddushim* 29b).

Saint Paul describes Jewish practice in first century Palestine: "A man who keeps his head covered when he prays... brings shame on his head; a woman, on the contrary, brings shame on her head if she prays... bareheaded.... A man has no need to cover his head, because man is the image of God, and the mirror of his glory, whereas woman reflects the glory of man." (1 Corinthians 11:4–7)

There are records stating explicitly that French rabbis in the thirteenth century uttered the benedictions bareheaded. Similarly, in the sixteenth century, Salomon Luria, a great rabbinic authority, expressly stated that he knew of no prohibition against praying with uncovered head. Still, by that time, the custom of covering one's head (though not always) seems to have been widely accepted. Thus, Maimonides, the great medieval Jewish philosopher and scholar (1135–1204), ruled that a Jewish man should cover his head during prayer (*Mishne Torah, Hilkhot Tefilah* 5:5).

Rubens, from whom much of the above material is taken, speculates that the custom of covering one's head may stem from medieval times when Jews were forced to wear the infamous "Jew's hat" whenever they stirred from their homes.

Although the custom of covering one's head when entering a synagogue, reciting prayers or engaging in a religious act is not based on any talmudic law, it has now taken on the force of law through tradition. The levels of observance differ: some wear a skullcap at home but not on the street; some put it on only when praying; and some wear it at all times. A ḥaredi Jew wears his *yarmulka* under his hat lest he be bareheaded for even an instant when he removes his hat—he even goes to sleep wearing it. In most Reform synagogues, covering one's head is not required.

In Israel today, and increasingly in the United States, the *kippah* defines the religious (and in a sense, political) affiliation of the wearer: a black *kippah* made of cloth identifies the wearer as belonging to one of the more fundamentalist groups, whereas a colorful crocheted *kippah* points to more moderate religious and political propensities.

Although *yarmulka* is a Polish word, folk-etymology sees in it the two Aramaic words *yerei malka* (awe of God). And that, after all, is the reason why Jews cover their heads—it is as a sign of reverence and respect in the presence of the Almighty.

48 Jewish Dress Codes

THE YEAR IS 1715 C.E., the place—Frankfurt am Main in Germany. If we were to visit one of the synagogues in the Jewish quarter on an ordinary Shabbat of that year, say July 13th, we would be struck by the disparity between the drab surroundings and the resplendent dress of the worshippers. The men look elegant in their silk and brocaded coats. The more old-fashioned among them still wear the ruffled collars and sport the powdered wigs of a bygone era.

On the balcony in the back of the sanctuary, the women, too, are lavishly garbed. Elaborate gowns in rich fabrics trimmed with much lace and decorated with real gold and silver threads make a colorful picture. It is clear that these people spend much money on their clothing and jewelry.

If we were to return one week later, we would be dumbfounded by the change that had taken place: no more multi-colored fabrics, no more silks and no more lace. Gone are the expensive furs and most of the jewelry. What has happened to change the glittering scene of the week before to the drab picture we now observe?

On Thursday of that week, the Elders of the *kehillah* (Jewish Community) had enacted a set of regulations that amounted to a dress code for the Jews of Frankfurt. These laws are known in the literature as "Sumptuary Laws." There was hardly a community in Europe that did not have similar regulations at one time or another. Sumptuary laws came in response to anti-Jewish agitation stemming from displays of luxury, ostentation and conspicuous consumption.

The laws announced publicly in Frankfurt on that Thursday, 18 July 1715, specified, for example, that, "all clothes made of velvet or with gold or silver thread, whether new or old, are forbidden." Women's clothes must not be made of fabrics with more than one color and could not cost more than a specified sum. On workdays, no taffeta or silk could be worn except for small silk caps of a single color. Silk gowns and pleated skirts were forbidden even on Shabbat. Married and unmarried women were forbidden to wear corselets or bodices without sleeves in the streets.

The regulations go on for pages. They specify the hairdo (no curls, ringlets, false hair or powdered hair), the shoes (no new shoes of any color except black or white, no embroidery or colored braid) and especially the jewelry, down to the buttons, spangles and buckles on the garments.

Several of these restrictions were relaxed for the bride and the mother of the bride while under the *ḥuppah* (wedding canopy). Either of them could wear up to four rings, three more than the usual limit.

Equally detailed proscriptions were passed for men. An especially interesting one states that, "No Bar Mitzvah should stand before the Torah wearing a wig."

THE SANCTIONS FOR FAILURE TO comply are interesting. In Frankfurt, as in many other places, it was excommunication! True, excommunication in Judaism does not mean to be cut off from the sacraments of the church, and thus salvation, as it does in Christianity. Still, it amounts to social isolation or shunning that must have been devastating in the closed society of the ghetto. Other cities imposed heavy fines. The regulations passed at Forli, Italy, in 1416, held that "Men shall be held responsible for the observance of these rules by their wives," and continued to the ultimate in punishments: "If anyone refuses to obey the ordinances, the community shall refuse to admit him to *minyan* or to read the Torah or to perform the *gelilah*." (*Minyan* refers to the quorum of 10 males traditionally required for public prayer and *gelilah* is the honor of dressing the scroll after reading from it.)

Besides trying "to avoid arousing the envy of the Gentiles," some of the laws were designed to minimize the effects of envy within the *kehillah*. They tried to get people to live within their incomes or, at least, to discourage them from trying to keep up with the Levines. In 1659 in Poland, for instance, rabbis were charged with setting the number of guests that could be invited to a circumcision or a wedding in accordance with the means of the host. In Moravia, the amount one could spend on wedding clothes was determined by the amount of the dowry. ("In case the bride's dowry amounts to 5,000 thalers or more, the bridegroom is allowed to wear whatever he pleases.") The laws also limited the value of the gifts that bride and bridegroom could exchange—usually from two to five percent of the dowry (Hamburg, 1715).

These regulations exhibit an overt classism to which most people today would strongly object. Still, it is refreshing to remember that the laws also made it easier to live in the crowded conditions of the ghetto and prevented the still widely-practiced custom of parents going deep into debt to provide their children a respectable wedding or even an unsurpassed Bar or Bat Mitzvah.

49 Jewish Cooking

WHY ARE THERE SHELVES AND shelves of Jewish cookbooks? Is there really such a thing as Jewish cooking? Of course, there are certain dishes one would expect to encounter more often in a Jewish home than in a Gentile home, and other dishes one would not expect to see on a Jewish table at all. Still, for the most part, Jewish dishes reflect the cuisine of the surrounding culture of the peoples with whom Jews had most contact in the recent or not-so-recent past.

Jewish cooking has adapted to the local foods the way Jewish dress, Jewish languages, Jewish music, customs and even beliefs have taken on the native coloration of the countries where Jews have settled. With very few exceptions, there is nothing global or unique about Jewish cooking. Dishes eaten in the Polish *shtetl* resembled those eaten by poor Polish Gentile peasants more than those served in the homes of Iraqi Jews.

On the other hand, our religious laws do circumscribe these adaptations to foreign ways. The laws of *kashrut* dictate, to some extent, the foods we can eat, or rather the ones we cannot eat. We would not expect to find recipes for pork dishes, rabbit stew or bear steak in a Jewish cookbook. Nor would we find seafood dishes or recipes for catfish, a fish that does not have both fins and scales, as required by law.

Although there are no geographic variations in the actual laws of kashrut, we find minor differences in their application in different Jewish communities. The sturgeon is a case in point. Because its scales do not overlap like normal scales, *Ashkenazi* authorities in England find the fish *treif*, unfit for consumption, while *Sephardi* authorities define it as kosher. In the United States, Orthodox authorities also exclude the fish, while the Committee of Laws and Standards of the Rabbinical Assembly of America (Conservative), which is just as strict when it comes to the dietary laws, allows both sturgeon and swordfish to be eaten. An interesting sidelight is the fact that those for whom sturgeon is out-of-bounds will also have to forego caviar. Except for honey, which is kosher although it comes from the non-kosher bee, the law forbids the consumption of products of unclean animals.

THE JEWISH RELIGION PRESCRIBES THE correct preparation of foods — animals have to be ritually slaughtered. *De facto*, this removes wild game animals from the Jewish cuisine, even if they are kosher. For instance, elk or moose meat may be legally bought in many countries, though it is doubtful that the Jewish butcher will have either in his display case.

Also, to prepare meat, all blood must be drawn from it through salting and repeated rinsing before cooking. This removes from the menu dishes like blood sausage and blood pudding which are so popular in Germany. Broiling, grilling or roasting on the spit are alternative ways of *kashering* meat, that is, drawing out the blood. These make it possible to have steak (except for certain cuts, see below) and chops for dinner — at least in principle. In reality, in many Jewish communities, people were too poor to afford these cuts and meat was seldom served other than for Shabbat and holidays.

Best known, of course, is the prohibition of mixing dairy foods and meat dishes in one meal. This law eliminates dishes such as beef stroganoff, Swedish meatballs and cheeseburgers from the Jewish table. It affects the menu in that dairy desserts, such as ice cream, could not be served after a meat dinner.

An additional limitation derives from the famous wrestling match our patriarch Jacob fought with the angel. Although he bested the angel, he received a blow that injured his sciatic nerve and left him limping. The Bible tells us: "Therefore the children of Israel eat not the sinew of the thigh-vein which is upon the hollow of the thigh until this day." (Genesis 32:33) Since it is very difficult, and therefore expensive, to remove the sciatic nerve from the hindquarters of an animal, it is not removed in the United States. Observant Jews, therefore, cannot enjoy a fillet mignon or a leg of lamb. In Israel, on the other hand, and in several *Sephardi* communities of the Middle East, the sciatic nerve, and the blood vessels surrounding it, are routinely removed. In England, this operation used to be performed through the reign of Queen Victoria. It is no longer.

It is not surprising that Jewish cooking is as varied and tasty as it is. It is exactly these restrictions which stimulate the culinary inventiveness of Jewish cooks to seek acceptable substitutes. Adaptation often requires substituting ingredients and seasoning as well as adjusting the method of preparation to achieve the qualities which, after all, give Jewish cooking its *ta'am* — distinctive character and flavor.

So far, we have considered the influence of religious laws on Jewish cooking, and the extent to which they limit the borrowing from the cuisines of the surrounding cultures. Is there, then, anything that is unique about Jewish cooking? Bagels and lox are hardly a Jewish dish. American tourists are always surprised that they cannot get a real bagel in Israel.

It seems to me that dishes made of *matzah*-meal have no counterpart in other peoples' foods. Here, for use during Passover, we take flour, bake *matzah* (unleavened bread) with it and then grind it up to make flour. Dishes made from this meal, for instance *matzah-knaidel* (dumplings), must surely be uniquely Jewish. But here, too, there are great regional variations in the recipes. In Alsace and in Southern France, the balls are made not from meal, but from *matzah* broken up between the palms of the hands. And then there is, of course, the ongoing dispute as to whether *matzah*-balls should be light as a feather or heavy like cannon balls. Because I come from the second persuasion, it took me several years to learn to appreciate my wife's super-light knaidlach; they did not strike me as substantial enough.

A MAJOR INFLUENCE ON JEWISH cooking which we have not discussed so far is the biblical prohibition, "You shall kindle no fire throughout your habitations upon the Sabbath day" (Exodus 35:3). Our Sages taught that this forbids us to light a fire but permits the use of one lit before the onset of Shabbat. In response to this prohibition, a dish was born that writers on Jewish food like to call the quintessential Jewish dish — *Cholent* ("ch" as in chopped herring). Because it is prepared on Friday before the Sabbath, and kept hot overnight until noon the following day, *cholent* became the ubiquitous hot dish for the main meal on Shabbat. Folk-etymology derives the name *cholent* from the French word *chaud* (hot), though there is no linguistic basis for this derivation.

Although we can find slow-cooked stews in many different cuisines, it is true that *cholent* has long been associated with Jewish cooking. With but little poetic license, it has been called "the sublime expression of Jewish identity." Heinrich Heine, the German poet, even wrote a parody of Goethe's Ode to Joy about it, the first two lines of which are:

Cholent, ray of light immortal!
Cholent, daughter of Elysium!

In pre-expulsion Spain, over 500 years ago, the dish was known as *adafina*. Like *cholent*, it was prepared on Friday. Unfortunately, after the expulsion in 1492 C.E., this practice became literally an identifying "dead give-away" of the *conversos* (Jews who outwardly converted to

Christianity but practiced Judaism in secret). It was among the tips the Spanish Inquisition gave in one of its Edicts of Faith to ferret out Jews. The dish went into exile with Spanish Jewry and is still enjoyed today by *Sephardi* Jewish communities in North Africa.

The typical *Ashkenazi* cholent calls for meat, potatoes, barley and small haricot beans. Some European recipes add *kishke* (a sausage stuffed with a mixture of flour, onion and fat) and various *knaidlach* (dumplings) to the pot. *Adafina*, on the other hand, generally includes chickpeas or large lima beans and rice instead of the barley. Lamb replaces the beef and raw eggs in their shells are gently placed in the pot. It is often sweetened with dates, quinces, apricots and sweet potatoes.

Variations on these recipes abound. In no version, however, is it a light dish. The Jewish joke has it that people who eat a hearty meal on Shabbat, then lie down for a nap and wake up again two hours later, are sure proof of the resurrection of the dead. The comedian Buddy Hackett tells the story that when he was drafted into the army and, for the first time was away from his mother's cooking, he feared that he was dying because his "fire had gone out." For the first time in his life, he did not have heartburn!

Besides the broad differences between *Ashkenazi* and *Sephardi* cooking that I mentioned, there are regional differences in each of these cuisines that are just as diverse. I shall never forget the horrified look on my wife's face when she took the first bite of my aunt's gefilte fish. It was sweet enough to serve as dessert. Actually, it was Polish cuisine at its best! Now when she buys a jar of gefilte fish, she studies the label very carefully. After all, Jewish foods differ as much as the Diasporas in which they are prepared.

What Jewish dishes do have in common is the fact that they resemble most closely the foods of the poorer strata of the countries from which they come. In many of these countries, the Jews themselves were abjectly poor over much of their history. Folk wisdom in the *shtetl* had it right: "When does a Jew get to eat a chicken? When either of them is sick!"

Heaps of Stones: Why We Put Stones on Graves

IN THE WAKE OF THE movie "Schindler's List," several people asked me about the significance of placing small stones on tombstones when visiting a cemetery. I expected this to be one of the easier questions to answer. To my surprise, I found no mention of the custom in the usually very complete, sixteen-volume *Encyclopedia Judaica.* I put the question out on the Internet and received a dozen or so responses. Finally, I used every opportunity I had on a recent trip to Israel, where the custom is well known and universally observed, to find out its origin and meaning.

I asked several people of different backgrounds if this was part of their tradition. I discovered that this *minhag* (custom) is practiced wherever Jews live. At Rosh Hanikra (the northernmost point on the Israeli coastline), a sari-clad elderly lady, a recent immigrant from India, answered my question about placing stones on tombs affirmatively. Several Yemeni Jews, as well as Jews from Morocco and from Iraq responded similarly. Because it is the custom also in *Ashkenazi* communities, It seems that placing stones on graves goes back to biblical times, certainly before the dispersion of the Jewish people into the various Diasporas.

I also found out that neither Christians nor Muslims (at least not in Israel) place stones on graves. Both communities use flowers or palm fronds, which are expressly prohibited by some Rabbis as *minhag hagoyim* (a non-Jewish custom).

The reasons advanced by my many respondents can be divided along religious lines. The completely secular suggested that the custom was a carryover from early days when the dead were laid in shallow graves and covered with heaps of stones (as Bedouins do to this day in the Sinai desert). With time, animals would scatter the stones and passers-by would add a stone or two in an attempt to keep the grave covered.

The religious respondents all included the "soul of the departed" in their answer: "To honor the soul," "to show the soul that it has not been forgotten," "when the soul comes up and looks around, it sees the stones, is reassured and returns to peaceful rest." Although there is a central belief in Judaism that death is the passage from this life to life everlasting, in our folklore, the soul in some undefined way remains tied to the place of burial. People go to the graveside not only for sentimental reasons, but to ask the soul to intercede with God on their behalf. The many supplicants who pray at Rachel's Tomb, the tomb that Jacob built for his beloved wife Rachel outside of Bethlehem, are a prime example of this practice.

Rachel's Tomb provides also the first instance in the Bible of the use of a *matzevah* (tombstone, see Genesis 35:20). Although earlier burials are mentioned, *matzevot* (plural) are not. Their use could have been discretionary. This, however, is not the case any longer: even if the deceased specified in his will that no tombstone be erected, it is a (religious) duty for the survivors to disregard the will and provide one.

Anthropologists see the small stones we place on graves as an extension of the slabs (or monuments) we use to cover the graves. Professor Issahar Ben-Ami from Rehovot, who specializes in Jewish Folklore, explained it to me as follows:

> The use of stones to cover graves is a very ancient custom and can be found in many cultures. It represents the ambivalent feelings of the living toward their departed. On the one hand, families want to keep in contact with members who died; on the other, there is the fear that the souls of the dead might return and cause harm to the living.

In his classic study, *Jewish Magic and Superstition: A Study in Folk Religion*, Joshua Trachtenberg devotes a whole chapter to "The War with the Spirits." He cites numerous references in the Talmud and medieval rabbinic writings that speak of the power of the dead. The souls of the deceased are thought to be aware of everything that goes on here on earth, and are not beyond coming back and interfering in the affairs of the living.

This is why we do not speak ill of the dead and this is why, in some communities, it is customary, at the time of a funeral, to confess any wrongdoing against the departed and to ask their forgiveness. The Jewish folk-belief in the *dybbuk* (the restless soul of a departed which enters the body and takes possession of a living person) belongs to this genre.

Originally, then, tombstones were both memorials and powerful barriers to keep the restless soul down. The custom has long since changed its meaning and now represents a sign of respect and love which keeps the memory of the departed alive.

ANOTHER EXPLANATION OCCURRED TO ME while writing this column: Four times a year, as part of the *Yizkor* (memorial) service, we offer individual prayers in memory of a departed close relative. In these prayers we find the following sentence: "May his/her soul be bound up in the bond of life," where "bond of life" refers to eternal life. (The first letters of the words in this sentence, ת נ צ ב ה, are often engraved on Jewish tombstones.) The word used for soul in this prayer, *nefesh*, has a second meaning which entered the language during the talmudic period, namely, tombstone. Moreover, the word used for bond, *tzeror*, also stands for small stones. The sentence can, therefore, be read: "May his tombstone be bound up (or heaped up) with small stones for life." What more explicit instruction to place small stones on tombstones could one want?

51 Why on the Ninth Day of Av?

TISH'AH BE'AV (THE NINTH DAY in the month of Av) has been called "the saddest day in the Jewish calendar." It is the day on which we remember and mourn the major tragedies that befell our people through the ages. According to the Talmud, disasters recurred again and again to the Jewish People because of the lack of faith the Israelites exhibited on that date, in the Sinai desert, on their journey from Egypt to the Holy Land.

In Numbers, Chapters 13 and 14, we read the story of the twelve scouts that were sent to tour the land of Canaan before the Israelite conquest. When ten of them came back with frightening accounts of fortified cities and powerful inhabitants, the people lost courage and "they wept that night." They railed against Moses and said to one another, "Let us head back for Egypt." Then, according to the Talmud (*Ta'anit* 28b), because their complete lack of faith, God, who had promised them the land, said, "You wept without cause; I will therefore make this an eternal day of mourning for you." And so, according to tradition, it was decreed on the 9th of Av that the generation that had left Egypt should not enter the Promised Land. Moreover, it was decreed that both the First Temple (built by Solomon) and the Second Temple (built by Zerubavel and beautified by Herod) would be destroyed on that day.

But that does not end the list of tragic coincidences connected with Tish'ah be'Av. The expulsion of the Jews from England in 1290, the expulsion from Spain in 1492 and many pogroms (especially during the crusades of the Middle Ages) are said to have occurred on that day.

The question arises: Does historical evidence support the calamitous nature of the Ninth of Av? Let us see. Dating the destruction of the First Temple by Babylonian King Nebuchadnezzar in 586 B.C.E. is problematical. According to Jeremiah (52:12), the Temple was burned on the tenth of Av; Chapter 25 of 2 Kings (verses 8–9) dates it on the seventh. Dating for the Second Temple fares no better. According to the historian Josephus Flavius, the Temple was destroyed on the tenth of Av.

Of the five tragedies enumerated in the Talmud, only the fall of the Beitar fortress, the last stronghold of the Bar Kokhba revolt against the Romans, in 135 c.e., occurred on that day. Influenced by the shock of this loss, the Rabbis fixed the date of the final destruction of Jerusalem one year later, on the ninth of Av. About that time, the Emperor Hadrian started building the Roman city Aelia Capitolina on the site of devastated Jerusalem, a city that Jews were forbidden to enter.

In medieval England, King Edward I found the Jewish communities so impoverished by special taxes and decimated by repeated massacres that he had no more use for them. On July 18, 1290, he issued an edict banishing all Jews from England as of All Saints Day, Nov. 1, that year. The Hebrew date of the day on which the edict was signed was the second of Av, 5050.

The "Edict of Expulsion" from Spain was signed by King Ferdinand in Granada on March 31, 1492: "Convert to Christianity or be banished!" In May, the sorrowful exodus began and the last Jew left Spain on July 31, 1492, on the seventh of Av.

In more recent times, the deportation of Jews from the Warsaw Ghetto—to the concentration camps of Treblinka and Auschwitz and to the gas chambers—began on the eve of Tish'ah be'Av.

Are these inaccuracies significant? Not at all! By accretion, the ninth day of Av has become the focal point of disasters and calamities which have befallen our people close to that day throughout history. It has become the symbol for the loss of the Temple and political independence and for the suffering in the Diaspora. It has become a fast day in the Jewish calendar (the only one, other than Yom Kippur, on which the fast lasts a full 25 hours) and the rules of behavior on it are those of deep mourning.

However, Jewish history does not end on a downbeat. Tradition holds that the Messiah will be born on the same date as the Temple was destroyed, that is, on Tish'ah be'Av. Thus, the day of deep mourning carries in it the promise of Redemption. It is in this spirit that we read the *haftarah* on Shabbat following the Ninth of Av containing that wonderfully heartening message of Isaiah 40:

> Comfort, oh comfort ye My people, says your God. Speak tenderly to Jerusalem, and declare to her that her term of service is over, that her iniquity is expiated; for she has received at the hand of the Lord double for all her sins.

52 Of Scribes and Scrolls and Torah Etiquette

THE *SEFER TORAH* (THE TORAH scroll), which contains the Five Books of Moses, is the most revered object in Jewish life. So precious is the scroll that over the centuries Jews have, repeatedly, given their lives to save a *sefer torah* from destruction. The reverence we accord the *sefer torah* explains the etiquette or code of behavior we adopt in its presence. We rise when the Torah rises, *i.e.*, is in the arms of the ḥazzan (cantor) or is carried around the synagogue. Only when it is laid on the *bimah* (podium) or held by a person sitting down, do we sit again. Moreover, it is customary to rise any time we open the *aron hakodesh* in which the Torah scrolls are stored.

It is bad form to turn one's back on the Torah. When the congregation stands and watches the *sefer* being carried around during the procession or recession, it is polite to follow its progress by slowly turning so as to face it at all times.

As a sign of the respect in which we hold the Torah, we kiss its mantle when it is carried close by us. Although it is perfectly all right to touch the mantle with one's hand, many people prefer to touch it with a corner of their *tallit* or even with their prayer book, which is then brought to the lips. In some congregations it is customary to bow as the Torah is carried past.

The honor and love which the Jewish people accord the holy scrolls are often expressed by the beautiful decorations with which we clothe them. Ornately stitched mantles and silver breastplates, crowns and *rimonim* (finials) have ever provided a favorite outlet for the creative imagination and skills of Jewish artists and artisans. This is in keeping with *hiddur mitzvah*, the obligation of beautifying ritual objects. However, our Sages warn us to do this in moderation and not increase our spending by more than one-third over the amount we would spend for a comparable object for everyday use.

Our behavior on the *bimah* also reflects the reverence we feel for the *sefer torah*. When honored with an *aliyah*, we don a *tallit*—if we didn't wear one already—and approach the *bimah* by the shortest route possible to show our eagerness to fulfill this *mitzvah*. Similarly, after the reading, we return to our seat by a longer route.

On the *bimah*, while we say the appropriate blessings and follow the reading of the *ba'al koreh*, we hold on to one of the two wooden rollers on which the scroll is rolled. In Hebrew, the roller is called *etz ḥayyim* (tree of life) and we hold on to it in keeping with the verse: "It [the Torah] is a tree of life for those who grasp it" (Proverbs 3:18).

When the reader points to the place where our portion starts and, after the reading, where it ends, it is customary to bestow a kiss on these places in the scroll. We touch the scroll and then, bring our fingers to our lips. Since we do not touch the parchment with our bare hands, we, again, do so with a corner of our *tallit*. Moreover, we do not touch the place itself, but rather the empty margin between the columns next to it.

The reason for this custom is mainly economic: The *sefer torah* is handwritten on parchment using a goose quill and specially prepared ink. It is painstaking work done by a devout *sofer*, whose concentration must be absolute. Any mistake makes the *sefer* unfit for public use. The *sofer* may not write even a short sentence from memory, though he may well know it by heart. He must copy it, word for word, from an error-free model copy in front of him.

If a mistake occurs, it can sometimes be corrected by removing it with the sharp point of a knife, for the ink does not penetrate into the parchment. If the mistake, however, occurred in copying the name of God, the entire piece of parchment has to be discarded to be buried ritually (because we are not allowed to erase the Holy Name).

By touching the writing repeatedly, we may cause a letter or part of a letter to flake off. To avoid having to have a *sefer* repaired—which is quite costly—we take care not to touch the writing itself, not even with the specially designed pointer, the *yad* (hand) with its extended index finger. Here again, as is so often the case, good manners go hand in hand with good sense.

53 Reading the Torah

THE PRACTICE OF READING CHAPTERS of the Torah and the Prophets in public on a regular basis goes back a long way. Scholars believe that regular Torah readings became part of our religious services perhaps as far back as the fourth or third century B.C.E. Prayer services were added soon after the destruction of the Second Temple (70 C.E.) when synagogue prayer replaced the Temple sacrifices. The Torah is read during Morning Prayer on Shabbat, the festivals and the New Moons. In addition, shorter "portions" are read on Monday and Thursday mornings and on Shabbat afternoons.

For the first 200 to 300 years, the selection of the readings and their lengths seem not to have been fixed for we find discussion among the talmudic Sages of these issues. Because there was no universally recognized division of the Torah into weekly portions, the *kohen*, who would be honored by being called up first, would read a short passage and stop where he felt it was appropriate. This was usually at the end of a topic, though he was expected to read a minimum of three verses and make an effort not to end his reading on a negative note. A *levi* would be called up next and he would start reading where the *kohen* had left off. Thus, it would continue for seven *aliyot* on a Shabbat morning, each person reading a few verses. It is, therefore, unlikely that any two synagogues heard the same passages from the Torah read on any given Shabbat.

The first reference to a fixed cycle of consecutive readings occurs in the Babylonian Talmud (*Megillah* 29b). There we learn that it was the custom in *Eretz Israel* to complete the reading of the Torah in three years. The Jewish communities in Babylon and the rest of the Diaspora read three times as much each Shabbat and completed the cycle in the course of one year.

After the period of Persian domination of *Eretz Israel* (539–333 B.C.E.), Aramaic slowly replaced Hebrew as the *lingua franca* of the country. (The later books of the Bible, such as Daniel and Ezra, are bilingual.) With the decline of Hebrew as the spoken language of the Jewish communities, it became customary both in *Eretz Israel* and in Babylon to translate the Hebrew text into Aramaic at the time of the reading. In other countries, the translation was into the vernacular: Greek, Arabic or Ladino. The reader would pause after each verse and a special synagogue official, called the *meturgeman*, would repeat the sentence in translation.

Halakhah requires that any public reading of the Torah be done from a hand-written *sefer torah* (Torah scroll). A printed text may not be used, although, of course, such a text may be used for study and preparation for the reading. Initially, each person called up to the Torah read his own portion, as we saw above, but because the scroll contained only the consonants of the text, in time, with the decline of scholarship among lay people, fewer and fewer people were able to do their own reading. Hence, a specialized reader, the *ba'al koreh*, read the portion while the person called to the reading recited the benedictions before and after the reading. The requirement of reading only from the scroll did not hold for the reading from the Prophets, the *haftarah*, which was done from a printed text that did include vowels, punctuation and accent marks. This reading required much less skill and the person called up for this honor (*hamaftir*) reads the selection himself or herself.

The Sages ruled that the Torah may not be read in a regular speech or recitation pattern. It must be chanted. The chanting (or *layning*, in Yiddish) uses melodic cadences which subdivide the biblical verse into phrases according to its meaning and the rhythm of speech. The purpose of *layning* is to make the text clearer. The individual accent marks, the *trope*, serve as our familiar punctuation marks—commas, semicolons and full stops. Moreover, they tell us which syllable to stress in each word to make the text more easily understood and therefore more meaningful. *Layning* does not attempt primarily to create a beautiful piece of music, although it undoubtedly adds to the spiritual value of the recitation. The musicologist Curt Sachs argues that the restriction of the individual accent marks to a small range of notes and limited ornamentation is intentional and not primitive. The purpose was to ensure that the melody would never interfere with the perception of the words and the comprehension of their meaning and spiritual message. He characterizes *layning* as "logogenic," where the musical element proceeds from the word and is subordinated to the communication of the text with no attempt at musical autonomy. (See the article "Masoretic Accents, Musical Rendition" in the *Encyclopedia Judaica*.)

For many centuries, the *trope* marks were passed on as part of the oral tradition. In fact, there were several competing systems of these cantillation marks. It was only when the Masoretes finally edited the Bible text in the tenth century C.E. that the marks we use today became the authoritative system. Jewish communities all over the world now follow this system; it is known (together with the Bible text and its vowels) as the *Masora* or Masoretic Text.

Although the system of musical accent marks is the same for all communities, the texts are chanted in many different ways. As our young *benei mitzvah* are well aware, the Torah *nusaḥ* (musical style) differs from that in which the *haftarah* (Prophetic portion) is chanted. There is a special *nusaḥ* for the High Holy Days and for several other occasions. There are also special melodies for the Scroll of Esther, the book of Lamentations and for the books of Ruth, Ecclesiastes and the Song of Songs. Even within a given *parashah* (weekly reading from the *Pentateuch*), a special text may have its own *nusaḥ*, for instance, the "Song of the Sea" (Exodus 15). It is considered wrong to substitute one system for another. Finally, the *Ashkenazi* and *Sephardi* systems differ from one another, and there are significant differences within each of these broad Jewish groups.

Because *halakhah* forbids adding any marks to the consonants in the Torah scroll, readers have to go to a printed text that contains the full array of vowel and *trope* marks to prepare for their *layning*. Such a text is called a *tikkun* (correction). A *tikkun* is a useful aid to prepare for one's *layning* because it reproduces the text as it appears in the scroll on one page and the full text with vowel and *trope* marks on the facing page.

BESIDES THE DIFFERENCES IN THE musical rendition of the *trope* marks, there are differences in the pronunciation of Hebrew between *Sephardi* and *Ashkenazi* readers. These differences consist not only of the well-known changes in vowel sounds but also of the less-well-known accentuation of words in the two idioms. *Sephardi* accents usually fall on the last syllable of the word, whereas *Ashkenazi* readers (following German language patterns) tend to emphasize the penultimate syllable. Yet, when it comes to reading the Torah, both groups follow the *Sephardi* accentuation of the text because that is what the Masoretic *trope* system calls for.

Initially, *trope* marks were taught in conjunction with a set of hand and finger movements, which served as *aides-memoire*. They mirrored the rise and fall in the pitch of each *trope* mark. The reader was assisted by a person (the *somekh*) who signaled the correct *trope* by his hand movements. This custom was still practiced until recently in Italy and

Yemen, but has now, unfortunately, fallen into general disuse. Wouldn't our *benai mitzvah* (and other *layners*) love to see this practice revived!

The Kabbalists of the Middle Ages, who saw mystical meaning in many of our practices, viewed the reading of the Torah to the assembled congregation as a re-enactment of the giving of the Torah at Mt. Sinai. The reader represents the Almighty, the person who is honored with an *aliyah* symbolizes the people who received the Torah, and the *gabbai rishon* (who stands to the right of the reader)—Moses. This helps explain why *halakhah* imposes strict requirements on the readers. They must stand erect and may not lean on the *bimah* for support, they must enunciate each word clearly (though not excessively), and must repeat any mispronounced word (especially if the word's meaning was changed by the mispronunciation). Finally, they must be of upright character which, of course, is clearly the case for the whole group of Beit Am's devoted *layners*.

54 The Changing Role of the Rabbi

ALTHOUGH MANY PEOPLE PLAY IMPORTANT roles in the social, cultural, educational, charitable and financial realms that make up a typical Jewish community, religious leadership rests, in general, in the hands of a rabbi.

Rabbis may fulfill different functions depending on the type of congregations they serve. The more traditional the congregation, the fewer the tasks a rabbi is expected to perform. According to *halakhah*, none of the rituals in the synagogue requires the presence of a rabbi nor do most of the events in the life of a Jew. A rabbi does not possess any special authority to perform a *berit milah* (circumcision) or officiate at a Bar Mitzvah, a wedding or a funeral.

As for the *berit*, any Jew (male or female) may perform the operation. The *mohel* (person performing circumcisions) is essentially a trained craftsman.

Young people become *benei mitzvah* simply upon reaching the age of religious maturity. No special ceremony is required, nor is a special person authorized by Jewish law to confer the status of *bar mitzvah* or *bat mitzvah* upon the youngsters.

Weddings, too, are private affairs—contracts between the two individuals involved. Although marriage is considered a sacred relationship (*kiddushin*), it is not a sacrament as it is in the Catholic Church. If certain conditions are fulfilled—the groom handing the signed and witnessed *ketubbah* to the bride, giving her something of value, and pronouncing the *harei at* formula—the couple is legally married. Again, no rabbinical authority need play any part in the ceremony. However, because certain unions are forbidden—*e.g.*, close relatives by blood or by marriage—a rabbi would be essential to rule on the *halakhic* permissibility of the marriage.

The final event in a person's life cycle, the funeral, is also a function that the community performs. The *ḥevra kaddisha*, the Sacred Society, prepares the body for interment, and the mourners follow the prescribed laws of mourning. Of course, the presence of a compassionate rabbi might lend comfort to the bereaved, as it might lend dignity to this or any of the other rituals discussed above, but Jewish law does not require a rabbi's presence.

What about the rabbi's role in the synagogue? Traditionally, the rabbi is not the *shali'aḥ tzibbur* (prayer leader). The rabbi may, of course, take a turn, with the rest of the knowledgeable members of the congregation in leading prayers, but this is regarded as a privilege, not a duty. The same is true for the *layning*, the chanting of the relevant portions from the Torah scroll. A congregation may have a designated Torah reader or a number of members capable of layning who take turns reading. That task, too, does not usually fall within the purview of the rabbi.

For most of the congregations with which we are familiar, the rabbi's sermon is an integral part of the worship service. The sermon, delivered in the synagogue or in the house of study, mainly on Sabbaths and festivals, is a very ancient institution. As far back as the end of the Second Temple period, sermons served as the chief means of instructing the people and imparting to them at least an elementary knowledge of the Torah and its teachings. The Sages used the sermon as a means of guiding the people, strengthening their faith and refuting heretical views.

This was the case throughout the Middle Ages and is still true today. But who delivered these sermons? Was it the rabbi? For most of our history, at least until the middle of the nineteen century when the role of the rabbi changed drastically, it was specialized professionals, *darshanim* and *maggidim*, who preached to the congregations. Some of these were appointed by a specific community and received a fixed salary, others were itinerant preachers who traveled from town to town and had to rely on irregular contributions. Traditionally, the local rabbis were expected to deliver only two sermons a year: on *Shabbat Hagadol*, the Sabbath before Passover, and on *Shabbat Shuvah*, the Sabbath between Rosh Ha-Shanah and Yom Kippur. On the first of these, they discussed the importance of the Exodus, the delivery from slavery, and the laws concerning the Passover Festival; on the second, they delivered a call for repentance appropriate for the Days of Awe.

We have seen so far that traditionally, and by Jewish law, the role of a rabbi is quite limited. In contrast to the clergy of other religions, a rabbi is not accorded a higher degree of holiness than any other person. Rabbis do not stand between members of the congregation and God. They do not administer sacraments nor do they have the power to absolve people from sin. It is difficult for those not having grown up in the Jewish tradition to realize that the rabbinate is not a calling, but a profession. Rabbis are not assigned to congregations as Catholic priests are to parishes; rather, they are hired by the congregations they serve, and, generally, are paid by them.

If a rabbi does not possess any special religious authority, what, then, are the specific functions that only a rabbi can fulfill? According to *halakhah*, only an ordained rabbi has the authority to render legal judgments and make decisions based on Torah. A rabbi (the title translates to My Master) is a person who has spent years studying the Jewish sources (Talmud, commentaries, etc.) and has received *semikhah* (ordination) from a teacher attesting to mastery of the material.

To render a *pesak halakhah* (legal decision) is, of course, not a trivial thing. It may decide the limited question of whether the meat of a cow with some minor blemish is kosher or not, or may have dealt (historically) with the complex allocation of charity resources within the community. In either case, the rabbi's decision is binding and may significantly influence the quality of life in the community. Rabbis who were known for their learning and piety were often called upon to render decisions and find practical solutions in financial matters that went far beyond disputes between two litigants. They dealt with more general problems: business practices between communities of different backgrounds, relations between employees and employers in small industries or ethical problems arising from conducting business.

We are familiar with many of these issues, for the rabbis' decisions were often collected in books of *Responsa*. These may contain a particular rabbi's answers to questions, or a collection of answers by a group of rabbis. *Responsa* make fascinating reading. For example, in the area of medical ethics, we find in them consideration of organ donation, the permissibility of selling parts of one's body to assist the study of medicine (pints of blood!), or the legality of autopsies—all in light of the principles of *halakhah*.

In the average congregation, the presence of a rabbi as judge is required mainly in only two situations: as a member of a *bet din* (rabbinical court) dealing with a divorce or presiding over a conversion to Judaism. In both cases, it is the function of the court to ensure that all the formalities required for the procedure are carried out according to law.

WHEN DID THE TRADITIONAL ROLE of the rabbi change and take on the attributes and functions of the modern rabbi? In the 1840s, a series of conferences were held in different cities in Germany that brought together a group of modernist rabbis. These were rabbis with traditional Jewish as well as secular university education. Their "primary concerns were the large-scale defections from Judaism in the age of Emancipation, and the absence of Western standards of aesthetics and decorum in the traditional manner of Jewish worship." (*Encyclopedia Judaica*) To solve these problems, they set about reforming the service by abbreviating the liturgy, supplementing the standard Hebrew prayers with prayers in the vernacular, and introducing regular sermons in the vernacular. They instituted mixed-gender seating, and choral singing with organ accompaniment in the synagogue. This was the birth of the Reform (or Liberal) Movement.

With these innovations, the nature of the service changed to resemble more closely that of a Protestant service, and the role of the congregational rabbi changed to resemble more closely that of a Protestant minister. The rabbi now started to take a leading role in conducting services of which the 20-minute weekly sermon became a major component. Rabbis officiated at Bar Mitzvah celebrations, marriages and funerals as a matter of course. Besides the pastoral work such as comforting the bereaved, visiting the sick and counseling those with problems, the modern rabbi is expected to take an active part in all social, educational and philanthropic activities of the congregation. An important part of the job is to represent the Jewish community and serve as its spokesperson in dealing with the larger community.

The article "Rabbi, Rabbinate" in the *Encyclopedia Judaica* summarizes the changed role of the modern rabbi:

> The Reform rabbi is judge no longer: he has become to a large degree, for the first time in the history of the rabbinate, a priest ordering the prayer service and leading it. In the United States in particular he is also becoming the social and even the socialite director of his synagogue congregation.

This characterization holds true, to a lesser or greater degree, for rabbis of the other religious streams in Judaism as well.

55 "Stretch Out Your Hand..."

WITH THE DESTRUCTION OF THE Temple and the dispersion of the Jews from their ancestral land, the specifics of the safety net which the Bible had mandated to help the indigent became largely irrelevant. That system was mainly devised to alleviate hunger and help the needy in an agricultural society. However, the principle underlying the system was still valid despite the changed circumstances, and the injunction to "stretch out your hand to the poor" was still a legal and ethical imperative. The Sages coined the term *tzedakah* (righteousness) for the act of giving and held that "*tzedakah* is as important as all the other commandments put together" (Bava Batra 9a).

The talmudic Sages spent much time discussing how to fulfill this *mitzvah*. In answer to the question of "who was eligible to receive *tzedakah*?" they defined a poverty line. Any person earning less than 200 *zuzim* (dinars) a year was considered indigent and was entitled to weekly financial support from the local charity fund as well as daily meals from the communal soup kitchen. From tractate Bava Metzi'a we learn that 200 *zuzim* amounted to about 25 percent of the average income at the time. (Interestingly, this is almost the identical level at which the United States government defines its poverty line.) The obligation of giving *tzedakah*, fell on everybody, even, according to Maimonides, on those who themselves lived entirely on *tzedakah*!

Although the obligation fell primarily on the individual, it soon became apparent that communal action was often called for. Many of the institutions that developed during the talmudic era (first through fifth centuries C.E.) in the Jewish communities around the Mediterranean and in Babylon survived in Europe through the Middle Ages and into the beginning of the twentieth century. They became increasingly important as Jewish communities in country after country repeatedly became impoverished through the actions of rapacious rulers, the devastation of the Crusades, the horrors of pogroms, wars, plagues and famines.

The many relief societies that existed to provide assistance for the needy in one Polish town are described in some detail in Yaffa Eliach's, *There Once Was a World, A 900-Year Chronicle of the Shtetl of Eishyshok*. In this magnificent study, the author describes the *tzedakah*-responsibilities these societies took upon themselves. *Bikkur Ḥolim*, for instance, not only fulfilled the religious duty of visiting the sick, but paid for medical care and medicines for those who could not afford them. *Linat Tzeddek*, which Eliach calls "a very prestigious society," provided more than personal nursing care for the sick. Its members, men and women of the upper classes in the *shtetl*, took turns spending nights at a poor sick person's bedside. Following a centuries-old tradition, the *Hakhnasat Kallah* society provided dowries for daughters of poor families and, where necessary, paid for the total wedding expenses including those of the *shadḥan*, the matchmaker, to find the girl a suitable bridegroom.

The list continues. There was a society to provide general financial assistance, a society to provide interest-free loans to those who wanted to start a business, and a society (*Malbish Arumim*) that provided clothing to those in need. It distributed new clothing for Pesaḥ and used clothing whenever needed during the rest of the year. (It even brought the clothing into the homes of the recipients to save them the embarrassment of being seen receiving handouts.) There was the *Hakhnasat Orḥim* society, which provided hospitality in a communal shelter or in private homes; the communal soup kitchen (which, by the way, fed as many hungry non-Jewish Poles as Jews); and the *Ḥevra Kaddisha* (Burial Society), which helped the grieving family make funeral arrangements, prepared the deceased for burial, and even provided the Meal of Consolation. It was an honor to belong to one of these societies, and membership was often a status symbol. It is quite clear that Jewish communities (of which the one in Eishyshok was fairly representative) took the obligation of *tzedakah* very seriously.

What about the recipients of these righteous donations? Did they feel demeaned by them? The folklore surrounding *tzedakah* suggests the very opposite: the *shnorrer* (Yiddish for beggar) did not so much beg as claim what was rightfully his. He saw himself as the agent of the Almighty who provided the better-off an opportunity to fulfill a *mitzvah* and helped redistribute the bounty that was God's gift to the rich. The Yiddish story about the beggar who came on his annual rounds to the door of the wealthy Jew has it right. When the rich man says: "I had a bad year and can't give you as much as usual," the *shnorrer* asks him indignantly: "Just because you had a bad year, I have to suffer?"

56 *Meḥitzah, the Physical Barrier*

SEATING MEN AND WOMEN SEPARATELY in *shul* (synagogue) is a practice that distinguishes Orthodox Judaism from other Jewish religious movements. Conservative synagogues have had mixed seating for many years, and Reform and the more recently formed Reconstructionist, Renewal and other movements never accepted the requirement of separate seating.

In strictly Orthodox *shuls*, not only do men and women sit apart, but the physical arrangements are such that men cannot see women during the service. This is accomplished by seating women behind a *meḥitzah*, a physical partition, such as a wall or a curtain, or by placing the women's section on a balcony from which they can follow the service without being seen.

The main reason given by the Orthodox for separating the sexes during worship is that this arrangement was ordained by God; it is claimed that men and women prayed separately in the Holy Temple in Jerusalem. This, however, is not attested to anywhere in the Scriptures, though the Talmud does indeed discuss the construction of a temporary women's balcony in tractate Succah (51b, 52a).

One way to help achieve the proper atmosphere in *shul*, say the Orthodox, is by creating a division between men and women during prayer. A rabbi of the Ohr Samayach Institute in Jerusalem explains that: the separation is "to promote modesty, and to prevent the distraction from prayer to both men and women by the presence of members of the opposite gender, to whom there is a natural attraction." Although the quote speaks of distraction from prayer to both men and women, the restrictions do not apply equally to both genders. Women may gaze upon the male worshippers from behind the *meḥitzah*, whereas men are prevented from looking upon the women's faces. Also, it is only a woman's voice, *kol ishah*, that is not to be lifted in song in a synagogue. Apparently, it is primarily women who distract men and make it more difficult for them to concentrate on prayer.

What is the reasoning of the Conservative Movement that allows mixed seating in their synagogues? Rabbi David Golinkin summarizes the arguments in his *Responsa for the year 5747/1987 (Vol. 2)*, published by the *Va'ad Halakhah* of the Rabbinical Assembly in Israel. Rabbi Golinkin disputes the assertion that the sexes were separated in the Temple. There is no mention of any separation during either First or Second Temple days. For most of the year, women and men mingled freely in the Women's Court. The temporary balcony, mentioned above, was erected only during *Simḥat Bet Hasho'evah*, the Feast of the Water-Drawing on Sukkot, when men danced round the altar with burning torches in their hands. It was explicitly constructed to protect women from what the rabbis called *kalut rosh* (excessive frivolity).

The Temple was built as a series of connected courts: both men and women worshipped in the Women's Court. Connected to it was the Priests' Court for those charged with the sacrificial service. Just inside this court was a small area called the Israelites' Court for representatives of the people (*Anshei Ma'amad*) during the sacrificial ceremony. Finally, there was the Holy of Holies, the repository of the Ark of the Covenant, to which only the High Priest had access. Various contemporary sources speak of the mixing of the genders in the Women's Court of the Temple. This court measured 40,000 square feet (almost an acre) designed to accommodate this mixed congregation of worshippers, whereas the Israelite's Court enclosed less than one-tenth of that area.

In the more than 100 ancient synagogues uncovered in *Eretz Israel*, archaeologists have found no evidence of women's balconies or enclosures. According to Golinkin, separate seating is not mentioned in any source prior to the eleventh century C.E. and then only in passing. The first *halakhic* source requiring separate seating did not appear until the end of the nineteenth century, in reaction to the growing liberal Reform Movement in Germany.

Based on these facts, Golinkin argues that separate seating in synagogues is a *minhag* rather than legally required by *halakhah* and as such is open to change. Over the centuries, many *halakhot* (pl.) have changed as the customs upon which they were based have changed. In Western societies, new mores prevail; men and women are accustomed to sitting together in all kinds of situations. Therefore, the argument of "distraction by the presence of the opposite sex" has lost much of its validity. Mixed seating, then, is justified by new customs, which, significantly, include the greater role women have assumed in synagogue affairs.

57 Hidden Treasures: The *Genizah*

THE HEBREW ROOT OF THE word *Genizah*, means to hide, to shelve, to archive or to store. Yet, the function of a *Genizah* is the very opposite of preservation: a *Genizah* provides a convenient way of getting rid of certain objects, the removal of which, in other ways, would present a major problem. According to Jewish law, we cannot simply throw away, burn or otherwise destroy sacred books (or ritual objects) which have become unusable. Often, these tattered prayer books, Bibles etc. are ceremonially buried in a Jewish graveyard. This is what our community did in 1989, when we rededicated the Jewish part of Waverly Cemetery in Albany. The grave is formally marked by a stone that has the word *sheimot* (names, *i.e.* of God) engraved on it, for it is not the paper but the Divine Name that we thus honor. For the sake of convenience, in lieu of immediate burial, the texts are often collected in a *Genizah*, that is, an out-of-the-way area in a synagogue where the *sheimot* are awaiting burial when they become too worn to be used.

The most famous of all the *genizot* is the Cairo Genizah which was discovered in the mid-1800s in the attic of the Fostat synagogue in Old Cairo. There are no doors or windows in the Cairo *Genizah*, and access to this room is via ladder through a hole in one of the sidewalls. It turned out to be a treasure trove of Jewish antiquities. Because of the length of time the synagogue had been used (it was built in 882 C.E.!) and the extremely dry climate, thousands upon thousands of priceless, well-preserved documents were recovered from it.

In 1896, the British scholar Solomon Schechter, after prolonged negotiations, was able to persuade the synagogue authorities that no terrible disaster would ensue (in contrast to what they strongly believed) if materials were removed from the *Genizah*. He transferred over 100,000 pages from it to Cambridge University. Since then, the *Genizah* has yielded several times that number of pages, which have found their way into various other university collections. Most of the ongoing work of analysis is taking place at the Taylor-Schechter *Genizah*

Institute in Cambridge; there is enough material there for scores more Ph.D. dissertations.

AN INTERESTING ASIDE IS THE fact that Solomon Schechter (1847–1915), who was a reader in Talmudics and Rabbinics at Cambridge University, realized the value of the *Genizah* treasures by identifying a single page, brought to him by two Christian travelers, as the original Hebrew version of the *Book of Ben Sira*. The book was known only in its Greek translation, and is included in the Apocrypha under the name *Ecclesiasticus*. It obviously never made it into the Hebrew Bible or else it would not have been lost. In 1901, Schechter accepted an invitation to come to the United States to head the Jewish Theological Seminary and the fledgling Conservative Movement.

Besides the *Ben Sira* original, the *Genizah* yielded hundreds of new *piyutim* (the medieval poems that make the High Holidays services so special), the existence of which was not even suspected. It included variant text readings of the Mishnah and Talmud, ancient liturgies, and much more. Because it contained many secular letters, contracts and documents as well, it provided new insights into periods of Jewish history about which little was known.

CAIRO WAS FOUNDED AFTER THE Islamic invasion of Egypt in the seventh century. There is evidence that Jews lived in Cairo from the very beginning. The history of Jewish settlement in Egypt, though, goes back much further than that. The *Encyclopedia Judaica* traces Egyptian Jewry back to the time of Jeremiah, though the great wave of immigration came at the time of Alexander the Great. Jews have lived in Alexandria since the third century B.C.E.—while the Temple in Jerusalem was still standing. Each quarter of the city had a synagogue, and the Jewish population had autonomous control over its own affairs. The Great Synagogue of Alexandria is mentioned in the Talmud because of its splendor and size. It is said that it was so large that worshippers in the back rows could not hear the *ḥazzan* and had to be alerted by waving of flags when to respond with "amen."

From the records, we know that the Jews of Alexandria, and Egypt in general, were mainly artisans, though a few were wealthy traders. They became significant in culture and commerce and, according to Philo, constituted 12–14 percent of the total Egyptian population by the first century C.E. They maintained close connections with *Eretz Israel* and with the Temple to which they sent regular contributions. They supported the war effort of the Jews against the Romans, and staged riots in Alexandria against the Roman rulers in support of the Bar Kokhba revolt. It was during these riots that the Great Synagogue of Alexandria was set afire and burned down.

THE MOST FASCINATING JEWISH SETTLEMENT in Egypt was the one at Elephantine. Nothing was known about it until 1953, when a collection of papyri dealing with it was published. Elephantine was a garrison city on an island in the upper Nile, which guarded Egypt from attacks by the Nubians. The papyri clearly show that the garrison force had several large units of Jewish mercenaries attached to it. Besides the soldiers, there was a good-sized civilian Jewish population in town. The Jews of Elephantine traced their origin in Egypt to the days of the prophet Jeremiah (seventh century B.C.E.), and as early as the sixth century they built a temple to substitute for the one they had left in Jerusalem. They, too, had kohanim (priests), and performed animal sacrifices. Of course, their temple was never recognized by the Jerusalem authorities.

Much of our history would be lost to us without the precious documents that afford us a glimpse into the past. In many cases, it was the genizot that preserved these documents.

58 To Choose the Right Name

To CHOOSE THE RIGHT NAME for a baby is not a trivial undertaking. In the Jewish tradition, names are extremely important. The Talmud (*Berachot* 7b) teaches that the name bestowed on the newborn influences future behavior and the destiny of the individual. Jewish mysticism, the Kabbalah, considers an individual's name connected to his or her essential self. A baby boy's Hebrew name is revealed for the first time during his *berit*, the ceremony of circumcision, which initiates him into the Covenant of Abraham; a baby girl's name is announced in the synagogue when her parent is called up to the Torah. Thus the naming becomes part of a religious ritual.

Traditionally, most Hebrew names come from the Bible and have meaning in the Hebrew language. Many of them give information about special circumstances attending the birth of the baby. Examples abound. The Egyptian princess who fished Moses out of the Nile, where he was set afloat to escape death, called him Moses, an Egyptian name. His parents had presumably given him a Hebrew name, but we are not told what it was. Instead, folk etymology saw in the Egyptian name the Hebrew word *mashah* (pulled out) and so his name remained Moses—"he-who-was-pulled-out-of-the-river." Similarly, Jacob, who followed his twin Esau out of the womb, was named Ya'akov (*akav*, followed on the heels of)—"he-who-was-born-second." A stranger case is the name given to the offspring of Lot and his older daughter. After the destruction of Sodom and Gomorrah, the daughter, fearing that there were no other males left in the world to propagate the human race, tricked her father into having intercourse with her. She named the son Mo'av (from-my-father). The Bible does not report whether the son resented having to go through life with a name that was a constant reminder of his being the issue of an incestuous union.

Not as drastic, but still disturbing, was the name that Rachel, Jacob's beloved wife, bestowed on her second son. Being near death, for she died in childbirth, she named him Ben-oni (son-of-my-sorrow). Fortunately for the baby's future peace of mind, Jacob renamed him (after Rachel's death?) Ben-yamin, which carries the exact opposite connotation of the name his mother gave him.

Parents may indeed be blessed with powers of prophecy when naming their newborn babies, as folk belief has it. This seems to have been the case with Noah, whose name in Hebrew comes from the word rest. Noah, though, was more than restful, comfortable, or relaxed—all traits implied by his name. A better translation might be complacent, for Noah is the silent man of the Bible. He utters not one word of protest when God announces the end of the world and tells him to build an ark. In contrast, Abraham argues and negotiates strenuously to save the inhabitants of Sodom and Gomorrah from destruction. Noah, true to his name, silently watches the destruction of the entire world, accepting it.

Harder to explain, but equally prophetic, are the names with which Elimelekh and Naomi saddled their two sons, as related in the Book of Ruth. Both of them, Ḥilyon and Maḥlon, have names meaning sickly in Hebrew. Living up to their names, both died young, leaving their Moabite wives widowed. This, of course, is the setting for the beautiful relationship between Naomi and her younger daughter-in-law, Ruth. But one has to wonder: what were the parents thinking when they put the stamp of failing health on their babies at birth? Moreover, had they chosen different names, might Ruth never have married Boaz, and thus David, their direct descendent, might never have become king? It boggles the mind.

The bitter rivalry between the two sisters, Leah and Rachel, for the affection of their joint husband, Jacob, was fought by means of the sons each gave him. Here, again, the names by which each of the wives called her children marked the progress in their prolonged contest-by-progeny. The Bible tells us that Rachel was Jacob's favorite wife, and that Leah was unloved. That is why, when Leah bore Jacob's first son, she called him Reuben (see, a son), adding, "now my husband will love me." Poor Leah! All in vain! Her second son she called Simeon (from the root *shama*, to hear) declaring: "The Lord has heard that I am unloved and has given me this one also." And so it went through six sons by Leah and two by each of the two handmaidens who bore sons to Jacob. When Rachel finally bore a son—hoping she was on a roll—she called him Joseph (*yasaph*, to add) saying, "May the Lord add another son for me!" The names of Jacob's sons, ten of whom became the names of ten of the tribes of Israel, tell the story of this bitter feud between the sisters.

So far, we have looked at biblical names that reveal something about the circumstances connected with the birth of the baby. Among the more than 1400 unique names in the Bible, we find, of course, many different categories. Thus, babies were named after animals and flowers, no doubt in the hope that they would grow up exhibiting the strength, grace or beauty of their role models. Many names incorporate some form of the name of God. We find *el* both as a prefix, as in Eliezer (God is my help), and as a suffix, as in Daniel (God is my judge). The syllables *ya, yo, yeho* and *yahu* (all abbreviations of YHWH) also show up ubiquitously as prefixes and suffixes of biblical names.

With rare exceptions, it was the mothers who named the babies. There is no record in the Bible as to whether husbands were involved in the decisions. It was the mothers of Samuel, Samson, Isaac, Jacob and Esau, to name just a few, of whom the Bible says "and she called him...." There are some notable exceptions to this generalization, two of which I will cite here. Moses named his son Gershom, for "I have been a stranger (*ger*) in a foreign land." Joseph who, though being a highly-placed Egyptian official, gave his two sons Hebrew names — his firstborn Menasheh, "for God has made me forget (*nashah*) my hardship," and Ephrayim, "God has made me fertile" (*peri*, fruit).

God Himself provided names on several occasions. It must have been He who named the first man Adam (Earthling), because there was no one else around to assign this fitting name. About 3,000 years later, God used the names of the three children of the Prophet Hosea to drive home a point. After the death of King Jeroboam II (743 B.C.E.), the Northern Kingdom of Israel was in moral decline and Hosea predicted the punishment to come. God told Hosea to name his firstborn Jezre'el, after the valley where idolatry was being practiced; his second child Lo-ruḥamah, not-pitied; and his third child Lo-ammi, not-my-people. These are bitter names to indicate God's bitterness toward Israel, His people. Equally powerful, though, was God's directive to the prophet Isaiah to take his son She'ar-yashuv (a remnant shall return) when going to meet King Ahaz of Judah, so as to provide hope to those whose destruction and exile Isaiah had predicted.

More beneficent were the occasions when God saw fit to change the names of Avram and Sarai and, later, of their grandson, Jacob. Avram's name meant exalted father or grand father, a fitting enough name for a tribal chieftain, which is what Avram was. God added a letter to his name and made it Avraham, thereby lending grandeur to the name ("for I have made you the father of a multitude of nations.") Likewise,

Sarai becomes Sarah, a princess. This recalls the custom of monarchs who, upon ascending the throne, assume regal names. Indeed, a similar change of name, and consequent change in stature, occurred when Jacob, who had wrestled all night with the mysterious stranger, was told by him in the morning "Your name shall no longer be Jacob, but Israel, for you have striven with God and men and have prevailed."

The custom of changing names has carried over from ancient times. The Talmud (*Rosh Ha-Shanah*, 16b) mentions it as one of the four ways of combating illness. An example from my own family: When my brother, David, was gravely ill as an infant, my father added the names Shalom before and Israel after the name David. As a result, the acronym of his new name became *Shaddai*, one of the names of God. It seems to have worked for—80 years later—he is still alive!

The folk-belief that the Angel of Death is rather stupid and can easily be fooled also underlies the custom among *Ashkenazi* Jews not to name an infant after a living relative. This is to prevent the wrong one being carried off in case there are two persons alive with the same name. Thus, we have no "the Second" or "Junior" after Jewish names. *Sephardi* Jews show no such concern and their children are named after dead or living relatives. The main purpose of naming a child after a relative is the same in both communities: to honor the person, or the memory of the person, after whom the infant is named, and to give the child a suitable namesake with desirable traits after whom the growing child can model his or her life.

Jewish mysticism points out that the word *neshamah* (soul) contains within it the word *shem* (name). It follows that a tight bond exists between the infant and the soul of the ancestor after whom it is named. They become, as it were, soul-mates.

59 What's in a (Family) Name?

COMPULSORY, HEREDITARY FAMILY NAMES ARE a relatively recent phenomenon among Jews. Formerly, people were often known by names that differentiated them as individuals rather than identified them as members of a family or clan.

About 200 years ago, European governments started insisting on fixed family names for administrative purposes — mainly army service and taxes. In 1787, Emperor Joseph II of Austria compelled all his subjects to register their family names. At that time, many individual names became transformed into family names. Often, people who were known by their father's name took the patronymic as a family name. Thus, Pinḥas ben Ya'akov became Paul Jacobson or, in Eastern Europe, Pawel Jakobowicz. In our community we have Aronson, Michaelson, Berlowitz (Berel's son) and, in a somewhat different category, Rabinowitz (the rabbi's son). An interesting example of the above is the name Yudelson (little Jew's son) which became Delson when one branch of the family dropped the first syllable.

Because Jews moved around quite a bit (whether voluntarily or forced out by edict), places of origin often identified individuals and later became family names. The following clearly show the provenance of their holders: Berlin, Brody, Englander, Frankfurter, Krakauer, Landau, Moskowitz, Warshawski and so forth. Both Bialik (the national poet of Israel) and Rachel Biale (the author of *Women and Jewish Law*) stem from Bialystok. Winograd, the wine city, is not far from there. Kuttner most probably comes from Kuttno, a small Polish town. An interesting example of the place-name category comes from a former member of Beit Am, Mike Gildesgame, whose family name derives from the German town of Hildesheim. The connection is simple: The Russian alphabet does not contain the letter H and uses G in its stead.

Uniquely Jewish are names like Cohen, Kahn, Kogan (remember the Russian H) and derivatives like Kaganowitz which indicate that an ancestor was once known as "So-and-so the *Kohen*" (priest). Katz, which is the acronym for *kohen tzedek* (righteous priest) belongs to this group. The status of *Levi*, too, is easily recognized in many family names: Levy, Levine, Loeb, Lowin, Loewe, Lewenstein, Lowenthal and the like.

Persons were often identified by the occupations they followed and family names were based on these. The names tell us much about the social structure of the Jewish communities. First of course, we expect the Jewish occupations: Rabi, Rabin and Kaplan (German for chaplain). Next to the rabbi we have the *hazzan* who often shows up as Kantor or Schatz (which is the acronym for *shali'ah tzibbur*—the congregational emissary). The Torah-roll scribe is Sofer or Schreiber; the ritual slaughterer without whom no community could exist is Shochet or Schecter; the important teacher is Melamed or Malamud, Lehrer or even Kinderlehrer; and the kid in the *heder* (Jewish preschool) who would rather have been outdoors playing, grew up to be a Lerner.

Of course, other occupations are represented as well. Because Jews could not own land or become members of the all-encompassing craft guilds in medieval Europe, many occupations are not represented. We would not expect to find a Fletcher (arrow maker) or Schmidt, but do find many Goldsmiths who performed the early banking functions. The name Wechsler or Wexler (money changer) belongs here. Kaufman (business man) was also a common and honorable occupation.

In the *shtetl*, though, many other occupations can be found. The butcher is represented by Metzger or by Fleischhacker, like the German-Jewish family after whom the San Francisco Zoo is named. (One of their great worries, I presume, must have been that one of the daughters might marry Dr. Milchiger, of Tevye the Milkman's fame.) There are, of course, Schneiders and Schusters (tailors and shoemakers in German) and Buchbinders and Plotnicks (carpenters in Russian). There are Shers or Sherers (barbers in Yiddish), Musikants and Fabrikants (manufacturers). An important (and much hated) man was Pachtman who collected the rents from the tenant farmers on a Polish nobleman's estate. Often, the hard-pressed peasants vented their anger not on the landlord who oppressed them, but on the Jew who collected the rents in the noble's name.

One of my favorites, though, is the name of a fellow economist, Bronfenbrenner. *Bronfen*, is Yiddish for that 100-proof, liquid-fire that one tips down one's throat in response to the *lehayyim* toast. Bronfenbrenner thus translates into distiller. Bronfen, of course, also appears in the name of the famous Canadian Bronfman family that made its fortune in liquor.

IMAGINE FOR A MOMENT THAT you are living in the Austro-Hungarian Empire about 200 years ago. A newly passed law (1787) requires that you officially adopt a family name, something you haven't done so far. You are suspicious of the law for you suspect—correctly—that one of its purposes is to speed the assimilation of the Jewish communities into the general population. Several of the new law's provisions (names, generally, could not be Hebrew or Yiddish, but had to be German or Hungarian) point to that fact.

Well, then, which name would you choose? Many families chose precious objects as their family name: Gold and Silber (and, of course, the many derivatives such as Goldberg, Goldwasser, Silberstein, etc.), Diamant, Brilliant (a diamond of a certain cut), Garfunkel or Finkelstein (sparkler, the Old-German word for diamond), Perlmutter (mother-of-pearl) and Bernstein (amber) are other, easily recognized examples. Some names like Margolis (Hebrew for pearl) slipped through, and the German word for jeweler, Schmukler, was a common occupation-based family name. Krane is the Yiddish pronunciation of the German *Krone* (crown), and Sapir, Safire, Saperstein *etc.* come from the Hebrew word for the gem Sapphire that occurs ten times in the Bible. The name Schatz that we mentioned above, despite the fact that the word means treasure in German, does not belong in this category—it is an acronym for *shali'ah tzibbur*, as we noted above.

In trying to register your new name, you quickly discover that the officials in charge have the power to accept or reject a name and view the process as a new source of income. If you have the money for a bribe, you may end up with a lovely name like Sonnenschein (sunshine) or Stern (star). If not—mean-spirited officials have no trouble coming up with names such as Nirenstein (kidney stones) or Knoblauch (garlic) to show their displeasure.

Assuming they had the money, Jewish families often chose names that portrayed desirable personal characteristics: Froehlich or the Yiddish Freilich (joyous), Suess (sweet), Ehrlich (honest), Freud (glad), Liebhaft (lovable), Gottlieb and Frum (devout), Baruch (Hebrew blessed) and the like. Many took the peace-ful names of Fried, Freed or Friedman.

The name Shane, which sounds like the Yiddish pronunciation of schoehn (nice, pretty), and should therefore fit into this category, does not. It too is a Hebrew acronym for cantor: *shali'ah ne'eman* (faithful emissary of the congregation).

Most intriguing are the many names with reference to nature. Because Jews could not own land in medieval Europe, they were largely an urban people. (Outside of Eastern Europe, the Dorfmans (villagers) or Feldmans were in the minority.) These names may well reflect a longing rather than the drab reality. We have flower names such as Blum, Blumfeld (or Bloomfield), Blumberg (which in Italian became the famous Montefiore), and we have specific flowers like Rosenberg and Rosenblatt (*berg* is mountain, *blatt* is leaf) and Lilienthal (*thal* is valley). Roses and lilies, though, seem to exhaust the list; I haven't found any forget-me-nots or honeysuckles. Lawns and grass are represented by names such as Wiesenthal and Raas.

Tree names are popular—not only fruit trees such as Birnbaum (pear), Apfelbaum (apple), Teitelbaum (date palm), Mandelbaum (almond) and Nussbaum (nut), but decorative trees like Tannenbaum (fir tree), Eichenbaum (Oak) and Buxbaum (box tree), as well.

Animals are well represented in the list of family names. There is Hirsch (deer), and the older Herz (hart) from which we get Herzl, Herzberg, Herzog, etc. There are wolves, bears (Berman), lions (Loeb—a name usually taken by a *Levi*), Elefants and eagles (Adler). Many of these names have biblical references.

Besides nature, there is, of course, the stomach, and many families are named after favorite delicacies. In our community we have several Weintraubs (grapes), Korn and Weitz (both stand for wheat), Zucker, Karp, Kalb (calf), Honig (honey) and Kugelman. Recently I met a Dr. Van Kuchen who told me that his family name used to be Pfannkuchen (pancake) in Vienna. The food names may actually represent occupations, that is, people who dealt in these commodities rather than the food items themselves. Thus we have both Ochs (ox) and Oxenhandler.

We have only scratched the surface of the long and fascinating list of Jewish family names. None of the illustrious *Sephardi* names are included in our list, nor are many of East European (Russian, Polish or Ukrainian) origin. Each of these deserves a study of its own, as does the long list of Hebrew names—both traditional and newly coined or translated.

60 Coming of Age

OVER THE YEARS, SEVERAL JEWISH adults have told me, some with real regret in their voices, that they had never been "bar mitzvahed." They implied that this failure to have gone through a formal ceremony in their youth somehow made them less Jewish or even threw their very Jewishness into question.

Nothing, of course, could be farther from the truth. At age thirteen and a day a boy becomes a *Bar Mitzvah* regardless of whether or not he took part in a ceremony to mark the event. The same holds true for a girl who becomes a *Bat Mitzvah* at age twelve and a day. What then are *Benei Mitzvah*? Originally, the term referred to children who had reached physical maturity; nowadays, it refers to children whose Jewish education is deemed sufficiently advanced to recognize right from wrong and, therefore, to have reached an age at which they are expected to fulfill the commandments.

Although the ceremony that nowadays accompanies this coming of age is of relatively recent origin, we do find the notion that a male child reaches religious majority at puberty as early as in talmudic times. Rabbi Eleazar directs the father of a boy who has reached the age of thirteen to recite the blessing: *Barukh shepetarani me'onsho shel zeh* (Praised be He who has relieved me from the responsibility for this one. *Genesis Rabah* 63:14). Given that from now on the child is regarded as a responsible person and liable for his own actions, the parent is free from accountability for the child's transgressions.

With responsibilities also go privileges. At age thirteen, the boy is counted in the *minyan* and may be called up to the Torah for an *aliyah*. And that is the basis of the modern Bar Mitzvah celebration. Since about the fifteenth century, a festive ceremony has evolved at which the boy is honored by being called for the first time to the public reading of the Torah.

A comparable ceremony for a *Bat Mitzvah*, though common today in most Jewish congregations, did not take place until less than a century ago. On Shabbat, March 18, 1922, Judith Kaplan, daughter of Rabbi Mordecai Kaplan, the founder of Reconstructionist Judaism, was the first girl to be called up to the Torah to read part of the weekly portion from the scroll, as well as the *haftarah*, the appropriate portion from the Prophets.

IN GENERAL, ASIDE FROM HOLIDAYS and Shabbat afternoons, the Torah is read three times a week: during morning services on Shabbat, on Mondays and on Thursdays. On Shabbat, seven people are called up for *aliyot* plus the *maftir*, the one who is privileged to read the *haftarah*. On Mondays and Thursdays only three people are called up for, after all, these are workdays. (The shorter readings on these days consist of only the first *aliyah* of the weekly portion that will be read on the following Shabbat.)

In many non-Orthodox congregations in the United States, it has become customary to honor both boys and girls on the first Shabbat following their thirteenth birthday. (This, as we pointed out above, is merely a convention; any public reading of the Torah would serve as well.) The *Benei Mitzvah* are called after the obligatory seven honorees have been called, and thus have the honor of reading the *haftarah* to the assembled congregation.

In Orthodox circles the *Bar Mitzvah* is often called to the Torah on a weekday morning. This allows him to put on his *tefillin* (phylacteries) for the first time—other than for learning purposes—because they are not worn during Shabbat and festival prayers. Also, it makes it possible for out-of-town guests who would not travel on Shabbat, to come to the ceremony.

Since no *haftarah* is read on weekdays, the *Bar Mitzvah* has to learn only the Torah *trope* (cantillations)—that he, most likely, will have picked up already during regular attendance at services—and prepare a *devar torah*, that is, demonstrate his erudition by giving a learned talk.

Usually, however, the preparation of the *Benei Mitzvah* for the happy occasion will include learning the special cantillations with which the Torah and the *haftarah* are chanted, as well as the blessings before and after each. No musical notations, no punctuation marks and not even the vowels of the alphabet are indicated in the Torah scroll. Thus, reading from the Torah is no simple matter, and the achievement of the young people, demonstrating their commitment to carrying on our tradition, is impressive.

It is traditional to throw a party in honor of the *Bar* or *Bat Mitzvah*. This has been justified by a *midrashic* interpretation of Genesis 21:8,

"And Abraham made a great feast on the day that Isaac was weaned." Weaned is taken to mean not from his mother, but from childhood to *mitzvot*, that is, on attaining his religious majority. In some circles, though, Abraham's "great feast" has become a very elaborate and costly affair. There are special consultants who, for a fee, will not only suggest a theme but also help with every detail in carrying out an African Safari, Star Trek, or A 1950s Bar Mitzvah. To the dismay of many, especially the rabbinic community, there is often more "bar" than "*mitzvah*" in these celebrations.

61 Temple vs. Synagogue

WHILE GROWING UP IN ISRAEL, I had never heard of a temple as a Jewish place of worship, much less seen one. The Hebrew term for synagogue is *bet keneset*, literally, a house of assembly. (The word synagogue, is an exact translation of the Hebrew term: it comes from the Greek word *synagein*, to bring together.) In Germany, the synagogue that my grandparents attended and where I also went to *ḥeder* as a young child, was always referred to as a *besmedrish* (*bet midrash* or house of study).

These traditional names for a synagogue (*bet keneset* and *bet midrash*) are both descriptive and highly appropriate. Historically, the synagogue was much more than just a place where Jews went to pray at fixed times of the day. Although synagogues existed already before the fall of the Holy Temple, they filled at most a marginal role—certainly within the Land of Israel. However, after the destruction of the Second Temple in the year 70 C.E., prayer supplanted animal sacrifices and synagogues replaced the Temple in Jerusalem and became the centers of Jewish religious life.

The synagogue was (and is) a democratic institution without the religious hierarchy that governed the Temple. The rabbi is, as the title indicates, a learned person and not technically a minister. Throughout its history, but especially since the Middle Ages, under ghetto conditions, the synagogue functioned not only as a place of worship and study but also as a communal center. It was the place where wayfaring strangers would be fed and housed, where marriages took place and births were announced. It was the center for proclamations, for legal decisions, and for the taking of oaths. In the synagogue, mourners were publicly comforted, and any person could demand redress of a wrong done to him or her, by stopping the reading of the Torah (!)—a custom which, though not often seen, exists to this day. Unfortunately, all too often the synagogue also served as a last stronghold where the Jewish community defended itself against attacking mobs set on its annihilation.

The learning and teaching functions, though, were the most important. A synagogue may be turned into a house of study, but the latter may not be turned into a synagogue, in accordance with the dictum that the function a religious object or building fulfills may only be changed so as to effect an increase in holiness. The names by which synagogues are called in different countries (*scuola, escolo, shul* or even *Judenschul*) mirror the religious-educational character of the synagogue.

Among the Ḥasidim, the *besmedrish* underwent notable changes in the direction of increased folksiness. It became structurally less imposing, replaced pews with tables, did away with professional *ḥazzanim* (cantors) and readers and was affectionately referred to as the *shtibl* (little room), reminiscent of the store-front churches in the United States.

WHEN DID TEMPLES COME ONTO the scene? The designation "temple" for a synagogue was one of the changes introduced by the Reform Movement in Germany at the beginning of the nineteenth century. The first reform temple was founded in Hamburg in 1818. The reforms in religious ritual came about in large part in reaction to the *Haskalah* (Jewish Enlightenment) movement, which prompted many young Jews to adapt their way of life to the non-Jewish world around them. Many abandoned Judaism as outmoded and irrelevant.

In response, some communities introduced reforms in both ideology and ritual. At traditional services, the number of prayers recited in the German language was increased greatly and all prayers referring to the coming of the Messiah and the Return to Zion were deleted. Temples introduced mixed-gender seating, counted women as equals, did away with the wearing of the traditional garb, *tallit* and *kippah* and introduced organ music into the service. The role of the rabbi changed to resemble more closely that of a Protestant minister.

By 1870, most German Jewish communities were beginning to favor reform, and actively engaged in formulating and consolidating the principles of reform. Briefly these were: "Israel's mission was not to remove itself from other nations and to re-establish a separate kingdom, but rather to unite with all other earthly creatures on the basis of common faith in one God." It follows that any custom, law or prayer that ran counter to this mission should be changed or abolished. Gone was the notion of a Diaspora and the thrice-daily uttered hope of redemption and return to Zion. Israel's mission was here and now, and the Reform temple became its symbol — the ultimate, rather than temporary, replacement of the Jerusalem Temple.

The mid-to-late nineteenth century immigration of German Jews brought Reform Judaism to these shores, where it flourished. The first two temples I encountered in the States (Temple Emanu-El in San Francisco and Temple Beth Israel in Portland) are both impressive, large structures with great domes arching above them. Basing myself on this sample of two, I believed that all Reform synagogues were trying to emulate the Jerusalem Temple not only in name but also in structural splendor. It was only when I started reading in the history of American Jewry that I learned that there was more to it than that: there was an ideology behind all this and not just an edifice complex.

62 *Kohanim:* **The Unbroken Line**

SOME TIME AGO, AT A party, I was introduced to two gentlemen, a Mr. Cohen and a Mr. Katz. Both names usually indicate that their bearers are *kohanim* (priests, plural of *kohen*). Since I am also a *kohen* I quipped: "What do you call a group of three kohanim?" To my surprise, Mr. Cohen answered that I'd better find a term for two *kohanim* for he was not a *kohen*. He explained that when his grandfather came to this country, the immigration officer at Ellis Island, who could not spell his grandpa's complicated Russian name, arbitrarily assigned him the name Cohen.

Mr. Cohen's story, of course, echoes the common—but probably false—belief among American Jews that their family names were changed at Ellis Island. However, with ships' manifests clearly spelling out the names of the immigrants, it is much more likely that Mr. Cohen's grandfather decided, either upon arrival or afterwards, to change his name to Cohen.

Most name changes, of course, went in the direction of more American-sounding names. Why would anyone want to change his name to Cohen? Traditionally, *kohanim*—members of the Priestly Caste—carried a level of prestige among Jews that is largely forgotten today. In traditional congregations, the first person accorded the honor of being called up to the Torah at the public reading of the weekly portion has to be a *kohen* (if there is one present); the communal recitation of the *birkat hamazon* (Grace after Meals) is prefaced with the phrase, *birshut hakohen* (with the permission of the *kohen*) if one is present among the diners; a first-born male child has to be brought to a *kohen* to be redeemed and, of course, it is the *kohen* who pronounces the Priestly Blessing at designated times during prayers.

Today, many congregations do not observe these time-honored customs. Usually, the Priestly Blessing is recited only by the cantor, or whoever leads the prayers, rather than by the *kohanim* present at the worship service. Only in Orthodox and the more traditional Conservative synagogues is this ritual (the oldest in Judaism) regularly re-enacted.

There, on the Festivals and High Holy Days, the *kohanim*, their heads and raised hands covered by prayer shawls, face the congregation and intone the well-known verses from Numbers, 6:24–26: "The Lord bless you, and protect you! The Lord deal kindly and graciously with you! The Lord bestow His favor on you, and grant you peace!" In *Eretz Israel*, the priestly benediction is recited daily.

This honored status of the *kohen* is the basis of the old joke about the Jewish man who says to a rabbi, "Rabbi, I'm willing to make a large donation to the Temple building fund on condition that you make me a *kohen*." Speechless, the rabbi finally asks, "Tell me, why do you want to be a *kohen* so badly?" "Well, Rabbi," answers the man, "my grandfather was a *kohen*, my father was a *kohen* and I want to be a *kohen* too...." The point of the joke is, of course, that if the man's father was a *kohen* he is automatically a *kohen* as well.

By Jewish law, the line of *kohanim* is passed on from father to son and goes back all the way to Aaron, older brother of Moses. Aaron and Moses belonged to the tribe of Levi, the only tribe that, according to tradition, did not join in the worship of the Golden Calf in the desert. As a reward, the tribe was chosen to carry out certain priestly duties. In the desert, those mainly involved the offering of daily and holiday sacrifices and of blessing the people. On Yom Kippur, the *kohen gadol*, the High Priest, had the additional important task of performing the ritual of atonement for himself, for the priestly community and for the people as a whole.

The duties of the *levi'im* (Levites), the remaining male members of the tribe, consisted mainly of guarding and transporting the Tabernacle—the portable religious shrine that housed the Ark of the Covenant—and its vessels during the Israelites' 40-year wandering in the wilderness. They were also responsible for assisting the *kohanim* in carrying out their tasks.

When the Israelites entered the Promised Land of Canaan, the special status of the tribe of Levi was underscored by the fact that it was the only tribe not allotted a specific piece of land. While the other eleven tribes were given clearly identified territories, the members of the tribe of Levi were scattered and lived among the rest of the Israelite tribes.

Because they had no land of their own to farm, special provisions had to be made for the maintenance of the Levites. According to the Torah, each tribe had to cede to them a certain number of cities and areas of pasture land. The 48 cities thus established included the six Cities of Refuge—three on either side of the Jordan—which served as asylum from the traditional blood revenge for anyone who had unintentionally killed somebody. (Given the size of the tribe of Levi at the time of the conquest of Canaan—about 50,000—these cities were, at best, large villages or small towns.)

In addition to this land, the *levi'im* received *ma'aser* (tithes) from the rest of the population—ten percent of whatever the land produced. They also received voluntary donations, especially of food, during the various festivals. From the *ma'aser* they received, the *levi'im* themselves had to tithe, that is, they had to allot ten percent to *kohanim* of their choice.

The *kohanim* were recompensed even more generously. They were entitled to a large portion of most of the animals brought as sacrifices to the altar, as well as to a portion of the money donated to the Temple. They were given the right to the firstborn of any domestic animal, to the first harvests of wheat, fruits and oil and to the wool from the first shearing of the sheep.

Besides these perks, the *kohen* had several other sources of income, including a *terumah* or portion (about two percent) of the harvest which farmers could donate to a *kohen* of their choosing. The *kohanim* also received five silver shekels for performing the *pidyon ha-ben* ceremony (redemption of the firstborn son), a ceremony still performed in traditional Jewish circles today.

ABOUT 300 YEARS AFTER THE conquest, around 1000 B.C.E., King David made Jerusalem the capital of his kingdom and transferred the Ark of the Covenant there, This move concentrated all religious worship in Jerusalem. When his son, King Solomon, built the Holy Temple there, it became the only place at which sacrifices could be offered to the God of Israel. The existence of the Temple regularized the services and greatly expanded the role—and the political power—of the *kohanim* and the *levi'im*.

The *kohanim* were the only persons usually allowed to enter the Priestly Court, approach the altar and perform the intricate rituals of the various sacrifices. They also served as administrators of the Temple treasury and of Temple affairs in general. Besides their sacred duties, they are mentioned as scribes in the royal court, as judges and as teachers. The *levi'im* served in the Temple as gatekeepers, as maintenance personnel, as musicians providing both choral and instrumental music during divine services and as teachers of the general population among whom they lived.

In order to qualify for ritual duties, a *kohen* had to meet several strict requirements. Besides being of impeccable moral character, the *kohen* also had to be physically presentable. The short sentence in the Torah, "He who has a blemish shall not approach to make offerings to God" (Leviticus 21:17) became the basis for a list of 140 physical blemishes. According to Maimonides, being intoxicated, in need of a haircut, having unkempt or disarrayed garments or being completely bald or left-handed (!) would render a *kohen* unfit for service in the inner confines of the Temple.

Most important, though, was the genealogical requirement: to be eligible for service, a person had to be the son of a *kohen*. The *Sanhedrin HaGadol*, the Supreme Court of the Jewish People, ruled on the genealogical suitability and fitness for service of the *kohanim*. The court maintained extensive and meticulous records of the lineage of each of the priestly families. In fact, these pedigrees were maintained even during the Babylonian exile (586–538 B.C.E.). They provided the basis on which even greater prestige and power was assumed by the priesthood when the remnant returned to *Eretz Israel* and rebuilt the Temple.

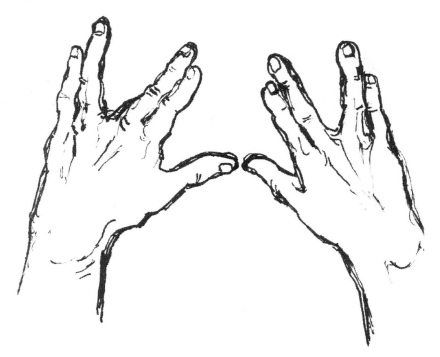

THE SPIRITUAL LEADERSHIP OF THE priestly caste and its preeminence in Israelite society ended with the destruction of the Second Temple by the Romans in 70 C.E. Prayer replaced the sacrifices and Rabbis replaced the Priests. It was Rabbinic Judaism which developed the laws by which Jews have lived ever since. The genealogical records have long since been lost and any claim to a kohanic status is based purely on an individual's family history. How creditable can such claims be after almost 2,000 years of life in the Diaspora?

The answer to this question is surprising.

Recent DNA studies have found a common set of genetic markers — the "*Kohen* Gene" — in over 80 percent of self-identified *kohanim*. These findings hold for Jews from different countries, for different groups such as *Ashkenazim* and *Sephardim* as well as for Jewish populations that have been separated geographically from one another for over 1,000 years. Modern science, it seems, has validated the claim of a common ancestry of the *kohanim* — a line that goes back 3,300 years to the first High Priest, Aaron, brother of Moses.

How Others See Us

63 Blood Libel

PESAḤ, THE FESTIVAL OF PASSOVER, is one of the most joyous holidays in the Jewish calendar. Passover is associated in most people's minds with the celebration of freedom and with warm feelings of family togetherness. Yet, over the centuries, this time of year was often the time when the most terrible accusation was leveled against Jews, an accusation that often brought pogroms in its wake—the infamous Blood Libel.

It is hard to imagine how anyone could believe so preposterous a lie, yet Jews have repeatedly been accused of ritual murder, that is, of using human blood for ritual purposes. As far back as the second century C.E., pagan Greeks accused religious minorities (Jews as well as Christians) of sacramental baby-killing, and the baby-eating that goes with it. By the Middle Ages, however, Jews were the main victims of this monstrous accusation. The allegation usually charged that Jews murdered innocent Christian babies and used their blood in baking *matzah*, the strange unleavened bread they eat during Passover. It is, of course, no accident that the Blood Libel surfaced during Passover, for Passover and Easter are closely related in time and religious fervor runs high around Easter. It was during that period that mobs used to ravage Jewish communities with the dread cry of "Christkillers" and the mocking "Hep! Hep!" (*Hierosalyma est perdita*— Jerusalem is lost) on their lips.

With the spread of Christianity, the Blood Libel became the hallmark of European anti-Semitism during the later Middle Ages and even, incredibly, into the twentieth century. The first case of Blood Libel goes back to Norwich, England where in 1144 Jews were accused of having "bought a Christian child before Easter and tortured him with all the tortures wherewith our Lord was tortured and on Long Friday hanged him on a rood in hatred of our Lord." Similar allegations, involving Jewish sadism and hatred of Christians, and echoing the Passion of Jesus, are recorded in Blois, France in 1171, Saragossa, Spain in 1182 and many other places in the twelfth and subsequent centuries.

One famous case from England concerns a Christian child, Hugh of Lincoln. The accusation states that in the year 1255 "the child was first fattened for ten days with white bread and milk and then… almost all the Jews of England were invited to the crucifixion." The victim, by the way, became known as "Little Saint Hugh" and is the subject of "The Prioress' Tale" by Chaucer. It is typical of medieval anti-Semitic tales.

In 1494, the citizens of Tyrnaua, a city in Slovakia, explained that the Jews need blood because:

> Firstly, they were convinced by the judgment of their ancestors, that the blood of a Christian was a good remedy for the alleviation of the wound of circumcision. Secondly, they were of opinion that this blood, put into food, is very efficacious for the awakening of mutual love. Thirdly, they had discovered, as men and women among them suffered equally from menstruation, that the blood of a Christian is a specific medicine for it, when drunk. Fourthly, they had an ancient but secret ordinance by which they are under obligation to shed Christian blood in honor of God, in daily sacrifices, in some spot or other.…

Although church authorities were often involved in the murder trials, no pope has ever condoned the Blood Libel. Several popes had the allegations thoroughly investigated and referred to them publicly as "sinful slander." Unfortunately, nobody listened.

From the seventeenth century on, Blood Libel cases spread into Eastern Europe where — skipping 300 years of recurring bloodshed — the last and most famous of the ritual murder trials, the infamous Beilis case, took place.

The case started on March 12, 1911, shortly before Passover, when the horribly mutilated body of a 12-year old boy was discovered in a cave near Kiev, Russia. Although a police investigation pointed to a gang of thieves as the perpetrators of the crime, four months later, the Czarist government, helped by a vicious anti-Semitic campaign in the press, arrested Mendel Beilis, the Jewish superintendent of a nearby factory, and accused him of the crime. What follows is termed "The Bloody Hoax" in the title of a recently translated book by Sholom Aleichem. Beilis was imprisoned for over two years before proceedings started. The trial, which lasted 34 days, was a sham. It quickly became apparent that powerful anti-Semitic groups and the authorities were engaged in a conspiracy to use the child's murder as a provocation for new pogroms to counter the rising tide of liberalism in Czarist Russia.

Some of the testimony was ludicrous. The main prosecution expert on Judaism, a priest by name of Father Pranaitis, kept insisting that he had learned about the custom of using Christian blood in baking *matzah* from an old woman by name of Baba Basra. Poor man: Somebody had told him what to say and he had confused the name of one of the tractates of the Talmud, *Bava Batra* (pronounced "Bobbe Basra" in Yiddish), with the Russian word for Grandma which it resembles. To demonstrate to the jury the incompetence of the witness, the defense lawyer, in an inspired stratagem, asked him, "Who was this Bobbe Basra and when did she live?" to which the learned Father answered, "I didn't know her." The Jewish part of the audience broke out in laughter.

The worldwide reaction to the vile accusation was astounding: Heads of state, hundreds of leading authors and scientists, the press and many organizations protested the Beilis trial. If the reaction of the civilized world had been of like magnitude in 1938–39, the Holocaust might well have been averted.

On October 23, 1913, the court reconvened to hear the judge's summation and charge to the jury. The two-hour talk has been characterized as "more fit for a prosecutor than for a judge." The mood in the courtroom, at least on the part of the Jewish audience, was depressed and pessimistic. The well-known author, Vladimir Nabokov, one year later wrote about the jury: "People were astonished and perplexed by the choice of jurors.... The jury consisted of practically illiterate peasants and commoners...." Still, this group of illiterate and, most probably, anti-Semitic Ukrainian peasants returned, after only one hour-and-a-half, a verdict of "Not guilty!"

It was only after the collapse of the Czarist regime that all the details of the conspiracy (including the name of the true murderer) came to light. A recent book by Ezekiel Leikin, *The Beilis Transcripts, The Anti-Semitic Trial That Shook the World*, makes fascinating reading. It presents the complete trial record in English. Likewise, in a gripping study, *Blood Accusation, the Strange History of the Beilis Case* (1966), the noted U.S. author Maurice Samuel gives real insight into the forces that staged this "most bizarre and extraordinary frame-up of modern history."

The world followed the Beilis case with horror and disbelief on the eve of World War I. People assumed that now that it was over, the terrible Blood Accusations would finally be laid to rest. Yet, 21 years later (May 1934), the "Big Lie" was revived in a special issue of *Der Stürmer*, the propaganda paper of the Nazi party in Hitler Germany.

ONE MIGHT THINK THAT THIS ridiculous calumny would have finally died out by the end of the twentieth century. Unfortunately, it has taken a bizarre twist in the last two decades, resurfacing in the media of Muslim countries all over the world. Whereas in the Middle Ages the Jews were accused of killing Christian babies for their blood, the updated version has them stealing body parts from defenseless Arab Muslims.

An article by Eric J. Greenberg in the December 31, 2004, edition of the Jewish newspaper *Forward*, reports that "Israel and America are being accused of stealing body parts from defenseless Arab Muslims." Greenberg describes an Iranian television series entitled "Zahra's Blue Eyes." Set in Israel and the West Bank, each episode opens with graphic scenes showing a Palestinian girl with eyes surgically removed, her face covered with bandages over the empty sockets. The first episode shows Israelis disguised as United Nations workers visiting a Palestinian school, ostensibly to examine the children's eyes for diseases, but in reality to select which children's eyes to steal for transplants. Subsequent episodes in the series cover the theft of other body parts. The whole show closely resembles similar anti-Semitic productions aired previously on Egyptian and Lebanese television.

This Iranian television series seems to have inspired an article written by Fakhriya Ahmad, originally published in Saudi Arabia's government daily *Al Watan* on December 18, 2004. Ahmad repeats the old Blood Libel but adapts it to his own purposes: Christian babies are transformed into Iraqi Muslims. Moreover, the perfidious Jews now become American soldiers. (This was readily accepted by his readers, for conventional wisdom proclaims that Jews control the United States and her policies. Iraqis often refer to American soldiers as "Jews.")

In his article, Ahmad asserts that, "Secret European military intelligence reports indicate the transformation of the American humanitarian mission in Iraq into a profitable trade in the American markets, through the practice of American physicians extracting human organs from the dead and wounded, before they are put to death, for sale to medical centers in America."

Ahmad also claims that Iraqi prisoners killed in Abu Ghraib and other prisons were forced to undergo operations for the purpose of extracting their organs. "Following their mutilations," he adds, "the bodies were discarded far from the prisons to conceal the facts."

The fact that a spokesman for the United States Department of Defense, LTC Barry Venable, called the allegations "garbage" has not kept the article from being reprinted in the Syrian daily *Teshreen* and in the Iranian daily *Jomhouriye Islami*. By now, it has become part of the conventional wisdom of the region. It is true: old lies never die; they are just being updated for new, receptive audiences.

64 "People of the Book"

JEWS LIKE TO REFER TO themselves as the "People of the Book." They believe that this sobriquet reflects the high value put on education in Jewish culture. No doubt, many of them are surprised to learn that the term "People of the Book" (*ahl al-kitab*) first appears in the Koran, the holy book of Islam. There, it refers to Jews as well as to Christians, that is, to all who accept the Hebrew Bible. Mohammed accepted large parts of both the Jewish Bible and the "New Testament" and pointed to places in them which allegedly predict his coming. It was only when the Jews of the Arabian peninsula rejected him as prophet and refused to convert to Islam that he became critical of and even abusive toward Jews. He changed the direction in which the faithful faced in prayer from Jerusalem to Mecca, and *yaum el jum'a* (the Day of Assembly) from the Sabbath to Friday.

Although Islam accepted "The Book" as holy, in general, there are some significant differences between the Muslim version and the Hebrew original. For instance, Muslims believe that it was Ishmael, Hagar's son (who became the progenitor of the Arab people), and not his son Isaac that Abraham was willing to sacrifice as proof of his faith. The annual festival of *eid al adha*, which comes at the end of the *haj* (the pilgrimage to Mecca season), commemorates the event. Another discrepancy concerns Miriam, the sister of Moses. She and Mary (Miriam in Hebrew), mother of Jesus in the New Testament, are rolled into one person, Maryam, in the Koran.

Muslims claim that their version is authentic because there is an unbroken succession of people (known by name) starting with those contemporary with Mohammed, who can testify to its correctness. They maintain that the Jewish version is a counterfeit, forged by the Jews to further their own claim of superiority.

DID IT HELP OR HURT the Jews and Christians who lived under Muslim rule to be regarded as the "People of the Book?" Actually it helped, for it conferred upon them the status of *dhimmi*, that is, "Protected People." Islam demanded conversion (by the sword if necessary) only of heathen and idolaters; Jews and Christians, as adherents of monotheistic religions, were spared that fate (except in some rare instances). In that respect, Jews living under Muslim rule were significantly better off than those living in many Christian countries, where they often faced the choice of conversion, death or, at best, banishment.

Although *dhimmi* were accorded freedom of religion, they did not enjoy full civic rights. Special restrictions were imposed against Christians and Jews, such as those specified in the *Covenant of Omar* (Omar ibn abdal Aziz, 717–720 C.E.). Both minorities were compelled to pay a special poll tax and could not testify against Muslims in a court of law. They could not ride horses or mules as their neighbors, but only donkeys and then only sitting sideways on packsaddles. They had to step off the sidewalk when encountering Muslims. Restrictions were put on the design and construction of their homes and places of worship. Interestingly, and an omen of darker times to come, the *dhimmi* had to wear identifying clothes and hats — Christians, blue; Jews, yellow!

The fact that different rulers repeatedly called for stricter enforcement of these restrictions seems to indicate that they were often honored only in the breach. Literacy and a high level of skills undoubtedly explain the fact that Jews were often employed in high administrative positions. Whatever the restrictions, they certainly did not stifle the tremendous flowering of scholarship, art, science and commerce under Moorish rule that we have come to call the Golden Age of Spanish Jewry. That Golden Age ended in 1492 with the expulsion of all Jews from Spain under Ferdinand and Isabella, the new Christian rulers of that country.

Medieval Disputations: Tournaments for God and Faith

FORCED DEBATES BETWEEN JEWS AND Christians were always a matter of deep concern to the Jews. These disputations, as they are called, were often staged as public spectacles at which representatives of the Jewish community were forced to debate with Christian clergy the relative merits of their respective religions.

Theological debates took place not only between Jews and Christians. The Mishnah records challenges to Jewish monotheism by Hellenistic pagan beliefs as far back as the second century C.E. From the seventh century on, debates took place in various Muslim countries, often among representatives of all three monotheistic religions. Yet most of the important debates took place during the Middle Ages in Christian Europe. Unlike the Romans or the Muslims, who were not necessarily interested in converting Jews to their faiths, Christian debaters had a very specific goal in mind: to show Jews the error of their ways and to induce them to accept Christianity. Disputations, then, were usually not debates between two opposing parties of equal standing in society who were trying to arrive at the truth. They were more like public trials in which the Jewish "debaters" had to defend certain passages from the Bible or the Talmud and justify their interpretation thereof.

Christianity had, of course, adopted the Jewish Bible as part of its own sacred writings, but saw it mainly as a series of prophesies presaging the coming of Jesus as the Messiah. Thus, the early debates dealt, on an unsophisticated level, with what Christian scholars believed to be hints in the *Tanakh* relating to Jesus. For instance, they point to Genesis, Chapter 48 in which Jacob before his death blesses his grandsons Menasseh and Ephraim. Their father, Joseph, had positioned them so that Jacob's right hand would lie on the older, Menasseh's head. But Jacob crosses his hands, thereby favoring the younger son. When Joseph points out what he thought was an error, Jacob says, "I know, my son, I know," and then, speaking of the first-born, he adds, "his younger brother shall be greater than he." Christians saw in the crossing of the arms a portent of the Holy Cross and of the superiority of the younger religion, Christianity, over the older, Judaism. Another argument concerned the fact that the most frequently used names for God in the Jewish Bible — *Elohim* and *Adonai* — are both plural nouns in Hebrew, which "clearly points to the existence of the Trinity."

In the thirteenth century, because of internal tensions within the Church, attempts to convert Jews to Christianity became more insistent. It was often the apostates, who had to demonstrate their loyalty to their new faith, who were arguing the Christian position. Thus, in Paris in the year 1240, Nicolas Donin, a former Jew, pointed to the Talmud as being full of foolish errors and blasphemies against the Church. He saw in it the source of Jewish stubbornness in clinging to their misguided religion. One of the arguments concerned anthropomorphism, the portrayal of God in human form or with human traits, which was so common in the Jewish Bible and in the Talmud.

Based on these accusations, the King of France ordered a public debate, or rather a public trial, at which the Jews were allowed only to defend themselves against the accusations brought against them. As usual, the occasion turned into a grand show with hundreds of the nobility and clergy in attendance to enjoy the spectacle and, as usual, the Jews were judged to have lost the "debate." As a result, Pope Gregory IX banned the Talmud everywhere and on Friday, June 6, 1242, twenty-four wagonloads of its volumes were burned. Because of this outcome, the number of conversions increased significantly, as it did after many of these Tournaments for God and Faith. Still, most of the Jewish population clung more fervently to their faith, which explains Martin Luther's frustrated exclamation that, "It is as easy to convert the Jews as the Devil himself!"

THE RELIGIOUS DISPUTATIONS THAT TOOK place in Christian Spain exhibited far less of the excessive fervor found in the less civilized countries of Germany and France. The more secure position of Spanish Jewry, both politically and socially, can be seen in the famous Great Disputation at Barcelona in 1263. King James I of Aragon asked Rabbi Moses Ben-Naḥman (also known as Naḥmanides or by his acronym RaMBaN), the leader of Spanish Jewry and the greatest sage of his time, to debate with the convert Pablo Christiani. Naḥmanides consented to do so if he could speak without restrictions: "I intend to speak in a decent manner, but it will be of my own free will." Before a dazzling crowd at court, Naḥmanides refuted the arguments leveled against Judaism and aggressively attacked the Christian notion that the Messiah had come: "The prophet says, "Nation shall not lift sword against nation, neither shall they learn war anymore." Yet from the days of Jesus until now the world has been filled with violence and pillage. The Christians, moreover, shed more blood than other nations; how hard it would be for you, your Majesty... and for these knights of yours if they were not to learn war anymore!"

At the conclusion of the debate, the King awarded Naḥmanides a prize of 300 dinars, declaring that never before had he heard "an unjust cause so nobly defended." At the urging of the Bishop of Gerona, Naḥmanides summed up his arguments in a book, *Sefer ha-Viku'aḥ* (*The Book of the Disputation*). Four years after the debate, Dominican friars brought Naḥmanides to trial on charges of blasphemy, and, despite the King's guarantee of his right to free speech, convinced the Pope that he be punished. Naḥmanides fled Spain and settled in *Eretz Israel* in the year 1267.

A PLAY, THE DISPUTATION, BY Hyam Maccoby, based on the actual Barcelona debate, was performed by the Jewish Repertory Theater in New York in May, 1997.

As WE HAVE DISCUSSED BEFORE (see Chapter 39, page 131), the division of the Bible into chapters, which we still use today, was a Christian innovation. It was introduced by Cardinal Stephen Langton, Archbishop of Canterbury (c. 1150–July 9, 1228), and forced upon the Jews during the period of religious disputations to provide both sides with a common system of reference to the Scriptures. Before that, the *Tanakh* was not divided into chapters, nor are Torah scrolls to this day.

Some of the chapter divisions the Cardinal instituted are inappropriate in terms of Jewish theology or *halakhah*. For instance, Chapter 1 of Genesis, which tells the story of creation, ends with the sixth day. The seventh day, Shabbat, clearly the culminating event of the story, instead of ending the chapter, is transferred to the first three verses of Chapter 2. Some editions of the *Tanakh* rectify these mistakes by the way the text is presented. (In this case, verses 1–3 are printed at the end of Chapter 1.) They do, however, indicate the traditional chapter divisions to conform to the accepted system of reference. See, for example, *The Torah, A Modern Commentary*, Rabbi W. Gunther Plaut, ed. (Union of American Hebrew Congregations, 1981).

66 The Roller-coaster History of British Jewry

THE HISTORY OF BRITAIN'S ATTITUDE toward Jews is not very admirable. Jews have lived in England as far back as Roman times. But even when Jews were tolerated in England, the attitude toward them was usually colored by British self-interest. William the Conqueror invited the first large groups of French Jews to come to England in 1066 C.E. because he hoped that their skills and talent would bolster the British economy. However, because they could not own land or belong to any of the guilds that controlled all manufacturing in the Middle Ages, Jews were forced into the one occupation that was forbidden to Christians—money lending. The results were predictable: Jews were hated for what they did and despised for their beliefs. Still, they were tolerated as long as they were able to pay the heavy taxes imposed on them.

Anti-Jewish atrocities, though, were frequent. The first Blood Libel accusation in Europe was leveled against the Jews of Norwich in 1144 C.E. The body of a 12-year old boy was found outside of town and the Jewish community was accused of ritual murder. Although the story was clearly a fabrication, Bishop William de Turbeville went to great length to spread the cult of the "boy-martyr." He hoped thereby to attract pilgrims—the tourist trade of his time—and with it considerable income for his town and diocese.

The twelfth and thirteenth centuries saw much shedding of Jewish blood in England. Only heavy ransom payments handed over by the threatened communities were sometimes able to avert the frequent massacres. Under King Edward I, 600 Jews were imprisoned in the Tower of London and 200 of them were hanged. (As an aside: it was he who required that the yellow badge that Jews had been forced to wear on their clothing be in the shape of the two Tablets of the Law.) Finally in 1290, when he had milked them dry and could extract no more taxes from them, Edward ordered the expulsion of the approximately 16,000 Jews left in England and the confiscation of their houses and goods.

Also with this expulsion, England led the rest of European countries, many of which followed suit over the next several centuries.

For 365 years, Britain was *Judenrein*, unsullied by the presence of Jews. In 1656, Oliver Cromwell, the Lord Protector of England, permitted them back into England. There is no question that Cromwell, Puritan that he was, believed in the prophet Isaiah's promise that God would collect His people from the "end of the earth." For wasn't that the very name of England—*Angle-terre*? Therefore, according to this fanciful etymology, it was God's will that Jews reside in England. But, it is equally true that he was well aware of the material advantages to be gained by readmitting Jews to England.

It was the celebrated Dutch scholar and diplomat, Rabbi Menasseh Ben-Israel, who made the case for readmission most convincingly. In a lengthy humble address, Rabbi Menasseh applauds Cromwell's decision and demonstrates the benefits of attracting the rich Jews of Amsterdam to London and, with them, their enormously profitable trade interests with Central and South America. He asks only for the free exercise of the Jewish religion in England.

In response to Cromwell's oral guarantee allowing them to practice their faith openly, a number of *Sephardi* Jews from Holland immigrated to London. They founded a synagogue in 1657; however, it was not until 1698 that the Act for Suppressing Blasphemy gave legal recognition to the practice of Judaism in England.

After this, an increasing number of (mainly) *Ashkenazim* of central European origin came to England and, generally, were well treated. Several were knighted and many served in Parliament. Famously among the latter is Benjamin Disraeli who became a distinguished Prime Minister under Queen Victoria. Disraeli was always regarded, and heckled in Parliament, as a Jew although he was not. His father had a falling-out with his *Sephardi* congregation and, as incredible as it may sound, had his children baptized.

Britain greatly benefited economically from the presence of Jews and they helped guide British policies, notably in the last two centuries. Among those we must mention is Sir Moses Montefiore, the great philanthropist, who helped resettle Jews in *Eretz Israel*, thereby supporting British policies in the Middle East. There is also Lionel Rothschild, who was responsible for many government loans, including those for the relief of the Irish famine, the financing of the Crimean War and the purchase of the bonds that gave Britain control over the Suez Canal. Rothschild had been elected to Parliament in 1847 (the first Jewish member), but the existing legislation prevented him from taking the necessary oath of office. He could not take his seat until a compromise was reached and this restriction was removed in 1858.

Even the Balfour Declaration, given in November 1917, which provided the long-sought-after British support for Zionism and was sympathetic to its goal of establishing a Jewish homeland in Palestine, was based in part on political considerations. After three years of devastating war in Europe, Britain sought to secure the financial and political support of American Jewry, and to enlist the Jews of *Eretz Israel* in its war with Turkey.

Not long before that, Britain had tried to induce the Arabs to revolt against the Ottoman Empire by promising Arab leaders political independence after the war. In a series of letters between Sir Henry McMahon, British High Commissioner in Egypt, and Hussein bin Ali, Sharif of Mecca (who later proclaimed himself King of Hejaz), Britain pledged to support Arab sovereignty over large areas of the Middle East. A year later, when the Balfour Declaration was given, the Arabs accused Britain of duplicity for making mutually irreconcilable promises to both Arabs and Jews regarding Palestine. Britain countered that Palestine belonged to the area explicitly excluded in the McMahon correspondence.

With Turkey defeated at the end of World War I, the League of Nations granted Britain a Mandate to guide Palestine in its economic development and prepare it for political independence. The Mandate's primary purpose was to put into effect the Balfour Declaration. But, rather than being supportive of the political aspirations of the *Yishuv*, Britain's attitude and actions became progressively more obstructive and repressive. Were it not for its infamous White Paper, which severely limited Jewish immigration, *Eretz Israel* might have been able to save hundreds of thousands from the hands of the Nazi butchers.

Of course, there have been many Englishmen sympathetic to their Jewish compatriots, but as the current wave of verbal and physical attacks shows, anti-Semitism was never far below the surface. There is an old saying that if you scratch a—Ukrainian, Pole, Hungarian,... you fill in the blank—you don't have to go very deep to discover an anti-Semite. England seems to belong to that list.

67 Anti-Semitism in the British Halls of Ivy

A FRIEND FORWARDED THE FOLLOWING message from the well-known Israeli author and columnist, Naomi Ragen:

Dear Friends,

Israeli Amit Duvshani, age 26, applied to Oxford for a doctoral position. This is the reply that he received from Andrew Wilkie, Nuffield Professor of Pathology, Weatherall Institute of Molecular Medicine, The John Radcliffe, Headington, Oxford, UK.

I think that we should all, every one of us, send the good professor a message on his Fascist tendencies and his disgusting Nazi-like tactics in dealing with Israelis (i.e. Jews, and don't we all know where you are coming from Herr Professor). My own letter to Herr Professor is below.

Naomi Ragen

From: Andrew Wilkie
To: Amit Duvshani
June 23. 2003
Subject: Re: Your PhD application

Dear Amit Duvshani,

Thank you for contacting me, but I don't think this would work. I have a huge problem with the way that the Israelis take the moral high ground from their appalling treatment in the Holocaust, and then inflict gross human rights abuses on the Palestinians because they (the Palestinians) wish to live in their own country.

I am sure that you are perfectly nice at a personal level, but no way would I take on somebody who had served in the Israeli army. As you may be aware, I am not the only UK scientist with these views but I'm sure you will find another suitable lab if you look around.

Yours sincerely, Andrew Wilkie
Nuffield Professor of Pathology,
Weatherall Institute of Molecular Medicine,
The John Radcliffe, Headington,
Oxford OX3 9DS, UK

THE EMAIL NAOMI RAGEN SENT to Professor Wilkie read as follows:

Dear Dr. Wilkie,

Ah the wonders of the internet. No longer can closet anti-Semites ply their trade under the cover of darkness. Now the entire world knows who you are, as your disgusting bias in dealing with Amit Duvshani is now out there for all to see. The Jews have been living in the Land of Israel for three thousand years. Indeed, as Disraeli pointed out, while your ancestors were still swinging from the trees, ours were priests in the Temple of Solomon.

You can accept or reject Mr. Duvshani on the basis of his academic qualifications. But to reject him on the basis of his qualifications as a human being because he served in the Israeli army and defended the Jews in their ancestral homeland shows me, an Israeli, a Jew, the author of six books, one play, and numerous articles that you Brits are still swinging from the trees in a Neanderthal morality that stinks of eras only lately ended.

For shame, Herr Professor. For shame, Oxford.

Naomi Ragen

FOLLOWING RAGEN'S SUGGESTION, I SENT the following email to Professor Wilkie:

Professor Wilkie:

The last time Jews were kept out of universities because they were Jews was in Nazi-Germany. Too bad that you chose to follow that nefarious example. I'm sorry you rejected Mr. Duvshani's application on the sole ground that he is an Israeli and that he served in the Israeli army, for such guilt by association somehow doesn't fit into my notion of British fair play. I'm happy that Israel does not operate by your standards of "morality," for otherwise the Arab students who constitute 1/3 of Haifa University's student body would find themselves out on their ears. (The various Arab members elected to the Israel Knesset would certainly not have stood still for that!)

I wonder whether a student of any of the countries whose record of human rights abuses (according to Amnesty International) far exceeds that of Israel's would have met the same rejection, or whether it was indeed anti-Semitism that motivated you. Only you know the answer.

Ze'ev Orzech, Professor emeritus,
Department of Economics
Oregon State University

A FEW DAYS LATER, MY friend forwarded to me a letter from Professor Shalom Lappin of King's College, London to the Chair of Wilkie's department. Subject: "A serious incident of bigotry in your Department."

Dear Professor Waldmann,

The correspondence below [he's referring to the letter from Wilkie to Duvshani on page 221] was forwarded to me by a colleague at SOAS. If Professor Wilkie's note to Amit Duvshani, an Israeli applicant to your D. Phil program, is indeed authentic, it constitutes direct evidence of a serious act of racist discrimination (on grounds of national origin) against Mr. Duvshani by a senior member of your Department. I would appreciate clarification of this incident as soon as possible. I have written to Sally Hunt, the Secretary General of the AUT, and to Professor Arthur Lucas, the Principal of King's College, London, where I am a professor, as well as other colleagues in the UK and members of the press asking them to investigate this matter. I find it extraordinary that this sort of blatant discrimination is tolerated in your institution. If this matter is not corrected internally, it seems to me that there are grounds for asking the Commission on Racial Equality and appropriate governments offices to take it up. I look forward to hearing from you at your earliest convenience.

Sincerely, Shalom Lappin
Professor, Department of Computer Science
King's College, London

IN RESPONSE TO THE MANY letters of protest that were sent to Professor Wilkie and Oxford University both the university and Professor Wilkie apologized. The latter stated: "I have been in contact with [Duvshani] to apologise, not just for my original email but also for causing his name to become so publicly prominent."

The matter was referred to Oxford's Visitatorial Board (which is made up of two High Court judges) which upheld the charges against Dr. Wilkie and suspended him from academic duties without pay for two months. Subsequently, Oxford University announced on behalf of Pembroke College that, in light of the ruling by the Governing Body of the College, the university accepted Dr. Wilkie's resignation as a Fellow of the College and as a member of its Governing Body.

IN HIS APOLOGY DR. WILKIE states: "I recognise and apologise for any distress caused by my email of 23 June and the wholly inappropriate expression of my personal opinions in that document." What is distressing is the fact that this well-known professor apologizes for the "distress" he caused to Amit Duvshany (and, presumably, to the university), but not for the personal opinion he expressed. At no time does he reject or convey regret for what many recognized as the underlying motivation of his action: racial discrimination and, specifically, anti-Semitism. Many commentators on the case have pointed out that Dr. Wilkie's rejection of Duvshani's application on the grounds that he (Duvshani) had completed the compulsory three-year service in the Israeli army, in fact, rejects all Jewish students from Israel under the umbrella of his humanitarian concerns for the Palestinians.

The sad fact is that Dr. Wilkie had no reason to camouflage his personal views or apologize for them; they were in perfect accord with sentiments prevailing in much of the environment in which he worked. The Duvshani incident was but part of the ongoing boycott of Israeli academic institutions and scientists. The attempt to isolate Israel, which is not unique to Britain but had started there, has led to the exclusion of Israeli academics from professional meetings and routine rejection of journal articles they submitted for peer review. Such isolation runs counter to the free sharing and exchange of ideas that is the *sine qua non* of academia. Given Israel's record of innovative research in electronics, medicine and science in general, it is beyond doubt that it is the countries that boycott Israeli scientists and products who will suffer in the long run.

68 Why Did the Jews Leave Morocco?

ON A TOUR OF MOROCCO, we were often told of the Jewish presence in this North-African country, but always in the past tense. "This is where the *Mellah*, the Jewish quarter used to be" or "these workshops once belonged to Jews." Such observations were often accompanied by a complaint:

> We don't understand why the Jews left Morocco. After all, Jews have been here for centuries. This is their country, their roots are here. Moreover, there were no anti-Jewish sentiments in Morocco. On the contrary, Jews were highly regarded because of their skill in metalworking and other crafts. It was simply not fair for Israel to seduce Moroccan Jews to leave here in order to give them lands taken from the Palestinians.

Half the argument is correct, of course. Jews had lived in Morocco for a long time—certainly since biblical times. (According to numerous local legends, possibly even since before the destruction of the First Temple!) Tombstones with Hebrew inscriptions found in the ruins of the Roman-built town Volubilis, dating back to before the first century C.E., attest to that. According to Ibn Khaldun, the great Arab historian, several Berber tribes had converted to Judaism before the coming of Islam to Morocco in the eighth century. Jewish communities existed in all major cities and trading towns throughout the country. Jews were among the first settlers of Marrakesh. By the tenth century, the city of Fez had become a center of Jewish learning renowned beyond the borders of Morocco.

The second part of the argument, however, is specious. True, many Moroccan Jews were skilled artisans, especially in the metal and textile trades, and their work was highly esteemed. We had a chance to see a priceless collection of their art when we stumbled upon the Belghazi Museum in Rabat—a private museum of traditional Moroccan arts. There were rooms upon rooms of richly embroidered kaftans, wedding shawls and bridal finery; intricate gold and silver jewelry and inlaid musical instruments and weapons—many attributed to Jewish artisans.

Yet, although their creations were highly prized, the craftsmen themselves were not. The same religious-social dynamics that drove Jews in Christian societies into money-lending—a despised activity—pushed many Moroccan Jews into occupations that were shunned by their Muslim neighbors or forbidden by the Koran (such as wine making or distilling). The *Encyclopedia Judaica*, under "Goldsmiths and silversmiths" speaks of "the contempt in which artisans were held by the Arabs." Because manual labor was disdained in Muslim countries, it was often religious minorities, the Jews among them, who worked in these occupations.

IT IS DIFFICULT TO GENERALIZE about a period that extends over 2,000 years. The socio-economic condition of Moroccan Jewry over these centuries varied in direct relation to the degree of political and religious freedom they enjoyed. Periods of relative freedom and prosperity, though, were the exception and were invariably followed by periods of intolerance and economic misery. Even when there were no massacres and forced conversions, Jews and Christians, as *dhimmi* (protected, non-Muslim minorities), became second class citizens under Islam and were denied many of their civil rights. They had to pay a poll tax, were forced to live in separate, miserable *mellahs* (walled Jewish quarter, specific to Morocco), could not sue a Muslim in court, had to wear a distinguishing yellow cloth on their hats, had to step off the sidewalk when encountering a Muslim and so forth.

There were periods when the restrictive laws were not enforced and the Jews of Morocco prospered. The fourteenth century and the end of the fifteenth century, when the Spanish exiles found refuge in the *Maghreb* (Muslim North Africa), were two such periods. Overall, though, the lives of Moroccan Jews have been described as being "subjected to such repression, restriction and humiliation as to exceed anything [done to Jews] in Europe."

The condition of the Jews did not improve until 1912 with the establishment of the French Protectorate, which granted them equality and religious autonomy. When, during World War II, Morocco came under the rule of Vichy France, King Mohammed V successfully fought the deportation of Jews, thereby saving the lives of thousands. Still, uncertainty about their future and grinding poverty induced many to emigrate. With the establishment of the State of Israel in 1948, they found an alternative. In 1948, the Jewish population of Morocco stood at 270,000. Except for the small number of better-off families who had emigrated to France or the United States, and the few who still live in Morocco today, all chose to make Israel their home.

A mass exodus of this magnitude cannot be explained solely by the pull of Israel. It requires powerful forces pushing families to abandon their homes: Moroccan Jews were escaping the anti-Jewish sentiments and poverty pressing on them in their own society, while hoping for a life of dignity and relative ease in the Promised Land.

69 The Shame of France: *Vel d'Hiv*

PREJUDICE AND VIOLENCE AGAINST JEWS go back a long way in French history. From the persecutions and forced conversions of the early Middle Ages to the massacres of Jewish communities during the Crusades; from the repeated expulsions, especially of the 12th and 14th centuries to the international scandal of the Dreyfus Affair of the 19th century—French anti-Semitism was never far below the surface. The 20th century saw the French police actively assist the Nazis during WWII in the round-up and deportation to the death camps of more than 76,000 Jews, few of whom survived the war.

The most infamous and brutal of these round-ups took place on the night of July 16-17, 1942. It has become known as *La Rafle du Vel d'Hiv*. (*Vel d'Hiv* was the name by which the *Vélodrome d'Hiver*, the indoor bicycle stadium that stood not far from the Eiffel Tower, was known.) On that night, in the pre-dawn hours of the morning, 4,500 French policemen rounded up 12,884 Jews—including 4,051 children—from Paris and her suburbs and carted them off to various collection points in the city. Over 7,000 of them were herded into the *Vel d'Hiv*. From these places, they were transferred to French transit camps and, from there, deported to certain death for practically all of them in the gas chambers of Auschwitz.

The conditions at the *Vel d'Hiv* were indescribably inhumane. For the five days that most of the dazed families were detained there, there was no food other than the little they had managed to pack in the few minutes given to them so early in the morning. There was one working water tap—real torture in the crowded conditions and the stifling July heat. The three available toilets (nine others had been blocked off because they were accessible from the outside) quickly overflowed and ceased to operate. Letters that were smuggled out speak of people dying because of lack of medical attention, of the many who broke down and the ones who went out of their minds or committed suicide.

After five horrible days, the families were transferred to three transit camps: the infamous Drancy on the outskirts of Paris and two others in the Loiret district, Beaune-la-Rolande and Pithiviers. Here, the horror increased. Upon arrival, the children (from the age of two) were separated from their parents. The parents were transported to Auschwitz to die in the gas ovens. The children were collected at Drancy, also awaiting transport to Auschwitz. Some waited as long as ten weeks, suffering greatly from the lack of medical care, insufficient food and the brutality of all but a few of the French guards. Records show that more than 6,000 Jewish children were arrested and transported to their deaths between July 17th and September 30th, 1942.

CAN THIS ATROCITY BE BLAMED on the Nazi forces that were then occupying France? Operation *Vent printanier* (Spring Breeze), the code name of the operation, was jointly planned by the German occupation administration and French police authorities. However, the French police not only collaborated but actively and eagerly assisted the Nazis in carrying out their death mission. The Germans had proposed to limit the arrests to Jewish men, sixteen years and older, and it was on the authority of Pierre Laval, Prime Minister of the Vichy regime that cooperated with the Nazi extermination of the Jews, that the decree was extended to include entire families.

Of course, not all French men and women collaborated with the Germans in carrying out "the final solution." Many Jews were saved through the selfless efforts of individuals who often risked their own lives in doing so. Over the years, *Yad Vashem*, the Holocaust Martyrs' and Heroes' Remembrance Authority in Israel, has recognized 3,000 French citizens among those honored as "Righteous Among the Nations." In January, 2007, French President Jacques Chirac conferred the prestigious Legion of Honor award to 160 of them for their efforts saving French Jews during World War II.

Yet, for more than fifty years, France had refused to accept any blame for what happened at the *Vel d'Hiv* in 1942. On Sunday, July 16, 1995, less than two months after his election, President Jacques Chirac, became the first French leader to break through the shroud of silence. He publicly recognized France's complicity in the arrests and deportation of the 76,000 Jews, including 11,000 children, who went to their deaths during the Holocaust. At a ceremony held to commemorate the *Vel d'Hive* round-up and subsequent deportations, Chirac acknowledged that, "France, homeland of the Enlightenment and of human rights, land of welcome and asylum, France, on that very day, accomplished something irreparable. Failing her promise, she delivered those she was to protect to their murderers."

UNFORTUNATELY, FRENCH ANTI-SEMITISM IS NOT a matter of the past. Even in the 21st century, newspaper accounts and letters to families and friends frequently tell of outrages against synagogues and attacks against Jewish individuals and institutions. French Jews feel that their position in French society has become precarious. They feel threatened and many have left France. Others are considering emigration. This is true not only for relative newcomers such as the children or grandchildren of recent immigrants who had to leave Muslim countries in North Africa because of anti-Jewish sentiments there, but also of families that have lived in France for centuries.

The French government proudly declares that it does not keep statistics by race or religion. Therefore, when the press reports these despicable incidents, they are usually portrayed as simple acts of vandalism rather than as hate-crimes. It is rare that a French journalist or politician will admit that France is riddled with anti-Semitic bigotry. True, the fact that there are now, in the year 2010, ten times as many Muslims in France as Jews has much to do with the recent epidemic of anti-Jewish violence. Still, public attitudes tend to condone these criminal acts and the French authorities do little to stop or control them. The *Vel d'Hiv* incident of almost 70 years ago was not as anomalous as one would like to believe.

70 Righteous Gentiles

ONLY A TINY FRACTION OF my very large family survived the Holocaust. They were the ones who had left Europe in time and immigrated to *Eretz Israel*. Of those that stayed in Europe, all the rest perished except for only one uncle and three cousins—two boys and a girl.

My uncle had joined the Polish army from which he later deserted in order to join the Jewish Brigade that had been formed in Palestine as part of the British army. The girl, Hadassah, who was eight years old when Hitler overran Poland, survived the war in a convent. At the end of the war, my uncle, who was still in uniform, found Hadassah and brought her to Israel. He had to abduct her from the convent because the nuns did not want to let her go, laying claim to her as a baptized Catholic.

The two boys' lives were saved by the actions of Righteous Gentiles—one by a Dutch couple, the other by a Japanese diplomat. "Righteous Among the Nations" is a talmudic phrase that is now applied to non-Jews who saved the lives of Jews during the Holocaust at risk of their own lives. In 1953, the *Knesset* (Israeli Parliament), directed *Yad Vashem*, the Holocaust Martyrs' and Heroes' Remembrance Authority, to establish a memorial to the Righteous Among the Nations. The aim was to honor individuals who, at personal risk and without remuneration, had rescued Jews during the Nazi period.

The youngest of the cousins, Eli, less than a year old at the outbreak of the war, was handed tearfully to neighbors in the town of Utrecht, Holland, the evening before my uncle and aunt were deported to Auschwitz. The International Red Cross found him after the war and he came to live with my family in Tel Aviv. The Dutch couple, who thought of Eli as their own, was unhappy about giving up the six-year old, but acknowledged the prior claim of the family. Eli later saw to it that they were recognized and honored as Righteous Gentiles.

Ya'akov, or Kuba as the family called him, was the oldest of the three. In 1939, at the age of thirteen, he had been enrolled for about a year as a student at the venerable, 150-year old *Mirer Yeshivah* (rabbinical seminary). Mir is a small town not far from Kovno in Lithuania, in which 50 percent of the pre-war population was Jewish. Kuba's parents, who lived in Warsaw, were not present when he became a Bar Mitzvah in December of 1939, three months after Hitler started his *Blitzkrieg* against Poland. They perished in the Holocaust as did all the others in the family. Kuba, however, and the rest of the Mirer student body and faculty survived because of the heroic, selfless actions of a Japanese official who set the dictates of his conscience above those of his government.

Once the German forces occupied Poland, 10,000 Polish Jews fled to Vilna in Lithuania—still neutral at the time—to escape the Nazi terror. After the Soviet Union annexed the country in late July 1940, it became clear that it would not serve as the hoped-for haven for either members of the Orthodox Jewish community or for the intelligentsia among the refugees. The Jews were caught in a trap: most Western countries would not accept refugees and the way East, through the Soviet Union, was barred to them as well. As foreign nationals (predominantly Poles, in this case) they were allowed to leave the Soviet Union only if they possessed a visa to another country. Their search for a way to reach the free world seemed hopeless. But then occurred what many of the survivors later referred to as a miracle. Actually, it was only the first of two miracles in our story.

Two *yeshivah* students who were Dutch citizens learned from Mr. Jan Zwartendijk, the acting Dutch consul in Kovno, that, "No visas are necessary for Curacao (a Dutch island in the West Indies). The Governor has exclusive authority to issue landing permits to foreigners, a power he rarely exercises." The students persuaded the Consul to write only the first sentence in each of their passports. Zwartendijk understood the desperate situation of the Jews and agreed to the ruse. He had a stamp made with this "Curacao End-Visa" statement, which he entered into thousands of Jewish passports once the word had spread among the refugees.

With this Dutch "visa" in hand, they now rushed to the Japanese consul general in Kovno, Mr. Chiune Sugihara, and asked for transit visas to Japan. Sugihara, who fully realized the spurious quality of the end-visa, nevertheless cabled the Japanese foreign ministry asking permission to grant transit visas. His request was denied. And here the second miracle happened: Sugihara decided, in direct contravention of his government's orders, to issue the visas. As the numbers of applicants swelled, he kept furiously entering Japanese transit visas into the no-longer-valid Polish passports—visas which provided their holders the key to escape and to life. Twice more, in ever more urgent tones, he sought his government's approval; twice more he was denied and ordered to desist.

Sugihara issued visas for about three weeks until his ministry removed him to a post in Berlin. During these weeks, he issued several thousand visas, working day and night. The exact number of visas can only be estimated (numbers run from 3,000 to 10,000) for he ended up putting his signature on plain sheets of paper when the official forms ran out, and kept handing out visas even as his train pulled out of the station.

Because of this Righteous Gentile, my cousin Kuba was able to get to Japan, from there to Shanghai, and, after the war, to New York. He was part of the *Mir yeshivah*—the only *yeshivah* whose total faculty and student body were saved from the Holocaust. On a list Sugihara prepared before he was dismissed from the Foreign Service, Kuba's visa appears as #1895, issued on August 17, 1940.

71 "Righteous" Nations

THOUSANDS OF POLISH JEWS WHO had fled Nazi-occupied Poland into Lithuania were saved from almost certain death through the heroic actions of one individual and the policies of two sovereign governments. The individual was Chiune Sugihara, the Japanese Consul General in Lithuania, who acted in defiance of direct orders in issuing thousands of transit visas and whom we discussed in the previous chapter. The two governments were: the Soviet Union, which allowed the refugees to traverse its territory and travel East when all avenues of escape to the West were closed to them; and Japan, which provided most of them with shelter first in Kobe and, after Pearl Harbor, in Shanghai until the end of the war.

What motivated the two governments to act in this lifesaving manner? Can we apply the term "Righteous Among the Nations" not only to individuals but to nations as a whole? Were the Soviet Union and Japan motivated by humanitarian considerations? Let us start with the easier of the two. In the case of the Soviet Union the motivation was straight self-interest or plain greed. It had decided that it was more profitable to hold the Jews for ransom than to ship them off to forced-labor camps in Siberia, as it had done with Soviet-bloc Jews who had indicated a desire to leave the country. And so, two Intourist offices were opened in Kovno just months before Germany invaded Lithuania to provide the necessary travel documents: each document at the cost of $200 and each ticket on the trans-Siberian railroad at $250— a sum of $450 payable not in the local currency, but only in dollars! That sum, the equivalent of about $10,000 today, was unattainable for the large number of the refugees who were penniless. Fortunately, the American Jewish community, in part through agencies such as the Hebrew Immigrant Aid Society (HIAS) and the American Jewish Joint Distribution Committee (JDS), was willing to perform the traditional *mitzvah* of ransoming prisoners and provided the means of passage to all who needed it.

The case of Japan is more complicated and more interesting. Japanese policies toward the Jewish refugees were inconsistent and mirrored the ambivalent attitude of the government toward Jews in general. On the one hand, we find Sugihara's superiors in the Foreign Office repeatedly ordering him not to issue any transit-visas to Jews for Japan. On the other, the authorities accepted the thousands of refugees who arrived with spurious end-visas in Polish passports that were no longer valid, and did not return them to the country whence they came—as many Western regimes had been doing. Moreover, even when it became clear that the refugees would far outstay the ten-day stopover they were granted and were piling up in Kobe as they had no place to go, Japan did not intern them.

How do we explain this strange behavior? Hillel Levine, author of the book *The Search for Sugihara*, ascribes it to what he calls a "Conspiracy of Goodness"—the uncoordinated humane actions of individual Japanese, both government officials and ordinary civilians. Levine speculates that Sugihara's courageous actions were contagious and somehow might have infected others who came in touch with the Jewish refugees.

More convincing is the explanation given by Rabbi Marvin Tokayer in his book, *The Fugu Plan*. In 1919, when 75,000 Japanese soldiers were fighting in Siberia alongside Russian soldiers against the Communists, they were first exposed to that greatest of anti-Semitic lies, *The Protocols of the Elders of Zion*. This Czarist forgery alleges that there was a plot by Jewish leaders to take over all the governments in the world; that Jews controlled most of the capital of the world, its presses and means of communication; that Jewish intellectuals such as Karl Marx were inciting the masses to revolution and, finally, that it was clearly the Jews who had started the war (WWI) in order to exploit the instability created in its wake.

For two young officers this was the first exposure to any information about Jews, as Japan had no experience with either Jews or anti-Semitism. Over the years, the conviction of Jewish power grew in their minds, and as they rose in rank, they collected around themselves a group of officers who were equally impressed with "Jewish power and financial skills."

By 1934, this group of officers had become influential enough to propose to the government a scheme to bring economic development to the Independent State of Manchukuo (Manchuria) that had fallen to Japan in 1905 as part of the peace settlement in the Russo-Japanese

war. The Fugu Plan, as it was referred to, was to invite 50,000 German
Jews to settle in Manchukuo and help bring this undeveloped area to
life. The Japanese Foreign Office which made the offer, hoped the plan
would guarantee the gratitude of American Jews, who, according to
the Nazi propaganda line, controlled the banks, the press, the movies,
and, above all, the Jewish president, Roosevelt, in the United States.
In exchange for saving 50,000 German Jews from Nazi concentration
camps, American Jewish wealth would pour into Manchukuo, and
America would end the economic boycott it had mounted against
Japan.

The one objection raised against the plan was the fear that the Jews
would become too successful in Manchukuo and ultimately take over
all of Japan. The need to proceed very cautiously was voiced repeatedly
and was expressed in the plan's name: Fugu is the blowfish which,
when carefully prepared, is delicious but, when done incorrectly, will
quickly kill those who eat it.

As late as 1940, and even later, the Jewish refugees admitted to
Japan benefited from the naiveté and the misconceptions on which the
Fugu plan was based.

Righteous Among the Nations: Ernst Leitz II

As WE HAVE SEEN, THE Righteous among the Nations is the name granted by *Yad Vashem*, the Holocaust Martyrs' and Heroes' Remembrance Authority, to non-Jews who risked their lives to save Jews during the Holocaust. As of January 1, 2009, there were more than 22,700 persons from 40 countries accorded that honor, among them 460 Germans. One German not listed, who should be on the list, is Dr. Ernst Leitz II, designer and manufacturer of Germany's most famous photographic product, the Leica 35 mm camera. The story of the Leitz family's efforts to save German Jews during the Nazi regime became generally known only when it was told at the 2002 Annual Convention of the Leica Historical Society of America in Portland, Oregon.

On January 30, 1933, Hitler was appointed Chancellor of Germany and two months later the *Reichstag* (German Parliament) gave him complete dictatorial powers. Within months, anti-Semitic legislation and acts of violence directed toward Jews followed in quick succession. In April, the Nazis issued a decree defining a non-Aryan as anyone descended from Jewish parents or grandparents. They also staged a boycott of Jewish stores and businesses. In May, they burned books with "un-German ideas." Nazi Propaganda Minister Joseph Goebbels, in a speech to university students, claimed portentously, "The era of extreme Jewish intellectualism is now at an end." (Incidentally, 100 years earlier, the German-Jewish poet, Heinrich Heine, in an insightful moment, wrote: "Where books are burned, human beings are destined to be burned too.")

With increasing intensity, the Nazis applied economic pressures depriving Jews of their livelihoods. They were prohibited from owning land and were banned from the arts and from the various professional occupations. They were prohibited from being newspaper editors or accountants; could not practice law, medicine or dentistry; could not teach or hold government jobs. They were stripped of many of their civil rights. This state-enforced anti-Semitism effectively expelled Germany's Jews from active participation in German society.

Many Jews—though, unfortunately, not enough of them—saw the handwriting on the wall and tried to leave. But that was made extremely difficult: although the Nazis at first encouraged emigration (before they seized upon extermination as the "final solution" to the Jewish problem), they made sure that whoever left did so penniless. Not only were Jews prohibited from engaging in a variety of commercial and professional activities, in April 1938, all Jews were ordered to register their wealth and property, and in December of that year the Nazis "Aryanized" all Jewish-owned stores and businesses. Deprived of their property and faced with increasingly higher emigration taxes, most of Germany's Jews were trapped, unable to leave.

However, the major problem facing families trying to emigrate was the fact that very few countries were willing to grant them entry visas. Nobody wanted the Jewish refugees. During 1938–1939, in a program known as the *Kindertransport*, the United Kingdom admitted 10,000 unaccompanied Jewish children on an emergency basis. The United States insisted on strictly enforcing its very limited immigration quota: by the end of June 1939, 309,000 German, Austrian and Czech Jews had applied for the 27,000 places available under that quota. A relatively small number of Jews were able to enter Palestine. Others found refuge in Central and South American countries and even in Japanese-occupied China.

These were the conditions that led Ernst Leitz, who had opposed Nazi ideology from the start, to help his many Jewish employees and dealers who were at risk and desperate to leave Germany. By diverting funds to the United States and by having his United States affiliates "hire" them, Leitz was able to secure exit permits to send these new "employees" to the United States, supposedly to generate sales. Leitz was able to affect this rescue because it promised to provide the hard currency from abroad that Germany desperately needed. The United States was the single biggest market for the firm's famous optical products.

In America, the Leitz subsidiaries worked hard to find jobs for these immigrants, and, in fact, supported them and their families until they found gainful employment. In all, it is estimated that between 200–300 people benefited from the program in the United States. Leica branches in other countries (for instance, France, Britain and Hong Kong) participated in the program, as well.

Members of the Leitz family and firm suffered for their good works. A top executive, Alfred Turk, was jailed for working to help Jews and freed only upon payment of a large bribe. Leitz's daughter, Elsie Kuhn-

Leitz, was imprisoned by the *Gestapo* after she was caught at the border, helping Jewish women cross into Switzerland. She eventually was freed but endured rough treatment in the course of questioning. After the war, Kuhn-Leitz received numerous honors for her humanitarian efforts, among them the *Palmes Academiques* from France in 1965 and the Aristide Briand Medal from the European Academy in the 1970s. In 2007, she accepted the Courage to Care Award presented posthumously to her father by the Anti-Defamation League of the United States.

The story was kept quiet because the Leitz family wanted no publicity for its heroic efforts. Only after the last member of the family was dead did the "Leica Freedom Train" finally come to light. It is now the subject of a book, *The Greatest Invention of the Leitz Family: The Leica Freedom Train* by Frank Dabba Smith, a California-born rabbi currently living in England.

(The last part of this column is based on an article in the Milwaukee Journal Sentinel of October 9, 2002. I am grateful to my brother David for drawing my attention to it.)

73 *Magen David Adom*

UNTIL THE YEAR 2006, WHEN one visited the Web site of the international organization to which the various national Red Cross Societies belong, two curious facts became immediately apparent. First, the name of the organization was (and still is) the International Federation of Red Cross and Red Crescent Societies. Second, although the membership list of the Federation contained 177 countries, running from Afghanistan to Zimbabwe, Israel was not among them. Why was Israel's highly regarded *Magen David Adom* Society (*MDA*) not recognized by the international umbrella organization? Sadly, it was a case of political discrimination against Israel.

The initial Red Cross was established in response to the call by Jean Henri Dunant, the Swiss philanthropist, for more humanitarian behavior on the battlefield. Representatives of sixteen nations met in Geneva in 1863 to found the International Committee of the Red Cross and to adopt the first of the Geneva Conventions. The emblem they adopted was based on the Swiss flag with its colors reversed—a red cross on a white field. Dunant was co-recipient of the first Nobel Peace Prize in 1901.

The initial symbol of Red Cross Societies and of the international organization was made up of five equal-sized squares and looked like a plus sign (+). It was not meant to represent a religious symbol. Still, Turkish soldiers refused to recognize the Red Cross emblem in 1875 when Turkey brutally crushed an uprising of its Christian provinces. When this Muslim country demanded to use its own symbol—the Red Crescent—permission was quickly granted in order to prevent further atrocities. The Geneva Convention of 1929 formally recognized both Red Cross and Red Crescent Societies and accepted them as members in the International Federation.

At that time, the Federation accepted a third symbol, the Red Sun and Lion, which was the emblem of Iran under the Shah. It was only in July 1980, when Ayatola Khomeini rejected the royal Sun and Lion, that Iran's emblem was changed to the Red Crescent.

In 1949, when Israel applied for membership in the International Federation, it was rejected by a vote of 22 to 21. It had met all but one of the ten requirements for membership: it wanted to retain the Red *Magen David* (Star of David) as its emblem of humanitarian relief. *Magen David Adom* is the only Society whose application for membership has ever been rejected! The list of countries who voted for and against the application makes it clear that the vote was politically motivated.

The history and growth of *MDA* parallels that of the *Yishuv*, the Jewish community in *Eretz Israel*. It came into being in response to the Arab riots of 1929–30 when it provided first aid and medical services to the *Haganah*, the self-defense forces of the *Yishuv*. In the following years, both the size and the scope of MDA grew. In 1950, the Israeli government officially recognized *MDA* as the Red Cross Society of the State of Israel.

The president of the Society is appointed by the President of the State of Israel at the recommendation of the Minister of Health. With a corps of over 10,000 volunteers and 1,200 emergency medical personnel, *MDA* maintains over 100 first-aid stations and conducts regular first-aid classes. It runs a fleet of 800 ambulances and mobile intensive-care units throughout the country and administers an efficient blood center. *MDA* performs tasks that may be specific to Israel; during times of war, *MDA* can become an auxiliary arm of the Israel Defense Forces. On a different note, it holds in readiness twice the usual number of ambulances for the night of the Passover Seder, for experience showed that the number of miscarriages climbs to twice the average on that night. Pregnant women having labored hard to ready the house for Passover, finally relax on the *seder* night—and go into a different kind of labor.

Although *MDA* was excluded from the International Federation, it was accorded official observer status. Its emblem, the Red Star of David had to be respected, under international law, as the symbol of the medical services of Israel's armed forces. *MDA* maintains good relations with many of the national Red Cross Societies, including the American Red Cross. Internationally, *Magen David Adom* is well respected in its tasks of saving lives and providing relief to victims of natural disasters. It does not discriminate: Whether it is a flood in Italy or an earthquake in Turkey or China, Israel is quick to dispatch trained personnel, medications and supplies to disaster-stricken areas around the world.

All along, the American Red Cross society and the American government had lobbied actively for Israel's inclusion in the international body. Starting in the year 2000, the American Red Cross began withholding its annual dues payments. It took seven years (a total of $42 million) to force the issue. The protest, obviously, had an effect: In June of 2006, the International Federation of Red Cross and Red Crescent Societies accepted *MDA* as a full member. To accomplish this, the umbrella organization first had to adopt a third protocol emblem,

equivalent to the Red Cross and the Red Crescent, but free of religious, ethnic or political connotation. The new symbol, the Red Crystal, is a red square tilted at 45 degrees so that it stands on one of its points. At home, Israel is free to display its own red *Magen David*—internationally it has to appear within the square: a childish stratagem to accord Israel full membership in the international organization that she should have had 58 years earlier!

74 A Visit to the Past

THE LAST TIME I VISITED Germany was as guest of the city of Wiesbaden where I was born. For some years Wiesbaden had been inviting groups of its former Jewish citizens to come and experience the new Germany. It was an attempt by the city of Wiesbaden not to undo something that all agreed could not be undone, but rather to clear the air. Many of the group that came the year I was there—and we assembled from the four corners of the earth—held lingering resentments. These were Jews who had once lived in Wiesbaden and had been fortunate enough to have left in time to escape the Holocaust. We came with reservations, but curious to search for places out of our past, see the houses we grew up in and the schools we attended before they kicked us out as *Saujuden* (Jewish swine). For the spouses who were not Wiesbadeners, it was an opportunity to put pictures to the stories they had heard for years.

The city government, working through the Christian-Jewish Friendship Organization, had allocated a considerable chunk of money to invite, over a number of years, as many of the former residents as they could locate. Of the 1,400 Jews who lived in Wiesbaden in 1938, 1,100 had been deported in 1942, 40 had committed suicide in August of that year, and of those of us who were still alive more than half a century later, about 150 had been willing to accept the invitation.

Wiesbaden went all out to make this a VIP experience: it paid for all travel expenses plus meals and lodging for two weeks for our group of ten returnees and six spouses. We had a special bus at our disposal, a free pass to all city institutions and a charming and competent guide. We were invited to a symphony concert, a ballet performance, a meeting with the mayor, a day cruise on the Rhine River and trips into the beautiful wine country that surrounds Wiesbaden.

Despite what any tourist would rate an A-1 experience, I felt very mixed emotions during my stay in Germany. I was glad to be shown the places where I had spent the first ten years of my life, though I had only vague memories of them. Fortunately, the group included people who were somewhat older than I and who had known my family at that time. They showed me where I had lived and where my parents' store had been. Unfortunately, each of these places also evoked the bitter memories connected to it. I remembered tiptoeing down the staircase from our apartment because the neighbor downstairs, a rabid anti-Semite, used to vilify me every time we met. My parents' store did not exist any longer, but I remembered the day two brown-shirted SA-men set up a movie camera across the street and filmed everyone entering the store. Whether they actually filmed the shoppers or only pretended to, I don't know—it had a disastrous effect on the business. One of the trips our group took was to the Nerobad, a restaurant and public swimming resort to which my family liked to go on hot summer Sundays. Although the view from this well-known spa was spectacular, all I could see—in my mind's eye—was the sign that had appeared one day at the gate forbidding Jews entry to the resort.

THE MOST POSITIVE RESULT OF the trip had to do with the members of the Christian-Jewish Friendship Organization we met. Each couple of our group was "adopted" by one of the Christian families that belonged to that organization and spent as much time as possible with them. The family we connected with consisted of a father who was a geologist, a mother with a Ph.D. in biology who worked as a librarian and two teenage boys. The family was genuinely interested in better understanding and better relations between members of the two faiths, was active on behalf of Israel and was working through the organization to construct an archive of the Jews of Wiesbaden. The organization was instrumental in getting the city to allocate the space and a budget to erect a memorial to the thriving Jewish community that once was. We are still in touch with the family and consider them our friends.

I cherish some positive memories from that trip. Our guide asked whether anyone of the group was interested in visiting a high school class to answer questions about the Nazi period the class was studying. The following morning I found myself facing a class of 20 seventeen-year olds intensely interested in what happened to me and my family and in everything I could remember of my youth. We talked for an hour-and-a-half and I came away with the feeling that these youngsters had no illusions about the evil their country had committed against the Jews. I felt that they were different enough in their education and outlook to allow one the fleeting thought that had they been alive instead of their grandparents, history might have been different. Maybe....

As PART OF THE PROGRAM to reacquaint us with our native city, the City of Wiesbaden arranged a visit to the synagogue. We were impressed. The interior of the synagogue was beautiful: fine woodwork along the walls, an impressive *aron kodesh* (Holy Ark), and stained glass windows all around the ceiling, just above the women's gallery. Although the location on Friedrichstrasse seemed familiar, I did not recognize the place. Only later did I find out that it was indeed the *shul* (synagogue) to which my parents had belonged—one of the several Orthodox *shuls* in town. Together with all the other synagogues in town, it fell victim to the *Kristallnacht* pogrom in November 1938. Because the *shul* stood in a courtyard, surrounded closely by other buildings, the Nazi hoodlums did not set it afire but only ravished its interior. Since the building itself had remained intact, the Headquarters Command of the United States Air Forces in Europe helped restore it for Jewish members of the Allied Forces based in Wiesbaden and for the few, mainly old Jews, who ultimately returned there. The dedication took place on December 22nd, 1946, almost exactly eight years after its destruction. Twenty years after that, reparation payments from the German Government enabled the community to rebuild the 86-year old synagogue and bring it to its present splendor.

The other Wiesbaden synagogues were never rebuilt. Those of the prewar Jewish community who had not managed to emigrate in time (primarily to *Eretz Israel* and the United States) had been deported and killed. There was no need for more than one *shul* for a community of fewer than 300 persons, made up of those who found their way back to Wiesbaden for one reason or another, and of Russian immigrants who fled the new wave of anti-Semitism there.

BEFORE THE WAR, THE JEWISH community consisted of two distinct groups: The old German Jewish families who were mainly Reform, and the *Ostjuden*, mostly Orthodox immigrants who had fled from the pogroms in Eastern Europe. The two groups experienced culture shock when they first encountered one another. The German Jewish community could trace its beginnings back to the Middle Ages, and was highly assimilated: it was educated, embraced Western culture and values and spoke pure German. Its members had fought and distinguished themselves in World War I as Germans, and, in general, regarded themselves as "Germans of Mosaic persuasion." They looked with contempt upon their East European brethren and were ashamed of them. Many of those came from poorer backgrounds, and looked different—they insisted on keeping their heads covered. Moreover, the foreigners spoke that despised, bastardized German called Yiddish.

The *Ostjuden*, for their part, were equally dismayed: "What kind of Jews are these who *daven* (worship) with uncovered heads, have an organ in their so-called temple and don't even talk *mame-loshn* (the mother-tongue, *i.e.* Yiddish)? It is, therefore, not surprising that "mixed" marriages were very rare. Not only were the cultures so very different, there were practically no occasions for young people of the two groups to meet socially and mingle.

There is an old joke about a Jew marooned on a desert island. When, after several years, he is rescued, he proudly shows off the various things he had managed to build for himself—including two synagogues. "How come two synagogues, you were all alone?" "Of course," he answered, "one, where I go to *daven* (pray), and one, I wouldn't set foot in it if you paid me."

As a youngster, growing up in Wiesbaden, I never entered the magnificent Reform synagogue on the Michelsberg, which, with its towers and high onion dome, its grand organ and choir loft, was an architectural landmark famous far beyond the city limits. For me, it might as well have been on the moon.

When I did not accompany my father to the Friedrichstrasse *shul*, I went with my grandfather and uncles to the *Talmud Torah*, one of the three *hassidic shtiblach* (small prayer-houses) in town. I preferred it by far. It was much more casual and spontaneous than my father's *shul*. There was no *hazzan*—the members took turns *davening*. During the Torah service, which seemed interminably long to us seven-to-ten-year-old youngsters, we used to roam around and get into all sorts of trouble. That kind of behavior was out-of-the-question in my father's *shul*.

It was at this *Talmud Torah* that we received our first Jewish education. For it was there, from the age of four, that we went to *heder* for two hours, every afternoon. We hated it. Not only was the learning by rote and boring, but the *melammed* (teacher) was an unkempt old man, who managed somehow to reach with his bamboo cane clear to the end of the table around which the dozen or so of us scholars were seated. Still, we learned to read the Hebrew prayers, plus some *Humash* and Rashi commentary. When, at age seven, I could no longer attend the German public school, I was enrolled in the Jewish school in Frankfurt, three-quarters of an hour away by train. When that school was forced to close, in 1936, my parents sent me abroad to a safer environment for a Jewish education: they enrolled me in a Jewish boarding-school in Bex-les-Bains, Switzerland.

Those were the memories that flooded my mind when I returned more than half a century later to the city of my birth. The comments expressed at the end of the visit by the members of our group were mainly positive. They appreciated the work of the Christian-Jewish Friendship Organization, which had sponsored the trip and the support of the City of Wiesbaden which had it financed it.

75 A Visit to What "Used To Be"

THREE YEARS AFTER OUR VISIT to Wiesbaden, my wife and I accepted an invitation from our German friends, who had hosted us there previously, to visit them in their new home in Darmstadt and tour the Black Forest region with them. When I left Germany in 1936, I was too young to appreciate what was happening to the German Jewish communities, except as it concerned my immediate family. And so, to get a broader view, we decided to accept the invitation to tour southern Germany with Andreas and Dorothee and, subsequently, visit Berlin on our own, even though we expected that it would evoke painful feelings.

Our fears proved to be true: the overwhelming feeling I experienced was sorrow, often mixed with rage. Wherever we went, we encountered the phrase "used to be"—recurring testament to the rich Jewish life that was destroyed by the Nazis. When asked, people seemed only too eager to show us the places where Jews once worked, owned businesses, worshipped—in short, lived. We kept hearing: "the town synagogue used to stand here," "this is where the rabbi used to live," "this store once was the kosher butcher shop," and so forth. Sometimes these places were marked by memorials, sometimes by simple plaques set in a wall, but often only remembered and pointed out to interested tourists.

One of the small towns we visited was Sulzburg, a town of 2,700 people in southern Germany. Our guide, an assistant to the mayor, led us to the synagogue, or rather to the building that once was the synagogue. Over the entrance to the building, a large two-story structure with stained-glass windows facing the street, were the Tablets of the Law in Hebrew. Inside, though, the sanctuary was bereft of Jewish symbols except for the *aron kodesh*, a niche in the eastern wall, in which the Torah scrolls were once stored. Inscribed over it was the traditional Hebrew phrase, "*da' lifnei mi ata omed*" (Know Before Whom You Stand). The building now belongs to the town of Sulzburg, which uses it for lectures and concerts. I wondered what might go through the minds of the people listening to a performance while facing that empty Holy Ark.

The most interesting part of the building was the women's gallery on the second floor, which extended along three sides of the hall. The town had set it aside as a museum, dedicated to the memory of the Sulzburg Jewish community. From the documents and photographs exhibited there, we learned that a Jewish *kehillah* (congregation) is first mentioned in the year 1528. With a short interruption (1604–1622), when the Jews were driven out of the district, the *kehillah's* history goes back half a millennium!

As in other small towns in the region, the Jewish community numbered no more than a few dozen families, though at its peak in 1864, it comprised 416 souls, one-third of the town's population. The *kehillah* of Sulzburg had a reputation for being very devout, and from 1787 to 1826 its rabbi served as Chief Rabbi for the whole district. The former synagogue we visited was dedicated in 1822 on what-everybody-called the *Judengasse* (Jews' Alley). With several renovations, it served the dwindling community until November 9, 1938, when, on *Kristallnacht* (Night of the Broken Glass), it was looted and its interior destroyed. Unlike so many other synagogues in Germany on that night, it escaped being set afire because neighbors, who stood idly by watching the outrage, were concerned about their own homes, which abutted the synagogue, and prevented the conflagration.

By that time, the number of Jews in town had declined significantly. Because of the harassment and restrictive laws, many of the 84 Jews that the census showed living in Sulzburg in 1933 had emigrated or moved to bigger cities. Following the *Kristallnacht* pogrom, the first group of Sulzburger Jews was deported to Dachau concentration camp. (The last 27 Jews were deported to the Gurs concentration camp on October 22, 1940.) Among the documents exhibited on the second floor is a letter from the *Gauleiter*, the Nazi leader of the region, to the local functionary of the party. It asks, after *Kristallnacht* and repeated attacks by Nazi thugs and the local police, "how many Jews had committed suicide." The answer still sends shivers up my spine, "I regret having to report that none, so far."

After the war, the building was sold to a private owner who used it as a warehouse. In 1970, the State of Baden-Württemberg in which Sulzburg is located, acquired the building. It was completely renovated and dedicated in 1988 as the "erstwhile synagogue, a place of memory and study." The good burghers of Sulzburg are proud of their "used to be" synagogue and list it in their tourist information among other worthwhile places to visit.

Berlin Holocaust Memorials

IN THE PREVIOUS CHAPTER I wrote about the synagogue that had become a memorial to the vanished Jewish community of Sulzburg, a small town in Southern Germany. There are many such towns in which the only evidence of a once-thriving Jewish community is the cemetery (unless it too was vandalized) and the memorials erected in memory of the murdered Jewish citizens.

On the other hand, there are many towns in Germany today that are experiencing an increase in Jewish population and a renaissance of Jewish communal life. However, most of the 200,000 Jews who now live in Germany are not former German Jews who survived the Holocaust. They are immigrants, mainly from Eastern Europe, who came to Germany in search of a better life. Berlin, the capital of Germany and its largest city, has the largest number Jewish residents. In 2010, the Jewish Community of Berlin (the official umbrella organization for the various congregations in the city) numbered about 11,000 members. It is estimated that there are, at least, an additional 5,000 Jews who are not affiliated with any of the organized congregations.

Berlin boasts the largest number of Holocaust memorials of any city in the world. Several of these are sites that served the pre-war Jewish community. Most notable among them is the magnificent New Synagogue (which dates back to 1861) with its gilded dome and its strangely out-of-place Oriental architecture. It can be seen from afar and is a Berlin landmark. In its heyday, it seated 1,800 men and 1,200 women for services; today it is mainly a tourist attraction requiring an entrance fee from those who wish to view the main sanctuary. A small chapel on the top floor functions as a Reconstructionist synagogue. There are several other former synagogues, community centers, cemeteries etc. that serve the revitalized Jewish community today, though most of the pre-Nazi era sites are just memorials.

There are also many memorials to the victims of the Holocaust that were erected after the war, both by the city of Berlin and by the

Federal Government. I shall describe only three of the ones that we managed to see during the nine days we spent in the city. The first is the Memorial to the Murdered Jews of Europe or, in short, The Holocaust Memorial. Like several others within the city, this memorial does not specifically commemorate the destruction of the 120,000-member Jewish community of pre-Nazi Berlin, but rather, as its name implies, commemorates the annihilation of a large part of European Jewry, the murder of 6 million souls.

The Holocaust Memorial is located in the center of the city, near the Brandenburg Gate, which once divided East and West Berlin. It consists of 2,711 rectangular concrete pillars laid out in a vast grid that covers an area of 5.5 acres. The pillars are of uniform size (about 3' by 8') but vary in height from eight inches to a towering sixteen feet. The grounds of the memorial slope downward toward the center. According to Peter Eisenman, the New York architect who designed it, the memorial represents a radical approach to memorials: it is completely abstract and uses no symbolism, Jewish or other. Although there is a below-ground visitors' center, which offers information on the Nazi war against the Jews, the memorial itself contains no plaque or other inscription mentioning either the victims or the perpetrators of the "final solution." One can look at the slabs of concrete, or even walk among them, as the architect envisioned people would, without having to contemplate the crimes this memorial is meant to memorialize. Though the visual impact was undeniable, I felt completely unmoved by it—I thought it devoid of any meaning.

In stark contrast are the Deportation Memorial at Grunewald Train Station and the *Gleis 17* (Track 17) memorial, adjacent to it. Grunewald, an affluent suburb of Berlin, was the main station from which over 60,000 of Berlin's Jews were deported to concentration and death camps. By establishing the Deportation Memorial the *Deutsche Bahn* (German railroad company) acknowledged the role its predecessor, the *Deutsche Reichsbahn*, played under Hitler in transporting some 3 million Jews to twelve extermination camps all over Europe. In 1991, it erected a 60-foot long wall at the station to honor the memory of those deported from there. The ten-foot high wall depicts human silhouettes deeply imbedded at irregular intervals into its cracked surface. An inscription tells the story of the deportations. The silhouettes elicit an immediate emotional response and evoke images of desperate men, women and children herded onto the trains nearby.

Outside the station one comes upon a second memorial, *Gleis 17*, the train track from which all of the deportations between 1941 and 1945 departed. Each section of the track now bears a steel plate that lists the concentration camp destination, along with the date of the transport and the number of passengers on it. One of the earliest of the 168 plates we saw read: "Transport of 1,252 Jews from Berlin to Lodz, October 18, 1941." The last plate bore the inscription: "Transport of 18 Jews from Berlin to Theresienstadt, March 27, 1945." Note the date—evil beyond comprehension! When it was already clear that it was losing the war, Germany was still diverting scarce transport resources from the war effort to haul Jews to the death camps in the East. I cannot stop thinking of these eighteen individuals, possibly three or four families, who had managed to survive five years of war, most probably in hiding, only to be caught and sent to their deaths less than six weeks before the end of the war.

Stolpersteine:
Holocaust Sidewalk Memorials

THERE IS ONE KIND OF memorial to the victims of the Holocaust that is very different from the memorials we have discussed so far. It is not as impersonal as The Holocaust Memorial in Berlin, nor does it memorialize entire groups of people. It is not a monumental structure and, thus, not a destination for groups of tourists interested in the Holocaust. Yet, to my mind, it is a more effective way of remembering the victims. It keeps their names alive, and serves as a reminder for generations too young to remember the events of the Nazi period. This memorial consists of small brass plates (4" by 4") that are neatly set into the pavement in front of the houses where Jews once lived. Each plate carries the name of one person, the date of birth, the name of the concentration camp to which the person was deported, the date of deportation and the date the person was murdered. Germans call these small personal memorials, *Stolpersteine* (Stumbling Stones or Tripping Stones).

The *Stolpersteine* are aptly named, for although we didn't literally trip over them while walking down a sidewalk, they caught our eye, made us stop and read the inscriptions on them. "Born... deported... murdered" — the information given does not seem adequate to describe a person's life, and yet, it set us thinking about the individuals whose names we saw embedded in the sidewalk. And this, after all, is what a memorial is supposed to do. Six million is too big a number to comprehend, but one person or two persons, or a whole family whose names one learns and whose last residence (before being deported) one views — these lose their anonymity.

The *Stolpersteine* are the work of Cologne artist, Gunter Demnig, who produced the first of the cobblestone-memorials in 1993. By the end of 2010, there were more then 22,000 of them in place in many towns in Germany. Each of the brass-covered stones sells for 95 euros, which is about $125. As a rule, they are not bought by the current inhabitants of the houses in front of which they are placed, but are projects of some civic or church group. Often, they are the end result of a unit of study by a high-school class that dealt with the Nazi period. The students research the biographies of the deported as a class project. In Berlin, it was usually individual neighborhoods that undertook and financed the memorial projects.

The first *Stolpersteine* Mimi and I saw were in front of our small hotel (a former private residence) in Freiburg. They were of Berthold and Else Weil (*née* Stern), aged 41 and 31, respectively, who were deported in 1940 to the Gurs concentration camp and murdered in Auschwitz in 1942. We also took a photograph of a group of five stones in Berlin which recall Philip and Gisela Kozower, ages 49 and 42, and their three children, Eva Rita (15), Alice (10), and Uri Aron (1-year old) who were deported in 1943 to Theresienstadt and subsequently murdered in Auschwitz.

Not everybody shares our opinion about the appropriateness of these memorials. Sometimes, householders object to having the stones embedded in the pavement in front of their homes. They fear lawsuits brought by the heirs of the previous owners reclaiming the property. Equally negative are the fears of an "inflation of memorials," expressed, for instance, by Christian Ude, four-time mayor of the city of Munich. Ude points to existing memorials and to the ceremony in memory of the victims of the Nazi terror held annually in the Dachau concentration camp. In response to this objection, the artist explained that, memorial services on annual days of remembrance may be attended... or not, and museums may be visited... or not. He hoped to bring the remembering exactly to the place where the expulsions began—at the last residences of the victims

More valid, in my opinion, are the objections which claim that the small memorials are simply inadequate to convey the enormity of the crime they are meant to memorialize. Seeing even ten or twelve *Stolpersteine* in front of a private residence, or several dozen in front of a former nursing home, may be heartrending, but it still does not fully express the horror of the Holocaust. Related to this argument is the notion that the small *Stolpersteine* may ultimately become substitutes for more substantial memorial structures. Finally—and this objection is most often advanced by Jewish communities—the paving stones lack dignity. Charlotte Knobloch, the President of the Central Council for Jews in Germany, opposes them strongly: "It is unbearable" she maintains, "to read the names of murdered Jews on tablets that are part of the pavement and regularly trampled on."

Most people, however, clearly do not share these reservations. In fact, more cities in Germany join the project each year, and since 2005, the small memorials have spread to Austria, Czechia, France, Hungary, Poland, The Netherlands and Ukraine.

The inscription reads: "Here lived Berthold Weil, born in 1899, deported to Gurs (concentration camp) in 1940 and murdered in Auschwitz in 1942."

This inscription commemorates his wife Else, née Stern, ten years his junior who suffered the same fate.

Upon Re-reading the Bible

Which Ten Commandments?

IN MARCH 1999, THE ARKANSAS House of Representatives passed a bill, on a 51–18 vote, to permit the posting of the Ten Commandments in classrooms and in public buildings. Unfortunately, the legislators neglected to specify exactly which Ten Commandments they had in mind.

There are at least a half dozen different versions of the Ten Commandments in English, and they differ in more than wording. Most people coming from a particular religious tradition are completely unaware of the existence of versions other than their own.

How can there be multiple versions of this core text, sacred to both Jews and Christians, since all of them are based on the original as given in the Hebrew Bible?

Some of the differences among the versions arise from the fact that the Ten Commandments appear twice in the Bible: once in Exodus, Chapter 20, verses 1–17, and again in Deuteronomy, Chapter 5, verses 6–22. Although the two passages are essentially alike, they are not identical. Another reason for the multiplicity of versions stems from the fact that the commandments are not numbered in the Bible. Both Hebrew versions comprise seventeen verses, which obviously can be divided in more than one way to make up ten commandments. The Bible tells us that, "[God] gave Moses the two Tablets of the Covenant, stone tablets inscribed with the finger of God." It does not describe the shape of the tablets, and certainly does not divide the ten commandments evenly between the two, neatly setting them off with Roman numerals.

In the Jewish tradition, the First Commandment is: "I am the Lord your God who has brought you out of the land of Egypt, out of the house of slavery." Both Catholics and Protestants, however, regard this as an introductory sentence and do not count it as a commandment. In a strict sense they may be right, for the sentence is not couched in the imperative mode. Yet the Bible never mentions Ten Commandments in the first place. It speaks instead of *Aseret HaDibrot*, the Ten Pronouncements. (The Greek term *Decalogue*—Ten Sayings—comes closer to the Hebrew original.) In our tradition, the opening sentence is not only counted as the First Pronouncement, it provides the authority for the remaining nine.

The Second Commandment contains three connected ideas: (a) "You shall have no other gods beside Me; (b) You shall not make for yourself a sculptured image or any likeness of what is in the heavens above, or on the earth below, or in the waters under the earth; and (c) You shall not to bow down to them or serve them ...." The Protestant version divides this commandment into two and uses part (a) as its First Commandment, and parts (b) and (c) as the Second Commandment. From here on, the numbering of the Protestant version parallels that of the Hebrew versions.

The Catholic version agrees with the Jewish tradition and sees the unity of the three ideas. The Second (Jewish) Commandment, thus, becomes the First Commandment for the Catholic Church. There is some controversy about this commandment. In the Catholic Catechism, it is reduced to part (a) alone: "You shall have no other gods beside Me." Because this leaves out the prohibitions against making graven images and bowing down to them, its detractors have accused Catholicism of condoning idolatry. Catholic scholars reply that the Catechism, which contains the principles of their faith, is merely a teaching device. The abbreviated form of the commandment is simply a mnemonic aid to facilitate learning.

The Third Commandment (second in the Catholic tradition) is usually translated as: "You shall not take the name of the Lord your God in vain. For the Lord will not leave unpunished him who takes His name in vain." The Jewish Publication Society chooses a different, probably more accurate, wording in the Bibles it publishes. This translation limits the scope of the commandment, rendering it as: "You shall not swear falsely by the name of the Lord your God; for the Lord will not clear one who swears falsely by His name." Talmudic sages, though, broadened the proscription against false oaths to include all perjury, fortune-telling, etc. and any frivolous use of God's name.

The Fourth Commandment is the first instance in which the two Hebrew versions, though clearly identical in intent, differ in their wording. Exodus 20:8 reads: "Remember the Sabbath day and keep it holy," whereas the version in Deuteronomy starts. "Observe the Sabbath day and keep it holy." Actually, the discrepancy is more substantial: The rationale given for the commandment differs in the two versions. Exodus (20:11) reads: "For in six days the Lord made heaven and earth ... and He rested on the seventh day; therefore the Lord blessed the Sabbath day and hallowed it." Deuteronomy (5:15) uses a historical perspective: "Remember that you were a slave in the land of Egypt and the Lord your God freed you from there with a mighty hand and an outstretched arm; therefore the Lord your God has commanded you to observe the sabbath day."

The Jewish sages felt that the variations had to be explained. Some maintained that both versions were uttered in one breath and heard simultaneously by the Israelites assembled at the foot of Mount Sinai. Others contended that each of the two tablets contained all ten commandments—each tablet inscribed with one of the two biblical versions.

Slight differences occur again in the Fifth Commandment. The text in Exodus (20:12) reads: "Honor your father and your mother that you may long endure on the land which the Lord your God is giving you." Deuteronomy (5:16) expands the commandment and adds to the reward for fulfilling this *mitzvah*: "Honor your father and your mother, as the Lord your God has commanded you, that you may long endure, and that you may fare well, in the land that the Lord your God is giving you."

The Sixth Commandment is unique in that most English translations distort the meaning of the original. The Hebrew reads: *Lo tirtzah* (You shall not murder). Yet most of the Christian, English-language Bibles render it as "You shall not kill." The difference is significant. Murder refers to the unlawful killing of a person, especially with malice aforethought, whereas killing is any taking of a life. The Bible clearly does not prohibit all killing; killing in war, even killing in self-defense is sanctioned. So is, of course, killing in the administration of justice (though we know that the courts imposed the death penalty only very rarely). In spite of this, the commandment has been used as an argument for pacifism, against abortion, against the death penalty, and even against the slaughtering of animals. Whatever the merits of these issues, the Sixth Commandment, as written in the original, takes no stand on them!

It is interesting to speculate why the Hebrew root *r-tz-h* was mistranslated as kill. The first translation of the Bible into English was by John Wycliffe (1525), who used the verb "kill." The Oxford English Dictionary suggests, however, that the meanings of kill and murder were practically synonymous at that time. The King James Bible (1611), which was largely based on the Wycliffe, continued the usage. When this, the most elegant and influential translation, became the authorized edition of the Bible, the use of kill became widespread and entered the language. It is interesting to note, though, that recent translations, such as the New King James Version (released in 1982) and quite a few others, have reverted to the original "You shall not murder."

Many Jewish philosophers, including the illustrious Rambam considered murder too narrow and interpreted the commandment more broadly. Ibn Ezra, for instance, a Spanish contemporary of Rambam, holds that murder can be committed by the tongue as well as by the hand. Thus, embarrassing a person in public, tale bearing and character assassination are all forms of murder. Even carelessness or indifference resulting in the loss of human life when it could have been prevented, are deemed to be murder.

The Seventh, Eighth and Ninth Commandments, "You shall not commit adultery," "You shall not steal" and "You shall not bear false witness against your neighbor," respectively, are identical in both Hebrew versions and faithfully translated in both Catholic and Protestant versions.

The Tenth Commandment is remarkable for a curious reversal in the order of the text. Exodus (20:14) reads: "You shall not covet your neighbor's house; you shall not covet your neighbor's wife, his male or female slave, his ox, his donkey, or anything that belongs to your neighbor." The Deuteronomy version (5:18), on the other hand, puts the neighbor's wife ahead of his possessions: "You shall not covet your neighbor's wife. You shall not crave your neighbor's house, his field, his male or female slave, his ox, his donkey or anything that belongs to your neighbor." How can one explain the shift in emphasis that occurred between the two versions?

The Jewish and the Protestant traditions view either of these versions as representing one idea and count it as the Tenth Commandment. The Catholic Church, however, separates the wife from the rest of a man's possessions and views "You shall not covet your neighbor's wife" and "You shall not crave ... anything that belongs to your neighbor" as separate imperatives. They, therefore, divide Deuteronomy 20:14 into two parts, which, respectively, become their Ninth and Tenth Commandments

The question of which version to use becomes even more complicated when the good legislators of Arkansas restrict themselves to the "New Testament." In Matthew 19:18–19, in answer to the question of which commandments to keep, Jesus lists only five of the ten commandments: "Do not murder; Do not commit adultery; Do not steal; Do not offer false testimony; Honor your father and mother." Then he adds, quoting Leviticus (19:18): "Love your neighbor as yourself."

One thing seems certain: no matter which version of the Ten Commandments is put up in a classroom, someone will take exception to it.

79 "The Hell!" You Say

THERE IS NO HELL IN the Hebrew Bible, and there is no devil. The "New Testament," of course, has many references to hell, and the fire that heats the place. There is much talk of the wicked being "cast into the furnace of fire. And there shall be wailing and gnashing of teeth" (Matthew 13:42). But the *Tanakh* does not have this concept. The irony, though, as we shall see, is that both hell and the devil himself end up with Hebrew names taken directly from the *Tanakh*.

The fact that we do not find hell (or paradise, for that matter) in the Bible does not mean that the Israelites thought that death spelled the end of a person's existence. They did have some notion of an afterlife in a shadowy place where people dwelled after death, *She'ol*. The term is often mistranslated—especially by Christian sources—as hell, but, it really refers to an underworld place (like the Greek *Hades*) to which the souls of all mortals, good and bad, are consigned after death. *Sheol* is not a place where the wicked are punished.

We can deduce this from the well-known story of King Saul and the witch at En-Dor (1 Samuel 7–25). Although the King had outlawed witchcraft and necromancy in his kingdom, he desperately wanted to talk to the deceased Samuel, the prophet who had crowned him, for things were not going well for Saul. Disguised, he went to the witch at En-Dor and persuaded her to divine for him the ghost of Samuel. When the ghost appeared, the first words he said to Saul were, "Why have you disturbed me and brought me up?" We see that he came up from some place below and that he was not pleased about having had to make the trip. It seems that the biblical resting place of souls, *She'ol*, was a summer resort compared with the hell Dante describes in his *Inferno*.

Ultimately, the concepts of hell, purgatory and paradise did become part of the Jewish religion. During the talmudic era, these entered rabbinic Judaism from Persian and Greek belief systems. However, there is no unanimity about either their nature or even their location. (For instance, in the Talmud we find a discussion as to whether hell was somewhere below or up in the heavens.)

Now, of course, there is a general belief in the reward and punishment for our deeds on earth. Yet, here again, there is no consensus within Jewish theology as to whether punishment can last forever or is of limited duration. Will the coming of the Messiah bring salvation for everybody or only for the righteous? Some Sages hold that reward and punishment are of this world: the reward for a good deed is the deed itself, and an evil deed is its own punishment.

There is a fairly general belief in the resurrection of the dead at "the end of days." Yet, it is not clear who will be resurrected—whether only the righteous or everybody—nor whether it will be a bodily resurrection or a more spiritual reawakening from the dead.

Back to the matter of the names: A word generally used by Jews, Christians and Muslims alike for hell is *Gehinnom* or *Gehenna*. *Gei Hinnom* (The Valley of Hinnom), is the place, south of Jerusalem, where, the Bible tells us, children were sacrificed in idolatrous rites to the god Moloch. A truly gruesome place—no wonder hell was named after it.

Satan, the devil incarnate in "New Testament" language, is mentioned repeatedly in the Hebrew Bible. However, there is no relation between the biblical Satan and Christianity's Prince of Darkness, ruler of hell. In our scriptures, Satan represents the Accuser or the Adversary, as, for instance, in the story of Job. There, we may remember, God points to Job as an upright, God-fearing man. Enter the Adversary (*Satan* in Hebrew): Big deal! Why wouldn't he be God-fearing? You've been good to him. "But lay Your hand on all he has and he will surely blaspheme You to Your face." Pretty nasty stuff that, but far from the accepted satanic behavior of post-biblical theology.

One other name by which the devil goes also comes from the *Tanakh*: *Ba'al Zevuv* (Hebrew for "Lord of Flies") is mentioned twice as the god of the Philistine city of Ekron. In transliteration, this became Baalzebub or Beelzebub. Pity the Canaanite god whose name became synonymous with that of the devil in the "New Testament."

So, although the Jews did not invent the devil, his name, his nickname and the name of the domain over which he rules, all originate in the Hebrew Bible.

80 Did Jephtha Kill his Own Daughter?

ONE OF THE MOST SHOCKING stories in the whole Bible is the story of Jephtha who, because of a rash, ill-considered vow, sacrifices his young daughter—his only child—as a burnt offering to God. Chapter 11 of the Book of Judges tells the dramatic tale.

"And it came to pass in the days of the Judges" the story starts, in the tribal period of our history, that the Ammonites, a neighboring people, waged war on the land of Gilead, that part of the land of the Israelites which lies east of the River Jordan. The Elders, much agitated, seek out Jephtha, a native son of Gilead who is described as a "mighty warrior" and ask him to head the defense of the country. Jephtha, though not eager to take on the commission, agrees to do so when the Elders press him and promise to make him head over all the inhabitants of Gilead. After repeated, unsuccessful attempts to settle the border dispute peacefully, Jephtha prepares for war. But before he sets out on his campaign—and this is the crucial part—he swears an oath to the Lord: "If You deliver the Ammonites into my hands, then whatever comes out of the door of my house to meet me on my safe return from the Ammonites shall be the Lord's and shall be offered by me as a burnt sacrifice."

Jephtha joins battle with the enemy and routs them completely. When he returns victorious to his home in Mitzpah, he is horrified to see his young daughter "coming out to meet him with tambourine and dance." He is in despair, but his daughter insists he keep his vow: "Do to me as you have vowed." She asks for a two-month reprieve during which time she and her companions would "bewail her virginity upon the hills." The Bible ends the tragic tale with the chilling words: "After two months' time, she returned to her father and he did to her as he had vowed."

Did Jephtha really bring his virginal daughter as a burnt sacrifice to the Lord? There seems to be little room for doubt in the biblical narrative. The talmudic Sages (*Ta'anit* 4a) certainly assumed it to be true; they regarded Jephtha as wicked and condemned him for what he did. The *Midrash* has it that Jephtha was punished and died a horrible death, being torn limb from limb.

The Bible, however, mentions no such punishment. On the contrary, it tells us that, after leading Israel as a Judge for six years, "Jephtha the Gileadite died and was buried in one of the towns of Gilead." The fact that the Bible does not rebuke Jephtha—even mildly—for his morally abhorrent act has been taken as an argument to throw doubt on the execution of the vow. Not only does the Bible fail to condemn Jephtha, in the only other instance where he is mentioned (1 Samuel 12:11), it refers to him as one of the saviors of Israel.

Medieval Jewish scholarship was divided in its view of Jephtha. For instance, Rabbi David Kimchi, known by the acronym Radak, (Provence, 1157–1236 C.E.), held that Jephtha's vow must be interpreted as conditional: "Whatever comes out of the door of my house... shall be offered by me as a burnt sacrifice..." —if it be suitable for a sacrifice. However, human sacrifice is not suitable; the Bible repeatedly refers to such offerings as abominations before the Lord. Therefore, Jephtha's vow was clearly illegal.

Since the vow was invalid, Phineas, the High Priest, had the authority to annul it. The Torah provides a remedy for this kind of dilemma—a money payment to the Temple treasury to take the place of the human sacrifice. Why, then, did Jephtha, who was clearly distressed by the unexpected outcome of his oath, not take advantage of this way out? And why did the High Priest not insist he do so? Our tradition tells us that both men, because of pride, refused to deal with each other. Phineas, like Jephtha, was duly punished. We are told that "the holy spirit departed from him, and he had to give up his priestly dignity." (Louis Ginzberg, *The Legends of the Jews*, JPS 1941, Vol. 4, p. 46)

Yet, the questions persist. What really became of the daughter? Did Jephtha actually carry out the oath? It has been suggested that, as a plausible alternative to murdering his daughter, Jephtha dedicated her to the Lord by forcing her to live a cloistered life as a virgin. To cite just one of the several Jewish sources that propose this way out of the moral dilemma: Adin Steinsalz, the contemporary Talmudist, reading the Scripture's account of Jephta's daughter bewailing her virginity rather than her death, and speaking no doubt from a male perspective, says, "Her fate was to remain a virgin throughout life, a tragic fate." Many others prefer this solution to the more violent one. Whether Jephtha's daughter preferred it, we do not know. At least it allowed her father to fulfill his sacred oath without committing the unspeakable act of shedding the blood of his only child.

In Handel's dramatic oratorio, *Jephtha*, composed in 1751, an angel appears and forbids the sacrificial rites to proceed—echoes of the sacrifice of Isaac! Handel, too, has the daughter devote her life to celibacy and the service of God.

There is an interesting choice of words in the Jephtha story. As is the case so often in the Bible, a person's name will telegraph an important event in that person's life (see Chapter 58 for examples). Jephtha's name in Hebrew is *yiphtaḥ* (he will open). And, indeed, in the dialog at the height of the drama, a close synonym of this verb appears twice instead of the verb to vow. Jephtha says to his daughter: "Alas, my daughter! ... I have opened my mouth to the Lord and I cannot retract." The daughter (who remains nameless in the Bible) answers: "My father, you have opened your mouth to the Lord, do unto me according to what came out of your mouth...." If there is a moral to this story, surely it must be that, had Jephtha not lived up to his name but had kept his mouth shut, he might have avoided the unimaginable—and unimagined—consequences of his vow.

81 Who Really Killed Goliath? Doublets in the Bible

WHO DOES NOT KNOW THE story of the valiant shepherd boy who slew the mighty giant? Chapter 17 of 1 Samuel has a vivid description of that dramatic event: How the Philistine forces are arrayed facing King Saul's army; how Goliath, a fearsome, ten-foot tall giant, armed to the teeth, struts in front of the Israelites challenging them to send him a warrior with whom he could fight *mano-a-mano* and thereby determine the winning side; how, for 40 days, there is no one among King Saul's warriors brave enough to accept the challenge; and how, finally, young David, youngest of the sons of Jesse, steps forward and fells the giant with his shepherd's sling and a stone he had picked up in the nearby riverbed. Is there any question who killed Goliath?

As a matter of fact, there is. Another description of the battle with the Philistines is given in 2 Samuel (21:19). There we learn that a man called Elhanan killed Goliath. The Bible goes to some length to equate this Goliath with the one David supposedly slew in 1 Samuel. How do we solve the puzzle of the true giant-killer? The Bible itself tries to do so by stretching a point. The author of the 1 Chronicles (20:5) resolves the contradiction by asserting that the Philistine giant whom Elhanan killed was the brother of the famous Goliath killed by David. The talmudic Sages were not happy with this solution and suggested that David and Elhanan were one and the same person. Elhanan, they said, was the given name of our young hero who later, upon ascending the throne, changed his name to David (the Beloved).

THERE ARE MORE THAN A few instances where the Bible tells the same story more than once, in passages that are similar yet differ in significant details. Scholars call these passages doublets. The question arises, if God revealed the Bible to Moses at Sinai, how is it possible that it contains mutually contradictory accounts of the same event?

To many biblical scholars doublets do not present a problem. They see the Torah as a divinely inspired document that evolved over centuries.

The doublet passages are presented as proof that the Bible was edited at some later date from more than one source. The editor either was careless or, for whatever reason, decided to retain the multiple versions of the event. This explanation is based on the Documentary Hypothesis—the theory that several different human authors composed the Torah. Traditional commentators who reject this hypothesis face the problem of how to reconcile the seeming contradictions.

The most famous of the biblical doublets is the Story of Creation—a doublet that, by the way, gave us Lilith, the "baddest" she-demon in our mythology (see next page). Here, at the very beginning of the Torah, we have two mutually contradictory accounts of this cosmic event. Chapter one of the book of Genesis lays out the order of creation day by day. According to this version, God created the infrastructure, as it were, on days one through four: light and darkness, day and night, the oceans and continents, the heavens and the heavenly bodies. On the third day, He also had the earth bring forth vegetation, seed-bearing plants of every kind and fruit trees of every kind. The creation of living creatures starts on the fifth day—all the sea creatures, large and small, and the birds. Finally, on the sixth day, God said, "Let the earth bring forth every kind of living creature: cattle, creeping things and wild beasts of every kind."

And then, as the culminating act of creation comes the creation of humans: "And God created *ha'adam* (a human being) in His image, in the image of God He created it; male and female He created them." In this version, there is no mention of Adam's rib, and no mention of Eve. Here, man and woman are created simultaneously. Moreover, only the first part of the sentence refers in the singular to *ha'adam* (which is not the proper name Adam because it is preceded by the definite article); all subsequent references are in the plural. The *Midrash* explains this duality by stating that the first human incorporated both male and female characteristics. Rashi clarifies the verse: "God created him first with two faces and then separated them."

The second version of the creation story, found in the very next chapter, differs substantially. In this version, Adam is created alone, before anything else is created, and only later is Eve fashioned. The order of creation here is the reverse of the one in Chapter 1: Man is created first, then the plants, then the animals, and finally, from one of the man's ribs, woman.

ANOTHER WELL-KNOWN BIBLICAL STORY WHICH appears in two different versions is the story of Noah. After God decides to destroy the world, He says to Noah (Genesis 6:18–19): "… you shall enter the ark—you, your sons, your wife and your sons' wives. And of all that lives, of all flesh, you shall take two of each into the ark, to keep alive with you; they shall be male and female." Yet in the following chapter, God amends His instructions and says: "Of every clean animal you shall take seven pairs, males and their mates, and of every animal which is not clean, two, a male and its mate."

The simple, straightforward idea of saving just enough animals to assure the survival of the species is blurred by the command to take seven pairs of the clean animals. Moreover, the division into clean and not clean in the second version is curious because the laws of *kashrut* were not formulated until at least 2,000 years after the flood. Even if the clean animals were to serve as future sacrifices by Noah's clan, as some commentators suggest, the number of *additional* animals—twelve of every clean species—seems excessive, given that most species multiply within a few months. It may be more reasonable to conclude that the clean-animal requirement refers to the dietary laws after all (as Rashi maintains), and was added to the account of the flood by a later author.

From these examples of many more, modern biblical scholarship posits two separate traditions that are combined in the biblical accounts. Scholars cite yet another piece of evidence for this hypothesis—the different Hebrew names for the Deity used by the presumed different authors. The first version of the creation story refers to the Creator 35 times as *Elohim* (God), and never uses the tetragrammaton (YHWH—usually translated as Lord). The second version, on the other hand, uses only the YHWH name and never uses Elohim. In the story of Noah, too, we again find the exclusive use of the two divine names: the first version uses only *Elohim* whereas the second version uses only YHWH.

According to the Documentary Hypothesis, the two names represent two (of several) distinct literary sources in the Pentateuch, referred to as the E (Elohist) and the J (Yahwist) documents. Richard Friedman's fascinating book, *Who Wrote the Bible?* presents an excellent exposition of the Documentary Hypothesis.

BASED ON THE FIRST VERSION of the creation story doublet, there is a Jewish tradition that Adam had a wife before Eve. It is based on the separation of the earthling (*ha'adam*) into a male human and a female human. The Bible does not mention this first mate, Eve's unnamed predecessor. However, an early medieval source, *The Alphabet of Ben Sira*, identifies her as Lilith, the fearsome she-demon who is mentioned several times in the Talmud. According to this legend, Lilith refused to submit to

Adam's domination, especially in sexual practices, demanding equal rights: "For was I not created at the same time as Adam and from the same dust of the earth?" After much strife and vain attempts to achieve equality, she flies off, leaving Adam — and Paradise.

Folklore has it that Lilith settled on an island in the Red Sea, from where she goes on nightly forays. She is blamed for endangering the lives of women in childbirth, the unexplained crib deaths of infants, and for the wet dreams of males with whom she couples in their sleep.

Because of her fiercely independent spirit, she has become the symbol of the Jewish feminist movement. She even has a magazine — *Lilith, the Independent Jewish Woman's Magazine* — named after her.

82 Safety Nets in Biblical Times

CARING FOR THE NEEDY IS ONE of the core values of Judaism. *Tzedakah* (the term coined for this *mitzvah* by the talmudic Sages) is usually translated into English as charity. Yet charity fails to convey the deeper meaning of the concept. In the Jewish tradition, charity is elevated to a religious precept. The care of the needy and the powerless is not dependent on the mood in which we wake up or how charitable we feel on any given day, but is undertaken as a divinely ordained duty, a *mitzvah*. The word *tzedakah* literally means, doing what is right.

Who were the disadvantaged that the Bible tried to protect in those early days of our history? In the mainly agricultural, tribal society that characterized most of our history in *Eretz Israel*, it was primarily the people who did not own land. In general, besides resident strangers, these were women who did not have a close male relative to support them. A widow is a case in point because she was specifically excluded from the succession of inheritance. She was, therefore, dependent on grown sons, a father or a second husband (if she remarried) for support. If she remained single and if there were no direct descendants, she was left without power or means of financial support. The same was clearly also the case with orphaned children. Indeed, the Bible enjoins us numerous times to take care of the fatherless and the widow in our midst.

The Torah is quite specific on how to assure that the needy are taken care of in an agricultural economy. It speaks of several sources of sustenance for the poor: *Pe'ah* refers to one corner of each field. That corner could not be harvested by the owner. It was left for the poor who could enter the field and harvest it for themselves. The Torah itself does not specify the amount but the Sages set the minimum at one sixtieth (about 2 percent) of the harvest. The poor did their own harvesting of the *pe'ah* to avoid the impression that what they got from the field was the result of the farmer's personal generosity. *Pe'ah* represents a privilege granted them by God, who is the real owner of the field, and not the gift of a farmer.

After a field had been harvested, the owner could not later reclaim any sheaves or bundles that had been forgotten in the field; the forgotten bundles (*shikhehah*) had become the property of the destitute.

The destitute had the right to follow behind the harvesters and pick up anything that accidentally fell from their hand (*leket*). This was what the biblical Ruth did in the fields of Boaz. Similar laws held for the grape harvest and the fruit harvests in the orchard. The Sages went so far as to suggest that non-Jewish workers, who might not be familiar with the above laws, should not be hired during harvest time.

Besides the above, a general social security tax, the *ma'aser ani*, was levied in the third and sixth years of every seven-year cycle. This consisted of a levy of ten percent of what remained of the produce (after all the above deductions). The farmer could give the *ma'aser ani* to a destitute person of his choice.

All these measures were in fulfillment of the basic command as given, among other places, in Deuteronomy (15:11): "...I am commanding you to open your hand generously to your poor and destitute brother in your land." But the biblical safety net was not limited to the brother, that is, Jewish inhabitants of the land. The Bible explicitly extends it to the *ger*, the stranger, (i.e., the non-Jewish alien) who lived among the Jews and who also lacked a power-base.

AFTER THE DESTRUCTION` OF THE Temple and the dispersion of the Jews from their land, agriculture became much less important as the economic base for the Jewish populations. New social and religious institutions had to be fashioned which would be appropriate for the changed circumstances. The talmudic Sages dealt extensively with the question of support of the indigent. The second-century Mishnah Sage, Joshua Ben-Korha, taught: "He who turns his eyes away (from a needy person) is to be considered as a worshiper of idols!" *Tzedakah* remained an important religious precept. One of the talmudic Sages, Rabbi Abin, puts it very graphically: "God stands together with the poor man at the door, and one should therefore consider whom one is confronting" (Leviticus Rabbah 34:9).

A surprising innovation of the times (appropriate for an urban population) was the public soup kitchen (*tamhui*), which the community maintained to feed the needy. The criterion was simple: "He who has food for two meals must not accept relief from the *tamhui*" or, put positively: one who did not have sufficient money for two meals a day was entitled to a free meal (*Shabbat* 118a).

(For the various forms that *tzedakah* takes in the mainly urban settings of post-biblical times, see Chapter 55, "Stretch Out Your Hand.")

83 Perchance to Dream

DREAMS IN THE BIBLE ARE not taken lightly. They often represent the means by which God communicates with an individual—a direct "communication link," to use the contemporary idiom.

An early instance of such a dream occurs when Jacob, on his way to Haran, lies down to sleep in a place that, upon rising, he was to name *Bethel* (House of God). In his dream, angels ascend and descend a stairway that reaches to heaven. More significant, however, is the fact that God, standing beside Jacob, repeats to him the promise He had first given to Jacob's grandfather, Abraham: "The ground on which you are lying I will give to you and to your offspring." This is the promise on which Jacob's descendants base their claim to the Land of Israel (Genesis 28).

In an earlier similar dream (Genesis 20), God appears to Abimelech, King of Gerar. In the dream, God confronts Abimelech and condemns him to death for having taken Sarah, Abraham's wife, when the couple traveled through his country. Abimelech protests the unfairness of the decree saying that Abraham had misled him purposely by presenting Sarah as his sister rather than his wife. Moreover, he, Abimelech, had not even touched Sarah. God accepts the King's arguments, changes His mind and exonerates the King.

God explains the connection between dreams and prophecy to Aaron and Miriam: "If there be a prophet among you, I the Lord make Myself known to him in a vision, I speak with him in a dream" (Numbers 12:6). The Bible clearly associates prophesies with dreams, as for instance, in Deuteronomy (13:2): "If there appears among you a prophet or a dreamer of dreams…" However, not all biblical dreams represent direct conversations between God and the dreamer. Still, dreams, providing visions of the future, are usually accepted as legitimate prophetic visions because they are believed to come from God.

Good examples of such prophetic dreams are the six dreams that feature so prominently in the Joseph story (a story so detailed that it takes up one-quarter of the book of Genesis). In the first two dreams, which set the plot in motion, Joseph sees himself elevated above his eleven brothers. Joseph is seventeen years old, naive and too full of himself for his own good. He relates his dreams to his brothers and barely escapes with his life. His brothers sell him to a passing caravan and he ends up as house-slave of Potiphar, a highly-placed official of Pharaoh in Egypt.

Falsely accused by Potiphar's wife, whose amorous advances he rejects as improper, Joseph is thrown in jail. There, by correctly interpreting the dreams of two fellow inmates, Pharaoh's chief steward and his baker, Joseph establishes his reputation. In consequence, he is called before Pharaoh to interpret two dreams that are causing the ruler much anxiety. Joseph correctly predicts seven years of abundant harvests followed by seven years of famine and suggests an economic plan to combat the predicted disaster. His plan concentrates all of Egypt's power and wealth in the hands of the Pharaoh, and, in a dramatic turnabout, Joseph the young Israelite slave and prison inmate is propelled to the center of power, second only to Pharaoh himself.

There is an interesting sidelight to Joseph's two dreams—the only ones whose realization lies a number of years in the future. Our Sages were disturbed by the heartless behavior of Joseph who, once elevated to power, could easily have notified his father, who was still grieving for his favorite son, that he was alive and well. Why the cruel behavior toward Jacob, his aging parent? Nachmanides, the noted thirteenth century, Spanish scholar, explains: Had Joseph revealed his identity too early, his brothers might not have bowed down before him and paid him homage. This would have run counter to the scenario of his dreams and the glimpse into the future God had granted him. What we have here, this explanation suggests, is the need to manipulate reality to make it conform to the dream. Not all our Sages agree with this rationalization.

Most prophetic visions related in the Bible do not come in the form of dreams. However, whether a prophet receives the message in a dream or while awake seems to make little difference. In the Book of Joel, God promises: "Your sons and daughters shall prophesy; your old men shall dream dreams, and your young men will see visions" (3:1). Indeed, as the following example demonstrates, sometimes it is difficult to know whether it was the one or the other.

Balak, King of Moab, wanted to wage war on Israel. To ensure his victory, he sent a delegation to Balaam, the mighty sorcerer, to enlist his aid. Balaam listened to the delegation's proposal and because it was evening said, "Spend the night here and I shall reply to you as the Lord may instruct me." Indeed, God comes to Balaam and tells him: "you must not curse that people for they are blessed." King Balak does not take no for an answer and offers a greater reward. Again we are told: "That night God came to Balaam..." The circumstances strongly suggest a sequence of two dreams, though the Bible does not report the event as such. The story has a happy ending. Despite his initial intention to curse Israel, Balaam, seeing the encampment of the Israelites, ends up with a blessing which we still recite upon entering a synagogue to pray: "How fair are your tents, O Jacob, your dwellings, O Israel."

What, then, can we say about the nature of dreams in the Bible? Modern psychotherapy theory holds that dreams arise from within the dreamer. Freud calls dreams "the royal road to the unconscious" and believes they express the basic drives of the individual. In contrast, biblical dreams are significant because they are imposed from the outside or, more specifically, from above. They represent one avenue by which God intervenes directly in the lives of human receptors.

84 Slavery in the Bible

IN THE FACE OF THE growing worldwide anti-slavery sentiment in the eighteenth and nineteenth centuries, the proponents of slavery had to find arguments that justified the ownership of human beings by fellow humans and proved the morality of such ownership. One argument that was often advanced was that slavery was beneficial to the black race: "White masters," it was said, "give them sustenance, Christianize them, and offer them hope for salvation." Thus, The *Spectator* (January 17, 1860) compares the "comfort and the protection of the slaves' Southern homes" with the "pitiable conditions of the original savage state from which they have been rescued," and asserts that "the intelligent, Christian slave-holder of the South is the best friend of the negro." The major argument justifying slavery, though, was based on the belief that the institution of slavery was ordained in heaven and had, in fact, "the positive sanction of God in its support." To make this point they invoked the Hebrew Bible, citing the various references to slavery.

It is said that the devil quotes Scripture for his own purpose, and the pro-slavery apologists followed his example. Whether knowingly or out of ignorance, they equated the slavery of which the Bible speaks with the heartless slavery practiced for over 200 years in our country. Indeed, they went one step further and pointed out that the Israelites in biblical Israel enslaved their fellow Israelites, whereas American slave-holders subjugated only heathens and barbarians who benefited from their enslavement, as pointed out above.

They could not have been more wrong! The error of the argument stems from the fact that the Hebrew word *eved* stands for both slave and servant. Wherever the Torah deals with an *eved ivri* (as for instance in Exodus 21:2–6), the term is best translated as a Hebrew bonded servant, or simply servant. For a non-Hebrew, *eved kena'ani*, the term slave may be more appropriate, although even in this case there is little resemblance between the Canaanite slave held by an Israelite in ancient Israel and an African slave held by a Southern owner, as we will see below.

The Torah is very explicit about the treatment due to a fellow Israelite who, usually because of reduced circumstances, had to sell himself as an indentured servant. In Deuteronomy 15:12–14, the Torah defines the rights of the Hebrew servant:

> If a fellow Hebrew... be sold to you by the courts for non-payment of a debt, and serve you six years; then in the seventh year you shall let him go free from you. When you let him go free from you, you shall not let him go empty: you shall furnish him liberally out of your flock, and out of your threshing floor, and out of your winepress; as God has blessed you, you shall give to him.

The Sages, as is often the case, amplified and expanded the terse Torah-command, "do not work him like a slave" (Leviticus 25:39). They forbade the master to impose on the slave demeaning tasks such as require him to wash his (the master's) feet, or put his shoes on him, or carry his things before him when going to the bathhouse, or carry him in a litter or a sedan chair as slaves do. The servant cannot be made to do any work other than that for which he was trained before he became indentured. Moreover, as for food, lodging, etc., a servant had to be treated as a member of the family. These restrictions were all designed to maintain the dignity and self-respect of the servant. With a bit of wry humor, the Sages summarized that, "He who acquires for himself an *eved ivri* is as one who has acquired for himself a master."

Rabbi Simchah Roth poses the interesting question: "What are the circumstances that bring about the Jewish servant?" I quote his answer in full:

> Abject poverty. The *eved ivri* has reached this status because he could not manage his own financial affairs successfully. He brought himself to penury and most often to theft. The simple solution of charity will not help: he had means and lost them; what he needs is education by example. During the time that he is "indentured" he has rights—which means that he is not a slave. But he does (or should) learn how a family should manage its affairs—in fact he becomes a member of the family. When, after six years, his time is up, he must go back into the real world and put into practice what he has learned; and he is given a substantial sum to start him off successfully! This is very different from the institution of "slavery" as the non-Jewish world understood it (and understands it). I think it also is a kind of blueprint for the Torah recipe for dealing with the social evil of destitution and what it brings about.

Finally, what about the Canaanite, that is, the non-Hebrew slave bought by an Israelite? He, too, had certain rights that were unthinkable in the slave-holding societies of the Western world. A slave who managed to escape could not be restored to his master. The slave was freed if the master caused him grievous bodily injury and was entitled to a compensation-payment from a fine assessed to his master. Like the rest of the members of the family, a slave was entitled to the Sabbath as a day of rest—something unheard of in those days in societies that had yet to discover the weekend. Finally, a non-Hebrew slave could not be held for more than one year by an Israelite owner, unless he renounced his paganism and converted to the faith of his master. In summary, slavery that existed in the United States was a very different institution from the slavery practiced in biblical Israel.

85 Wild Beasts

IN ONE OF HIS *MISHNAH* lessons, Rabbi Simchah Roth made the following intriguing statement: "In *Eretz Israel* in earlier times the countryside was infested by wild animals such as wolves, lions, bears, snakes and so forth." The *Mishnah* in question (Sanhedrin, 1:4) deals with the question of capital punishment, and extends the sentence to "wolf, lion, bear, tiger, leopard and snake" that have killed a human being.

The statement by R. Roth caught me by surprise. My notion of life in biblical times did not include images of people losing their lives to wild animals. Yet, indeed, the Bible contains numerous references to dangerous wild beasts, so called "beasts of the field."

Rabbi Roth cites three examples of wild beasts in the *Tanakh*, but there are many others. The first is from the period of the Patriarchs: Joseph's brothers, who had sold him to a passing caravan of Ishmaelites, had little trouble convincing their aging father that his favorite son had been killed by a wild animal. They presented Jacob with the bloody striped tunic (the famous coat of many colors) he had given to Joseph and saw their ruse succeed when the inconsolable father exclaimed: "My son's tunic! A wild beast devoured him! Joseph was torn by a beast!"

The story of Samson provides us with examples of two additional animals that roamed the landscape and endangered human lives and property. On the way to his engagement to a Philistine woman of Timnah, "a full-grown lion came roaring at him." Samson "tore him apart with his bare hands." (Judges 14:5) Some time later, enraged by the fact that during his absence his father-in-law had given his wife to someone else in marriage, Samson caught 300 foxes and tied them into pairs by their tails. He then stuck a burning firebrand into the knot and—with complete disregard for the environmental impact of this field burning—chased the animals into the wheat fields of the Philistines.

Being a shepherd may well have been one of the high-risk occupations of biblical days. We see this from a piece of legislation in Exodus (22:12) which requires that a man guarding another's animal must make restitution to its owner if the animal is stolen from him. But, he does not have to replace it if the animal was torn by wild beasts! The most famous of all biblical shepherds, David son of Jesse, who later became King of Israel, answered King Saul, who questioned his qualifications to fight the Philistine giant, Goliath: "Your servant has killed both lion and bear." (1 Samuel 17:36)

Finally, we have the strange tale of the Prophet Elisha and the bears. Elisha was on the road to Bethel when he met a group of youngsters who made fun of him calling him, "Baldy, baldy" (2 Kings, 2:23). Elisha gave them a piercing look and cursed them, whereupon two she-bears came out of the forest and mauled the 42 boys. The story is so horrifying—and uncharacteristic of the usual behavior of Elisha—that people must have been reluctant to accept it as true. Maybe that is the basis for the Hebrew idiom *lo dubbim velo ya'ar* (there were no bears and no forest) used to reject a story as an unbelievable fabrication, as something that never happened. (The original idiom appears in a different context in the Talmud, *Sotah*, 47a.)

GIVEN THE INFESTATION OF ANIMALS of prey, it is no wonder that they are regarded as one of the "four terrible punishments of the Lord: the sword, famine, wild beasts and pestilence" (Ezekiel 14:21). The threat of divine retribution for unacceptable behavior using the beasts of the field must have been very frightening and highly believable. One of many examples is found in Leviticus (26:21–22): "If you remain hostile toward Me and refuse to obey Me... I will loose wild beasts against you, and they shall bereave you of your children and wipe out your cattle. They shall decimate you, and your roads shall be deserted."

Conversely, protection from wild beasts often is an important part of the divine promise of reward for good behavior. The Lord obviously recognized that wild beasts are more likely to roam through abandoned villages or towns than through inhabited areas. Therefore, while promising to wipe out all the enemies of His people, He adds this thoughtful note on damage control: "I will not drive them out before you in a single year, lest the land become desolate and the wild beasts multiply to your hurt" (Exodus 23:29).

Time, Calendars and Holidays

86 It's About Time...

MANY JEWISH RITUALS AND OBSERVANCES are connected in some way with time. There is a time before which we are not supposed to start reciting the Morning *Shema* or the Evening *Shema* prayers, and there is a time after which we are not supposed to light Shabbat candles. The first accurate mechanical time-keeping devices did not appear until the end of the Middle Ages. How did Jews know the proper time for any observance before then?

The methods used to keep track of time were based on observation of the sun, the moon or the stars. One may not start reciting the evening *Shema* until three medium-sized stars—the Sages differentiated between stars by size—are visible in the sky. The degree of darkness required to see these stars occurs at about 25 minutes after sunset. Curiously, for *Havdalah* (the end of Shabbat), one must be able to see three small stars in the sky. This more stringent requirement—about 40 minutes after sunset—is meant to express our unwillingness to let go of the sacred time of Shabbat and enter the period of weekday drudgery.

THE JEWISH DAY IS DEFINED as going from sunset to sunset in contrast with the Western day, which starts at an unobservable moment, midnight. Both the Western and the Jewish day are divided into 24-hour sections. For the Western calendar, an hour represents a fixed length of time. This means that the number of daytime hours and nighttime hours changes from day to day over the course of a year. We all know that there are more daylight hours and fewer hours of darkness in summer than in winter. In contrast, in the Jewish calendar the number of daytime hours and nighttime hours are fixed: the time from sunrise to sunset is divided into twelve hours, and the time between sunset and sunrise is also always twelve hours. This means that the length of an hour changes over the course of the year, making the daylight hours longer and the nighttime hours shorter in summer, and vice versa in winter. These proportional hours are called zemanim in Hebrew. For the year 2009, for example, the longest hour (on June 21) was 77.97

minutes long, and the shortest (on December 21), only 44.23 minutes long. These times are for Corvallis, Oregon, for obviously they change with the latitude of the location.

Halakhah requires that the morning *Amidah* prayer must be said before the end of the fourth hour. What does this mean? The first hour of the day begins at sunrise, noon is at the start of the seventh hour, and the twelfth hour ends at sunset. Therefore, we can easily calculate by what time the morning *Shema* had to be recited, say on June 21, 2009. We add four proportional hours of 77.97 minutes each to the time of sunrise at 5:27 am. and arrive at about 10:45 am.

IN SPECIFYING SHORT TIME INTERVALS, a span of eighteen minutes is often used. Shabbat candles, for example, must be lit at least eighteen minutes before sunset, and *halakhah* stipulates that, when baking *matzah* for use on Passover, no more than eighteen minutes may pass between the time flour and water are mixed and the time the dough is put in the oven.

What is so special about the number eighteen? It is tempting to cite the fact that eighteen is the numerical value of the two letters that make up the Hebrew word *ḥai* (life). Because of this, our donations to charity or to synagogues are often in multiples of $18. Surprisingly, the real reason is more prosaic and goes back to a Roman measure of distance and time cited in the Talmud. The distance a Roman legion could cover in 1,000 paces was called a "mil"— obviously the source of our modern word for mile. How much time would it take to cover this distance? The Talmud states that on an average day, a person can cover 40 Roman miles from sunrise to sunset. A simple calculation shows that on such an average day of twelve sunlit hours, this energetic person would walk a total of 720 minutes (12 hours times 60 minutes each). If we divide these 720 minutes by the 40 miles covered, we arrive at a speed of 18 minutes per mile. Now, tractate *Pesaḥim* (46a) stipulates that the maximum permissible kneading time for *matzot* is the equivalent of the time it would take someone to walk from the village of Migdal Nunya to the town of Tiberias, a distance of one Roman mile. This walk, as we have just seen, would take 18 minutes—the time allowed for the matzah-baking procedure until this very day.

In many parts of the world, time is still defined by non-mechanical means. As a youngster in *Eretz Israel*, going on hikes, we would occasionally inquire of a Bedouin how far it was to the next town. The answer we received might well have been: "two and a half cigarettes."

87 The Moon and the Biblical Festivals

THE JEWISH CALENDAR IS BASED on the lunar year. This means that the dates on which the holidays fall are fixed with respect to the lunar months. It is essential to fix the beginning of each month accurately in order to celebrate each holiday on the correct day, as specified in the Bible. While it is impossible to pinpoint the beginning of a solar month by observation (nobody can tell when the month of January ends and February begins by looking at the sky), it is easy to identify the start of a lunar month by direct observation. The appearance of the crescent of the new moon signals the beginning of a new month. In fact, this was the method used in ancient Israel to determine the first day of a month: on the eve of the thirtieth day of each month, members of the *Sanhedrin* (High Court) would assemble to receive testimony about the sighting of the new moon crescent. If two creditable witnesses testified to its reappearance, that day would be proclaimed *Rosh Ḥodesh* (beginning of the new Month). Conversely, if no crescent was sighted that night, the day would become the thirtieth day of the current month and the new month would start on the following day. Thus, the Jewish year would consist of six 29-day months and six 30-day months for a total of 354 days. (The monthly testimony was required because the 29-day months and the 30-day months do not alternate regularly.)

If the new moon was sighted, the news was quickly transmitted throughout the land via a chain of bonfires from mountaintop to mountaintop. However, distant Jewish communities, outside *Eretz Israel*, that could not be reached in this fashion, always celebrated the thirtieth day of the month as *Rosh Ḥodesh*. To insure that they would celebrate the festivals on their proper dates, the custom arose of adding a second day to the celebration of each biblical festival. Yom Kippur remained one day for it was deemed too difficult to extend the fast to two days. This remained the custom in the Diaspora even after the fourth century C.E., from which time on the New Moon was determined by astronomical calculations rather than by direct observation.

Before artificial illumination made it possible to turn night into day, the rebirth of the moon after several days of darkness must have struck early civilizations as a symbol of hope and an occasion for rejoicing. The Bible mentions *Rosh Ḥodesh* as a holiday that is on a par with the major festivals. On that day each month, special offerings were brought to the Temple and families gathered for festive meals. Even today, the beginning of each month is a half-holiday on which special prayers are added to the synagogue liturgy. Early on, the monthly waxing and waning of the moon was identified with the female menstrual cycle, and *Rosh Ḥodesh* became a women's holiday. On that day, women refrained from working as they would on any of the major holidays. During talmudic times, this rule was modified to forbid only heavy work, such as weaving, while allowing light work, such as sewing. In modern times, this custom has been forgotten completely, though the Jewish feminist movement has appropriated the holiday as its own. In all streams of Judaism *Rosh Ḥodesh* groups are being formed by women who meet on this day to study Torah and deepen their understanding of their heritage.

ALL BUT ONE OF THE biblical feasts that have a connection to agriculture or to nature are celebrated in the middle of the month, at the time of the full moon. Thus, Pesaḥ, the Spring Festival, begins on the fifteenth day of Nisan, the spring month, and Sukkot, the feast of the ingathering from

the threshing floor and wine press, starts on the fifteenth of Tishrei at the end of the agricultural year. This is not surprising. An agrarian society had no effective or cheap way of lighting its homes and public places and went to bed with the sun. The full moon provided an opportunity to extend both family and public celebrations beyond the daylight hours. Long before religious-historical overlays overshadowed the importance of the agricultural base of the festivals, the native populations celebrated the increases of their flocks in spring on Passover, the bounty of first fruits and the wheat harvest on Shavu'ot (Pentecost or the Feast of Weeks) at the beginning of summer, and the largesse of nature on Sukkot at the end of the year. Surprisingly, though, Shavu'ot is the only one of the three pilgrimage feasts celebrated one week before the full moon, on the sixth day of the month of Sivan.

The explanation lies in the different interpretation of a single word. In contrast to the other festivals, the Bible does not give a specific date for Shavu'ot. It simply says: "From the day after the Sabbath... you shall count 50 days, until the day after the seventh week. Then you shall bring an offering of new grain to the Lord" (Leviticus 23:15–16). It all hinges on the interpretation of the word Sabbath in these verses. The Sages took it to refer to the first day of Passover (which was, of course, a Sabbath, that is, a day of rest). Thus Shavu'ot falls 50 days later, on the sixth of Sivan when the moon is still waxing. Other groups, for instance the Karaites who do not accept rabbinic law, understand the term Sabbath literally, as the seventh day in the week. Hence, for them, Shavu'ot always falls on a Sunday. It is, however, entirely plausible that the word "Sabbath" refers to neither of these but to the last day of Passover, which is also a day of statutory rest and religious celebration. (In fact, the Torah mentions this day of rest just prior to the reference to Shavu'ot.) If this reading were accepted, the festival would fall one week later. It would follow the pattern and would also fall right in the middle of the month, at the time of the full moon!

What Makes Ḥanukkah so Jumpy?

WHY DOES ḤANUKKAH JUMP AROUND so? Why isn't the date on which the holiday falls fixed? In the year 2009, the Festival of Lights started on December 12 and ended on December 19. Four years earlier, in 2005, Ḥanukkah did not start until December 26 and ran through the end of the year into 2006!

Of course, the dates on which Ḥanukkah and all other Jewish holidays fall are fixed but, as we saw in the previous chapter, they are fixed according to the Jewish calendar. Unlike the western (Gregorian) calendar, which is based on the earth's orbits about the sun, the Jewish calendar is a modified lunar calendar, that is, its dates are based on the orbits of the moon. Jewish holidays fall on variable dates in the common calendar because the lunar year (twelve rotations of the moon around the earth) is shorter than the solar year (one rotation of the earth around the sun).

If we disregard fractions of a day and round off, the solar year is 365 days long, giving us the combination of 30-day and 31-day months (plus February) with which we're all familiar. The lunar year, on the other hand, rounding again, is only 354 days long—a difference of eleven days. It is this difference that causes any given date in the Jewish calendar to creep backwards by eleven or twelve days a year relative to the common calendar.

The same is true of the Muslim calendar. It, too, is based on the moon and, therefore, loses eleven days each year. Thus, the Muslim month of fasting, Ramadan, wanders slowly around the calendar, showing up in turn in each season of the year over a 33-year cycle. Because Muslims do not have any holidays that are tied to nature, or to events in the agricultural cycle, it does not matter that a given date falls sometimes in summer and at other times in autumn, winter or spring. (Of course, it is much more difficult to refrain from eating and drinking from sunup to sunset for a whole month in the heat of the summer.)

In contrast to the Muslim calendar, the main purpose of the Jewish calendar was to fix the times at which the festivals were celebrated. Each of the major festivals has an agricultural component, which is reflected in its very name. Thus, Pesah is *Hag ha-Aviv* (Festival of Spring), Shavu'ot, *Hag ha-Katzir* (Harvest Festival) and Sukkot is *Hag ha-Asif* (Festival of Ingathering—the final harvest of fruits from the fields). Obviously, it would not do to have Passover, the spring festival, occur in mid-winter, nor have Sukkot, the fall festival, come in the spring. Therefore, enough days have to be added periodically to the Jewish lunar year to keep it in step with the solar year which determines the seasons. In practice this means that a thirteenth month is intercalated (inserted) before the month of Adar, as needed to bring the two calendars into harmony. (Thus, the new month becomes "Adar I," which makes the original month "Adar II.") Because the lunar year is about eleven days shorter than the solar year, about every third year becomes a leap year with thirteen months.

While the Temple was still standing, and even somewhat later, the decision to have a leap year was arrived at *ad hoc* each year. If toward the end of the month of Adar (about March), it was still cold and spring was not in the air, the Sages of the Jerusalem *Sanhedrin* declared the year to be a leap year. This pushed Nisan, the Spring month which follows Adar, off by one whole month—by which time, it was hoped, spring would have sprung.

Often, economic considerations entered the decision. If it appeared that the harvest might be poor that year, the Sages (and later, the High Court in Yavneh) hesitated to declare the year a leap year. According to biblical law (Leviticus 23:14) the new grain could not be eaten before the 16th of Nisan. Therefore, in a year of hunger it made sense not to insert an additional month before the new harvest could come into the markets. (Passover starts on the 15th of Nisan and the prohibition against eating and storing of *hametz*—leavened stuff—may originally have been a device for cleaning the house and barn of last year's grain to make space for the new harvest. This also kept the yeast starters from going too sour.)

One specific application of this concern for food is the sabbatical year, during which fields must lie fallow. That year and the year after, during which food is likely to be scarce, may never be intercalated.

All this changed in the year 358 C.E., when the sage Hillel II published his calculations which fixed the Jewish calendar—the calendar still in use to this day. It provides that every 3rd, 6th, 8th, 11th, 14th, 17th and 19th year in a 19-year cycle be designated a leap year and contain thirteen months. For instance, the Jewish year 5771 (or 2010 C.E.) is year 14 in the current 19-year cycle.

This arrangement is much more complicated than adding a 29th day to February every four years. However, we are dealing with a much more difficult problem: to devise a calendar that, while fixing Ḥanukkah according to the moon year, yet assures us that it will always come back to "shed its sweet light" when we need light most—during those long winter nights.

89 The Times We Live in: A.D. or C.E.

THE BEGINNING OF A NEW year, whether Rosh Ha-Shanah or January 1, evokes thoughts about the passage of time. As I write this column, we recently entered the year 5770 according to the Jewish calendar. In the western calendar we still have a few days left in the year 2009. The Muslim calendar gives us yet a third number for the current year. These three constitute only a small sample of the different calendars that have been used in the past, or are still in use today.

It is clear that there is more than one way to measure the passage of time. We get different answers for a specific point in time depending upon which calendar we use. Different calendars count time from different points of origin and, in some cases, the years they count even differ in length. For example, Muslims start their count from the year of the *Hegira*, the year that the prophet Mohammed fled from Mecca to Medina. Because the *Hegira* took place in 622 C.E., one would expect the current Muslim year-count to be 622 less than our current date 2009, i.e., 1387. This is not the case, though. The Muslim year is based on the lunar calendar and is about 11 days shorter than one of our standard years. Thus, more years have elapsed since then and, indeed, this year in the Muslim calendar is 1431 rather than 1387.

What about the Jewish calendar? According to tradition, the Jewish calendar measures the time elapsed from the creation of the world. On a Sunday morning (actually on the eve before), 5770 years ago as I am writing this, God started working and by Friday afternoon He had created the world and all that's in it. The date of that Friday? According to tradition, it was 1 Tishrei, the first day of Rosh Ha-Shanah. Our calendar counts the years elapsed since then.

There are several problems with this scheme. For the first 4,000 years nobody seems to have kept track of the time elapsed since creation. The Bible certainly does not date events with reference to creation. The first time we see this chronology presented is in the second century midrashic work, *Seder Olam Rabbah*, which calculates specific dates for all important events since creation. This *Anno Mundi* (Year of the World) scheme did not come into general use until the eleventh century. Moreover, there is a Jewish tradition that ours was not the first world God created, but the first—after several previous attempts—with which He was satisfied and which He decided was a "keeper."

Our Sages were not the only ones to calculate the time of creation. According to James Ussher, Anglican Archbishop of Armagh and Primate of all Ireland (1581–1656), the world was created on October 23, 4004 B.C.E., at exactly 12:00 noon.

What about the calendar in general use? Whereas the Jewish and Bishop Ussher's calendars are universal and neutral with respect to religion, the Gregorian calendar measures time from a very specific, parochial event—the birth of Jesus of Nazareth. It designates years since that event as A.D. (*Anno Domini*, Year of our Lord) and events that happened before as B.C. (Before Christ). However, the accuracy of the zero-point for this calendar is highly suspect, because the date of birth of Jesus can be pinpointed, at best, to within a ten-year period. Moreover, the calendar itself changed when an edict of Pope Gregory XIII corrected the previously used Julian calendar in 1582.

Many people are troubled by the designators A.D. and B.C., because they refer to Jesus as "our Lord" and as "Christ," that is, the Messiah. Not being Christians, they object having to date historical events with reference to the life of Jesus. To get around this problem, the terms C.E. (Common Era) and B.C.E. (Before the Common Era) are sometimes substituted. We find these designators with increasing frequency in history books, scientific publications in various fields and even in some unexpected places. Microsoft's recently released *Encarta Africana* uses these "scientific" time designators. Also, on a recent tour of Turkey, we were surprised to hear the tour-guide, a Muslim, use C.E. and B.C.E., so as not to offend the non-Christians in the group.

Have we solved the problem by changing to a Common Era? Common to whom? The fact remains that we still divide history into those events that occurred before the birth of Jesus and those that occurred after it. We may reject the notion of Jesus as God and Savior, but still measure the course of history by it. Is there a way out of this dilemma?

What we need is a neutral point-in-time upon which we can all agree. My own suggestion is January 1, 1980—the year in which IBM introduced the personal computer and the date to which all PCs default when their batteries are disabled. Any event before 1980 would be B.C. (before computers), and any event after would need no designation, for that is the brave new world in which we live. This, however, is the stuff of which social science fiction is fashioned.

In Six Days God Created...

AFTER DARWIN AND MORE RECENT discoveries in geology, paleontology and archaeology, the question of the age of the world emerges within the broader debate of evolution vs. creationism. In this clash between scientific discoveries and the biblical account of creation, the question takes on the form: "When was the world created and what exactly was created at that time?"

Christian fundamentalists (we'll look at the Jewish position next) take the Bible at its words: God created the world in six days, and—no nonsense about it—each day was of 24-hours duration. This creation took place almost exactly 6,000 years ago. Since that time, nothing has evolved and nothing has changed; God created exactly what we see today. Biblical literalists have no trouble explaining the seeming contradictions between the Bible and the apparently very old geologic structures, fossils and artifacts that science has discovered. They maintain, "When God created the world, He created rocks and fossils that looked millions of years old, as well as bones of human-like creatures and animals that never lived on this earth." Granting that God created these objects as little as 6,000 years ago, but made them look as if they'd been created millions of years earlier, why would He want to trick us in this fashion and mislead us about the true age of the world? The usual answer, "to test our faith," I do not find satisfactory.

What is the Jewish view of the age of the world? As I am writing this, at the beginning of the year 2010, we are, according to our tradition, in the year 5770 after the creation of the world. Of course, the date of creation is not specified in the Bible, nor is it an article of faith. The date is arrived at by adding up the generations since the creation of Adam as recorded in the Bible. But not even all of those who take the Bible literally as the word of God believe that the world was created only 5770 years ago. On the contrary, our Sages are agreed (*Vayikra Rabbah* 29:1) that the count starts after the creation of Adam, at the end of the sixth day of creation. It is this sixth day, Friday, on which the process of creation was completed, to which we refer when we exclaim each year on Rosh Ha-Shanah: "Today is the birthday of the world." Thus, in the Jewish tradition, the age of the world is 5770 years plus six days!

These six days are significant. They set up two separate calendars, one from Adam forward, which uses human time, and the other for the Six Days, the period of creation before humanity appeared on the face of this earth. Many Orthodox Jews will readily admit that the first six days do not necessarily represent 24-hour time spans. Because the sun was created only on the fourth day, to speak of a 24-hour first, second or third day is meaningless, in any case. References to a much older age of the world and universe abound in classical Jewish literature.

Rashi starts his explanation of the Book of Genesis with the statement that the conventional translation of the first sentence, "In the beginning God created the heaven and the earth..." is wrong. Grammatical considerations lead him to the conclusion that the text does not regard the creation of the heaven and the earth as the absolute beginning of creation. Many modern Jewish translations (see, for instance, the Jewish Publication Society) follow Rashi and translate this crucial sentence as: "When God first created the heaven and the earth..." or, "When God began to create the heaven and the earth...." This admits the possibility of a long process of creation before our earth was created. Indeed, the *Midrash* speaks of many worlds that God had created but found wanting before He created our Earth, suitable for sustaining living beings, including, of course, Adam and Eve.

These insights did not come about in reaction to the contemporary controversy between religious fundamentalism and science; they predate it by some 1,600 years. The Talmud (*Hagiga*, Ch. 2) tells us that the entire account of creation in Genesis is given in parable form, a poem with a text and a subtext. Of course, nobody at that time put the age of the earth at four and a half billion years, or the age of the universe at fourteen billion. How could they have? Even we did not know the age of the universe—nor, in fact, that it had a beginning—until 1964, when Penzias and Wilson discovered the echo of the Big Bang. Some people have tried to force an interpretation, which upholds the modern dating of the universe, on verses such as "A thousand years in Your [God's] sight are like a day that passes..." (Psalms, 90:4). This is not necessary; these verses are simply beautiful poetry. No unbridgeable gulf exists between Jewish faith and modern science.

91
Ḥanukkah, O Ḥanukkah

IN ITS DISCUSSION OF ḤANUKKAH, the Talmud asks an unexpected question, *Ma'i Ḥanukkah*? (What is the reason for Hanukkah?) It offers the following answer:

> When the Greeks entered the Temple, they defiled all the oils therein. When the Hasmonean dynasty prevailed against and defeated them, they searched and found only one cruse of oil which lay with the seal of the High Priest. This cruse contained sufficient oil for one day's lighting only; yet a miracle happened and they lit the lamp therewith for eight days. The following year these days were appointed a Festival with the recital of *Hallel* and thanksgiving.

What is astonishing about this answer is the fact that this is the first time the cruse of oil is mentioned anywhere! The only contemporary information about Ḥanukkah comes from two books of the Apocrypha, 1 Maccabees and 2 Maccabees, which are not incorporated into the Hebrew Bible. These books fail to mention the miracle of the oil!

Why would the talmudic Sages introduce extraneous "facts" to explain the great revolt which occurred five centuries earlier, in 167–164 B.C.E.? From the discussion (*Shabbat* 21b) it appears that, although the festival commemorating the victory over the Syrian forces was still celebrated for eight days each year, the reasons for the celebration and for some of the customs connected with it had, obviously, been forgotten. Thus, we see, for example, that the two great schools in the Academy disagree about the order of lighting the Ḥanukkah candles: The School of Shammai maintains that the candles should be lit in descending order, starting with eight candles on the first night and ending with one candle on the last night, whereas the School of Hillel holds that the candles should be lit in an increasing order—one candle the first night, two on the second night, etc. We, of course, know that the School of Hillel prevailed in the dispute.

There may, however, be a deeper reason for focusing on the little cruse of oil. The Books of the Maccabees describe in great detail the battles which Mattathias, the priest from Modi'in, and his five sons had fought—first against their fellow Jews who had forsaken strict adherence to their religion, and then against the armies of Antiochus who was determined to wipe out Judaism in order to impose Greek culture on the population. The books credit the ultimate victory over the Syrians entirely to the courage, wisdom and determination of Judah Macabbee and his brothers. What the narrative does not contain is any account of miracles. The story clearly glorifies human military prowess rather than divine intervention.

Several hundred years later, in Babylon, the rabbis of the Talmud faced a different reality. They were no longer looking for a human hero who could lead the dispersed Jewish communities from the Diaspora to their ancestral homeland and restore the political autonomy they had lost. Now, they prayed for the coming of the Messiah, a spiritual force, to rebuild Jerusalem. They hoped for divine intervention and looked for examples of it in past periods of our history. And so, the emphasis of Hanukkah changed; it became the Festival of Lights, and we were enjoined, in every generation, to publicize the miracle by placing lights outside of our homes or in the windows where they could easily be seen by all passers-by.

This remained the emphasis of Hanukkah for more than a millennium and a half. The blessing we say before lighting the candles speaks of "the miracles God performed for our ancestors in those days at this time of year," and our children spin *dreidels* that proclaim "a great miracle happened there."

With the birth of modern Zionism, the meaning of Hanukkah changed again. To build a new nation, courage and determination were needed and the Macabbees, who had established an autonomous Jewish state so long ago, provided inspiration and good role models. Thus, for example, the international Zionist sports organization, *Maccabi*, was named after them and every Hanukkah their birth place, Modi'in, became the starting point of a torch relay race to Jerusalem.

The name of Judah, or rather his sobriquet, Macabbee, reflects the different perceptions of the holiday. In Hebrew, the "k" sound can be represented either by the letter *qof* or by the letter *kaf*. If we spell Maccabee with a *qof*, the word suggests *maqevet* (hammer); if we spell it with a *kaf* the word becomes an acronym of the phrase, *mi khamokha ba'elim Adonai* (Who is like You among the mighty, O Lord?). The former emphasizes the secular view of the hero and of the holiday as commemorating a mighty victory against great odds in the first war for religious freedom. The second spelling of the name reflects the religious view and celebrates the divine miracle of the victory and of the lights.

Which of the two spellings of the name is correct—the one with a *qof* or the one with a *kaf?* There is no way to know, for the only account that came down to us was written in the Greek language and there the name Maccabeus is spelled with *kappa kappa.* We make our choice and choose our own version of history.

Purim and Noise Making

THERE'S BEEN A PURIM HOLIDAY in each year of my life, yet only a few of them stand out in my memory. The one I remember best occurred when I was eight years old. That year, a clever woodworker and friend of the family made me a special *grogger* (noisemaker). It wasn't your usual kind that you whirl round and round making whatever noise a measly piece of wood or tin can make on a ratchet drum. No, Sir! Mine looked like a well-shaped tree. From the trunk (a wooden dowel that served as the handle) branches came out and from each of these numerous smaller branches. On each of these branches there was a little wooden hammer pivoting on a pin. When I shook my noisemaker, dozens of pieces of hardwood hit other pieces and made the most unbelievable racket. My "Purim rattle" was by far the loudest in the *shul* and I was the envy of every kid that year.

I was reminded of my glorious *grogger* a few years ago when my wife and I spent *Erev Purim* in New York. The meetings we attended had finished and we had a free evening. When we asked one of the locals for the closest synagogue to our hotel, he suggested the venerable Spanish and Portuguese Synagogue, the oldest in New York (going back to New Amsterdam, 1654). We were a little awed by the magnificence of the huge sanctuary with tiers of seats ringing the hall on three sides according to the *Sephardi* tradition, and the elevated *bimah* (reader's podium) in the center. When the people came in our eyes popped: the sparkle of diamonds on the women's necks and wrists was blinding, and the black top hats on the men reminded us of an age gone by. Even the little kids wore suit jackets and ties. I was waiting for the reading of the *Megillah*, for I figured that even this illustrious crowd would relax when it came time to drown out the name of Haman. But what a shock! Haman's name was uttered time and time again in absolute silence. It was unreal; I thought maybe my hearing was gone. Later, upon asking, I was told that the congregation regarded it as undignified to make a racket in the synagogue.

Why then all this noise on Purim in the synagogue? The Hebrew language is not rich in curses. The worst Hebrew curse is the biblical *yimah shemo!* (may his name be erased). So, the purpose of making all that noise at the mention of Haman is, of course, to erase the name of the evil fiend who tried to wipe out all the Jews of Persia so long ago.

I remembered our silent Purim—almost nostalgically—when Mimi and I attended a *Megillah* reading in a small *hasidic shtibl* in the Old City of Jerusalem that reminded me very much of the *besmedrish* of my youth. No top hats here, but beautifully made *streimels* (wide-brimmed hats made of sable or mink fur) covered that evening in plastic wrapping against the impending rain, which, fortunately, never materialized.

The place was overrun with kids, all in costume. I didn't see the women, for they were safely tucked away behind a curtain on the balcony in back of the room. It was clear that many of the men had started early to fulfill the *mitzvah* of drinking until they couldn't tell the difference between blessing Mordecai and cursing Haman.

And then the reading started. Every time Haman's name was uttered, the noise rose to a level that threatened to blow the roof off the building. Everybody had a noisemaker of some sort, and men and kids got off the wooden benches on which they sat and banged them against the stone-tile floor. I was reminded of the one time I attended a rock-and-roll concert, and—as on that occasion—tried to keep my mouth open lest the noise burst my ear drums. It was clear that the people here were taking their biblical curses seriously. They tried to erase Haman's name by drowning it in noise.

93 Purim Parodies and Purim Spiels

WHEN THE BEIT AM NEWSLETTER featured a Purim supplement for the first time, several people expressed their concern about making fun of serious religious practices or institutions. They thought that an article which proved, by means of traditional, talmudic argumentation that Queen Vashti and not Queen Esther was the true heroine of *Megillat Ester* (the Scroll of Esther; see next chapter), was somehow unbecoming, possibly even sacrilegious. Yet, parodies of sacred texts in the form of learned sermons or discourses, known as Purim Torah go back in the *Ashkenazi* tradition at least as far as the Middle Ages.

On Purim, even our talmudic Sages who, in general, were not known for their light-hearted banter, were not above poking fun at biblical themes and their own methods of exegesis. A well-known passage in the Babylonian Talmud (*Hullin* 139b, fifth century C.E.), tells of a visiting scholar who was challenged to find references to Haman, Esther, Mordecai and even Moses in the Torah. Since the story of Esther deals with events that occurred many centuries after those described in the Torah, and because the name of Moses is cited there a mere 770 times, the request for references was obviously made in fun. Indeed, the visitor acquitted himself quite well by means of clever puns and anagrams. Not all subsequent scholars, however, saw the humor in the passage. Thus Rashi (eleventh century, France) earnestly explains why it was necessary to look for an allusion to the name of Moses in the Torah!

Scholars were divided on toning down the hilarity connected with this holiday commemorating the miraculous deliverance from annihilation. The noted talmudic scholar Rava declares that, "A man is obligated to get drunk on Purim to the point where he can no longer distinguish between "cursed be Haman" and "blessed be Mordecai" (*Megillah* 7b). But later authorities could not condone drinking to excess even on Purim and limited imbibing to the amount sufficient to make one sleepy.

In the course of the centuries, Jews borrowed from the cultures of the various peoples among whom they lived. In the second half of the sixteenth century, in northern Italy, the clever, "upside down" sermon of the *Purim Torah* slowly expanded under the influence of the *Commedia Dell'arte*. It started to involve groups of players wearing costumes, and relied on stereotypical characters and masks. The rabbis explained the masks by the fact that God's face was hidden in the Purim story; His name does not appear even once in *Megillat Ester*. Even the strongly worded negative commandment in the Torah against transvestism is suspended during Purim.

The subject matter of early Purim plays was the Purim story, though often with a parody approach to the main characters. Later, the plots expanded into other areas. The plays were known by the collective name of *Purim-spiels*. From the early 1700s, the *spiels* became more complex and resembled contemporary European theater in literary style and sometimes even in their non-biblical subject matter. Besides the traditional parody element, the plays now often contained material which might be objectionable to some viewers, as well as vulgar language. The *Encyclopedia Judaica* states that, "the printed version of the *Akhashverosh-spiel* was burned by the city fathers of Frankfurt in 1714, presumably because of the play's indecent elements." The *Encyclopedia* goes on to speculate that, "this was probably the reason for a public notice of 1728 in which the leaders of the Hamburg [Jewish] community banned the performance of all *Purim-spiels*."

Irreverence continues to be the order of the holiday. I close with the couplet with which we begged for coins in my youth while making the rounds of our Jewish friends to deliver the traditional *shalaḥ manot* (gifts of food and goodies). In loose translation:

"Today is Purim, tomorrow it's done;
gimme a *groschen* and away I'll run!"

94 A Call To Action: A Purim Spoof

WE, THE VIGILANTES AGAINST SUBVERSION of Historical Truth, Inc. (VASHTI), have organized to redress an historical outrage, a nefarious plot unequalled in history. We refer to the displacement of the hero figure in the Scroll of Esther in the Bible. Instead of the true heroine, Queen Vashti, we are presented with two figures, Mordecai and Esther, and asked to accept them as the protagonists of the marvelous events that took place in Shushan, Persia during the reign of Ahasuerus, 2,450 years ago.

Here are the points that first aroused our suspicion. Each taken alone may not be conclusive, but, when taken together, they provide overwhelming evidence of a conspiracy:

Mordecai, the Jewish hero of the tale is named for Marduk, the chief deity of the city of Babylon. What nice Jewish boy would be named for a foreign deity? It is as if we had named one of our sons Christopher! Worse: Mordecai insists that his adopted niece, who bore the lovely Hebrew name of Hadassah (a name that conjures up at one and the same time the fragrance of the myrtle and the comeliness of generations of Jewish women), go by the name of Esther, after the pagan goddess Ishtar.

Where other parents have been known to sit *shiv'ah* when their daughters married outside the faith, Mordecai thrusts his niece into a beauty contest with the hope of marrying her off to a *goyishe* king. Worse yet, he demands she hide her Jewish origins. Did he really think she could hold on to her *Yiddishkeit* in the palace? Would not somebody become suspicious of her vegetarianism? Was there a *mikveh* in the harem? How long would the king put up with her "Not tonight, I have a headache" for twelve to fourteen days out of every month? No, for Mordecai no price was too high to have Ahasuerus as his *mishpoche*. The scheme, obviously, paid off because we're told in the *Megillah* that he had some kind of government job as an undercover agent and hung out at the palace gate all day long.

Moreover, the story, as told in the *Megillah*, sounds fishy: We are told that Haman's hatred of the Jews started because Mordecai refused to bow down before him, the king's vizier. This could not have been because of religious scruples. Later commentators find his behavior puzzling for Jewish tradition enjoins us to honor highly placed personages—Jewish or not.

All right already, so Mordecai is no hero. But how about Esther? Unfortunately, Esther is tarred by the same brush. She went along with her uncle's designs, married a Gentile king and lived in his harem. In fact, she had to be threatened with exposure and death before she was willing to do anything to help save her own people from extinction.

Compare this with the noble figure of Vashti. A truly modest queen who would not expose herself to her vain husband's drunken guests. She dreaded the howls of "take it off, take it off, take it all off" that she knew would surely follow her appearance at the banquet. And so, she refused to come, was deposed... and the rest is history.

We must point out that Vashti's decision was not an impulsive one; she knew the consequences of her courageous act. The letters of her name in Hebrew when read backwards (*yod, tav shin, vav*) spell *yiteshu* which is the future tense of the verb to drive out, evict, or oust. Her tragic fate was sealed in her name, for the king, indeed, banished her. (Esther's secretiveness, too, was concealed in her name: *samekh, tav, resh*.)

Finally, the conclusive proof by means of *gematria* (the mystical adding up of the numeric values associated with Hebrew letters): *Vashti Hamalkah* (Queen Vashti) adds up to 816. If we add to this the number of provinces over which she reigned, 127, and subtract 3 (for the ill-fated feast took place in the third year of her reign), we end up with 940—the exact value of that paean to the "Woman of Valor" of Proverbs 31: *Eshet hayil mi yimtza?* There can be no doubt: Vashti is that woman of valor, the true heroine, by the *Megillah's* own reckoning!

This concludes our proof. And so, we urge you to join forces with us, the Vigilantes Against Subversion of Historical Truth, Inc. Help vindicate noble Queen Vashti and restore her to her rightful place in history!

Purim Torah

SHORTLY AFTER I TOOK OVER as editor of *Kol Ha'am*, the Beit Am newsletter presented what it grandiosely called "the First Annual Purim Supplement." In it, I tried to revive a traditional way of marking the holiday by presenting what is known as *Purim Torah*. *Purim Torah* purports to be an erudite discourse on a traditional subject—possibly a portion of scripture or a passage from the Talmud—which uses traditional terminology and methods of analysis. However, it only appears to be authentic. The point is that the sermon or piece of writing must sound believable, but, of course, be utter nonsense.

In March 1995, in the second issue of our Purim supplement, I tried my hand at a piece of *Purim Torah* that resulted in a set of quite unexpected reactions. The greatly revered spiritual leader of the Chabad-Lubavitch Hasidic movement, Rebbe Menahem Mendel Schneerson, had recently passed away, and many articles had appeared about him in the media. I figured that if I ascribed a really far-out idea to him, people would quickly realize that it was a piece of *Purim Torah*. To make sure that readers would recognize it as such and not take offense, I put the Hebrew date of Purim (14th day of the month of Adar) into the last line of the dispatch. Here is what I wrote:

CROWN HEIGHTS, N.Y. A veritable shock-wave ran through the Lubavitch Hasidic community when it was learned that their venerated Rebbe, Menahem Schneerson, who went to his reward recently, had left a most unusual Ethical Will. In this will, which he had left to the Chabad community, Schneerson suggests that the Law Committee re-examine the rule that excludes women from being counted in the *minyan* (the quorum of ten Jewish males necessary for communal prayer). The Rebbe explains that the separation of the sexes became the custom, which by now had taken on the force of law, for reasons of *kevod hakahal* (public sentiment) during the early Islamic period. He suggests that today public sentiment would favor counting women as equal to men in the matter of public prayer. Usually reliable sources from within the ḥasidic community report that a stormy session of the Law Committee, lasting seven hours, debated the issue. Though the majority of the religious leaders were opposed to so radical a breach with tradition, the Rebbe's authority carried enough weight to force a compromise: Basing themselves on Leviticus 27:2–4, where the value of a female servant is explicitly set at 60% of that of a male servant, they suggested that women be counted at 0.6 of a man. Thus a group of seven male and five female worshippers would constitute a *minyan* for communal prayer.

The concern was expressed that with women praying alongside of men in such a mixed *minyan* and possibly wearing *tallitot* (prayer shawls) as men do, young children would not be able to tell the difference between the genders and might grow up with ill-defined sexual orientations. Although the danger of this was deemed slight, it was decided in the spirit of "building a fence around the Law" to require women to wear *tallitot* with pink stripes while men continue to wear the traditional garment with the blue or black stripes.

An official announcement of the decision is planned for the 14th of Adar.

Unbeknownst to me, a friend posted the above "news release" on a Jewish website. The reactions were both numerous and mind-blowing. Among the very first was a phone call by a reporter from the *Village Voice*, the weekly New York newspaper, who wanted to write a special article on the "highly significant" change in the Rebbe's stance toward women. She was very disappointed when I explained that it was a Purim hoax. Another caller, who wanted a reference to the Rebbe's will for a history of the Lubavitch movement he was writing, saw the joke immediately when I pointed to the date and was amused by the piece.

Many e-mail messages (from all around the world!) were highly complimentary. They appreciated the allusions to Jewish Law and thought it was a fitting piece of upside-down *Purim Torah*. However, not all the readers were amused. An ambivalent reaction by one of them read:

Purim Torah is all fine and good, but it must not be harmful either intentionally or unintentionally. With all the bashing that Lubavitch has been suffering at the hands of its detractors such a posting is inappropriate. (I am assuming that it was all meant in good humor and not intended to offend anyone.) I got about two lines into it before I started looking for the date or other indication that it was Purim Torah. As it was there, I have no problems with the message.

I, for one, cannot imagine anyone needing a clearer sign that it was Purim Torah. I can only assume that the people taking it amiss were actually fooled on something so obvious, and are allowing their gullibility to speak for them.

On the other hand, another reader was clearly outraged. Fortunately, he was one of only a few who felt this way:

I realize that it is before Purim and some have started to drink a little earlier then required by the halocheh. I would just like to point out to the writer here what the Mordechai *brings* in his commentary on *Yoma*, "There is a *Tekuneh* and a *Cherem* from the previous generations to not say evil about those who are dead and rest in the earth". As you have posted this in a public place, where there are at least three men who have seen it, it is a public act. You are REQUIRED, to appear before the gravesite of the Rebbe, and in front of ten men remove your shoes and ask *mechileh* from him, as the halocheh requires. I AM SERIOUS, and I have not been drinking. *Der Velt is Nisht Hefker.*

For the sake of peace in the world, I fought the impulse to respond to the writer and ask whether I could substitute seven men and five women for the required 10 men.

Glossary for the above email message:

Halocheh–*Ashkenazi* pronunciation of the Hebrew word, *halakhah*—Jewish law

The Mordechai–Mordechai Ben-Hillel, 13th C. German rabbi and talmudic commentator

Brings– Cites

Yoma – A treatise of the Talmud

Tekuneh – *Ashkenazi* pronunciation of the Hebrew word,

takkanah– an enactment which revises a law

Cherem – Exclusion from the community

Mechileh – Ashkenazic pronunciation of the Hebrew word, *meḥilah*—Forgiveness

Der Velt is Nisht Hefker – Yiddish: The world is not chaos. (There are rules!)

Passover Bunnies?

PASSOVER IS THE YEARLY JEWISH Festival of Freedom. We are enjoined to celebrate it as if each one of us personally had been freed from Egyptian slavery. The *seder* ceremony is an integral part of this celebration. Although the *seder* is held at home, it is no less an act of worship than services held in a synagogue.

Jews worship not only through prayer, but also through study and learning, in this case, through the retelling of the Exodus story. Like other Jewish religious ceremonies, the *seder* follows a strict order, which is laid out in the *Haggadah*. Indeed, the very name of the ceremony, *seder*, means order in Hebrew.

The core of the text was already established by the second to fifth centuries, in the days of the great centers of Jewish learning in *Eretz Israel*. The first complete text we have dates to the tenth century, when *Haggadot* (plural of *Haggadah*) were still hand-written and illustrated. The text continued to evolve with many later additions such as the hymn *adir hu*, added in the thirteenth century, and the children's favorite, *had gadya*, incorporated in the fifteenth century.

Because the order was so important, various mnemonics evolved to jog the memory of the celebrants when no books were available to guide them. Before the advent of printing, not every household could afford an expensive hand-written *Haggadah*. The best known of these devices is the rhyme that traces the thirteen steps (the meal is step ten) of the *seder* ceremony. It can be found on the opening pages of every printed *Haggadah*, and begins with the rhymes: *kaddesh urehatz, karpas yahatz, maggid, rohtzah, motzi matzah*....

Another well-known memory aid is the acrostic made up of the first letters of the ten plagues the last of which finally induced Pharaoh to let his Israelite slaves go: *detzakh, adash, be'ahav*. Although the words themselves have no meaning, they helped keep the order of the plagues straight. Some people even arrange the foods on the *seder* plate in the order in which they are used during the service.

MANY OF THE EARLY *HAGGADOT* were illustrated with pictures of rabbit hunts, in addition to the more conventional illustrations of the ten plagues and Moses parting the Reed Sea. These curious rabbit-hunt pictures—so alien to the theme of the *seder* and to Jewish culture—can be found only in *Ashkenazi Haggadot*. What is the story behind these strange illustrations?

When the night of the *seder* falls on a Saturday night, as it does from time to time, the usual order of the service changes slightly. To mark the end of Shabbat, a special *Havdalah* service is inserted into the normal sequence. The initials of the words denoting the steps of the new sequence are combined into the nonsense word *yaKeNHaz*. To *Ashkenazi* Jews, speaking German or Yiddish, this sounds very much like the two German words *Jagen Haas* (hare hunt). Thus, because of the coincidence of sounds of a Hebrew acrostic and a pastime of the German landed gentry, we have illustrations of rabbit hunts in our *Haggadot*—the better to remember the sequence. All in the pursuit of order!

In later *Haggadot*, such as the *Augsburg Haggadah* of 1534, the pictures of rabbit hunts are often accompanied by sequels in which the rabbits escape from the net into which they had been driven. This represents, allegorically, the persecution and ultimate redemption of the Jewish people. These illustrations are hard to find in contemporary *Haggadot*. Pictures of Jews depicted as rabbits pursued by dogs, their enemies, don't seem to fit well into our age of political correctness.

Superstitions and Other Odd Notions

97 The Horned Moses

IN THE ART OF MOST European countries throughout much of the Middle Ages and the Renaissance, Moses is depicted with horns sprouting from his head. This strange representation can be seen in the famous statue by Michelangelo, the equally well-known portrait by Rembrandt, the

magnificent stained-glass windows of the cathedral of Chartres, and those of Ste. Chapelle in Paris. Moses is depicted with horns in thousands of Psalters, Bibles and other illuminated manuscripts. From where does this horned image come?

Until not so long ago, I would have given the traditional, facile answer that it was all due to a mistake in translation. When Jerome (342–420 C.E.), one of the Church Fathers who was later to become St. Jerome, translated the Hebrew Bible into Latin, he made an error in the translation of verse 34:29 in Exodus. The verse relates that, as Moses came down the mountain for the second time with the two tablets of the Pact, "he did not know that the skin of his face was radiant because he had spoken with Him." The verb used in the sentence is *karan*. The problem arises from the fact that the Hebrew noun *keren* can mean both ray of light and horn. Jerome chose the second meaning and rendered the phrase, "...and he knew not that his face was horned (*cornuta*, in Latin) from the conversation of the Lord."

What a silly mistake! And yet, is it reasonable to conclude that Jerome, who had settled in Bethlehem, had studied Hebrew for years with a series of Jewish teachers, had translated the Bible from the

Hebrew and the New Testament from the Greek into what became the generally accepted version of the Catholic Church (the Vulgate), would make such an elementary mistake? And is it reasonable to assume that for centuries afterwards the mistake would be perpetuated by thousands of scholars and artists who drew their inspiration from the Bible?

Recently, I came across a book which tries to explain this puzzle. In *The Horned Moses in Medieval Art and Thought* (Berkeley, 1970), Ruth Mellinkoff argues that the horns on Moses' head could be viewed as a symbol of honor, power or victory rather than as a symbol of dishonor. She shows that throughout history, horns were a universally used motif in many different cultures. Many of the major deities were represented with horns or horned headdress, and horns were often used to indicate kingship or leadership. As far back as 2000 B.C.E., statues of the Babylonian creator-god Marduk usually show him wearing the horned-headgear power symbol.

There seems to be little doubt that Jerome meant to convey grandeur when he translated *keren* as *cornuta*. In his Commentaries on the Bible, he says of the face of Moses that it "showed splendor" and then adds *cornuta*. Moreover, he repeatedly refers to Moses as the "great commander" (worthy to wear horns).

In re-reading *Ki Tissa*, the relevant weekly portion from Exodus, I suddenly had doubts: Does Mellinkoff's explanation really make sense? The Torah tells us explicitly (and repeatedly) that, as Moses came down from the mountain, "the skin of his face was radiant." How does that translate into sprouting horns? Our classic sources explain that Moses' radiance was a "reflection of the divine radiance," for God is often portrayed as "bathed in light." Moreover, the Torah relates that Moses would "veil his face" (except when he spoke to the Lord or conveyed His word to the Israelites). Surely, Moses was not trying to hide horns sprouting from his head, for a veil could not hide those. Rather, it must have been the overpowering immediacy of God's radiant glory (a divine radiation burn, as it were) from which Moses tried to shield the people in his day-to-day dealings with them.

THERE IS, HOWEVER, ANOTHER ASPECT to the symbol of the horns, not necessarily connected with Jerome's translation but very disturbing in its sinister implications. It explains the widespread occurrence of the image in the Middle Ages. In the Christian world of medieval Europe, Jews were thought to be in league with the devil and to have taken on some of his physical attributes: cloven hooves, tail and, of course, horns. With the decline in importance of the Hebrew Bible in Christian scholarship in the later Middle Ages, illustrations of Jews as devils proliferate and the horns of Moses turn from being a symbol of honor and station to one of infamy and evil. Although there were rare exceptions, such as the artist Rembrandt, whose portraits of Jews are full of admiration and respect, the great untutored, superstitious masses in the Middle Ages often envisaged Jews as devilish, horned creatures.

At the end of the day, Mellinkoff's learned analysis may be irrelevant as an explanation for the horned images that we find on stained glass windows and ceilings in many of Europe's cathedrals. For, whatever Jerome intended to convey with his description of Moses descending from the mountain, it does not correspond to the later picture of the Jew in the popular mind. For Jerome, horns may indeed have represented divine power and glory; for the masses of true believers, listening to the Sunday morning sermon, they changed into a satanic symbol. Maybe not so surprisingly, this medieval superstition of Jews having horns has continued well into the modern period and has been documented in the not-too-distant past even in the United States.

98 *Mazal Tov!*

MAZAL TOV (OR, AS WE say in Yiddish, *mazel tov*) is a strange expression: *mazal* in most people's minds stands for luck, and *tov* we know to mean good, yet the combination does not stand for good luck but rather for congratulations. The expression is often misused by people who don't know what it means. For instance, Guenther Grass in *The Tin Drum* has one character wish success to a friend who is about to go on stage by saying: "*Mazel tov*, break a leg!")

The reason for the confusion is simple; the word *mazal* in Hebrew stands for a sign of the zodiac. So, when we wish somebody a *mazal tov* we actually express the hope that the event to which we are referring may have taken place (or should take place) under a good sign. (In English, we are more likely to say, under a lucky star, which comes to the same thing.) Somebody got married—*mazal tov!* Somebody had a baby—*mazal tov!*

Having said this, the question arises: Do we Jews believe in the influence of the stars on human affairs? Do we believe that constellations have the power to render events lucky or unlucky for us? The answer, as it turns out, is not a simple yes or no.

In the Bible, we are explicitly commanded not to bow down or worship the sun, the moon, the stars and the whole heavenly host (Deuteronomy 4:19). Then the sentence continues, "these the Lord your God allocated to the other peoples everywhere under heaven..." Heathen nations believed in the power of the stars and prayed to them. Had the Israelites adopted these practices as well, so that they had to be warned against them? Jeremiah's words (10:2) are very explicit: "Learn not the way of the nations and be not dismayed at the signs of heaven for the [Gentile] nations are dismayed at them."

What, then, do Jews believe? Do the stars affect human lives or don't they? Rabbi Yoḥanan, the early third century C.E. talmudic Sage, resolves the problem by dividing it: "Israel is immune to planetary influence" (*Shabbat* 156a); by implication, Gentiles are not. The answer, it seems, is both yes and no.

But things are never simple. Rabbi Hanina b. Hama, (R. Yohanan's teacher), takes the opposite view and states that planets do affect Israel too: "The constellation of the hour is the determining influence in our lives." This belief in the power of the stars explains why we find constellations playing a part in early Jewish folk-culture. One should add, though, that Jews never really got involved with astrology to the extent their neighbors did. Moreover, the belief in the power of the stars did not negate the central belief in the free will with which each person was endowed by the Creator.

By the beginning of the Christian era, the zodiac, with its twelve constellations (the invention of early Chaldean astronomers), had insinuated itself into popular Jewish belief and culture. It provided the theme for some of the most beautiful mosaic floors found in excavations of early Byzantine synagogues in *Eretz Israel*. It figured (and still figures) as decoration on many *ketubbot* (marriage contracts) with the accompanying good wishes, *bemazal tov u-vesiman tov*—wishing the newlyweds the luck of a good constellation and a good celestial sign.

The zodiac provided the basis for a long piyut (medieval poem) which was read in synagogues on the Festival of Shemini Atzeret. This poem can be found in old *mahzorim* (Holiday prayer books) usually accompanied by pictures of the twelve *mazalot* (pl. of *mazal*). In modern *mahzorim* this *piyut* is purged, for belief in heavenly signs is not quite politically correct any longer.

In the Jewish lunar-year calendar each sign of the zodiac corresponds directly to one of the months of the year. The names of the signs are translated from the Latin.

In their effort to connect the signs to Judaism, the rabbis interpreted them symbolically. They were made to stand for the twelve tribes of Israel, or were tied to Jewish beliefs and history. Thus, *Moznayim* (Libra or balance) corresponds to the month of Tishrei in which Rosh Ha-Shanah and the Day of Judgment fall, i.e., the period in which the human fate is in balance. *Aryeh* (Leo or Lion) is the sign for the month of Av, on the ninth day of which the Holy Temple—often referred to as *Ariel* (the lion of God)—was destroyed. These are homiletic explanations that try to make the presence of foreign astrological ideas within Judaism more palatable. Still, the hearty *mazal tov* we wish one another on happy occasions retains an echo of early idolatry.

99 Jewish Superstitions

— GRANDMA, ARE THERE JEWISH SUPERSTITIONS?

— God forbid! There are no Jewish superstitions, my precious! There are some customs that may strike you as strange, but they're all based on solid ground. But what an intelligent question! Such a precocious child, *kineahora!*

— Grandma, what does *kineahora* mean?

— It wards off the Evil Eye.

— But Grandma...!

Grandma is clearly wrong. Joshua Trachtenberg's classic study, *Jewish Magic and Superstition*, discusses hundreds of Jewish superstitions and traces their origins, sometimes even back to the Sages of the Talmud. Still, some customs are based on Scriptural passages and may therefore escape, in the minds of some, the label of superstition.

For instance, Jews like to set out on a trip or start a new venture on a Tuesday, but avoid, if possible, doing so on Mondays. Why? In the story of Creation in Genesis, on five days the Bible relates that God looked at what He had wrought "and saw that it was good." This phrase is missing from the account of Day Two, Monday, but occurs twice on Tuesday. What better proof that Tuesday is indeed a very good day for a trip?

Speaking of travel, it is customary to give someone who sets out on a journey a small amount of money to be contributed to charity at the destination. This is called *mitzvah gelt* (money to perform a good deed) and is based on an old *midrash* which holds that no harm can come to a person engaged in the performance of a *mitzvah*, for that person is under divine protection.

One does not count Jews. To count people is regarded as highly unlucky. This custom is probably based on the passage in Exodus (30:11-13): "The Lord spoke to Moses, saying: When you take a census of the Israelite people according to their enrollment, each shall pay the Lord a ransom for himself on being enrolled, that no plague may come upon them through their being enrolled." Indeed, when King David ordered a general census of his domain (2 Samuel 24:1–16), a plague struck the kingdom and killed 70,000 of his people.

Maybe the phobia about being counted stems from the real fear of having one's name on a list, for lists often become tax-rolls or armed services recruitment rosters.

The custom, however, lives on in strange ways. It is not good form to count people in the synagogue to see if a *minyan* (a quorum of ten adult Jews) is present. One does hear, however: "Not one, not two, not three..." Also, those present may be counted by means of a biblical verse consisting of ten words—each word one person.

Recently, a friend told me about asking a teacher of hers (an educated, Orthodox woman) how many grandchildren she had. The woman replied tersely, "I don't count my grandchildren!"

The fear of bringing about unwanted consequences underlies many customs (superstitions?) in the Jewish home. As a child I was often admonished not to run around in socks. Barefoot—yes, but in socks—never! Years later I came to understand the reason: because people who sit *shiv'ah* (in deep mourning) remove their shoes, the connection between going around in socks and death was felt to be too immediate. Moreover, there was an element of causal relationship implied.

The same fear explains my grandmother's agitation whenever two people were helping my brother or me get dressed: A dead person is washed and dressed prior to burial by a group of people (the *hevrah kaddisha*), but a living being—never!

Do these examples imply a belief in evil spirits and demons? Probably yes, for it is believed that the Angel of Death roams the world and is attracted by behavior usually associated with a house of mourning.

Fortunately, the Angel of Death and most other evil spirits are deemed to be pretty stupid and easily deceived. From this stems the custom of changing the name of a critically sick person in order to mislead the Angel of Death. My brother, David, had pneumonia as a baby (no small matter in those days before antibiotics) and in a ceremony in *shul* his name was changed to Shalom David Yisrael. The protection here was twofold, for the acronym of his new names spells *Shaddai*, one of the names of God.

In the *Ashkenazi* tradition we do not name a newborn after a living person, but rather after a dead relative. This too is based on the attempt to trick the Angel of Death into assuming that the name belongs to one already dead. The error will allow the baby to escape unscathed. The explanation that we name the baby to honor an ancestor is, as are so many later explanations, meant to lend a measure of rationality and respectability to the custom. Naming a boy after his father by adding Jr. to his name is surely also meant as an honor, yet Jews do not do this.

In many families the baby's name is not discussed or mentioned openly before birth. But this custom is probably more connected with belief in the Evil Eye than belief in evil spirits.

THE QUESTION ARISES: HOW DO we combat the evil spirits, demons and the like, the *mazikim* (purveyors of harm) that figure so prominently in Jewish "folk religion," to use Joshua Trachtenberg's term? What can we do to ward them off?

First, colors. The colors red, white and blue are very effective in repelling evil spirits. In Israel, we often saw babies with a red ribbon tied to their wrists or around their necks, on their strollers or baby-buggies. This is especially true among the *haredim* (ultra-Orthodox).

White, too, is an effective prophylactic. Trachtenberg maintains that this is why brides and grooms wear white at traditional weddings. (Now, of course, we give more spiritual explanations to this custom.)

Blue is thought to be an effective anti-demonic color all over the Middle East. Arab villages in Israel often look colorful because many window shutters and doors are painted blue to guard the entrances to the home. An educated Arab friend justified this practice to me, saying, with a straight face, that many types of disease-spreading insects are repelled by the color blue, which makes inhabitants, thus protected, less prone to illnesses.

When it comes to substances, salt ranks very high on the demon-repellant scale. Demons just do not like salt. In biblical times, newborn babies were bathed and rubbed with salt before being swaddled (Ezekiel 16:4). We scatter salt in the corners of rooms in new houses to drive out the spirits that might have been displaced from the site by the new construction. This also explains the well-known custom of welcoming new neighbors by presenting them with bread and salt. However, because the salt might not always be effective, wealthy families used to hire squatters to break-in a new dwelling before they felt safe to move in themselves.

In some communities of Eastern Europe a bit of salt was put into the pockets of new garments to keep the mini-sized types of spirits from lodging there. Salt is so powerful because the combined numerical value of its letters, *mem-lamed-het* (78), is three times the value of the letters in the name of God, Y-H-W-H (26). The Kabbalists were very explicit: "It drives off the spirits. Therefore one should dip the piece of bread over which the benediction is recited, three times into salt." Which is what we do, religiously.

Now let us turn to the *Ayin Hara* (Evil Eye). Some of the methods of avoiding harm done by *shaydim* (evil spirits) are equally effective against the Evil Eye. The belief that a glance from someone who has the Evil Eye can bewitch or cause harm shows up in many cultures. It certainly is not a Jewish invention. It is, however, almost universal in Jewish folklore and dates back at least to the period of the Talmud. The Evil Eye can do harm to individuals, cause damage to property and can turn joy into sorrow. People therefore firmly believed that it was wise to wear amulets to ward off the Evil Eye—though rabbis were often just as firmly opposed to the custom. One of the more effective means of warding off the Evil Eye is a *ḥamsa*, an amulet in the shape of a human palm. Its use is widespread among Oriental Jewish communities.

The most-often heard protective expression is undoubtedly *kineahora* (from Yiddish *kein*, without, and Hebrew *ayin hora*, evil eye). It is used whenever one speaks of someone dear, something beautiful, or, in general, something that might evoke envy or jealousy.

Often, rather than using counter-magic (amulets etc.), it is best to avoid certain envy-inducing occasions (such as baby showers before the birth of the baby) or any mention of praise, beauty, success or joy. People often try to camouflage a beautiful baby by using an ugly name, or cover it with an old rag or a worn bedspread when guests come to visit. We break a valuable object to disguise periods of great joy, which is the origin of breaking a precious glass goblet at the end of the wedding ceremony. We attempt to fool the evil spirits into thinking that those present are sad because of the loss of the treasured object. (Nowadays, the goblet has been transformed into a light bulb, and dozens of more politically correct explanations are advanced for the custom.)

The strangest custom I've come across in my research for this column is that of pulling the lobe of one's ears when one sneezes. Though I had never heard of it, I received several versions of this custom over the internet, and had them confirmed by several Beit Am members. For example, a friend wrote as follows:

> Following a sneeze, my wife and her family pull the ears of the sneezer. Three small pulls to the top of each ear are followed by three tugs on the ear lobe. This procedure is repeated three times. It is expected that the sneezer will perform this ritual him/herself. However, should

the sneezer not comply, they think nothing of rushing up and pulling the sneezer's ears. I first discovered this quaint custom while driving in the car with my wife and my mother-in-law. Following a sneeze, I was shocked as the mother began pulling my ears from her position behind me in the back seat!

Well, at least she kept the evil spirits from interfering with his driving; she kept them safely on the road. *Tfoo, tfoo, tfoo!*

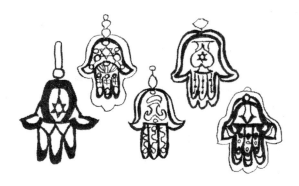

100 Giving the Devil His Due

IN THE PREVIOUS CHAPTER ON Jewish superstitions we saw that there are various ways of dealing with the *shaydim* (demons) that are all around us. Of course, the easiest way is not to alert or provoke them in the first place. Thus, we do not whistle inside our homes nor mend a garment while it is worn by somebody without giving the person a piece of the thread to chew on vigorously (lest the Angel of Death mistake the garment for a shroud that is being put on a corpse and carry the person off). However, if there is a chance that we might run into one of these evil spirits, we can take countermeasures, as we have seen, carry a piece of red cloth or an amulet when we go on a long journey or scatter salt to ward them off.

There is, however, a third stratagem and that is to appease those who have the power to inflict damage on us. This is done by bribing them, by sharing with them or, in other words, by "giving the devil his due." The most ancient forms of this practice were the sacrifices (human, animal or other) brought to appease the anger of these powers or to ask for their benevolent intervention on our behalf.

We tend to believe that the practices of our own people while the Temple in Jerusalem was still standing were somehow different, their purpose loftier than those of the pagan peoples surrounding them. For, although the Torah prescribes a long list of different sacrifices (both animal and other foodstuffs) for different occasions, these were seen by the ancient Israelites as a means of coming closer to God. After all, the word for sacrifice in Hebrew, *korban*, derives directly from the root *k-r-v*, meaning to bring near.

There are, however, those among our Sages who recognized the primitive nature of the sacrificial rituals. Maimonides, the famous Rambam, saw them as a temporary but necessary stratagem. He argued that, having spent 400 years in Egypt as slaves, the Israelites were not ready for a more spiritual intercourse with God. Only with the destruction of the Temple were sacrifices replaced by prayer. The names of most of our prayer services today mirror those of the various sacrifices of yore. (Thus, for example, *Minḥah*, the afternoon prayer, replicates the name of the lamb and grain offering brought to the Temple in the mid-afternooon.)

All religions absorb primitive practices which predate them, and Judaism is no exception. Some of these practices are elevated to a higher spiritual level, as was the case with animal sacrifices. Others are incorporated to varying degrees—sometimes disguised only by a thin veneer of respectability. An example of the latter, a ritual that clearly was an attempt to placate evil spirits, is the custom of *kapparot*, or *kaporess* in Yiddish.

On the eve of Yom Kippur, in a traditional home, the father twirls a live chicken three times over the head of each member of the family and recites this formula: "This is in exchange for you. This is in place of you. This is your atonement. This chicken will go to its death, but you will go on to a good and long life and to peace." The chicken is then slaughtered and given as charity to the poor. Sometimes, a live fish is substituted for the chicken, and in a Modern Orthodox home it is likely that *kapparot* takes the form of money, which is then donated to charity.

The scapegoat or appeasement aspect of the ritual becomes clearer when one learns that in the past the entrails of the chicken were thrown onto the roof (the site where the spirits were believed to congregate). No wonder that generations of rabbis tried to banish the custom.

Ten days before Yom Kippur, on the first day of Rosh Ha-Shanah, we encounter the custom of *tashlikh*. In the afternoon, we go to a body of flowing water, recite a prayer and symbolically cast our sins into the water. The ceremony seems innocuous enough, turning out one's (empty) pockets into a river does not pollute it nor do we really believe that we can slough off a whole year's transgressions this easily. Why then the strong rabbinic opposition to this centuries-old custom? People tended to carry (and often still do) breadcrumbs to the river and throw them into the water. This clearly was a way of buying off water-dwelling demons by feeding them. When rabbinic opposition failed to put a stop to the custom, the rabbis decreed that in years in which the first day of Rosh Ha-Shanah falls on a Shabbat, *tashlikh* is postponed to the following day, the second day of the holiday. That way, people were at least spared the transgression of carrying on the Sabbath while performing this ritual, even though it has superstitious roots.

And speaking of crumbs, in an observant household, crumbs are carefully brushed off the table and disposed of before *birkat hamazon* (the Grace after the Meal) is recited. That way, no one could mistake the crumbs for a food offering to the demons. The highly revered talmudic Sage, R. Eleazar Ben-Pedat, is quoted as saying, "He who leaves crumbs on the table is to be regarded as a worshipper of heathen gods."

Offerings of wine during festive or religious ceremonies used to be quite common. Some wine used to be poured on the ground during weddings. Though the custom is recorded as late as the nineteenth century, it has fallen into disuse today. Again, wine used to be poured on the ground during the *Havdalah* ceremony, which marks the beginning of a new week. Today we use the wine to extinguish the *Havdalah* candle. These are both examples of libations which, like many of the other customs discussed in this chapter, had very different purposes in Jewish folk-religion from the more lofty ones we ascribe to them today.

101 The Ten Lost Tribes of Israel

THE MYTH OF THE TEN Lost Tribes of Israel has been with us for close to 3,000 years. The kingdoms of Judah and Israel had existed for about 200 years after the breakup of the great empire of King David and his son Solomon. Upon Solomon's death, as a result of dynastic squabbles, the United Monarchy split into the Southern Kingdom of Judah, with its capital in Jerusalem, and the much larger and richer Northern Kingdom of Israel, with Samaria as its capital. The two tribes of Judah and Benjamin inhabited the Southern Kingdom and the population of the Northern Kingdom was made up of the remaining ten tribes

In the year 721 B.C.E., after a three-year siege, Samaria fell to the superpower Assyria. Sargon II, king of Assyria, exiled a good part of the Israelite population, and replaced them with people from other provinces of his empire. The Israelites, both in exile and at home, intermingled with the societies around them, assimilated and lost their identity. They, as well as their country, which had become a province of Assyria, ceased to exist and faded from history.

These, then, are the Ten Tribes of Israel whose fate has excited the interest of so many explorers, theologians and writers over the centuries. Many devoutly believed that the Ten Lost Tribes cannot truly be lost, for that would fly in the face of direct biblical prophecies to the contrary. The prophesies of Isaiah, Jeremiah and, above all, Ezekiel explicitly foretell the eventual reunification of all the tribes of Israel. For instance: "For days are coming, declares the Lord, when I will restore the fortunes of my people Israel... and I will bring them back to the land which I gave to their fathers, and they shall possess it." (Jeremiah 30:3) The sense of this quotation, as well as of many others, is that the ten tribes are hidden in some undisclosed place, waiting for the coming of the Messiah and the promised ingathering.

Indeed, Jewish belief going back to Second Temple times holds that the Ten Tribes of Israel are settled in a mythical land, "on the other side of the river Sambatyon," awaiting their redemption. Sambatyon is the legendary river that hurls stones in all directions for six days in the week, and on the seventh it rests. During weekdays, the tribes dare not approach it, and on the seventh day they cannot cross it because of the prohibition against travel on Shabbat.

Not everyone accepts the Sambatyon location for the Lost Tribes of Israel. A miraculous existence has been adduced for them in many remote corners of the globe. Early medieval biblical commentators saw Khorasan (the name of modern-day Afghanistan in Hebrew sources) as the location of the tribes. Interestingly, Afghani sources, too, trace some of the Afghan tribes to Hebrew origins. Ibn Hawqal, an Arab geographer of the tenth century, refers to Kabul as a Jewish settlement.

Benjamin of Tudela (Spain), the famous Jewish traveler whose extraordinary accounts survive in his *Sefer ha-Masa'ot* (Book of Travels), visited Kurdistan in 1170 and found more than 100 Jewish settlements in this northern corner of Iraq. He reports an ancient tradition that traces the origin of Iraqi Jews to the Ten Lost Tribes.

There is also a tradition among the Jews of Georgia, which describes them as descendents of the Lost Tribes of Israel. The *Encyclopedia Judaica* mentions a fifth century source according to which several kings and Georgian aristocrats were of Jewish descent.

One could go on for quite a while listing the sightings of the lost tribes. The one by Antonio de Montezinos, a Portuguese *Sephardi* Jew, is typical. He reports that on a trip to South America in 1641–42, he discovered a group of natives in Ecuador who greeted him by reciting the *Shema*. Many of these tales surfaced in medieval Europe when conditions for the Jews were desperate. They tended to give a much-needed psychological lift to their Jewish audiences by assuring them that an independent Jewish kingdom had miraculously survived. The tales raised messianic hopes and helped counteract the pernicious propaganda of the Church that contended that the Jews had lost their independence, as well as forfeited their covenant with God, because of their rejection of Jesus of Nazareth.

There are numerous myths held by groups or nations that claim direct descent from the Ten Tribes of Israel. We find these beliefs among the Japanese, the Ethiopians, Native Americans, ancient Celts and others.

Some modern-day Britons are among those who claim this Jewish ancestry. The British-Israel movement in England (British-Israelism, or Anglo-Israelism), espouses the belief that Britain is the geographical home of the lost tribes of Israel and that the inhabitants of the British

Isles (or most of them) are the direct descendants of the Lost Tribes. The organizational arm of the movement is the British-Israel World Federation (BIWF) with branches in Great Britain, Canada, Australia, South Africa, the United States and other English-speaking countries. It was founded in 1919, though many of its constituent groups existed long before then. Up to World War II, it had a large membership including British nobility and some of the royal family. The BIWF declares: "The Federation believes that Christ is our Personal Saviour. We also believe that the Lost Ten Tribes of the Northern House of Israel's descendants are to be found in the Anglo-Saxon-Celtic and kindred peoples of today." This belief has widespread currency in Britain.

Publications of the BIWF point to a number of places in the Hebrew Bible that show the connection between ancient Israel and the British Isles. They note the similarity in the ceremonies of crowning British monarchs with those of anointing Israelite kings. They trace the lineage of the Royal House of Britain to the Israelite King David. They view the similarities between numerous Hebrew and English words (for example the English seven and the Hebrew *sheva*) as proof that the original inhabitants of Britain spoke the language of the Bible. Some of their arguments are quite far-fetched: Is the word British really composed of the two Hebrew words *brit* (covenant) and *ish* (man)?

Still, elements of the Anglo-Israel myth have entered deep into English culture. The well-known hymn "Jerusalem" makes the point clearly. "Jerusalem" is cited in modern history books as one of the British Empire's anthems, among such songs as "Rule Britannia," "God Save the Queen" and "Land of Hope and Glory." Here are the words to the first stanza:

> And did those feet in ancient time
> Walk upon England's mountains green?
> And was the Holy Lamb of God
> On England's pleasant pastures seen?
> And did the Countenance Divine
> Shine forth upon our clouded hills?
> And was Jerusalem builded here
> Among these dark satanic mills?

The most insidious in its implications is the argument by some fundamentalist Christian groups that the Ten Lost Tribes are indeed lost — but not their genes! Therefore, through dispersion and intermarriage all Christians are now "of the seed of Abraham," and the prophecies concerning the coming of the Messiah refer to them. The Jews have forfeited redemption. This is the supersessionism doctrine that I discussed in connection with the question of "Jewish Bible vs. Old Testament" in Chapter 43. Clearly, the Lost Tribes, whether lost or found, serve someone's purpose.

I am struck by the contradiction between this attempt to identify with the Jews of old and the recurrent anti-Semitism we find in British history, anti-Semitism that is rampant in England today and is tolerated even in academic circles and in polite society. How do these self-styled descendants of Jews reconcile their beliefs with the hatred of their contemporary brethren? Does Anglo-Israelism, which identifies the present day Anglo-Saxon people as God's Chosen People, require the vilification of those from whom this title was purloined?

102 *Magen David*

ON OUR TRIP TO GUATEMALA our guide pointed out, in an exhibit of pre-Columbian artifacts, a ceramic pot that contained a *Magen David* in its design. He then proceeded to explain that the symbol on the pot was evidence of the presence of Jews in the New World in pre-Columbian times. Although it is, of course, entirely possible that Jews, or Israelites, had reached the Americas even before the common era, the *Magen David*, literally the Shield of David, cannot serve as proof for that assertion.

The six-pointed star (hexagram), which today is universally identified as the Jewish Star, has been recognized as such only in the last 200 years. Before then, it served, at most, as the emblem of individual European Jewish families or communities. Moreover, it is important to note that, although the *Magen David* has become, over time, a symbol of Jewish identity, it never had any religious significance nor, of course, any connection with the biblical King David.

The hexagram can be found in many ancient (non-Jewish) cultures, where it was usually associated with magic. On early Jewish artifacts, too, we find representations of the *Magen David* as decorative motifs. I remember seeing it in an ornamental frieze in the second century C.E. synagogue at *Kefar Nahum* (Capernaum), at the north end of the Sea of Galilee. The six-pointed star, which appears there in a row of rosettes, along with clusters of grapes, five-pointed stars and the swastika, was purely decorative and had no special Jewish significance at the time.

Gershom Scholem, the preeminent historian of Kabbalah states in his article in the *Encyclopedia Judaica* that the magical uses of the hexagram continued into the Middle Ages. At that time, the star was most often referred to as the Seal of Solomon rather than the Shield of David. But then, Scholem relates:

> In 1354, Emperor Charles IV granted the Jewish community of Prague the privilege of bearing its own flag—later called in documents "King David's flag"—on which the hexagram was depicted. It therefore

became an official emblem, which explains its wide use in Prague in synagogues, on the official seal of the community, on printed books, and on other objects. Here it was always called *Magen David*.

From Prague the usage spread, but it was only toward the end of the Middle Ages (fifteenth century) that the current name, *Magen David*, became generally accepted. The star had evolved from an occult symbol in books of magic and on amulets to ward off demons and fires, to a more general printers' sign in Jewish books. It still had no general Jewish significance.

At that time, though, another symbolism sprang up, which imparted some Jewish meaning to the *Magen David*. In kabbalistic circles, the Shield of David now became the Shield of the Son of David—the Messiah. This messianic interpretation of the sign was current among the followers of Shabbetai Tzevi, the seventeenth century false Messiah who claimed to be a direct descendant of King David. His followers transformed the *Magen David* into a secret symbol of redemption. In his article, Scholem maintains that this interpretation remained an esoteric one, and was not generally known—much less accepted.

From Prague, the acceptance of *Magen David* spread to the Jewish communities of Moravia and Bohemia, as far north as Amsterdam, and then eventually to Eastern Europe.

The *Magen David* found its way into the synagogue with the Jewish emancipation in nineteenth century Europe. Jews began to look for a symbol to represent them, comparable to the cross used by their Christian neighbors. Architects, mostly non-Jews who were commissioned to build the new synagogues, used the six-pointed star to distinguish them from the churches, which they resembled.

In 1897, the Zionist flag that Theodor Herzl presented to the delegates assembled for the First Zionist Congress in Basel, displayed the Magen David prominently in its center. Herzl had chosen the Star of David as a symbol of the new Zionist movement because of its wide acceptance and because it had no religious associations. In 1948, that flag would become the national flag of the newly born Jewish State of Israel.

Unfortunately, the very familiarity of the *Magen David* and its connection with the Jewish people resulted in its use as an instrument of humiliation and death. During the Nazi period, Jews were forced to wear it prominently as a badge of shame on the front of their garments. Later, when the "final solution" scheme was put into action, this badge served to mark them for extermination.

Today, the Star of David is the most popular and universally recognized symbol of the Jewish People. Many wear it as an item of jewelry. In Israel, it became fashionable for soldiers to carry it in battle as an amulet of good luck and safety. Thus, besides serving as a secular symbol of Jewish identity, the *Magen David* functions again, as it has centuries ago, as a magical symbol of protection from harm.

103 The Thirty-Six Hidden Saints

ARE THERE SAINTS IN JUDAISM? Well... not quite. It all hinges on the translation of the Hebrew word *tzaddik*. The literal translation is righteous or, possibly, just. Often, though, authors refer to the 36 *tzaddikim* as saints. Still, this sobriquet does not imply sainthood in the familiar sense: we don't see statues of these *tzaddikim* in our synagogues, we don't pray to them, asking them to intercede for us and there are no days in the year named after them. Who, then, are these saints? What about the number thirty-six? And in what sense and why are they hidden?

The legend of the 36 *Tzaddikim* has wide currency in *Ashkenazi* Jewish folklore. It has inspired many literary works, not only in Yiddish, but in world literature. The legend originated in the Kabbalah, the mystical strand in Judaism, and was adopted and popularized by the Ḥasidic movement. It is based on a passage in the Babylonian Talmud which states that in every generation there are 36 righteous people alive on whose merit the world rests. Without them, the world would cease to exist. As usual, the Sages of the Talmud base themselves on a passage in the Bible. Proverbs 10:25 reads: "When the whirlwind passes, the wicked person is no more, but the righteous is the foundation of the world." From this, it is but a small step to the conclusion that it is the *tzaddikim*, these righteous persons, on whom the continued existence of the world depends.

With respect to the number of saints, there is a difference of opinion between the Sages of *Eretz Israel*, who compiled what is known as the Talmud Yerushalmi, and those of Babylon whose deliberations are recorded in the Talmud Bavli. The former believed the number to be 30, whereas the Babylonians concluded it to be 36. Both numbers were arrived at, and justified, on the basis of gematria, intricate numerological calculations. The Bavli prevailed and the number 36 became part of our tradition. Since the letter *lamed* of the Hebrew alphabet carries the numeric value of 30 and the letter *vav* the value of six, this group of 36 righteous persons is generally known as the *lamed-vav tzaddikim* or, in Yiddish, simply, the *lamed-vovniks*.

As to the third question, who these *lamed-vovniks* are and what makes them so special—there is no difference of opinion. According to the legend, the *lamed-vovniks* are humble, self-effacing individuals whose compassion for all those who suffer is boundless. Tradition has it that, because of their piety and saintliness, the *Shekhinah* (Divine Presence) rests upon them. Most important, though, is the fact that they are hidden, that is, anonymous. Nobody knows their identity, they do not know one another's identity and, according to most versions of the legend, they are not aware of their own greatness. This anonymity is an essential element of the legend. They are the *tzaddikim nistarim*, the hidden righteous ones.

The *tzaddikim* are simple, humble folk, ordinary people who live ordinary lives. They perform their acts of loving-kindness without fanfare and the community does not suspect their greatness. It is only in times of extreme danger to the Jewish community that their strength is revealed. Because of their piety they are able to avert the danger, ward off the evil decree, or turn away the assailant. After the threat is passed, they retreat into their anonymity.

It was only natural that the legend of the *lamed-vovniks* became interwoven with the belief in the coming of the Messiah. Being powerless and persecuted during much of their history in the Diaspora, Jews saw in these holy and unknown heroes the promise of deliverance from danger and the hope for the ultimate messianic redemption. And so, many believed that one of the 36 is—or has the potential to become—the long-awaited *Mashiaḥ*.

In a Ḥasidic community, the Rebbe (spiritual leader) is referred to by his Ḥasidim (followers) as the Tzaddik. Hasidic lore is replete with stories about Rebbes who, by the power of their own great piety and deep compassion for their fellow humans, were able to accomplish feats that seemed impossible. As a consequence, Rebbes were often considered able to perform miracles. As an extension of this belief, many Ḥasidim saw in their charismatic and highly revered Rebbe one of the *lamed-vovniks*. (Whether Ḥasidic Rebbes, who often presided over elaborate courts and even created dynasties in which the leadership was passed on to their descendants, fit the image of a *lamed-vovnik*, is a moot point, at best.)

Although it is based on a legend, the belief in the 36 Righteous Ones provides those who are oppressed with comfort and hope, knowing that the world is based on justice and righteousness, and that in every generation there are individuals who guarantee the world's survival. Moreover, because the saintliness of these individuals is hidden, the legend encourages greater sensitivity for the feelings of others and more compassionate behavior toward our fellows. After all, any one of those around us — even we ourselves — may be one of the hidden *lamed-vovniks*, carrying the messianic potential within.

104 **False Messiahs**

THE HOPE FOR THE COMING of the Messiah, and with it the end of all persecution and oppression, is deeply embedded in the consciousness of the Jewish people. Three times a day, at morning, afternoon and evening prayers, we ask that God rebuild Jerusalem "soon, in our days, and speedily establish in it the throne of David" — a clear reference to the Messiah, as we shall see. In the Grace after Meals, we are even more explicit. We ask that "the Merciful One grant us life in the days of the Messiah," and, quoting Psalm 18, continue: "He gives deliverance to His King, loving-kindness to His anointed, to David and his descendents forever." The Hebrew word for anointed is *mashi'ah*, or Messiah.

Although the coming of the Messiah is connected with the concept of "the end of days," the hope for his coming expresses the immediacy and urgency of "soon, in our days." In my grandfather's house, so we were told, the main course was served before the soup "in case the *mashi'ah* should come between courses...."

Unfortunately, it was this same absolute faith which prevented my grandfather, and his extended family from leaving Poland, as my father had urged him to do, in time to escape slaughter by the Nazis. My grandfather, who was a Ḥasid (follower) of the Gerer Rebbe, obeyed when this religious leader forbade his Ḥasidim to emigrate to *Eretz Israel*: "We will return to the Holy Land when the *mashi'ah* comes. To hasten the end of exile through our own actions is a heretical rebellion against the Kingdom of Heaven." Because this was the stance of quite a few Orthodox rabbis, many perished in the Holocaust who might otherwise have found refuge in *Eretz Israel*.

Who is this anointed one for whose coming devout Jews so fervently wish? Although there is no coherent, unified concept of the Messiah in Jewish belief, it is clear that he was pictured, at least originally, as a Warrior King. He is regal and human. The *Encyclopedia Judaica* describes him as "a charismatically endowed descendent of David who the Jews of the Roman period believed would be raised up by God to break the yoke of the heathen and to reign over a restored Kingdom of Israel to which all the Jews of the exile would return." Over time, this picture was spiritualized but remained vague as to details. From being the national redeemer of Israel, the Messiah turned into a universal redeemer who would bring about the Kingdom of Truth, Peace and Justice. Still, he was seen as a man and not an incarnated God. Maimonides, the great medieval Jewish sage, maintained that the Messiah was not supernatural and would not perform miraculous changes of nature. He would die of old age!

BECAUSE OF THE PROMISE OF national redemption and an end to servitude to alien nations connected with the Messiah, hope for his quick coming ran especially high during periods of great national misfortune. When the lot of the Jewish people seemed hopeless, the messianic hope sustained them. These were also the times when false Messiahs tended to appear. Driven by their hopes, the people followed eagerly a charismatic leader who promised salvation. The leader, in turn, was sustained by his followers' belief in him. Alas, according to Jewish belief, each hoped-for-savior has so far turned out to be a false Messiah. After his disappearance, conditions were usually worse than before his coming.

The first and second centuries C.E. in *Eretz Israel* was a period of great disorientation: Rome ruled the Land of Israel, Jewish religious practices were heavily proscribed, and strife between the various Jewish factions practically amounted to civil war. No wonder that several messiahs, some self-proclaimed and some acclaimed by their disciples, appeared during this period. Josephus, the Roman-Jewish historian recounts the histories of some of them. Most founded movements whose aim it was to oppose Roman domination. At the end of the day, none of them produced the end of oppression and the hoped-for millennium of universal peace and justice. Because none brought about the Messianic Age, we adjudge them to have been false Messiahs.

It is curious that none of the contemporary Jewish or Roman sources mentions the central figure of Christianity. In Josephus (c. 38–c. 100 C.E.), who wrote very detailed accounts of the period, we do find Jesus mentioned twice (see Chapter 5). However, most scholars question the authenticity of the passages, believing that they represent later interpolations into the text. Jesus himself did not see himself as breaking away from Judaism; he lived and died an observant Jew. Nor did he proclaim himself to be the *mashi'aḥ*. However, in the Gospels, which were written in Greek years after his death, he is referred to as Jesus Christ. *Christos* is the Greek word for anointed, and millions of believers accept him now as the promised Messiah.

The majority of Jews did not accept Jesus as the *mashi'ah* for he did not correspond to the traditional image of the redeeming Warrior King. Nor had their world changed for the better with his passing. On the contrary, the situation had become much worse and culminated in the war with the Roman Empire and the ultimate destruction of the Holy Temple. The promise of a second coming seemed an unacceptable answer to their prayers.

I heard the late Professor Pinḥas Pelli, the eminent Bible scholar, tell a class of Christian philosophy students that,

> the difference between us is not so great: you believe in the coming of the Messiah and so do we. You are waiting for his second coming while we are still waiting for him to come for the first time. The issue will be resolved, as will all unresolved theological questions, at the time of his inevitable appearance. We shall ask him: "Excuse me, Sir, is this your first visit to the Holy Land, or have you been here before?"

SIXTY-TWO YEARS AFTER THE ROMAN army had destroyed Jerusalem and the Holy Temple, in the year 70 C.E., a heroic figure came onto the scene who seemed to be the answer to the people's prayers for the appearance of the Messiah. Shim'on bar Kokhba, who was a descendent of the House of David (as prophesied) fit the image of the fighting Anointed King and was believed by many to be the longed-for *mashi'ah* and savior of his people. For three-and-a-half years he prevailed against the mighty Roman army, liberated Jerusalem and much of Judea and proclaimed a free Jewish state. In 135 C.E., when Rome finally succeeded in squashing the revolt, it exacted terrible retributions: most of the country lay in ruin, many of the citizens were deported, the sympathizers of the revolt, including, many of the Sages, burned at the stake and Jerusalem was rebuilt as a Roman city. When Bar Kokhba failed to bring about the Kingdom of Heaven, the Rabbis of the *Sanhedrin* declared him a false Messiah. (For more details, see the Chapter 4 on the Bar Kokhba revolt.)

Bar Kokhba was only one of a long line of Jewish leaders with a passion for liberty who accepted God alone as their master. Would-be Messiahs arose in practically every century. One of the most influential of these, a man who answered the messianic yearning of Jewish populations everywhere, showed up 1,500 years after Bar Kokhba.

THE SEVENTEENTH CENTURY WAS NOT the best of times for Jews. In Portugal and Spain, the Inquisition was still hounding *conversos* (converts to Christianity who practiced Judaism in secret), burning at the stake those it found. In Italy, Pope Paul IV established the Roman ghetto and withdrew letters of protection he had extended to various Jewish communities, thereby sealing the death warrant of many. In the Ukraine, hundreds of Jewish communities were totally destroyed in the most barbaric pogroms imaginable by Chmielnitzki's Cossack hordes. The times were clearly ripe for a heaven-sent protector and redeemer.

Into this Messiah-hungry setting came Shabbetai Tzevi. Shabbetai was born in Smyrna, Turkey, in the year 1626. He finished his *yeshivah* education at the age of fifteen and immersed himself in the mysticism of the Kabbalah—a study traditionally restricted to mature men. He was subject to great mood swings and it has been suggested that he suffered from manic-depression. Several years later, this deeply pious and learned *Sephardi* rabbi, in one of his moments of religious exultation, proclaimed that he had heard the voice of God declaring him Messiah.

Slowly, over the opposition of most of the rabbis, Shabbetai Tzevi gained a following. However, it was not until another young rabbi, Nathan of Gaza, became his Prophet Elijah—the one who by tradition heralds the coming of the Messiah—that the movement grew into a groundswell. The messianic fervor inflamed Jewish communities throughout Europe and the Middle East. In Hamburg, Amsterdam, Paris and London, in the cities and villages of Russia and Poland, excited crowds paraded with banners depicting Shabbetai Tzevi. Records show that even several Christian governments fully expected him to be crowned King of the Jews in Jerusalem within a very short time. Jewish families sold or gave away their possessions, waiting confidently to join Shabbetai Tzevi on his triumphal march to the Holy Land.

In 1666, a year believed by many to be the year of redemption, Shabbetai Tzevi marched into Constantinople to take over the throne of the Sultan. He was imprisoned by the Turkish authorities and given the choice of death or conversion to Islam. Shabbetai Tzevi converted.

The disillusionment in the Jewish world was heartbreaking. Still, many of his followers also converted, believing his conversion to have been a stratagem. The belief in this would-be Messiah was kept alive by various Sabbatean sects till late in the eighteenth century and his influence extended beyond this. It is surely no coincidence that Hasidism was born and flourished exactly in those parts of the Jewish world where the Sabbatean influence was strongest.

Martin Buber, the respected contemporary Jewish philosopher, ties the disproportionate involvement of Jews in the world's reform movements and revolutions to the undying Jewish belief in a perfect world, the Messianic Age. That this belief is indeed alive is evidenced by the words of Maimonides that are still part of the daily liturgy, 800 years later: "I believe with perfect faith in the coming of the Messiah, and though he tarry, nevertheless do I believe."

105 Jerusalem, Above and Below: The Jerusalem Syndrome

MANY YEARS AGO, BEFORE THE establishment of the State of Israel, a fellow student at the University of California in Berkeley asked me from where I had come. I said, "Tel Aviv." When he looked nonplussed, I tried "Palestine"—with no more success. Finally, stretching geography a bit, I said: "Jerusalem." He looked at me accusingly and said: "Now I know you're pulling my leg, Jerusalem exists only in heaven!" The student was, of course, referring to the concept of *yerushalayim shel ma'alah*, the heavenly Jerusalem above, which exerts such powerful influence on the religious consciousness of millions of people. These days, however, it is *yerushalayim shel mattah*, the terrestrial Jerusalem below, which usually commands the attention of the world.

The boundary between the two Jerusalems, the one above and the one below, was not always sharply drawn. It was clearly the vision of the heavenly Jerusalem which led the poet Yehudah Halevi (twelfth century Spain) to lament: "My heart is in the East, and I am [stuck] in the farthermost West." Again, it was not the Jerusalem below, a poor and drab city, which, over the ages, drew the countless pilgrims who went searching for the Sacred City on the basis of an image they held in their mind's eye. Even down-to-earth, medieval cartographers succumbed to the dominance of *yerushalayim shel ma'alah* over physical reality by drawing their maps of the known world so that Jerusalem was located smack in the center. Jerusalem was, after all, the "navel of the universe."

Today, too, the boundary between the mystical city above and the reality of stones and concrete below sometimes becomes blurred in the minds of some. Each year, a goodly number of tourists are so overwhelmed by the intense spiritual aura of the city that they lose touch with reality. Their personalities transcend the ordinary and they turn into heroic or historic figures: Moses, King David, Jesus, Mary, or the Messiah. These tourists, often clad in what they believe to be biblical garb (i.e., white flowing robes), drift around the Old City, the

Via Dolorosa, and especially near the Western Wall. It is not difficult to find in today's Jerusalem ancient prophets wandering the streets, and, truth to tell, they may not look much more out-of-place than their role models did two to three thousand years ago. Jerusalemites are tolerant of these touched people; they believe them to lend a bit of color to the "City of Gold." The police take action only when one of the biblical characters insists on running around in the altogether or becomes a nuisance.

Not all the victims are quaint, though, or non-violent. According to Dr. Jordan Sher, a Jerusalem psychiatrist, the Holy City, and especially the walled Old City, attracts all sorts of disturbed persons. A good example of these is Dennis Rohan, the young Australian tourist who, upon hearing voices telling him to do so, set fire to the Al Aqsa mosque in 1969.

The phenomenon occurs frequently enough to have been given a name — the Jerusalem Syndrome. When concerned family members or harassed tour guides seek help, the afflicted persons are usually taken to the Sarah Hertzog Memorial Hospital in Jerusalem, the oldest psychiatric hospital in Israel. Dr. Ya'ir Bar-El, former head of the hospital, who was the first to describe the syndrome and give it its name, explains: "We are not trying to cure these patients. They are temporarily mentally unbalanced. In the four to five days they spend with us, we can usually help them regain their sense of reality enough to go home where they can be treated in a more familiar environment." He adds that 90 percent of the tourists and pilgrims the hospital sees had previous psychological problems.

Who are these patients? Based on the fifty or so smitten that the hospital sees a year, Dr Bar-El generalizes that about half are Jewish, and half Christian; there are practically no Muslims who succumb. The patients come in about equal numbers from North America, mainly the United States, and from Western Europe. Christians are most likely to come during Christmas and Easter, and Jews during the High Holy Days and Passover — all periods of high religious impact. To these danger periods Dr. Bar-El adds the months of high summer heat, July and August.

The process of psychic disintegration seems to proceed in a predictable progression. The first symptoms occur as early as the day after the tourists arrive in the Holy City. They exhibit signs of high anxiety and tend to seek isolation from whatever group they are with. Typically, they undergo rites of purification, taking shower after shower or immersing themselves in a *mikveh*, before turning into heroic personae of the Bible or the "New Testament" or assuming divinity.

According to Dr. Moshe Kalian, another psychiatrist at the Hertzog Hospital, the syndrome may be due to "the thrill of visiting a place previously only known as a sublime dream," and "the disappointment of discovering that the reality of Jerusalem with its traffic snarls and strip malls does not correspond to this dream. Unwilling to accept reality, they withdraw from it." Their problem, in terms of Jewish tradition, is their inability to differentiate between the two Jerusalems: *shel ma'alah* and *shel mattah.*

106 **The *Dybbuk***

JEWISH FOLK-BELIEFS AND FOLK-TALES ABOUND with ghosts, evil spirits, demons and the like. This was especially true of the culture of the *shtetl*, the small Jewish town of Eastern Europe—a culture that was consumed in the Holocaust and is no more. A *dybbuk* is such a spirit. It is the disembodied soul, usually of a person who committed some unforgiven sin, which cannot find rest; it enters the living body of another person and possesses it. Although stories of possession and *dybbukim* go back in Jewish literature to talmudic times, the term itself—stemming from a Hebrew root meaning to cling or hold fast—first appears in the eighteenth century. With the publication of S. Ansky's play *The Dybbuk* in 1916, the term enters the vocabulary of Western cultures. (A *dybbuk*, by the way, should not be confused with a *golem*, an artificially constructed creature in the form of a human being and endowed with life.)

Ansky's famous play deals with such a case of possession. Leah, the beautiful young daughter of a rich family, is secretly in love with Hanan, a poor *yeshivah* student. Hanan, on his part, pines for Leah whom he met while boarding with her family. Neither of them knows that they were promised to each other—even before they were born—by their fathers who were close friends. Hanan's father has since died, and Leah's father plans to marry her to the son of a wealthy family.

Hanan is deeply disturbed. He has been immersing himself in the study of Kabbalah, the mystical writings of Judaism, to find a way to make Leah his own. He consults a rabbi reputed to work miracles and calls on supernatural forces for help. All in vain. Just before the wedding, upon hearing the news that the groom's party approaches, he collapses and dies. His soul, however, cannot find rest and enters Leah's body. She is now possessed by the *dybbuk* of her star-crossed lover, Hanan.

No wonder Jewish tradition forbids anyone below the age of 40 and without a strong grounding in the more traditional fields of study to delve into Kabbalah. The Talmud records incidents of madness and even death resulting from entering the "forbidden garden."

It is a spine-chilling moment in the play when Leah first cries out, not in her own but in Hanan's deep voice: "You have buried me! But I have returned to my promised bride and will not leave her!"

A rabbinical court is quickly convened to exorcise the evil spirit from Leah. Because folk-belief has it that the possessed is guilty of some secret sin which opens the door to the *dybbuk*, the court investigates. However, it finds that it is her father's guilt in breaking the vow he had made to his friend that is visited on his beloved daughter.

The court imposes a heavy penance on the father, and, in a dramatic climax, Hanan's spirit is forced to leave Leah's body. The exorcism is successful. Or is it...? On her way to the *ḥuppah* (wedding canopy), Hanan's soul joins Leah's soul. Her voice is heard as from a great distance: "My bridegroom, my destined one. I am united with you for all eternity." She dies.

The dark mood of the play is mirrored in the dark settings in which it takes place. The flickering candles that light the old wooden synagogue in which most of the action occurs, leave the corners in darkness. And yet, it has been called a brilliant darkness—for right and true love triumph in the end. It has been said that Ansky saw in the play the "Jewish spirit struggling to maintain itself against forces of overpowering destruction"—the Russian revolution.

Ansky (pseudonym of Shloime Rappaport) was a victim of that revolution. Although a revolutionary activist himself, he had to flee for his life once Lenin seized power in Russia. He escaped the Bolsheviks disguised as a priest and reached German-occupied Vilna. Most of the material he had collected in years of ethnographic researches of Yiddish folklore in the small Jewish towns of Eastern Europe was impounded by the Soviets. He died not long after of diabetes and heart disease.

ANSKY DID NOT SEE HIS play performed; the first performance took place one month after his death. He had finished the play in 1916 and offered it repeatedly to the Vilna Troupe (the most famous of Yiddish theater companies) which rejected it. When Ansky died, his friends in the company decided to prepare the play quickly and present it as a memorial to him. It opened on December 9, 1920, to coincide with the end of the *sheloshim*, the traditional Jewish 30-day mourning period. The play was an immediate success.

Within a few years it was performed in Vilna, Moscow, New York, and San Francisco in Yiddish, Hebrew, and English. In 1922, the new Hebrew version (translated by H. N. Bialik) was presented in Moscow by the recently formed *Habimah* theater collective. *The Dybbuk* and *Habimah* became virtually synonymous. When the group immigrated to *Eretz Israel* and *Habimah* became the National Theater of Israel, *The Dybbuk* remained an integral part of its repertoire. For the next half-century. Hanna Rovina (1892–1980), the First Lady of Theater in Israel, who had performed the role of Leah in the premiere performance, continued in it until 1960 — a total of 1029 performances.

The story of *The Dybbuk* resonates in many cultures. The play, the only one Ansky wrote, inspired artistic creativity in many media. It has been performed, with only two actors playing all the roles, as puppet theater and wholly in sign language. It has inspired three films, several ballets (one composed by Leonard Bernstein) and several modern dance compositions. There has not been a time when this Yiddish theater classic was not performed somewhere in the world, in one or another of its many translations, in the last 90 years.

107 Harry Potter and the Bible

WITH THE HULLABALOO SURROUNDING THE publication of the Harry Potter books, it may be appropriate to take a look at magic and sorcery in Judaism. I am not referring to the Christian attitude in Europe during the Middle Ages which saw the Jew as sorcerer and justified the massacre of great numbers of Jews on the basis of this view. I am asking rather whether magic appears in the Bible and what was the early Jewish attitude toward witchcraft and the people who practiced it?

There is no question that the Bible recognizes the existence of magic and of people who engage in it. Thus, Pharaoh calls upon his own sorcerers to duplicate Aaron's feat of turning his rod into a serpent. Again, Balak, King of Moab, calls on Balaam, the well-known sorcerer, to help him defeat the Israelite armies on their way to the Holy Land by putting a curse on them. To enlist Balaam in his cause, Balak sent out noble messengers who themselves were "well-versed in divination."

As a final example among many others, let us recall the witch at En-Dor whom King Saul visited in disguise before his decisive battle with the Philistines. He wanted her to conjure up the ghost of the prophet Samuel so that he could ask him for advice. The king had to go to En-Dor in disguise for he himself had "forbidden [recourse to] ghosts and familiar spirits in the land."

During biblical times, the belief in the existence of diviners and sorcerers and in their powers was widespread. However, this belief in witchcraft and sorcery was absolutely condemned. In one of the many passages dealing with the issue (Deuteronomy 18:10–12), we read: "There shall not be found among you any one that... uses divination, or an observer of times, or an enchanter, or a witch, or a charmer, or a consulter with familiar spirits, or a wizard, or a necromancer, for all that do these things are an abomination unto the Lord." The Bible is actually more direct than this. In Exodus 22:17 we find the stark commandment: "You shall not suffer a witch to live." The penalty for engaging in any of the forbidden occult practices is death by stoning.

The Bible distinguishes between black magic and what I am tempted to call "white magic" (though this is not a Jewish concept). There are numerous instances in the Bible in which natural phenomena were caused by supernatural means: Moses holding out his rod, thereby splitting the Reed Sea so that the Israelites could cross it on dry ground, surely must have looked like magic to the host of newly-freed slaves. Another is when Joshua makes the sun stand still in Gibeon because he needed additional daylight to win the war against the five confederated kings who attacked Israel. A similar occasion occurs when the prophet Elisha raises from the dead the son of the Shunamite woman who had shown him much kindness.

In all these cases, the biblical account leaves no doubt that it is the power of God that has brought about the miracle. Our Sages, though, were concerned that the people realize this and not confuse human craft with the intervention of heaven. They had good reason to be concerned: While still in the desert, on one of the frequent occasions when Israel murmured against God and Moses, God sent serpents against the people and many died. Later, when the people repented, Moses, at the instruction of God, "made a copper serpent and mounted it on a standard; and when anyone was bitten by a serpent, he would look at the copper serpent and recover." With the passage of time, the people forgot all but the magical element in the healing power of the serpent's image. The Talmud (*Hullin* 6b) tells us that this serpent was preserved for several centuries; it became an object of veneration and was given the name *Nehushtan*. Six hundred years later, in the early seventh century B.C.E., Hezekiah, King of Judah, destroyed the serpent as part of his religious reforms designed to uproot all idolatry (2 Kings 18:4).

Nine hundred years after that, the Mishnaic Sages use this incident to stress the difference between magic and miracle: "[You] can say: 'Make yourself a serpent and set it on a pole: every person who was bitten will see it and recuperate.' Can a serpent kill or can a serpent give life?" The implied answer to this rhetorical question is clearly, "No!" Then they go on to make their point: "Whenever Israel raised their eyes aloft and subjected their heart to their Heavenly Father they were cured, otherwise they withered away."

Harry Potter's world of supernatural powers may not be so very different from the world of the Bible, after all. In both, magic, though officially outlawed and abominated, exists as an underground "folk religion" to use J. Trachtenberg's felicitous term.

108 Bible Codes: "Ask me Anything"

BIBLE (OR TORAH) CODES HAVE become a major topic of interest. Michael Drosnin's book, *The Bible Code*, published in June, 1997, occupied bestseller lists for many months. It is based on an article by Doron Witztum, et al., "Equidistant Letter Sequences in the Book of Genesis" (*Statistical Science*, 1994), which I'll discuss below. Both the article and Drosnin's book have generated much discussion and a great amount of searching for examples of coded passages in the Bible. I am amazed at the vast amount of material written on the subject and at the passions the various claims, counterclaims and counter-counterclaims aroused. What exactly are these Torah Codes that provoke such heated controversies?

The discoverers of the Torah Codes, and the subsequent believers in them, claim that beneath the clear text of the Hebrew Torah much information is hidden in the form of coded messages. This information pertains to events that happened thousands of years after the Torah was written, and may relate even to such secular incidents as the assassination of Israel's Prime Minister Yitzhak Rabin, the 9/11 attack on the Twin Towers and the outcomes of Presidential elections in the United States. Of course, the information is not immediately apparent for it is presented in encoded form. It is, however, accessible to anyone with a reading knowledge of Hebrew, a good deal of patience and a fair-sized computer to reveal the hidden messages.

The method of encoding consists of forming Equidistant Letter Sequences (ELS). The letters which make up the words of the hidden message are not necessarily written next to one another, but are separated from each other by a given number of skipped letters. For example, this sentence that you're now reading demonstrates **t**he method of encrypting **a** secret, **h**idden message within the surrounding text. The five **underlined** letters in bold type starting with the "t" in the word "the" spell the word "Torah." Every seventh letter is part of the message and the ELS here, therefore, equals seven. TORAH now becomes our Key Word. This, by itself, is not especially revealing nor really amazing. Within the 304,805 letters which make up the Torah, one would expect to find many such words in which the individual letters are separated from one another by equal distances. These, by themselves, do not constitute a complete, hidden or encoded message.

To show that there is indeed a hidden message in the text we must now find additional ELS words, conceptually related to our key word and in close proximity to it. To do this, one must rewrite the text in a two-dimensional array. The length of each row is the ELS, which can run from 1 (where the letters are next to one another) into the hundreds.

Let us construct an example with an ELS of 7: "This seemingly clear sentence illus<u>trates the method of encrypting a secret h</u>idden message within the surrounding text." Now we re-write the underlined part of the sentence in array form:

"This seemingly clear
sentence illus...

t	r	a	t	e	s	*t*
h	*e*	*m*	*e*	*t*	h	*o*
d	o	f	e	n	c	*r*
y	p	t	i	n	g	*a*
s	e	c	r	e	t	*h*

... idden message within the surrounding text."

The related words may appear in various patterns: with skips or without, spelled forwards or backwards, up or down, or even diagonally. Together, these words make up the encoded message. In our example, we find the word torah as the last column of the array (that is, formed by every seventh letter) and the sequence e-m-e-t, which spells "truth" in Hebrew, in the second row. Is this just a coincidence, or is it meaningful, telling us that the Torah represents truth?

This is where the controversy lies: How likely is it that the words which make up the hidden message will occur in such close vicinity to one another? The larger the samples (where the skips, and therefore the rows, are hundreds of letters long) the greater the likelihood of finding related words. It is essentially a mathematical-statistical question: if the occurrence of the words can be explained by random chance, no special meaning need be attached to the words — they do not constitute a message. If on the other hand, the likelihood (that is, the probability) of the words occurring as they do is so small as to rule out a random occurrence, then one must conclude that someone has introduced the message deliberately into the text. Moreover, because the method of encoding is so complicated as to have been practically impossible before the invention of the modern, high-speed computer, the conclusion is inevitable: the author of the hidden messages must be divine. The arguments thus quickly turn into a theological debate.

OVER THE AGES, JEWISH SCHOLARS who believed that the Torah represents the word of God have gone beyond the literal text and searched for deeper meaning in the Scriptures. Not only the Kabbalists, but also less esoteric students of mainstream Jewish thought, looked for mystical contents hidden below the surface of the text. The existence of Equidistant Letter Sequences had been suggested already hundreds of years ago. About 70 years ago, Rabbi Michael Ber Weissmandl, a Moldavian rabbi, actually demonstrated the pattern in single words.

The coincidence of key words and clusters of words with related meanings was first shown to exist in the Torah by three Israelis: Doron Witztum, a physicist, Eliyahu Rips, a mathematician, and Yoav Rosenberg, the computer-maven who perfected the software used to unravel the codes. In the article mentioned above, the three authors (WRR) show that the names of certain famous rabbis, who lived and died many centuries after the Book of Genesis was written, appear there (in ELS form) and for each, his dates of birth and death appear in close proximity to the name! The respected journal *Statistical Science* offered the paper to its readers as a "challenging puzzle." It was this oft-quoted article with its astonishing results that originated the idea of Bible Codes.

Three years later, Michael Drosnin, a journalist, provided the spark for the explosion of popular interest in the Codes. In his successful mass-market book, *The Bible Code*, Drosnin went beyond WRR's discovery and argued that the author of the Torah had encoded in the Hebrew text clear references to such contemporary events as, the Gulf war, the Oklahoma City bombing, the Kennedy assassination, the election of Bill Clinton and even the collision of a comet with Jupiter. Drosnin discovered references to the Holocaust, the moon landing, the attack on the Twin Towers, etc. The centerpiece, however, was the prediction of the assassination of Israel's Prime Minister Yitzḥak Rabin, which Dronin decoded in 1994, and its dramatic confirmation one year later.

By now, world-wide attention was focused on the Codes: interviews on CNN and the major talk-shows, articles in the daily press and the various news magazines, appearance on Oprah's program, all discussing the pros and cons of the phenomenal discovery.

The challenges were not long in coming. WRR were charged with "cooking" the data and making grievous errors in calculating the probabilities involved. The major criticism came from mathematician Brendon McKay of the Australian National University and his colleagues in an article that was also published in *Statistical Science* (1999). McKay claimed that WRR changed the spelling of the rabbis' names in their famous experiment to suit their own needs. The most telling argument against the validity of the Codes was the fact that many of the results could be replicated in the Hebrew translation of *War and Peace*.

In response, Drosnin challenged McKay in a *Newsweek* article: "When my critics find a message about the assassination of a prime minister encrypted in *Moby Dick*, I'll believe them." McKay countered by finding assassination predictions in the English text of Melville's *Moby Dick* for Indira Gandhi, Rene Moawad, Leon Trotsky, Rev. Martin Luther King and Robert F. Kennedy.

By then, though, the debate had shifted. *Aish HaTorah*, the world's largest Orthodox Jewish outreach program, had endorsed the Codes and declared it a *mitzvah* to teach them. A group of well-known Orthodox rabbis had published a "Torah Opinion" in support of the Codes and the belief in their divine origin. Critics were now labeled scoffers, accused of arguing on the basis of preconceived theological notions and warned that they "will be brought to account" on the Final Judgment Day.

Several months ago, a friend asked me for my opinion of the Torah Codes. At the time, I was highly skeptical of it. I considered the fact that there had been many versions of the Hebrew Bible in circulation until the Ben-Asher codex was accepted in 900 C.E. as the authentic one. The significant variations in these previous versions from our own Masoretic text cast doubt on the divine authorship of any codes based on our current Bible. This, of course, is even more true of translations into other languages. Have messages predicting the Second Coming of the Messiah, which Christian researchers have found in the King James Bible, really been put there by the author of the original Hebrew text? Moreover, even if one accepts the Torah as the source of all truths, would one really expect the Wright brothers' first flight or the fall of Russian communism to be encoded in it?

And so, in spite of the fact that the Web now offers dozens of software programs that will allow me to find my own name in the Bible or to do my own code research, I am more than skeptical. I am not a statistician, but, after reading hundreds of pages on the subject, I accept the opinion of the impressive list of professionals who, in a "Mathematicians Statement on the Bible Codes" published on the web, declare that any claims for the existence of the codes are, in their words "entirely unconvincing." In my own, less polite terms, they are "sheer bunk"!

109 *Gematria*

OUR SAGES TAUGHT: "THE TORAH can be interpreted in 70 different ways." The great contribution of rabbinic Judaism was that they did not take scripture "at face value," but tried to find meaning by delving below the surface of the written word. As is often the case, the number 70 here stands for any large number. Indeed, the literal interpretation of Scripture (*peshat*) is only the first of the levels on which a text can be interpreted.

One of the methods that go below the surface is known as *Gematria* (Jewish numerology). *Gematria* has been called the "Mathematics of the Torah." Each letter in the Hebrew alphabet has a numerical value. By adding up the values of the individual letters, one can find the numerical equivalent of a word or a phrase. *Gematria* tries to find meaning and additional insights by comparing the numerical values of different words and ideas.

Let us take two (non-Scriptural) examples of *Gematria* related to the holiday of Purim. Although traditionally Jews are moderate in their consumption of alcohol, on Purim it is customary to imbibe until one "can't tell the difference between 'Blessed is Mordecai' and 'Cursed is Haman'." The numerical value of both phrases is the same, 502, so maybe it was thought that it wouldn't take too much wine to mistake one for the other.

Basing themselves on *Gematria*, our Sages, though, suggest a deeper reason for drinking wine on Purim. In a different context, the Talmud says: *Nikhnas yayin, yatza sod* (*Sanhedrin* 38a): "When wine goes in, secrets come out." (The secret in this case is the presence of God, who is not mentioned even once in the Scroll of Esther.) Both "wine" and "secret" share the same numerical value, 70. Based on this equivalence, it is believed that wine attunes us to the underlying reality of God's presence.

YHWH, the four-letter, ineffable name of God in Hebrew, provides another example of the idea that words having the same value have correspondences in meaning. The four letters *yod-heh-vav-heh* have a combined value of 26. If we add together the values of *ahavah* (love) and *eḥad* (unity), each of which is 13, we arrive at the value for God!

The two examples above use the simplest form of *Gematria*—one value for each letter. The first ten letters of the alphabet carry values from 1 to 10, the next eight letters, values from 20 to 90, and the last four letters carry the values 100, 200, 300 and 400, respectively. There are, however, a great many more complex systems of *Gematria*, which generate much higher values for each word. By increasing the range of possible values for each letter, these systems greatly increase the choice of word-equivalences. The danger is that they thereby also open the door for more farfetched Scriptural analyses. All it takes is a mathematical bent of mind and enough time (or a high-speed computer, these days) to enable one to prove almost any correspondence one seeks.

Because of this, we are enjoined from starting with a conclusion and then looking for ways to verify it with *Gematria*. Yet, it is difficult to resist temptation and not look for a word—or a number of words—whose values fit our purpose. Because of this, in the Jewish tradition *Gematria* is never used to derive a *halakhic* or binding legal principle. It is used mainly for mnemonic purposes, to illustrate a point or to derive a new insight.

NUMEROLOGY ANTEDATES ITS FIRST MENTION in Jewish sources by about a 1,000 years. We find it first mentioned in an inscription of Sargon II, King of Babylon (727–707 B.C.E.), whereas the first reference to it in our sources is later, from the Mishnaic period. As one would expect, its use there is restricted to the *Midrashim* (interpretations), which the talmudic Sages used to explain and amplify Torah texts. A thousand years later, the Kabbalists, that is, the Jewish mystics of the twelfth and thirteenth centuries, developed *Gematria* into a major tool of exegesis. Rabbi Yitzchak Ginsburgh, a respected authority on Jewish mysticism, explains the rationale for this:

> The assumption behind this technique is that numerical equivalence is not coincidental. Because the world was created through God's "speech," each letter represents a different creative force. Thus, the numerical equivalence of two words reveals an internal connection between the creative potentials of each one.

Even among the mystics, though, *Gematria* served primarily to support existing ideas rather than to develop new ones.

The same is true of the way Ḥasidic commentators used (and still use) *Gematria*—almost as an intellectual exercise in which clever constructions of numerical equivalences is highly admired. A well-known example may illustrate the point: In Genesis (14:14) we are told that when Abram heard that his nephew Lot had been taken captive by marauders, "he mustered his retainers, born into his household, numbering 318, and went in pursuit as far as Dan." Careful readers were struck by the number 318 for the Bible rarely goes into such detail and, in fact, usually gives round numbers. A fanciful application of *Gematria* showed that the numeric values of the letters in the name Eliezer, the only servant of Abraham's mentioned by name, add up to 318. There you are! There really was only one retainer but he was the equivalent of a small army of warriors.

A final note: *Gematria* is not in any way connected to the Bible (or Torah) Codes that we discussed in the previous chapter. It is an additional, possibly more fanciful, method of finding meaning in the written word. The Codes, on the other hand, look for hidden facts encoded in Scripture.

110 The Wandering Jew

THE TERM WANDERING JEW IS widely known but often misunderstood. Google has about 300,000 "hits" for it and there is even a common houseplant which bears that name. Until quite recently, I had blithely assumed that the image came from our own Jewish tradition, possibly even from the Bible. Was it Cain who, in punishment for his fratricide, was condemned to be *na vanad* (a ceaseless wanderer) and served as the prototype for the Wandering Jew? Or is the term a metaphor for the Jewish people as a whole who, since they were exiled from their homeland 2,000 years ago, have been wandering the globe waiting for the Messiah?

It was only after seeing a performance of Glen Berger's successful play "Under the Lintel," which deals with the subject, that I realized that the answer to the above questions is: "None of the above." The Wandering Jew is not of Jewish origin at all, but rather is the main character in a Christian myth of the Middle Ages. The myth was commonplace in Europe over the centuries and has often been used to justify anti-Jewish outbreaks and, in fact, to incite them. In its most common form—which was concocted by medieval monks—it concerns a man (we'll see in a moment who that might have been) who offended Jesus on his way to the crucifixion and was therefore cursed by him to walk the earth alone until the Second Coming.

As is so often the case with legends and folklore, the myth of the Wandering Jew appears in many versions. A thirteenth century version speaks of Cartaphilus, a Roman gatekeeper in Pilate's service, who struck Jesus and mocked him for walking too slowly while carrying the cross to his place of execution. It was not until the sixteenth century that the figure was definitively identified as a Jew—a shoemaker named Ahasuerus who had taunted Jesus and was condemned by him to roam the earth until Judgment Day. By that time, so the *Encyclopedia Judaica* states, various publications in Germany portrayed Ahasuerus as, "a fully fledged personification of the Jewish people, incorporating the themes of participation in the crucifixion, condemnation to eternal suffering until Jesus' second coming and the bearing of witness to the truth of the Christian tradition."

From that time on, the myth helps to shape reality. "Sightings" of the Wandering Jew are reported from virtually every major European city (among them: Luebeck, 1603; Paris, 1604; Brussels, 1640; Leipzig, 1642; Munich, 1721; London, 1818). The appearances are described in innumerable diaries, pilgrims' travelogues and chronicles. Although the individual descriptions differ, most accounts depict the Wandering Jew as speaking the language of the place of his appearance and as having converted to Catholicism. Still, he is condemned to immortality and to repeating the cycle of growing old normally to the age of 100 and then returning to the body of a 30-year old. The legend becomes tailored to changing times and local conditions and shows marked national variations. However, it always exhibits strong anti-Semitic sentiments. In many places, the Jew's appearances presage some calamity; for example, in France they are connected with storms, epidemics or famine.

IT IS NOT SURPRISING THAT the figure of the Wandering Jew has become a major theme in Western literature and in the arts. In *Queen Mab*, Shelley has an angel of death (instead of Jesus) cursing Ahasuerus by exclaiming indignantly, "Barbarian! thou hast denied rest to the Son of Man: be it denied thee also, until He comes to judge the world." The Jew appears in stories by Nathaniel Hawthorne; in a novel by Eugene Sue, *Le Juif Errant* (where the Wandering Jew is depicted as a socialist hero); in a short story, *The Wandering Jew*, by Rudyard Kipling and in the satirical novel, *The Memoirs of Mister von Schnabelewopski*, by Heinrich Heine (which became the basis for an opera by Richard Wagner, *The Flying Dutchman*)—to name just a few. Mark Twain in his *Innocents Abroad*, includes a local version of the legend told to him by his guide while walking down the Via Dolorosa in Jerusalem. The Nazis referred to the myth in the title of their 1940 viciously anti-Semitic propaganda film, *Der Ewige Jude* (*The Eternal Jew*), produced under the supervision of Joseph Goebbels himself. The film depicts the Jews of Poland as corrupt, filthy, lazy, ugly and perverse: they are an alien people who have taken over the world through their control of banking and commerce, yet still live like diseased rats, spreading disease and corruption.

What is surprising is the extent to which Jewish authors and artists have made use of this purely Christian myth. Marc Chagall has a painting—a study of an old man for one of his *shtetl* scenes—that he called "The Wandering Jew." A 1933 Yiddish language film depicting the plight of the Jews in Nazi Germany borrows the concept in its title, *Der Vanderner Yid* (The Wandering Jew). Similarly, Abraham Goldfaden, "Father of the Yiddish theater," has a Yiddish poem, *Der Evige Yude* and David Pinski has a one-act Yiddish play, *The Eternal Jew* (1906). There are many others.

Jews tend to impute both relevance and positive value to the figure. In answer to a question about the name Wandering Jew for a plant, Rabbi Yehuda Appel of *Aish Hatorah*, the worldwide Jewish outreach program, writes, (23 July, 2000):

> Any botanist will tell you that the "Wandering Jew" is a unique species of plant which—when given minimal sustenance—will nevertheless spread and grow. Similarly, if you cut out its roots and plant it in other soil, it will regenerate itself and start anew. This plant's nomenclature is, of course, a comment on the Jewish People's ability to adapt to varied environments and conditions.

Whether Rabbi Appel is aware of the history behind the myth of the Wandering Jew or not—and most people are not—he still sees in it a positive statement about the ability of the Jewish People to survive.

Afterword

IN THE EARLY YEARS OF writing the columns which make up this book, no sooner was an issue "put to bed" than I started worrying about what to write the next month. I wondered whether I could find enough interesting subjects to engage my readers month after month. As the years went by, I stopped worrying. There was never a lack of topics to discuss. The problem soon became which subjects to tackle first and how to cover them in just a page or two.

Sometimes my readers asked me to write about my personal experiences. On the whole, I tried to stay away from answering these kinds of questions. I hoped my readers would learn something worth knowing from each column—as I did in writing it. Sometimes, though, I did introduce a personal note when I believed it would complement the subject I discussed.

Legend has it that Alexander the Great wept upon having reached India believing that he had run out of worlds to conquer. Unlike him, after 16 years and more than 150 short excursions into Jewish life, I know that there is still a whole world to explore and study. I look forward to doing so for a while longer.

About Ze'ev Orzech

ZE'EV ORZECH WAS BORN IN 1926 in Wiesbaden, Germany. In 1936, when attending public school as a Jewish child became impossible, his parents enrolled him in a Jewish boarding school in Bex-les-Bains, Switzerland. In 1938, he rejoined his family on their way to Eretz Israel (then Palestine). After graduating from Balfour College in Tel Aviv in 1947 he came to the United States to study economics at the University of California in Berkeley. In 1957, he and his wife, Mimi, moved to Corvallis, Oregon, where he began a teaching career at Oregon State University from which he retired after thirty-two years. The couple has three children and six grandchildren.

In 1974, Mimi and Ze'ev were among the founding members of Beit Am, the Jewish Community in Corvallis and have been much involved in its activities ever since. After retirement, Ze'ev started editing Kol Ha'am, the monthly community newsletter, from whose columns this book was created.